Games
without
Rules

Afghanistan

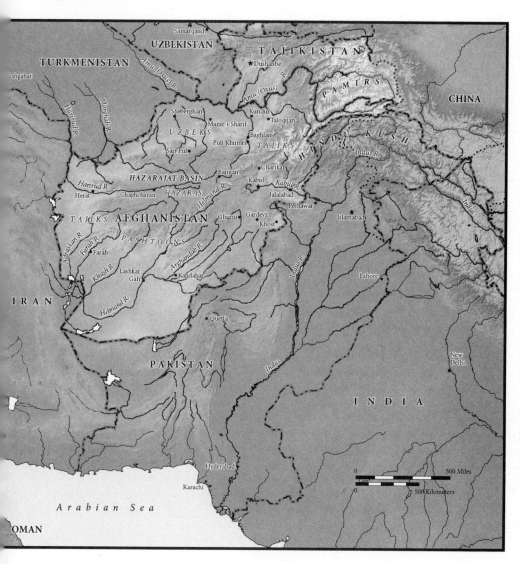

Games
without
Rules

**THE OFTEN INTERRUPTED
HISTORY OF AFGHANISTAN**

Tamim Ansary

PUBLICAFFAIRS
NEW YORK

Published in the United States by PublicAffairs™,
a Member of the Perseus Books Group

PublicAffairs books are available at special discounts for bulk purchases in the US by corporations, institutions, and other organizations. For more information, please contact the Special Markets Department at the Perseus Books Group, 2300 Chestnut Street, Suite 200, Philadelphia, PA 19103, call (800) 810-4145, ext. 5000, or e-mail special.markets@perseusbooks.com.

Designed by Pauline Brown
Text set in 12 point Adobe Garamond Pro

Library of Congress Cataloging-in-Publication Data

Ansary, Mir Tamim.
   Games without rules : the often-interrupted history of Afghanistan / Tamim Ansary. —.1st ed.
       p.   cm.
   Includes bibliographical references and index.
   ISBN 978-1-61039-094-1 (hardcover : alk. paper) — ISBN 978-1-61039-095-8 (ebook) 1. Afghanistan—History. 2. Afghanistan—History, Military. 3. Military occupation—History. 4. British—Afghanistan—History. 5. Russians—Afghanistan—History. 6. Americans—Afghanistan—History. 7. Afghanistan—Strategic aspects. 8. Afghanistan—Politics and government. I. Title.
   DS361.A755 2012
   958.1—dc23
                                                                                2012025651

First Edition

10 9 8 7 6 5 4 3 2 1

Night and day our people's lamentations reached the skies
and no one asked "Whose voice is that, uttering those cries?"
KHALILULLAH KHALILI
FROM "HOUSE OF LAMENTATION"

CONTENTS

LIST OF MAPS

CAST OF CHARACTERS

Abdul Haq Pushtoon Mujahideen leader, killed by the Taliban 2001.

Abdul Majid Zabuli Afghan entrepreneur, founded National Bank.

Abdul Rashid Dostum Uzbek leader, affiliated with both Communists and Mujahideen.

Abdul Rasool Sayyaf Prominent Islamist, head of a major Mujahideen party.

Abdullah Abdullah Ahmad Shah Massoud's top aide, presidential candidate 2004, 2009.

Ahmad Shah Baba Founder of the Afghan empire, first Durrani king, head of the Sadozai clan, "father" of Afghanistan, ruled 1747–1773.

Ahmad Shah Massoud Military commander of the Mujahideen party Jamiat Islam, minister of defense 1994–1996.

Ahmad Zahir Influential Afghan pop singer of the 1960s and '70s, often called "the Elvis Presley of Afghanistan."

Alexander Burnes Macnaghten's political agent in Kabul, 1839–1841.

Amir Abdu'Rahman, "the Iron Amir" Dost Mohammed's grandson, Sher Ali's nephew, reigned 1880–1901.

Amir Amanullah Son of Habibullah, grandson of Abdu'Rahman, ruled Afghanistan 1919–1929.

Amir Habibullah Abdu'Rahman's son and successor, reigned 1901–1919.

Amir Sher Ali Son and successor of Dost Mohammed, ruled twice: 1863–1866, 1868–1879.

Babrak Karmal Afghan Communist president, 1980–1986, headed Parcham faction of the PDPA.

Bachey Saqao (Habibullah Kalakani) Tajik bandit, deposed Amanullah, reigned February to September 1929.

Burhanuddin Rabbani Islamist professor, founder and head of Mujahideen party Jamiat-i-Islam, president of Afghanistan 1994–1996, assassinated 2011.

Charkhi family Staunch allies of Amanullah, crushed by the Musahibbans after the fall of Amanullah.

Dost Mohammed the Great First king of the Mohammedzai clan, reigned twice: 1826–1839, 1843–1863.

Durranis Ahmad Shah Baba's tribe, Durrani monarchs ruled Afghanistan from 1746–1978 except for the nine-month reign of Habibullah Kalakani (Bachey Saqao).

Frederic Roberts Commanded British forces in the Second Anglo-Afghan War, 1878–1880.

Ghilzais Major Afghan tribal confederation, long-standing rivals of the Durranis.

Gulbuddin Hekmatyar Radical Islamist, founder and head of Hezb-i-Islam.

Hafizullah Amin Khalq Party leader, architect of the 1978 coup, Taraki's right-hand man, president of Afghanistan September to December, 1979.

Hamid Karzai President of Afghanistan, 2004–2014.

Hashim Khan Nadir Shah's brother and prime minister, ruled Afghanistan from behind the throne 1933–1946.

Hazrats of Shor Bazaar Revered leading members of the religious Mujadeddi family.

Hezb-i-Islam Islamist party founded and led by Gulbuddin Hekmatyar.

ISI (InterServices Intelligence) Pakistani military intelligence agency through whom the United States funneled arms and money to the Mujahideen.

Ivan Vitkevich Russian agent in Kabul 1837–1838, claimed to be the czar's envoy.

Jalaludin Haqqani Prominent Mujahideen warlord of the 1980s, affiliated with the Taliban after 2002.

Jamaluddin-i-Afghan Radical Islamic modernist intellectual, Sher Ali's tutor.

Jamiat-i-Islam Islamist party led by Burhanuddin Rabbani and Ahmad Shah Massoud.

Khalq One faction of PDPA after the party split in 1967.

Lord (George Eden) Auckland Governor general of India 1836–1842, launched first British invasion of Afghanistan, 1838.

Lord (Edward Bulwer) Lytton Governor general of India 1876–1880, launched second British invasion of Afghanistan 1878.

Louis Napoleon Cavagnari Headed up British mission in Kabul, 1879.

Mahmoud Tarzi Prominent modernist intellectual at Amir Habibullah's court.

Malalai Iconic Afghan heroine, rallied the troops at Maiwand.

Malalai Joya Feminist activist, elected to Afghan Parliament 2004.

Massouma Esmatey-Wardak Pioneering feminist intellectual, head of Afghan Women's Council, 1979–1990.

Mohammedzais Dost Mohammed's clan, the royal branch of the Durranis, ruled Afghanistan 1826–1978.

Mujaddedis Noted religious family.

Mujahideen Islamic resistance groups who fought the Soviets in the 1980s.

Mullah Akhtar Osmani Prominent Talibanist insurgent and drug lord in Helmand province, killed by NATO 2007.

Mullah Baradur Leading Talibanist insurgent, southern Afghanistan, arrested and imprisoned by Pakistan in 2010.

Mullah Dadullah Insurgent leader of southern Afghanistan, associated with Taliban, killed 2007.

Mullah Farooq Insurgent leader in Ghazni Province, active after 2002.

Mullah Omar Reclusive one-eyed cleric considered to head up the Taliban.

Musahibbans Ruling family of Afghanistan 1929–1978, descended from Dost Mohammed's brother.

Nadir Shah Head of the Musahibban family, king of Afghanistan 1929–1933, won military victories against the British in the Third Anglo-Afghan War.

Najibullah, "the Ox" Member of Parcham, head of the secret police organization KhAD, president of Afghanistan 1988–1992.

Naseerullah Babar Pakistan interior minister under Benazir Bhutto, one architect of the Taliban.

Northern Alliance Confederation of Mujahideen parties opposed to the Taliban; organized by Ahmad Shah Massoud.

Nur Mohammed Taraki Afghan Communist president 1978–1979, head of Khalq faction of the PDPA.

Osama Bin Laden Radical Jihadist, founder of al-Qaeda.

Parcham One faction of the PDPA after the party split in 1967.

PDPA (People's Democratic Party of Afghanistan) Afghanistan's main Communist Party, founded in 1965.

Qasim Fahim Led Northern Alliance after Ahmad Shah Massoud's death.

Queen Soraya Tarzi's daughter, Amanullah's wife, leading Afghan feminist.

Quetta Shura Taliban leaders loyal to Mullah Omar, operating from Quetta, Pakistan after 2002.

Sadozais Ahmad Shah Baba's clan, a branch of the Durranis. Sadozai kings ruled from 1747 to 1826.

Sardar Ayub Sher Ali's son, beat the British at the Battle of Maiwand.

Sardar Daoud Nadir Shah's nephew, ruled Afghanistan as prime minister 1953–1963, and then as president 1973–1978.

Sardar Na'eem Nadir Shah's nephew, foreign minister 1953–1963.

Shah Mahmoud Nadir Shah's brother, ruled as prime minister, 1950–1953.

Shah Shuja Ahmad Shah's grandson, reigned twice (1803–1809, 1839–1842). Installed by the British in 1839.

Sher Agha Mujadeddi Leading opponent of Amanullah's reforms in the 1920s.

Siddiq Barmaq Filmmaker, directed the film *Osama*.

Wazir Akbar Khan Son of Dost Mohammed; leading Afghan general during First Anglo-Afghan War, 1839–1842.

William Hay Macnaghten Headed the British mission in Kabul, 1839–1841.

Yaqub Khan Sher Ali's son, installed as king by the British, 1879.

Zahir Shah Nadir Shah's son, king of Afghanistan 1929–1973.

Zalmay Khalilzad Afghan neoconservative intellectual and diplomat, advisor to the Reagan and Bush administrations on Afghan affairs.

INTRODUCTION

FIVE TIMES IN THE LAST TWO CENTURIES, SOME GREAT POWER HAS TRIED to invade, occupy, conquer, or otherwise take control of Afghanistan. Each intervention has led to a painful setback for the intervening power, and the curious thing is, these interventions have all come to grief in much the same way and for much the same reasons—as if each new power coming into Afghanistan has vowed to take no lessons from its predecessors.

The British invaded Afghanistan in 1839, suffered a disaster, and yet invaded the country again some forty years later only to make nearly the same mistakes. The predecessor from whom these folks failed to learn was themselves! Forty years later still, a third war broke the British grip on the country entirely. Sixty years after that, the Soviets invaded Afghanistan and ended up in the same tar pit as the British. Now, the United States and NATO are mired in Afghanistan, and the familiar patterns have emerged again.

What accounts for this historical amnesia?

I think back to an interchange I had in Kazakhstan a couple of years ago. I was there to promote a book I had written about world history as seen through Islamic eyes, but, everywhere I went, the conversation quickly narrowed down to Afghanistan—which was natural, I supposed, for I was an American citizen born and raised in Afghanistan, and the US intervention in my original homeland was hitting a critical stage just then. The topic had, however, a special urgency for Kazakhs, as I came to realize, because their country had been part of the Soviet Union, and many of the men in my audience had been in Afghanistan with the Soviet army of occupation during the 1980s.

One open-ended question kept coming up. How would I compare the US involvement in Afghanistan to the Soviet one? I gave the answer I had given often in America: I saw disturbing parallels. The United States seemed to be sinking into the same morass as the Soviets. The United States had made commitments it could not easily keep for practical reasons and could not easily back out of for political reasons. The United States was squandering lives and money in Afghanistan without being able to explain exactly why. The United States was able to control the cities but could not seem to quell a rural insurgency carried out by people who believed themselves to be acting in defense of Islam.

This answer failed to satisfy. One guy, I recollect, kept pressing me for follow-ups with questions so vague, I couldn't tell what he wanted. Finally I said, "Look: I can see you've got some answer of your own in mind. What am I not seeing?"

"You keep talking about the similarities," he complained. "What about the differences?"

"What differences? Tell me."

"Well, sir, *we* went into Afghanistan because we were invited. Afghans were in trouble and they turned to a neighbor for help. *We* didn't just send troops, we sent expert advisors in to help the progressive forces of the country. With you Americans, it's just a military invasion. That seems like a pretty big difference to me."

I could only shake my head and sigh. "Really? You think the Soviets went into Afghanistan because they were *invited*? To help progressives save the country from reactionaries? In that case you've just articulated another parallel between the US and the Soviet involvements, because that's pretty much how many Americans would describe what we're doing in Afghanistan today. Afghans needed help, the United States came to drive out the thugs, not to conquer Afghans, and the United States is still there today to support development and bring about progressive change."

The whole interaction got me to thinking about how the story from the outside looking in contrasts with the story from the inside looking out. From the inside, the various foreign powers and their intentions seem pretty much the same. Out in the countryside, where the fighting is hot right now, the insurgents make scant distinction between the Americans, the Russians, and the British.

From the outside perspective, it is Afghanistan that seems never changing, Afghanistan that presents ever the same challenge, the same terrain of rugged mountains, burning deserts, and endless steppes, the same warlike people who are always thought to be religious, xenophobic, and "tribal"—the very word conjuring up images of turbans, beards, robes, scimitars, and horses, as if membership in a tribe precludes wearing a three-piece suit or playing in a heavy metal band.

Actually, Afghans have a story of their own, the story of a zigzag journey toward some end point despite regular interruptions by foreign interventions. And what is this Afghan story apart from its many interruptions?

There is a game called *buzkashi* that is played only in Afghanistan and the central Asian steppes. It involves men on horseback competing to snatch a goat carcass off the ground and carry it to each of two designated posts while the other players, riding alongside at full gallop, fight to wrest the goat carcass away. The men play as individuals, each for his own glory. There are no teams. There is no set number of players. The distance between the posts is arbitrary. The field of play has no boundaries or chalk marks. No referee rides alongside to whistle plays dead and none is needed, for there are no fouls. The game is governed and regulated by its own traditions, by the social context and its customs, and by the implicit understandings among the players. If you need the protection of an official rule book, you shouldn't be playing.

Two hundred years ago, buzkashi offered an apt metaphor for Afghan society. The major theme of the country's history since then has been a contention about whether and how to impose rules on the buzkashi of Afghan society. Over these same centuries, however, Afghan territory has also provided the field of play for another game entirely, what British author Rudyard Kipling disingenuously called "the Great Game," which involves world superpowers tussling for strategic position. Like all jockeying among sovereign nations, this too is a game without rules and it is not about Afghanistan per se; the stakes are global. Afghanistan is involved only because it happens to be situated on the line of scrimmage.

Inevitably, when two unrelated games are in progress on the same field, the players crash into each other and the action gets intertwined. This has been happening in Afghanistan since the early days of the nineteenth century. Each game affects and complicates the other, but if you don't realize there are two different games going on, the action is apt to seem inexplicable.

The great power interventions in Afghanistan truly make a compelling story, to be sure; but the intervened-upon have a story of their own as well, which keeps unfolding between interventions as well as during. In *this* story the interventions are not the main event but interruptions of the main event. And if the foreign interventions tend to follow the same course, it's partly because they keep interrupting the same story, a story that never quite gets resolved before the next intervention disrupts the progress made.

This is not to rehash the old "graveyard of empires" lament, the conventional wisdom that great-power interventions in Afghanistan are doomed to fail because this place is impossible to conquer. The tough terrain and the fractious people do present a special challenge to would-be conquerors, and yet Afghanistan has in fact been conquered many times. The Aryans did it three or four thousand years ago, which is why this area was originally called Ariana. The Persians conquered this country in ancient times, which is why Persian (a.k.a. Farsi, a.k.a. Dari) is the lingua franca of Afghanistan, spoken at least as a second language by 90 percent of the people. The Greeks conquered it, which is why Hellenic kingdoms flourished here for two centuries and green-eyed blonds still sometimes pop up in pockets of the country. Even Buddhists conquered this territory, which is why the unique art style known as Greco-Buddhist originated and flourished only here.

The Arabs conquered Afghanistan, which is why 99 percent of Afghans are now Muslims. The Turks conquered Afghanistan, again and again. The Mongols swept across this land, and it didn't prove to be the graveyard of their empire—quite the opposite: they made this land a graveyard for countless Afghans. In the fifteenth century, a Turko-Mongol conqueror took over Kabul just before driving on into India to found the Moghul Empire. Afghanistan is not really impossible to conquer. It's just that all the successful conquerors are now called "Afghans."

The earlier conquests made Afghanistan what it is. This book tackles the puzzle of the last two centuries, during which time Afghans have fought five wars (depending on how you count) with great Western powers attempting to dominate their country. In these centuries, the story of Afghanistan and the story of the foreign interventions have interwoven like two strands of a single narrative, each strand driven by its own dynamics but each affecting the other. The global story explains why Afghanistan keeps getting invaded; the Afghan story helps illuminate why the interventions keep foundering.

Here, I offer the story from the inside looking out, the story of a country that began to form around the same time as the United States but is still struggling to coalesce, because of constant outside interruptions and its own internal demons, and this story begins with a man named Ahmad Shah.

PART I: AFGHANISTAN BECOMES A COUNTRY

1

Founding
Father

AROUND THE TIME GEORGE WASHINGTON WAS COMING OF AGE IN North America, a tribal warrior named Ahmad Khan was cobbling together an empire in central and south Asia. Afghans would later call this man Ahmad Shah Baba, which means "King Ahmad the Father," because in retrospect they saw him as the founder of their country.

By all accounts Ahmad Shah was a dashing figure: a big man with a broad, fair face and the romantic, almond-shaped eyes typical of his people. At the age of sixteen, he caught the notice of the king of Persia, a savage warlord named Nadir Afshar, who briefly reconstituted the Persian Empire, storming as far as India and plundering it of such treasures as the priceless Peacock Throne. Ahmad became the conqueror's trusted aide, commanding an elite corps of four thousand horsemen: quite a prestigious job for a teenager.

Then one night in 1747, Nadir Afshar was assassinated by his own generals. They killed him in the camp where he and his army had stopped for the night. Chaos broke out, of course, with the generals fighting to seize command, and the common troops commencing to loot. The king had been traveling with his harem, and, in that context, women were loot. Legend has it that Ahmad Khan was guarding the harem that night, and, when a mob of rowdies drunk on plunder approached the women's area, he backed them down single-handedly, saving the women from the mob. Then he called his cavalry together and rode hard for home.

That's the story I heard in school, and it sounds apocryphal, but historical evidence does confirm one feat Ahmad pulled off that night. The murdered king had an immense treasure with him, and, when Ahmad made good his escape, he got away with that whole hoard of gold, and gems, including one of the biggest diamonds in the world, the famous Koh-i-Noor, or "mountain of light." (I saw it in the Tower of London, where it is now displayed as one of the crown jewels of the British royal family.)

Meanwhile, Ahmad's people, the Pushtoons, were in an uproar. The Pushtoons acknowledged no overall king but were a multitude of tribes who ordinarily spent most of their time and energy fighting one another. Now, with the neo-Persian empire collapsing, they knew they had better unite behind one man at least temporarily to cope with the chaos that was coming. They called a grand assembly of the tribes, a *loya jirga*, a tradition in Pushtoon culture. All the most eminent men of all the most important tribes were there. Many respected scholars, judges, and clerics flocked to Kandahar as well to help pick a chieftain. Some writers claim that the other important ethnic groups of the area were also represented—leading Tajiks, Hazaras, Uzbeks, and others. Ahmad attended the jirga but didn't say much because he was only twenty-five years old and, in the culture of this area, the young must defer to their elders.

For nine days, the elders confabulated, but no man among them would stand down and accept another as his king. Finally, an old *dervish*, one of those mystical wanderers renowned for religious devotion, stepped into the circle, pointed to young Ahmad, and said "*There* is your leader. Can't you see? No other has his majesty and nobility! It's *that* man." Ahmad modestly demurred that he was not worthy, whereupon the dervish took a makeshift crown woven out of wheat sheaves and placed it on Ahmad's head, and, lo, the moment all those grizzled warriors saw the crown on Ahmad's head, they saw his charisma, and in his very modesty they recognized heroic power.

At least, so the story goes.

A cynic might note that Ahmad possessed some other assets too. He still had thousands of mounted warriors loyal to him personally, and he still had the dead king's treasure. But the apocryphal story expresses interesting aspects of Pushtoon culture. It legitimizes Ahmad Shah's ascent by spotlighting the endorsement he got from a wise old religious figure, the vote he received from tribal elders, and the fact that he demonstrated that most kingly of all traits: self-effacement. Those three factors turned plain young Ahmad into Ahmad Shah, king of all the Pushtoons and their local allies and subordinates.[1]

WHO ARE THE PUSHTOONS? THEY ARE A PEOPLE WHO INHABIT A contiguous area from the Hindu Kush mountains to the flanks of the Indus River. Today, they number about forty million: a little more than the population of California, a little less than that of Spain. Pushtoons speak Pushto, a language related to Persian (although the two are as mutually unintelligible as, say, Portuguese and Italian) and they share a distinct culture. The Pushtoons may or may not be the original inhabitants of this area—their own legends trace their line to one of the lost tribes of Israel—but they have lived here for at least two or three thousand years, so this is certainly their homeland.

The Pushtoons have always been organized—or, should one say, disorganized?—into numerous tribes, subtribes, clans, and extended families. Each tribe and subtribe traces its ancestry back to some great forefather. Most therefore have a name that ends in -zai, which means "children of." (It's like the prefix Mac- found in the names of Scottish clans.) Ahmad Shah belonged to the Sadozai clan, which means he and his relatives were descended from a man named Sado. About Sado little is known except that he didn't die childless. Another powerful clan was called the Barakzais, their name showing that they were all descended from Barak. No one now knows much about him either, except that he and Sado were brothers. Clusters of clans made up tribes, and tribes were loosely associated as great confederations. The Sadozais and Barakzais, for example, were two of many clan/tribes that belonged to the Abdali confederation, which means that they all descend from some much more remote ancestor named Abdal.

The Abdalis in turn had an archrival in the Ghilzais, another great confederation, also made up of numerous tribes and subtribes. Both the Abdalis and the Ghilzais lived in the city of Kandahar and spread south from there; the Ghilzais more to the east, the Abdalis to the west. The Ghilzais had been the dominant Pushtoons for centuries, much to the resentment of the Abdalis. In the fifteenth century, they had ruled northern India as "the Sultans of Delhi." In the 1730s, they had briefly ruled Iran. In 1747, the year of the landmark loya jirga, the Ghilzais were still the dominant confederation, but the balance of power was about to shift because of Ahmad Shah.

Although he wowed the elders with his modesty, Ahmad Shah began his reign by awarding himself a grandiose nickname: *Durri-i-Durran*—"the Pearl of Pearls." As his fame and stature grew, everyone even vaguely related to him sought to advertise the connection by calling themselves *Durranis*, which in English might be rendered as "the Pearly Ones." Finally all the Abdali Pushtoons were calling themselves the Durranis, and the very word *Abdali* passed right out of history.

That all came later. When he was first elected, Ahmad Shah wasn't really a king. He was the superchieftain of a ramshackle collection of tribes that had come together in the face of a common danger. Everybody assumed the alliance would be temporary. "It's me against my brothers, it's me and my brothers against our cousins, it's we and our cousins against the invader"—so goes an old Pushtoon saying. Right now, the Pushtoons had to brace themselves for possible Persian armies from the west and Turkish armies from the north. It was safe to suppose that as soon as the tension waned the confederacy would dissolve again into separate tribes, the tribes into clans, and the clans into the extended families that are the basic unit of Pushtoon culture.

This was the core challenge for Ahmad Shah: he headed up a population comprised ultimately of extended families, each of which saw itself as sovereign. Indeed, within each family every individual man saw himself as sovereign. It's true that tradition assigned to each person a role, a rank, a level: men stood higher than women, old stood higher than young, the son of a great man stood higher than the son of an obscure man . . .

Beyond these norms, however, hierarchy among men was not determined by the offices they held or the powers attached to those offices but by the qualities each individual brought to his personal interactions. If some people acquired leaderly stature, it was only because others deferred to their decisions. They earned this deference by the expertise with which they played the game of family/clan politics. In this game, deeds counted for something but not for everything. Inherited prestige counted for something but not for everything. Eloquence, gracious behavior, allies, marriage connections—all counted for something, but none was definitive. The authority of one man over another was always fluid and open to challenge; it could always be squandered by social errors, careless insults, clumsy etiquette, or graceless moments.

And what was true within a family was also true among families, and what was true among families was also true among clans and whole tribes. The same patterns reappeared at every level. Ultimately they all went back to personal interactions and how those interwove with the intricate dynamics of family politics, invisible to outsiders. When many tribes formed a common front against some threat, leadership had to be negotiated constantly, because even superchieftains like Ahmad Shah couldn't order about their near-peers: if they did, they might lose face, which could erode their authority.

Ahmad Shah gained his power from the network of personal followers he built up over time, loyal strongmen bound to him by reciprocal obligations that could never be quantified or reduced to quid pro quo, for the dynamics of leadership were those of a family, not of a marketplace. This is worth noting because the nature of leadership in Afghan culture has bedeviled every wave of foreigners that has tried to govern Afghanistan through proxy Afghan "leaders," mistakenly assuming that attaching a formal "office" to a given individual makes that man a leader.

In order to keep his people united and himself at the head of them all, Ahmad Shah had to wage war. His predecessor had sacked India, so he would sack it too. This was good politics, for Indians were mostly Hindus and their worship involved idols. Ahmad Shah's people, by contrast, were Muslims who believed that anyone who destroyed idols stood higher in God's favor. The more idols Ahmad Shah destroyed, the more prestige he gained among his own.

Sacking India was good business too, for the idols he broke were crusted with gems and located in temples that contained gold plate and other valuables: so his campaigns gave him a revenue stream, which enabled him to dispense favors to an ever-wider network of followers who were then bound to him by the debts they owed. Waging constant war kept enlarging this emperor's territory, but it also helped him consolidate the territory he already possessed.

Ahmad Shah must have been ferocious in battle, but his people didn't admire him for his military prowess alone. As a Pushtoon, he also had to perform great feats of hospitality, throw splendid feasts, lavish charity on the less fortunate, and demonstrate munificence. Even as he exerted mastery of every situation, he had to stroke the egos of the men he dealt with, for only by giving the appearance of modesty could he grow colossal. Pushtoon culture also values eloquence, and here again Ahmad Shah excelled. His martial poetry is still savored by Pushtoons (although it must be admitted that his work does not survive translation very well).[2]

In short, though his enemies feared him, his own people saw him as wise, diplomatic, and fair. Far from behaving despotically, he set up a council of nine advisors to help him rule. Each was the chief of a major Pushtoon tribe, and all civil decisions had to go through the council. By flattering the dignity of other Pushtoon chiefs, he kept them loyal.

Much has been said about *Pushtoonwali*, the code of the Pushtoons, which demands that men take care of guests even to the point of sacrificing their own wealth and lives if need be, that they avenge injury to their own kin with an equal injury dealt to the injuring clan, that they defend to the death the "honor" (that is, the inviolate sexual purity) of the women in their family, that they stop fighting an enemy the moment the enemy surrenders—and so on and so on and so on . . .

But although the Pushtoons may honor this code in the extreme, similar values flavor the folkways of other groups throughout Afghanistan. Tajiks, Hazaras, Uzbeks, and others all tend to revere generosity and treat guests as privileged celebrities. All tend to feel that a man's self-respect rests on the unsullied sexual modesty of the women in his family, especially the unmarried young ones. Whatever influence Ahmad Shah built up among Pushtoons, he cast a similar spell for his other subjects too. Non-Pushtoons may have had some cultural differences from Pushtoons, but they got along well enough under this Pushtoon lord, in part because Ahmad Shah pretty much let everyone run their own affairs. He did tax people, but that's what kings do. He did draft people of every ethnic group into his armies, but that was not so much an imposition as a way of sharing the spoils of war.

Ahmad Shah's empire ended up stretching from eastern Iran to the Indus River. Many earlier conquerors had flung up essentially the same empire. In the eleventh century the Ghaznavid sultan Mahmoud had sacked some of the very same temples as Ahmad Shah Baba. In the sixteenth century, the founder of the Moghul Empire fought a key battle at Panipat, where Ahmad Shah Baba routed the Hindu Marathas two centuries later.

If Ahmad Shah stood out from the other conquerors, it was mainly because he united the Pushtoon tribes more than anyone ever had. He mended the fault line between Barakzais and Sadozais. He reconciled the Durrani Pushtoons and the Ghilzai Pushtoons. He also created a fragile association among Pushtoons and other ethnic groups within his realm, governing a dozen ethnicities under one great umbrella. Farsi-speaking Tajiks, Shi'a Hazaras, Turkish-speaking Uzbeks and Turcomans of the north, and Farsibans whose roots ran west into what is now Iran, all thought of themselves as loyal subjects of this single great emperor. And, in his multifarious armies, the beginnings of a common national consciousness began to form. The many ethnic groups serving shoulder to shoulder in Ahmad Shah Baba's armies built up among themselves the beginnings of a national spirit, a sense of *Afghaniyat*, or "Afghan-ness."[3] This is why, in Ahmad Shah's lifetime, the area that was called Ariana in ancient times and Khurasan in medieval times came to be known as Afghanistan.

Ahmad Shah's Empire

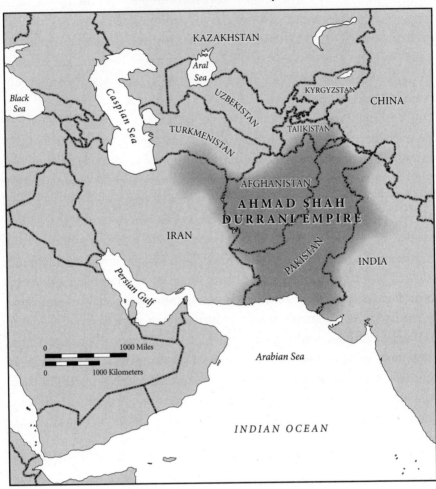

2

Ahmad Shah's Afghanistan

WHAT AHMAD SHAH BABA CREATED WAS NOT A COUNTRY IN THE MODERN sense. Today, "country" means at minimum a definite territory enclosed by a continuous border, within which one government makes and enforces all the rules for public life and issues a currency that all the inhabitants use for their transactions. In that sense, a country could not have existed in Ahmad Shah's time and place, for no man could have exerted much control at a distance. The geography was too daunting, the inhabitants too diverse, and the technology of communication and transportation too primitive. Ahmad Shah's empire was instead a loose affair characterized less by borders than by centers, a network of garrisons and cities laced through a mostly rural landscape.

Borders were more zones than lines. Each city and town had a strongman who dominated the surrounding countryside, but this strongman's power waned as one moved away from his seat, like the force field around a magnet. Kabul, for example, was one great power center and Kandahar another, but between those cities stretched a great deal of territory in which neither city's strongman mattered much.

In these locales, someone weaker but closer made the rules: he might be the lord of the nearest town or, if there was no town, the headman of the nearest village or, in a place even more remote, a big landowner with a fort of his own and a few hundred relatives and retainers living with him.

In this sort of state, the emperor's power consisted of his ability to tax and draft and his personal relationships with a network of local lords. Any place fitting this description was part of his empire. Accordingly, the most important power centers were governed by men loyal to the emperor, often his close relatives—his brothers, uncles, or sons.

Of the big cities, three defined Afghanistan: Herat, Kandahar, and Kabul. Two others were important as well: Peshawar in the south and Mazar-i-Sharif in the north. No matter who called himself king of this region, these five cities were usually part of his empire, an enduring nexus. Four are still part of Afghanistan, but the fifth, Peshawar, lies outside the country's borders, which has been a burr under the saddle throughout Afghan history and continues to generate trouble today.

In Ahmad Shah's era, each city had a high surrounding wall and one or more gates, much like the cities of medieval Europe. The bigger the city, the higher its walls and the more numerous its gates. Mighty Kabul, for example, had five gates facing five different directions. Through one came the road from Kandahar, through another the road from Peshawar, through another the road from Mazar-i-Sharif, and so on. Inside the walls, these roads became boulevards that converged on some definitive complex at the city's heart. In Kabul, all the big boulevards led to a vast covered market called the Grand Bazaar, a labyrinth of shops and stalls vending produce, handicrafts, and manufactured products from surrounding civilizations. The Grand Bazaar was situated along the Kabul River, which ran through a notch between two sets of mountains. Citizens' houses covered the slopes north of the Grand Bazaar. On the other side of the river, a royal palace known as Bala Hissar perched atop a promontory, a fortress with thick walls of sunbaked brick and immense towers dotted by small windows. The neighborhoods on this side of the river were known as Shor Bazaar or "Hubbub Market"—for it was, to locals and even to many travelers, the liveliest urban center ever seen.

Other cities had different flavors. At the heart of Kandahar, one found a thick cluster of mosques ringed by garrisons. This ancient capital of Pushtoon culture was always a conservative religious city and the capital of its major tribes.

At the heart of Herat, by contrast, one found schools and shrines, for this had long been an important capital of art, literature, and learning. It

Major Cities of Afghanistan

was the birthplace of Behzad, the greatest painter of Persian miniatures, and the home of vaunted Sufi poets such as Jami and Ansary.*

Mazar-i-Sharif means sacred shrine, and indeed the core of this city was and is an immense mausoleum embellished and expanded generation after generation no matter who ruled the country, a tomb believed by locals to be the actual burial place of Khalifa Ali, the Prophet Mohammed's fourth successor and the most revered figure to Islam's Shi'a sect. Here, also, the region's most spectacular New Year's Day celebration takes place, a festival featuring rituals and ceremonies dating back to Zoroastrian times.[1]

---

* Not an ancestor of mine—different branch of Ansarys.

Over the centuries, men who called themselves kings ruled by virtue of controlling at least a plurality of these strongholds. Most of the people they ruled, however, did not live in cities of any kind. The bulk of them lived in the countryside. Rural Afghanistan was in many ways the real Afghanistan, and the social fabric of this universe of villages is a key to this story because it still exists and its tenacity continues to affect the politics of the country.

———

AFGHAN HISTORIAN MOHAMMED ALI CLAIMS THE AFGHAN VILLAGE-republic attained its classic form around the same era as the Italian Renaissance.[2] Thousands of these villages dotted the hills and plains of this region, each of them a more or less autonomous political and economic unit. They sprang up throughout the mountains, in the steep valleys, along the hundreds of rivers and streams running down from snowy peaks. In general, every Afghan village had at its heart a stronghold or *qala*—a large compound with cob walls. Many but not all qalas had stout earthen towers rising from their four corners.

The people of any village were all related in some way or another because virtually all marriages took place within this village world, and yet the villagers typically regarded themselves as belonging to a number of different clans and kept track of their lineages in order to maintain a sense of separation. This allowed a social hierarchy to obtain among the clans. The most privileged families lived in the qala, along with their poor relations and servants. Others lived in compounds clustered around the qala. Fields and farmlands surrounded the cluster of compounds, extending as much as a day's walk away or more. On the slopes above the fields, the villagers grazed their numerous sheep and their less numerous goats.[3]

Some kept cattle, but not too many, for cattle took too much tending. Rarely butchered for meat, cattle were kept within the compounds for milk. Taking the sheep out to graze was a man's job, tending the cattle a woman's. Most farmers had buffalos as well to do the heavy work of pulling plows. People walked where they had to go, or, if they had to go far, they rode donkeys. Donkeys hauled loads as well: timber, mounds of grain, sacks of bricks—nothing was too bulky or heavy to load onto a donkey. Mules were not unknown but not common. In the mountains, few had horses: average folks could not afford them, and donkeys were far more practical. Horse country lay mainly in those rolling, grassy plains of the north.

Ali uses the term *village-republic* for these little social units because they had no formal ruler. The patriarchs of the clans were the leaders of the village. Some clans had higher status, and their patriarchs and leading men had more authority. But their authority was more like that of a father in a family than like that of a prince in a state—which illuminates what Ahmad Shah really was: the patriarch of all the patriarchs. That's why he was called Ahmad Shah *Baba*—Father Ahmad Shah.

Locally, the most important patriarchal lords were known as *khans*. They were the feudal barons of Afghan society, their status hereditary. Every village usually had a *malik*, as well, a formal "headman." Maliks were elected (sort of), but the chances were pretty good that the chosen malik's father had been a malik too or was at least recognized as a khan. If a crisis faced the community, the leading khan assisted the malik in deciding what should be done. The leading khan and the malik might very well be the same person, but they might not be.

Formal decisions were made by a council of the most important men of a village in a protracted discussion called a *jirga*. (In Dari-speaking villages, it might be called a *shura*.) The council was a standing body but didn't meet regularly—only when some issue came up. The jirga couldn't arrive at a decision by a simple vote. It had to stay in session until the group arrived at a consensus. This was a way to disarm future conflicts, because a decision by simple vote would likely leave a majority triumphant and a minority smoldering. Any such resentment was bound to flare again later in some seemingly unrelated context. Best to come out of a jirga with a consensus. Traditionally, anyone could speak up during the meeting, but, once a jirga made a decision, everyone was bound by it.

The malik was elected by the jirga, but his authority was not clearly separable from the informal authority he derived from prestige, social status, and family eminence. In "electing" a malik, the jirga was usually just acknowledging the stature of a fellow known by all to be the most eminent. Villages could operate by these informal, tacit rules because they were so small: everybody knew everybody. The malik did have some formal duties. He was responsible for dealing with the outside power, whomever that might be: the strongman of the nearest town, the king in the capital, the emperor, if there was one. If the king knew about a village, he collected taxes from it in the form of commodities. The malik was in charge of gathering what was due and delivering it to the king's agent.[4]

In any village, there were a few titled roles in addition to malik. Every village had at least one *mullah*, and perhaps more. A mullah was the basic, all-purpose Muslim cleric. He wasn't a "holy man." Mullahs had wives and children, they might own land, they went to war—they were no holier than thou or anyone else in the village. They just knew how to read, and they *had* read the Qur'an front to back. They supposedly knew at least the rudiments of the religious law. They oversaw the various rites of the life cycle insofar as these concerned religion. For example, when a child was born, the mullah was called in to whisper words from the Qur'an into the baby's ear, thus inducting him or her into the community of faith. When someone died, the mullah was the fellow who recited the necessary prayers to accompany the lowering of the body into the grave. Later, he'd be the one to organize the communal reading of the Qur'an that honored the deceased. And when two people got married, the mullah presided over the ceremony that joined the couple in matrimony and also over the all-important meeting of family elders to sign the contract—for every marriage was fundamentally a tribal-business transaction between families, not the culminating moment of a romance between individuals.

At the times of prayer, especially in the early morning and at sunset, the mullah might well be the fellow who climbed into the minaret (if the town had one) or onto some tall rooftop (if it didn't); from there he loudly chanted the Arabic verses that let people know that the time for prayer had come. In a larger village, the mullah might have a *muezzin* to perform this duty, an assistant with a particularly melodic, booming voice.

And every village did have some sort of mosque, some building that functioned as a gathering place for Friday prayers, for daily sunset prayers, for ceremonial gatherings on religious holidays, and for jirgas, a building that also served as shelter for travelers if any came by. Taking care of the mosque might be one of a mullah's duties, although not every mullah had a mosque of his own to look after. Those who did were known as *imams*, and when the people gathered for prayer the imam generally led the prayer—led it by doing just what everyone else was doing except that he stood in front of the group, facing the same way as all the others (toward Mecca) and speaking certain verses out loud while the others spoke them silently. He set the rhythm of the ceremony by chanting Allahu Akbar at the appropriate moments to let the group know when to go into its pros-tration or assume a sitting position or stand up or bow at the waist. In short a mullah was like a religious mechanic. He took care of the physical details of daily life in a world so permeated by religion that religion was indistinguishable from daily life. He had no special virtues otherwise.

Indeed, there is a robust tradition of the mullah as rascal, typified by Mullah Nasruddin, a fanciful figure featured in a rich body of humorous folk anecdotes. One such anecdote, for example, relates that the mullah's neighbor came to borrow his donkey. The mullah was reluctant. He said, "I'm sorry but my donkey died yesterday." Just then the donkey began to bray behind the house. "What's this? What's this?" the neighbor said. "Mullah-sahib: your donkey isn't dead, I can hear it braying." The mullah was indignant. "Who are you going to believe?" he snorted. "A mullah or a donkey?"

Another figure who roamed the village world was the *dalak*, a charac-ter who handled many of the less pleasant but necessary details of daily life. A dalak was not a religious figure at all, but many matters he handled were governed in some way by religion. At a young age, for example, boys had to be circumcised. A dalak did this. Dalaks pulled teeth, cut hair, and performed a variety of other personal services. Dalaks often had no homes of their own but moved around from household to household, sleeping wherever they happened to be and eating what the family fed them. The village world (and traditionally Afghan life in general) was strictly divided into a private realm (inhabited by both men and women) and a public world (inhabited exclusively by men). Dalaks moved between the two realms. They knew intimate details of every household since they dealt with matters most personal. They heard all the gossip, therefore, and they spread the gossip—they were a village version of a news service. Also, they knew which households had young men antsy to get married and which ones had girls of marriageable age, so they provided matchmaking services. This was especially useful because dalaks often served not just one but several villages in an area.[5]

The dalak was the lowest end of a scale that ran through the mullah on up to more respected figures. One such was the *mirab*, or water arbitrator. A man had to have acquired a high reputation for wisdom and good judgment to achieve this role. Even though a mirab adjudicated *only* disputes concerning water, his was a powerful role, for in this desert country, land per se was not worth much. Water was the precious resource.

At the top of the scale were hugely respected figures such as *mawlawis* (religious scholars). The *qazi* or judge was definitely a most eminent religious figure, but not every village had one. A qazi was needed only in difficult and complicated cases, often ones involving disputes between people of different villages or tribes—because disputes within a family were handled by the family, and those within a clan by the clan, and those within a village, in the case of criminal matters—a murder or a theft, for example— by the jirga. The qazi was qualified to judge complex matters because he had earned a broadly accepted reputation as a scholar and devout.

Some matters baffled even the typical qazi—matters involving subtle religious interpretations of a legal issue. In such cases, a qazi might consult with a *mufti*, a religious scholar whose reputation for learning was so immense, communal consensus accorded him the authority to issue *fatwas,* interpretations of religious law. These were not judgments about particular disputes but rulings about the law itself. Here was legislation derived, not from any government, not from any elected body, not from any political appointee, not from any warlord or general or ruler, nor from the will of any living individual or entity, but from the Muslim scriptures and the theological works of ancient devouts. The only way to achieve the authority to issue these rulings was to mature into the role by winning the approval and respect of the existing muftis and qazis. It was inherently a conservative system, deeply so.

Internally, these village-republics operated pretty much without money. They didn't even use the barter system. Personal service stood in for economic exchange: everyone was someone with respect to all other persons in the village—everybody was a son or a daughter, a niece or uncle, clan chieftain or grandfather or poor relation or whatever.[6] Some people had a duty to serve other people and had, in their turn, a right to be served by certain others. Children had to serve the whims of their elders. Young women had to obey the dictates of older women within their tribe of household womenfolk.

Women had command of certain spheres upon which men did not typically intrude. They made decisions about household food supplies and children, and they handled the initial negotiations and bargaining that led to marriages. As a group, however, the masculine encircled the feminine, and the women's corporation was contained within and ruled by the men's corporation. In this universe of village-republics, there were lords and there were lieges, and everyone did what was expected of them and demanded what tradition entitled them to.

Afghan villages were pretty much self-sufficient. They produced their own food, did their own carpentry, made their own shoes, and shod their own horses, if they had horses. Women did the spinning and weaving and made the garments. They cooked food and baked bread—all this was done privately, every compound in a village having its own pit oven. The women churned milk into butter and made cheese, and they dried yogurt to make the base for the coveted sour sauce called *q'root,* and they used techniques they knew about to preserve meats and vegetables for winter storage, and they pounded nuts and dried fruits together to make an edible leather that men could carry on long journeys. The men did the heavy work outside the home: they dug the irrigation works, they dammed and apportioned water, they plowed and harvested the fields, and they dealt with any strangers who approached the village. And of course, if there was fighting to be done (and there often was), men did the fighting.

Though largely autonomous, villages were not completely isolated. People of one village knew people of nearby villages, and any of the village men might sometimes go to larger local towns, their donkeys loaded high with q'root or felt or other goods they sold for cash, which they used to buy more sophisticated manufactured goods—matches, spoons, cosmetics, and the like. On these sojourns, they heard about events and affairs in the larger world. No one far away had much effect on their daily life, however. For most villagers, the governor was a story. The king was a rumor, some tough guy with a big army crashing around in the distance somewhere, his relevance to daily life near nil. If he came around, he was the boss; as soon as he left, he became a tale to tell the kids: "I saw the king once. Yes! Standing right there, he was, real as that horse!"

Yet even villagers who didn't travel anywhere might come into contact with the pastoral nomads who constituted some 10 percent or more of the population. They were a minority but a big minority: hundreds of thousands of people, and, because they lived on the move, they permeated the land. Farsi speakers called them *kuchis*: "the ones who move." Pushtoons called them *powindas*. They made their way across the land in bands of a few score to a few hundred people, stopping for several days in favorable spots—or at the most several weeks—and then traveling on.[7]

A small nomad camp might have ten tents and a big one up to fifty, but they were never much bigger. Any given band might have hundreds of sheep and dozens of camels, which roamed along with them and had to be herded and guarded wherever the band went and wherever it stopped. Every nomad band therefore had its own dogs, which weren't elegant Afghan hounds but mastiff-like beasts maybe twice the size of your average Labrador, with bulky bodies and large heads and jaws like those of a pit bull. When I was growing up in Afghanistan, no one seemed to think nomad dogs were any special breed. People regarded them simply as scary mongrels; yet these dogs all looked so similar, I have to think they were de facto purebreds. The ones I saw in Kabul as a boy were feral and frightening, but the nomads' own dogs trotted along the outside of the band as it moved, and they skulked around the edges of the camp when it stopped, and, if you were a stranger, these dogs were one more reason not to go wandering casually into a nomad camp.

This makes sense because nomads led an inherently perilous lifestyle. They were always in foreign territory. They were always subject to raids by other nomads or by bands of men who practiced marauding rather than herding as a way of life. In old Afghanistan, especially in the north, such marauders were legion. You might suppose that nomads would not offer a tempting target because, after all, what did people with such a spare lifestyle have to steal? The answer is herds. Food on the hoof was very valuable indeed. Also, they had women. And because marauders might make off with their women, the nomads tended to form up in the same way as covered wagon trains crossing the plains of America in pioneer days: in phalanxes with women and children in the center and men on the outside.

When they stopped and set up an encampment, the same physical pattern emerged: women and children hung out in the heart of camp, surrounded by tents. Men formed up on the outside and kept watch for hostile forces. If anyone approached the encampment, the men went to them and found out who they were and what they wanted.

Whenever a nomad band roamed close to a village, a potential for conflict arose because both groups had animals to graze, both needed pasture. The villagers could hardly be blamed for taking a proprietary view: they were here first, this was *their* turf, and so they were apt to resent a nomad band letting loose hundreds of sheep to swarm over *their* grassy slopes.

This is not to say nomads and villagers were at war. Hardly. Some villagers were closely descended from pastoral nomads; some nomads had been sedentary villagers until some misfortune such as a drought uprooted them, whereupon they took to a lifestyle they knew well because their tribal kin or near-term ancestors practiced it—and took to it gladly, it seems, for many preferred the nomadic to the sedentary way of life. But the relationship between nomads and townsfolk, though fragile, was symbiotic, especially for nomads because, unlike typical villagers, they were *not* self-sufficient. Kuchi bands produced their own food, to be sure, but they had to go into towns and bargain in the bazaars for items such as utensils and metalware and the very cloth from which they sewed their tents; plus they leaned on farmers for fruits and vegetables and the flour they needed for the staple of the Afghan diet, bread. For such goods they traded milk products, dried meat, hides, embroidered cloth, beaded garments, and other light portable craft items.

Nomads, then, were not separate from the general population. They belonged to tribes and felt tribal affiliations; they could trace their lineage to the same ancestors as some of the settled folk. They had mullahs, they acknowledged certain qazis as legal authorities, and they respected certain scholars in common with villagers. The difference was, a villager might live and die without ever having gone twenty miles from the spot where he was born. The nomads, by contrast, routinely traveled hundreds of miles in a year, deep into India going south, and beyond the Amu River going north. Borders? They hardly knew the meaning of the word. Even though they tended to be hidebound, suspicious, and deeply conservative, nomads had seen the world and could routinely speak three languages or more. For a king, governing an area in which many of the inhabitants were nomadic was like trying to serve soup with a sieve. The nomads were difficult to count, much less tax. And the hell of it was, they sometimes took umbrage with kings and lords and joined rebellions, so they could not be ignored.

Although kings such as Ahmad Shah Baba had little presence in the lives of their subjects beyond taxing and drafting, they could interact with their people in one further way. If people felt they were owed justice and weren't getting it from their jirga or the qazi or any other traditional source, they might petition the king, for, in addition to the traditional law, there was the king's law. Traditional law was a blend of religious rulings and folkways mistakenly regarded as religious rules plus local customs supported by generations of consensus. The king's law expressed the whim and wisdom of the king's officers and factotums—and ultimately of the king himself.

Since the king had the military power, his word superseded all other rulings. But anyone who went to the king for justice was taking a chance, for the king's rulings were final and might be arbitrary. Also, anyone who sought the king's justice had to gird for a long struggle getting into the system and getting heard by someone who mattered, because there was only one king, his corpus of officers was limited, and only a few people, therefore, were going to be heard. No one would even attempt to go to the king for judgment on some trivial dispute, and few would try unless they knew someone who knew someone who gave them some connection to the court. So only khans and other great men were likely to go that route. For the average villager, a wise king might be better than a stupid one, and a kind king better than a cruel one, but a change of dynasty produced little reverberation on the ground level. "Better a strong dog in the yard than a strong king in the capital," says an Afghan proverb.[8]

3

Farangis on the Horizon

AHMAD SHAH MAY HAVE BEEN THE FIRST KING OF AFGHANISTAN, BUT HE was the last of a long line of conquerors who amassed a tribal army and flung together an empire stretching from central Asia to India. He was the last because the political map was changing drastically by the time he died. New powers were moving into the region, powers no local warrior could beat in open battle. Some called them the *Farangi*, a corruption of "Frank," the name of the tribes that had come out of Europe seven centuries earlier to storm Jerusalem and trigger those centuries of battle the Farangis called the Crusades. Since then, *Farangi* had become the generic term for Europeans. Now one group of Farangis was coming to the forefront in India.

Local people called them the *Engrayzee*, a Farsi/Pushto corruption of the word "English." The Engrayzee had been in India for more than 150 years at this point. The first English trading post had been planted on the Indian coast in 1613 not by the government of England but by the East India Trading Company, a private English corporation looking to enrich its shareholders. In 1707, England and Scotland merged to form Great Britain, after which it was no longer just the English but the British who were in India, but they were still there mainly as merchants and traders, operating humbly out of little stations that the great and powerful Moghul dynasty allowed them to construct on a shoelace of land along the coast.

The British were just one of several European groups competing to do business in India at that time. They did some fighting, but not with the Indians: they fought each other. First, the French and English drove out the Portuguese. Then the French and British turned upon each other. In 1743, just before the Pushtoons named Ahmad Shah their king, the British began battling the French on the east coast of India. This became just one front in a global conflict that, in Europe, was called the Seven Years War and, on the North American continent, the French and Indian War. By 1763, the British had won this war and in India had won it decisively. After that, the French could live in India only "under British protection."

The British didn't realize they were conquering India itself as they battled the French, because they weren't out to rule India. Their interests remained strictly commercial. The British government had no officials on this soil. The British presence on the subcontinent was still limited to the East India Company, which was technically a private venture, even though it had the full endorsement of the British government and served as an agent of British interests. The company was just striving to maximize its market share, which happened to coincide with the interests of the British state.

In 1756, trouble broke out between the Indians and the British at the trading post of Calcutta. The minor Moghul governor of that province, the *Nawab* as such governors were called, arrested a few dozen British citizens and clapped them into a small cell, which the European press soon dubbed the Black Hole of Calcutta. The room was intolerably small, and by morning many of the British prisoners were dead. When news of the outrage reached East India Company headquarters at Pondicherry, the company deputized its agent Robert Clive to march north and punish that governor. Clive went to Calcutta with a small force, casually removed the Nawab, and installed his nephew in his place. The operation was called the battle of Plassey, but it hardly merits the term "battle." It was more like an administrative procedure. This was not the moment when the British took control of Bengal but the moment when everyone, including the British, realized they already controlled Bengal. No one could pinpoint exactly when the conquest took place, but, from then on, the East India Company did as it pleased in Bengal and anywhere else in India that caught its fancy.

The affair of the Black Hole of Calcutta took place on the eastern coast of the subcontinent in the same year that Ahmad Shah was sacking the city of Delhi. At that moment the Afghans might have seemed even more powerful than the British. After all, the British merely replaced one nawab with another; the Afghan king replaced the Moghul emperor with a more compliant puppet. Just as the British were revealing their naked power in the east, Ahmad Shah was asserting his naked domination in the west. The bare facts suggest a showdown brewing between the British and the Afghans.

But that would be getting ahead of the story. Delhi was nearly a thousand miles from Calcutta, and Ahmad Shah's home city of Kandahar was another five hundred miles farther west. There was no intersection between the British and the Afghans, no reason yet for the two to clash.

In the several years that followed the Black Hole of Calcutta affair, the British secured their hold on Bengal and began moving west. Their expansion began just as the Moghul empire was dissolving into smaller states. One by one, the British took control of these successor states. Where necessary, they took charge directly. When it was more convenient, they let an indigenous elite keep on ruling but set strict parameters for them.

Eventually, London decided that India was too important, fragile, and vast to be administered by a private company, especially because that company mismanaged Bengal pretty badly. In 1773—just as their North American colonies were beginning to break away—Great Britain sent a governor general to oversee India. The East India Company continued to operate on the subcontinent as a formidable power, but formal British rule of India had now begun. The colonial government was later called the Raj, and although its governor was appointed by the Parliament in London and his decisions were subject to Parliament's approval, he was pretty much sovereign in India, with his own cabinet and foreign policy.

Ahmad Shah died of jaw cancer in 1772. In that same year—just to put the event in perspective—American patriots in Massachusetts were planning the Boston Tea Party, an act of rebellion not just against the British government but against the East India Company, the same corporation that had such a stranglehold in India. Afghanistan, at that moment, was an empire stretching from the heart of modern-day Iran to the

Indian Ocean and included modern-day Kashmir in the northeast. As a power in the Muslim world, it was second only to the Ottomans.

But the Afghan empire was already beginning to crack. The emperor Ahmad Shah had been ailing for a few years before his death. After he died, just as British power was expanding, Afghan power shrank. The British had nothing to do with this. Their impact would come later. Ahmad Shah's state crumbled for internal reasons. It was a dynastic empire, which is an inherently unstable form of political organization because it depends on the genius of its ruler. Ahmad Shah was a towering figure, but his sons were less remarkable, and his grandsons even less so. The sons and grandsons fell to fighting over the throne. The crown changed hands six times in three decades. Finally, the fragmentation devolved into a grisly civil war between two Pushtoon clans, which was much like England's War of the Roses, when the Yorks and the Lancasters hammered at each other for several decades.

Out of the English conflict came the gigantic figure of Henry VII, the first of the Tudor dynasty and in many ways the founder of England as we know it. Out of the Afghan civil wars came a giant too: a man whom Afghans still call "Dost Mohammed the Great." The grandsons of Ahmad Shah all ended up blind, dead, or in exile. They themselves had done most of the blinding, killing, and driving into exile. In 1826, Dost Mohammed declared himself amir, and thus began the reign of his clan the Mohammedzais. Though not directly descended from Ahmad Shah, they were closely related to his clan and belonged to his larger tribal group, the Durranis: they too were Pearly Ones.

Amir Dost Mohammed Khan was a lanky, long-bearded, black-eyed man of imposing stature. In his youth he had been something of a wastrel and a drinker, but he had matured into an austere and soft-spoken monarch who impressed everyone he met as a perfect gentleman.[1] Obviously, he could not have been *perfectly* gentle, or he would not have come out of those civil wars victorious. When rougher manners were needed, he could no doubt sink to the occasion; but he was perfectly at home in genteel settings, the soul of sophisticated social grace.

Dost Mohammed set out to weld a coherent nation that could be ruled from his chosen capital, the city of Kabul. This would become the fundamental project of Afghan history, a project thwarted and distorted by both outside and inside forces. It is with Dost Mohammed, then, that the Afghan story really begins.

Within a few years, this king restored order to his territory. His countrymen could not have been more grateful. Life could now return to normal. Farmers could get back to farming, herders to herding. Women could tend their gardens and plot political marriages. Men could loll about in the bazaars and gossip with their friends. Trade could resume. Camel caravans wended their way out of the northern steppes once again, transporting wool and hides and flax oil, lapis lazuli and gorgeous carpets, horses, camels, and other livestock, over the Hindu Kush and down to the plains of India to exchange for rice, tea, spices, calico, cotton fabric, and other coveted goods.[2]

Dost Mohammed had recovered the core of Ahmad Shah's empire, yet he was not content. He was not content because he did not have the whole of the empire back. The city of Mashad was gone, but, oh well: that loss Dost Mohammed could swallow, because Mashad traditionally fell within the sphere of influence of the Persian monarch. But Dost Mohammed had lost Peshawar as well and with it all the fertile lands flanking the Indus River. Those lands had been seized by a formidable warrior-king named Ranjit Singh, who was not even a Muslim but a Sikh. Peshawar and its environs were inhabited by Muslim Pushtoons, and Peshawar was also the traditional winter capital of Afghan kings. The ruling clan of Afghanistan, being Pushtoons, found the loss of this city particularly galling. Dost Mohammed's determination to get Peshawar back launched a conflict that was never resolved and that continues to generate trouble to this very day.

4

Between the Lion
and the Bear

AT THE SAME TIME AS THE CIVIL WAR THAT RAGED IN AFGHANISTAN
before the rise of Dost Mohammed—roughly 1792–1826—Europe was
going through massive tumult of its own. The 1700s capped a period
of unprecedented European expansion, made possible by their mastery of
the seas. Over the course of just a few centuries, the English, French,
Dutch, Portuguese, Spanish, and others sailed to the furthest shores of
the five oceans, planting colonies and trading posts. As their dominance
increased around the globe, European nations fell to fighting one another
for commercial advantages and for possession of vast territories distant
from their own. During this same period, throughout western European
culture, science was replacing religion as a method for understanding nature, a development that spawned technological advances such as steam
engines, railroads, mechanized factories, and mass production, all of
which had profound political and economic implications.

In 1789, one of history's greatest social revolutions erupted in France.
The French overthrew their monarchy and landed aristocracy. The bour-
geoisie stood revealed as the new ruling class and the potential power elite
of the future. The conservative forces of Europe united to crush the new
order, but the revolutionaries beat back the monarchists, and out of the
turmoil marched a new kind of conqueror, a petty-journalist-turned-soldier,
Napoleon Bonaparte. Not content with defending France, he took the

war to France's enemies, conquering much of Germany and eastern Europe and ringing his empire with docile client states such as Italy and Spain.

Napoleon did not, however, manage to win a single significant battle against Great Britain, and his grand attempt to conquer Russia ended in disaster. Finally, beaten decisively at Waterloo, he was exiled to a lonesome little island to die. This whole dramatic episode—the French Revolution and the Napoleonic Wars—altered global politics. Britain emerged as the most powerful nation on the planet, a power derived largely from its navy: no one could beat the British at sea, and the Napoleonic Wars confirmed that sea power was now one key to global dominance.

Technology was the other key, and there too Great Britain held the lead. Britain was the first nation to build railroads and the first to harness steam power for mass production. To be sure, it needed an abundant supply of raw materials to feed its factories, but, even though it was a little island, Britain had a commanding advantage. It possessed India, probably the most valuable piece of colonial real estate in the world. With its unbeatable navy, its advanced technology, and the resources of India at its disposal, Britain had power no other country could match.

The Napoleonic Wars also left one other country snorting with newfound ambition: Russia. It was Russia that had dealt Napoleon his real deathblow, for Napoleon lost his entire army in a catastrophic march to Moscow. Russia was in many ways the polar opposite of Britain. Instead of tiny, it was vast. Instead of technologically advanced, it was primitive. Britain had (for its time) a sizable and well-educated middle class—Adam Smith supposedly described it as "a nation of shopkeepers."[1] Russia had virtually no middle class. It was a nation in which a handful of aristocrats ruled over millions of serfs and didn't even speak the same language as their subjects.

Russia had long been expanding east across the Ural Mountains and into central Asia, but it did not have colonies in distant places because of another crucial difference from the island nation of Britain: Russia was essentially landlocked. It did have an ocean to its north, but that ocean was the Arctic, which was frozen most of the year. Russia had ports on the Black Sea, but the Black Sea itself was surrounded by land except for the choke point of the Dardanelles strait. In this new age of naval power, a country needed better access to the world's oceans to compete globally.

Russia had one way out of its predicament. If it could expand east far enough and then move south through Afghanistan, it could gain access to ports on the Arabian Sea. From there it would have unlimited access to the Indian Ocean. Now *there* was a goal worth fighting for. Only Afghanistan stood in the way.

Britain could not look kindly on a Russian expansion to the Indian Ocean, for it would bring Russia right to the borders of Britain's precious India. For Britain, the issue wasn't just a port or two; the very source of British power and wealth seemed at stake. India must be defended! Russian expansion must therefore be blocked! At all costs, Russia must not be allowed to take Afghanistan! And so these two global powers began struggling for dominance in central Asia. Rudyard Kipling, in his novel *Kim*, famously called the contest "the Great Game," but it was a frivolous name for a drama that would turn so dark and so bloody.

The Great Game

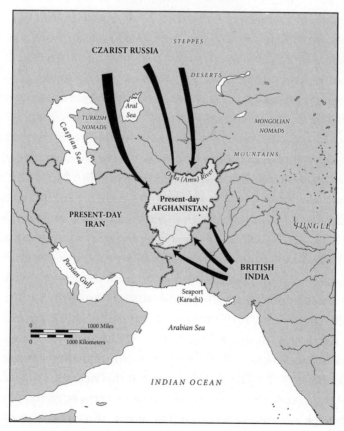

In 1831, the East India Company dispatched an eager young man named Alexander Burnes to explore the upper reaches of the Indus River and thence to proceed across Afghan territory to Bukhara and the other famous central Asian cities of the old Silk Route to see what commercial opportunities might exist up there. Burnes was new to the East and raring for adventure. He kept a diary of his travels in which, with a journalist's eye for detail, he recorded the sights and sounds of the worlds he passed through.

Burnes first stopped in the town of Ludhiana to see two former Afghan kings, Shah Shuja and Shah Zeman.[2] Both were grandsons of Ahmad Shah Baba. They were brothers. Both had briefly held the throne of Afghanistan. The man who dethroned Shah Zeman poked his eyes out to make sure he would cause no further trouble. The man who did this was Shah Shuja, the brother with whom Shah Zeman now lived in melancholy companionship.

Burnes is always generous about the Afghans: clearly he liked and admired them, and he tries to say nice things about these two. Both had a kingly dignity, he declares. Yet the scene he describes feels very dark. The blind brother seems intolerably gloomy. Shah Shuja comes across as a whiner and a fop. He greets Burnes wearing a pink gauze tunic and a velvet cap from which hang emeralds and tassels. A fat, sour man, he complains to Burnes about his many misfortunes. When he lost his throne, he fled to the court of the Sikh king Ranjit Singh, lord of Peshawar, seeking refuge. He was hoping to pay for that refuge with the Koh-i-Noor diamond, which he had stolen from the treasury before taking flight. But Ranjit Singh simply took his diamond and put him in a dungeon.

The renegade king tunneled his way into the sewer system and escaped the city. During his brief reign, he had curried favor with the British and in fact had signed a treaty ceding control of his foreign policy to the British. This was a canny move, as it turned out, for it gave the British a reason to think he might be useful to them one day. The British gave him an estate and a stipend sufficient for him and his harem of several hundred women (and his brother). Shah Shuja wasn't happy, however. He wanted a kingdom. When Burnes told him that he still had many friends in Sind,

Shuja dismissed the reassurance. "Oh! Friends like that are worse than enemies. They do nothing to help me."[3] Burnes reluctantly concluded that Shah Shuja didn't have the temperament or judgment to rule a country.

After leaving the Afghan brothers, Burnes visited the court of Ranjit Singh. He found this place brimming with luxury and pomp. Ranjit Singh was a military leader, a drunkard, a drug addict, a sensualist, and a religious devout. He read to Burnes from the Sikh scriptures, the Granth, which was wrapped in ten layers of cloth, each a different color. The outermost cloth was yellow because, at Ranjit's court, each day had its own color and that day's color was yellow. Everyone Burnes saw was wearing yellow garments, yellow turbans. All the flowers displayed around the room were yellow. Canaries released in the garden gave the foliage twinkles of yellow. After he had finished reading from his scriptures, Ranjit Singh proudly displayed the Koh-i-Noor diamond. It was, wrote Burnes, "about half the size of an egg."[4]

From Ranjit's court, Burnes and his group struck north and west to Peshawar, a city inhabited entirely by Pushtoons.[5] Although ruled by Ranjit Singh, it was governed by Dost Mohammed's brother Sultan Mohammed. The Pushtoon lord came to the city gates to meet Burnes, cutting a fine figure in his fur-lined coat ornamented with peacock down.

Braced for his first encounter with Afghan savages, Burnes was surprised to find the First Man of Peshawar a civilized and educated gentleman. That night, Burnes and his friends dined with the Durrani chieftain, feasting on milk-fed lamb simmered in sweet-and-sour stew, on baked rice dishes garnished with orange peels, and on sweetmeats followed by fresh fruits and sherbets. Burnes described the Afghans as sociable, well informed, noisily good-humored, and refreshingly free of prejudice. Nothing he told them about Europe put them off. "Every country has its customs," they shrugged.[6] The lord of Peshawar moved about his city freely, Burnes noted, without guards, attended only by his relatives and servants, who addressed him as a social equal.

From Peshawar, the expedition continued up the Kabul River. At the end of April 1831, they reached Dost Mohammed's capital, a burg so boisterously busy, said Burnes, that on the streets in the afternoons two men walking side by side could not hear each other well enough to carry on a normal conversation. The Kabul River dividing the city was lined with shade trees of every description. Countless orchards filled the air with the aroma of fruit tree blossoms: mulberries, apricots, pear, and quince. Kabul was a wide-open town—except for liquor. Dost Mohammed, once an enthusiastic drinker, had reformed, and in his zeal he had outlawed alcoholic beverages entirely. Armenians and Jews, who had been the city's main brewers and distillers, were leaving now because the new laws robbed them of their livelihood.

Burnes dined with Dost Mohammed in an immaculate apartment furnished only with a gorgeous carpet.[7] The men sat on the floor and ate with their hands. Burnes found the amir of Afghanistan solemn but impressive. He plied the Englishman with intelligent questions. How many kings in Europe? How did they coexist? How did the British collect revenue? What were British conscription policies? The amir heard they had filled their Indian armies with foot soldiers drafted from the native population. Did they have similar designs on Kabul? How did the British manage to produce such cheap goods? Burnes told him about steam engines, which interested the amir greatly.

Dost Mohammed seemed to like Burnes, and why wouldn't he? Burnes was an intense, brilliant, and charming young man, fluent in both Hindi and Persian. He not only spoke the local languages but could read the Arabic script in which Sufi poetry was written. His visit with Dost Mohammed laid the basis for a likely friendship between his country and Afghanistan; at least that was how Dost Mohammed interpreted it.

Burnes went on to publish a book about his great adventures, which became a best seller in London and made him the toast of the town. The young man became a coveted dinner guest at all the best houses. An adoring public dubbed him "Bukhara Burnes" because of his penchant for wearing turbans and other Oriental garb. They also called him the Iskandar of the East. Iskandar was the Persian pronunciation of Alexander, the great Greek conqueror. British accounts marveled that Burnes had made his way to remote regions so few had seen.

Actually, of course, lots of people had seen those places and saw them every day: they lived there. To them, the exotic element was Alexander Burnes. Nor did they think of themselves as particularly "remote." Those cities of the north—Balkh, Bukhara, Samarqand, Tashkent, and others—were entrepôts on the old Silk Road, which had long been the busiest highway of human commerce in the world, a network of roads and routes that connected China to Europe and both to India. People who lived in or around these cities traveled to India routinely on trading expeditions; and, of course, because people here were all Muslims, not a few had gone as far west as Mecca. In short, these were not unsophisticated primitives. Few, however, had been as far west as Europe—now *there* was a remote and exotic place, if ever there was one!

DOST MOHAMMED DID BATTLE WITH RANJIT SINGH SEVERAL TIMES, trying to regain Peshawar. He didn't lose those battles, but he didn't win them either. Peshawar remained in Sikh hands. Finally, Dost Mohammed decided that he needed help, and so he cast about for some alliance that would tip the scales.

He had two options, both of them attractive, both of them problematic. One was the British Raj, which dominated the subcontinent now. The source of British dominance wasn't clear to Afghans. The British homeland was far away, and they hadn't stormed in with a huge army. No, they had sent only a few military men, mostly officers, and had hired local folks to serve as troops. In fact, the British had two such armies in India. One took its orders from the British monarch, and its soldiers were called Queen's Company (because incredibly enough, Britain was ruled by a *woman*!). The other took its orders from the East India Company, which had pioneered English penetration of the subcontinent. Those soldiers were commonly called John Company. The two armies followed different masters yet somehow worked together. The British armies were about 90 percent Indian, yet Britain dominated India. This was certainly a new kind of force, and no one knew quite what to make of it, except that it was formidable.

The other option was Russia, whose king was called a czar. Like the British monarch, he ruled from a capital thousands of miles away, and it was a testament to his might that he could send his armies so far and make his power felt at such a distance. His troops had crossed the Caucuses, had taken Azerbaijan, had crossed the Caspian Sea and reached the shores of the Aral Sea. The czar's troops were close and getting closer. In fact, the Russians had even helped the Persian shah attack the Afghan-held city of Herat. The attack failed, but it showed that the Russians too were a force to reckon with.

Soliciting Russian help, however, was a little like asking a dragon for help building a bonfire. The czar's forces might offer too much help, as it were. Then again, asking the British for help posed similar risks. A third possibility existed: to play one power against the other, using each to keep the other out of Afghan territory. But, in that case, who would help Amir Dost Mohammed Khan recover Peshawar? How would he reconstruct the whole of Ahmad Shah's empire?

He inclined toward the British. Both of the new powers possessed menacing might, and both showed aggressive tendencies, but the amir felt that on balance the British were less expansionist, and, besides, Alexander Burnes, that young Scotsman who had come to Kabul in 1831, had left such a favorable impression.

Also, the new British viceroy in India, Lord Auckland, had sent a letter to Dost Mohammed assuring him quite directly, "My friend . . . it is not the practice of her majesty's government to interfere with the affairs of other sovereign nations."[8] Of course, he had said this in response to a guarded inquiry about getting British help for undermining Ranjit Singh, but if noninterference was really Britain's policy, they might be the safest ally for Afghanistan after all.

Then one day, in 1837, Dost Mohammed received good news: Lord Auckland was sending a trade mission to Kabul headed up by none other than—Alexander Burnes! The king welcomed the delegation and lavished upon his guests the sumptuous hospitality that Afghans consider their highest claim to fame. Officially, Burnes was here to (again) explore commercial opportunities on behalf of the East India Company. Actually, he had come with no authority to negotiate agreements of any kind. Just before he left India, Lord Auckland had specified that Burnes's mission was to spend as much time as possible in the palace and find out all he could about Russian influence at the Afghan court but avoid offering any hint of British aid for any of the amir's schemes or even discussing what the amir wanted. Mr. Burnes had come to Kabul purely as a spy.

His mission was limited in this way because Auckland was listening to another advisor, an older, higher ranking foreign policy expert named William Hay Macnaghten. Macnaghten was a British version of those American anti-Communist witch-hunters of the 1950s: everywhere Macnaghten looked he saw—*the Bear*. Britain *was*, of course, confronting "the Russian Bear" on a long front stretching from central Asia to eastern Europe, and, as an expert on central Asian affairs, Macnaghten believed the menace was centered in central Asia. He also knew what the Russians wanted—they wanted India!

A strong alliance with a friendly Dost Mohammed might have been one good way to block Russian expansion, but Macnaghten and Lord Auckland didn't trust "the Dost," as they called him. The Dost was too strong to be trusted. Strength gives a man ideas.

During those fine banquets at the Afghan court and the quiet conversations afterward, Burnes avoided all discussion of Peshawar, military aid, treaty alliances, and closer ties. Dost Mohammed began to realize that Burnes was going to return to India without having made him a single promise.

JUST ABOUT THEN, A STRANGER BY THE NAME OF IVAN VICTOROVICH Vitkevich pulled into town. He said he was the envoy of the Russian czar and he wanted to have a chat with the amir. To this day, no one is sure who or what he really was. The czar's foreign minister later said he barely knew the fellow. The czar denied that Vitkevich spoke for him. Maybe they had reasons of state for such denials. Maybe Vitkevich was a spy; or maybe he really was an adventurer, a freelance diplomat fishing for an agreement with Dost Mohammed that would please the czar and win him a job in Moscow.

In any case, Vitkevich met with Dost Mohammed and suggested that he might form a relationship with the Russian monarch. He wasn't suggesting a marriage—both kings would be free to see other people. It would be a friendship. By no means did Vitkevich suggest a joint Russo-Afghan invasion of India; he just thought a few Russian diplomats might take up residence in Kabul . . . and a few military people might come along to protect the diplomats . . .

Dost Mohammed made no secret of his meeting with Vitkevich. He wanted Auckland to know about it. He reported selected details of his conversation with the Russian to Burnes. To Dost Mohammed, the whole point of meeting with Vitkevich was to worry the British and push them into making a move. The amir was feeding scraps to a bear in hopes of making a lion jealous—because he couldn't let go of lovely Peshawar.

NEWS OF THE MEETING CAUSED AN UPROAR IN INDIA. MACNAGHTEN fumed. The Dost was proving just as treacherous as he had predicted. Lord Auckland composed a huffy letter. "Sir, . . ." he warned the amir. "You must desist from all correspondence with Persia and Russia. You must never receive agents from them . . . without our sanction."[9] This hardly seemed like the same Lord Auckland who, just two years earlier, had written to tell the amir, "It is not the practice of the British government to interfere with the affairs of other sovereign nations."

Even then, Dost Mohammed tried not to alienate the British. He was still hoping for an alliance. Instead of reminding Lord Auckland that he was a sovereign king, he said he wanted Lord Auckland to put his terms in writing, especially with regards to Peshawar.

In writing? The British high command in India huddled to consider this. Why was the Dost rolling over, as it seemed. What trick did he have up his sleeve? Macnaghten thought Dost Mohammed was already in the czar's pocket and thus would have to be ousted. Britain had an excellent replacement monarch living on a British pension in India: Shah Shuja. If it came down to legitimacy, well, Shah Shuja had a right to the Afghan throne. He was an actual grandson of Emperor Ahmad Shah Baba. He had even clocked some previous time on the Afghan throne. He had been king from 1803 to 1809, in the heart of that bloody period when kings were toppling kings and men were murdering monarchs and brothers were blinding brothers. He was part of that melee.

Dost Mohammed himself tipped the scales. When he heard nothing back from the British, he met with Vitkevich again. Well, that did it! Auckland decided to go with what he called the Forward Policy. Instead of just sitting back and waiting to see what happened, he would move into Afghanistan and *make* things happen. He issued the Simla Manifesto, a public statement announcing that "every consideration of policy and justice" led the governor general to "espousing the cause of Shah Shuja-ul-Mulk" and aiding "the restoration of the Shah to the throne of his ancestors . . . [by which] it may reasonably be hoped that the general freedom and security of commerce [and] the union and prosperity of the Afghan people" would be promoted."[10] The Simla Manifesto made a claim that would become grindingly familiar over the next 170 years: the British were not out to conquer Afghans but to see "the independence and integrity of Afghanistan established." Once this job was done, the British would withdraw.

5

Auckland's Folly

In the last months of 1838, Lord Auckland assembled the Army of the Indus, a force of 31,800 total, counting Sikh troops contributed by Ranjit Singh.[1] By December it reached Quetta. In March 1839, it took Kandahar without a battle. By summer, it was moving east, on the road to Kabul. Only the city of Ghazni stood in its way, and Afghans considered this city impregnable because of its imposing walls. They thought the British would never get past Ghazni.

The British appeared at the foot of those walls one hot July day and demanded the city's surrender. The Afghans refused. A few nights later, under cover of darkness, British cannons boomed, solders yelled, and bullets zinged—but it was all a ruse. When the Afghans rushed to the point of attack, they left the other side of their city undefended. Artilleryman Henry Durand sneaked to the foot of those walls, dug some holes, packed them with explosives, and down came the gates. Ghazni was in British hands.

The fall of Ghazni stunned Afghans. Dost Mohammed abandoned his capital and fled north to seek refuge with his relative the amir of Bukhara. But his relative was secretly on the British payroll and put Dost Mohammed in prison. Hundreds of miles south, the British marched into Kabul unopposed. They installed Shah Shuja in Bala Hissar, the formidable fortress-palace perched high above Kabul on a flank of Lions-Gate

Mountain, overlooking the Kabul River and the neighborhood known as Shor Bazaar.

The Dost soon broke out of prison and gathered an army of Uzbeks. The British rushed to meet him, but he beat them soundly in the mountains of Kohistan, just north of Kabul. For the next week or two, the Dost and his men harassed the British troops guerilla style, driving them back toward the city. Then, just when the British cause seemed lost, a strange thing happened. Dost Mohammed rode into their camp with just one aide and surrendered to Macnaghten. No one knows why, but you can be sure of one thing: this cagey man had a plan. In any case, he retired to India—to live in the very residence just vacated by Shah Shuja—on a British pension!

THE BRITISH HAD PROMISED TO WITHDRAW THEIR TROOPS AS SOON AS Shah Shuja got his throne back, but they decided to postpone the withdrawal. For one thing, Shah Shuja wasn't acting like a real king yet. He spent a lot of time with his harem, which had grown to more than eight hundred women.[2] Also, disturbances were still breaking out here and there. It wasn't really rebellion at first, just crime, but lots of crime. Most of it was petty, but still, it disrupted daily life. It wasn't unexpected, though, since Kabul was brimming with *badmashes*, "bad seeds"—thugs and gangsters. Some of the thugs were probably working for the ousted Mohammedzais, Dost Mohammed's clan, which gave the crime a political cast; some might even have been agents of the czar. In sum, the British brass decided it was best to stick around for a bit and help Shah Shuja settle in.

Macnaghten headed up the mission as Her Majesty's envoy in Kabul, and he agreed to act as the king's chief advisor. He got his staff busy establishing an administrative system, recruiting an army, and building a police force.

Alexander Burnes was the number-two man in the mission. It was his job, as a political agent, to sniff out plots and snuff out conspiracies. Dost Mohammed had a firebrand son Akbar hiding in the north somewhere.

The British built a garrison at the mouth of the pass into Bamiyan valley to keep Akbar and his forces from coming south. They erected garrisons in Kandahar and several other cities too. They got the country locked up so tight that, aside from crime, they had nothing much to worry about.

Apparently they didn't feel Dost Mohammed's sister posed much of a danger, even though, after her brother went into exile, she went roaming north, traveling from village to village on foot, calling upon men to fight the British in defense of Islam. The villagers felt honor bound to lavish hospitality on this highborn guest, but she threatened to refuse all food and drink unless the villagers pledged to take up arms. Everywhere she went, therefore, men vowed to join the jihad to avoid dishonor.[3]

Afghanistan had been almost laughably easy to conquer, but the British didn't rely on force alone to keep the country in hand. Money had defanged the Dost (or so they believed), so they used money to secure the passes between Peshawar and Kabul. That is, they paid handsome subsidies to the Ghilzai Pushtoons living along that stretch of road. There was some pretense that the Ghilzais would supply troops in exchange for the subsidies, but really they just took the cash and kept quiet. That was good enough, for as long as the locals made no trouble, traffic could flow freely between Kabul and British India, allowing Calcutta to absorb this wild frontier area into the realm it governed.

Within a few months, the British officers and their Indian subordinates sent for their families, concubines, and servants. A tidy little British community sprang up in Kabul. The amenities of British colonial life were transported over the Hindu Kush mountains: fine furniture, good glassware, musical instruments suitable for playing Western-style music, wines, liquors, and liqueurs, as well as cigars. The officers could enjoy a "chota peg," a small whiskey, before dinner and afterward a good smoke.[4]

The British lived in a large complex, which they called a cantonment. It stretched for almost a mile along the Kohistan Road. It had living quarters and offices as well as barracks surrounding a large yard. A wall surrounded the whole complex, but it didn't provide much protection because cantonments were situated on a plain flanked by high hills. Some British officers lived outside the residency, in compounds of their own, elsewhere in the city. Alexander Burnes, for example, had a house near Shor Bazaar.

Within their compounds and in cantonments, the British created a simulacrum of their life at home: they had balls and tea parties and played cricket matches and polo, and some of the women even organized amateur theatricals. From the slopes above, Afghans looked down into cantonments and tried to puzzle out what these people were doing, these Farangis who had come among them and with whom so few Afghans ever had any actual truck.

———

UNFORTUNATELY, THE BRITISH NEVER MANAGED TO ESTABLISH REAL order. Kandahar remained unruly. The roads between the cities remained unsafe. One day, a Mrs. Smith traveling toward the Bolan Pass with a guard was attacked and killed by unknown Baluchi tribesmen. One day, Lieutenant Jenkins and several dozen of his men were killed in an ambush in Khurd Kabul Pass, close to the capital itself. One day, Captain Sturt was stabbed in the face right inside the city, by a youngster who was never caught.[5]

In fact, episodes of lawlessness were increasing at the very time that Macnaghten wrote to Calcutta to say that Afghanistan enjoyed "profound tranquility." Alexander Burnes encouraged him to send such reports, because as soon as Afghanistan was stabilized Macnaghten would move to a new post in India, and Burnes would replace him as envoy, a tremendous honor for a man so young.

Then one day, Dost Mohammed's charismatic son Akbar popped up in Bamiyan, alarmingly close to Kabul. Already, Afghans were calling him *Wazir* Akbar Khan. A wazir (vizier) is a king's right-hand man, his chief executive officer and often the real power in a kingdom. Although only in his early twenties, Akbar had a formidable reputation already as a man of war. The best-known portrait of him shows a young man wearing chain mail and a sharply pointed iron helmet. His moon-like face has something cherubic about it, but his eyes belie the innocence. In battles against Ranjit Singh, he had proved himself a daring and bloody adversary. In Kohistan, just north of Kabul, a region already hot with rebellious clamor, disgruntled chieftains began flocking to his standard.

General Willoughby Cotton had led British troops into Kabul, but, in early 1841, he had finished his term and returned to India, and a new man had taken his place. William Elphinstone hadn't asked for the job and didn't really want it. He had done some fine soldiering during the Napoleonic Wars—twenty-five years ago. Now he had gout, his shoulders hurt, and he was slow, but he accepted his commission like a good soldier.

Meanwhile, Parliament had decided Afghanistan was costing too much, especially since the mission there was done. Why keep pouring rivers of money into a place that enjoyed "profound tranquility"? Why keep paying the Ghilzai tribes, for example? They made little trouble. They seemed rather docile, actually. Parliament therefore ordered that the subsidies to the Ghilzai be cut.

The Ghilzai commenced to seethe. And with Wazir Akbar Khan on the scene, Kohistan was moving toward full rebellion. Even in Kabul Afghans were getting restive. In the rest of the country random violence turned endemic. And a dithering old man was in command of the British military forces. Was the mission in trouble?

Macnaghten didn't think so. In late August of that year, he wrote to an associate in India that "the country is perfectly quiet from Dan to Beer-sheba."[6] On November 1, one of Burnes's Afghan agents came to tell him the city was about to go up in flames, but Burnes declared that all would be well as soon as he took over from Macnaghten.[7]

———

IT'S HARD TO BELIEVE THAT BURNES REALLY DIDN'T KNOW TROUBLE WAS brewing. Perhaps he and his fellows failed to realize the gravity of their situation because the real trouble wasn't random street crime or the chiefs of Kohistan. It had to do with women. Apparently, some members of the British community were "fraternizing" with Afghan women. Maybe "fraternize" isn't the right word. The alleged relationships were not so sibling-like. Most of them might actually have been innocent. Possibly, most of the British men were behaving in ways that would have raised no objections in London. Perhaps it was just a case of courteous young gentlemen making the acquaintance of friendly young women. It's just that much of what was courteous in London was offensive in Kabul. In Afghan society, there is no courteous way for a young man to lead a young woman to a corner of a room during a reception and engage her in genteel conversation, sometimes touching her shoulder or perhaps her arm to emphasize a point—with her father and brothers looking on.

And it wasn't all courteous. Among the lower ranks, rumor had it, some of the Tommys were taking "the Forward Policy" too literally. As British historian and diplomat Fraser-Tytler later put it: "Necessity is the mother of invention and the father of the Eurasian."[8] One account written by a British soldier decades after the fact defended his comrades by pointing out that young men far from home and long separated from the company of women get lonely. "And," this soldier went on to add, "the Afghan women were almost frighteningly willing."[9]

I don't believe that, in 1841, respectable Afghan women in Kabul were "almost frighteningly willing." It's true that, in a private setting, Afghan women can tease aggressively and act flirtatiously—verbally—but in an all-Afghan social setting, everyone knows the parameters. They know what can't be said or done, what lines cannot be crossed. Everyone knows but no one articulates it—or even could—because that's how culture works. I'm guessing that, in Kabul in 1841, many social situations cropped up in which the British inadvertently gave offense and the Afghans couldn't believe the British didn't know they were giving offense.

Nor was *all* of it innocent. The Afghan chieftain Abdullah Khan once went to visit a British officer and caught a glimpse of a woman hiding in the next room—one of his own mistresses! She was visiting this British guy, apparently! He complained to Alexander Burnes, and Burnes said he'd look into it but never did. Maybe he was planning to, but events moved too fast.[10]

On November 2, the day after Burnes said all would be well, a crowd of men surrounded his house to abuse him for British treatment of their womenfolk. Poor Burnes—he had real regard for Afghan culture: he liked Afghans, and his writings show it. He thought Afghans liked and accepted him because he spoke their language. But he also liked women, and, as a bold adventurer and a handsome wit whose accomplishments had made him the toast of London, he had good reason to believe that women found him irresistible. The day that crowd of angry Afghan men gathered around his house, he had a couple of local women inside with him. Strictly speaking, they were Kashmiris, not Afghans; but the crowd was not making fine distinctions that day.

From his second-story window, Burnes tried to placate the crowd. He offered them money to go away, but this only sparked the rumor that Mr. Burnes had gold in the house. Some pushing and shoving broke out. Burnes's bodyguards fired a few shots into the air, which only turned the crowd into a mob and the protest into a riot. When the melee ended, "Bukhara Burnes," "the Iskandar of the East," lay dead.[11]

News of the murder reached British cantonments and sowed panic. Suddenly, the high officials decided they had better look for the quickest way out of this country. While Macnaghten was trying to bribe various tribal chieftains into helping the British, the insurgency roared into a blaze. Two British outposts near Kabul fell bloodily. Macnaghten decided he'd better strike the best deal he could get: time was of the essence now. He reached out to the man he took to be the leader of all the Afghans, Wazir Akbar Khan, son of the ousted king.

Akbar wasn't the leader Macnaghten needed. The leader he needed did not exist, not at that moment. In ousting Dost Mohammed, the British had uncapped the chaos that the great amir had brought to heel. Many chiefs had leaderly prestige but none had undisputed top standing. There was no one, therefore, with whom the British could strike a deal. Akbar may have been the most prominent Afghan leader, but his prestige was tied to his prowess as a warrior. The moment the two sides pulled back from violence, the source of his authority would start to fade, reducing his ability to strike a deal. A similar dynamic applied to all the chiefs, for all were now in competition for top standing, and, under the circumstances, intransigence toward the British added to a man's power; striking deals with the British weakened him. Anyone the British tried to negotiate with became the man who wasn't worth negotiating with.

Wazir Akbar Khan finally offered Macnaghten terms. He would guarantee the British community's safety if they would pay him a subsidy, let him be the power behind the throne, and leave the country by the following summer. Akbar was promising something he couldn't deliver and he probably knew it: he was a Durrani Pushtoon; the tribes controlling the passes out of the country were the Durranis' longtime rivals, the Ghilzais.

He couldn't tell them what to do or not to do. Macnaghten should have known this, but he was so grateful to get a promise of any kind, he seized upon the deal and arranged to meet with the Afghan leaders two days before Christmas to work out details.

Unfortunately, in the weeks before the meeting, the British made two mistakes. First, Macnaghten wrote to General Nott in Kandahar, urging him to bring his large force to Kabul as soon as possible. Macnaghten wrote that he would keep the Afghans talking until Nott arrived. Maybe then, together, they could crush the rebels. Somehow, this letter fell into Afghan hands.

Second, Macnaghten's son-in-law John Connolly wrote a secret letter suggesting that 10,000 rupees be offered for the head of each rebel chief—and this letter also fell into Afghan hands.[12] Ironically, this letter not only outraged the chiefs on the list but also those who were not, because their exclusion implied they were less formidable.

Meanwhile, Akbar Khan double-crossed Macnaghten. He showed the terms of his deal to his fellow rebel leaders to prove that the British had tried to buy him off and would try to buy off others, whereupon several other chiefs revealed that they too had been tendered similar offers.

On December 23, 1841, a group of British officials met with a group of Afghan chieftains in the middle of a large open field, a site that neither side could fire upon from their strongholds. Considering all the secrets, double-dealing, and hostility the two sides brought to the meeting, it's no surprise that the negotiations broke down and the two sides fell to fighting. Someone—perhaps Akbar Khan—killed Macnaghten. Later, the rabble that stormed the field cut off his head and displayed it on a pole near the river.

Both top British leaders were now dead, which left General Elphinstone in charge. The terrible events had discombobulated the old man. Outside the cantonment, Kabul had dissolved into a massive, formless, leaderless insurrection. What was left of the British leadership huddled in their enormous compound to hatch a plan. One option would have been to leave the cantonment, fight their way across the city, and gain the security of Bala Hissar, the fortress-palace on the heights. But there was no telling if the gates would be opened to them. Their puppet Shah Shuja held the fortress, and, in these last few weeks, having read the writing on the wall, he had recast himself as an Afghan patriot opposed to the British.

So the British chose plan B—the insane one: they decided to abandon Kabul and march out of the country over the Hindu Kush on foot in January. They left on the 6th of the month, a long column of 4,500 active troops and about 12,000 wives, retainers, servants, camp followers, and whatnot—Kabul's entire British-Indian community.[13] They had about sixty miles to go, not counting the twists and turns of the road, if road is the right word for the dangerous path through canyons so narrow one of them is called the Silk Gorge because the space between the steep canyon walls feels as slender as one silk thread. Snow was already beginning to fall. In the next few days, most of the marchers were felled by the weather. The rest were cut to pieces by Ghilzai tribal warriors in the passes. A few were taken as hostages and eventually released, but of the group that left Kabul on that terrible day, only one European made it to Jalalabad to tell the world what had happened: a surgeon named Dr. Brydon.

———

FOR NINE MONTHS THE BRITISH LICKED THEIR WOUNDS AND PONDERED their setback. During that time, some nameless nobody assassinated Shah Shuja. One of his many sons briefly claimed the throne but found the seat too hot and fled to India. The late Shah Shuja's bodyguard dug up another youngster of the king's clan and slapped the crown on him. This puppy invited the British to come back, assuring them they were welcome in Afghanistan any time. That fall, two British armies converged on Kabul, led respectively by General Pollock and General Nott, both determined to leave "some lasting mark of retribution" on the city.

After careful consideration, the generals ordered their chief engineer, a man named Abbott, to destroy Kabul's famous Grand Bazaar, the city's commercial heart. They told him to burn it down in such a way that the fire wouldn't spread to adjacent neighborhoods and damage sections of the city inhabited by the king and other British clients. But they gave Abbott only a few days to complete the work, and, in that amount of time, Abbott saw no feasible way to do the job except with gunpowder and matches. Not only did the whole bazaar burn down and the fire spread, but British soldiers ran amok through the city, smashing what they could, whereupon random Afghan citizens jumped in and began to loot and pillage, using the chaos as cover to enrich themselves or expiate old grudges. "In the mad excitement of the hour, friend and foe were stricken down by the same unsparing hand," said British historian John Kaye, writing less than a decade later. But he goes on to note:

> When we consider the amount of temptation and provocation, when we remember that the comrades of our soldiers and the brethren of our camp followers had been foully murdered by the thousands in the passes of Afghanistan, that everywhere tokens of our humiliation and the treachery and cruelty of the enemy, rose up before our people, stinging them past all endurance and exasperating them beyond all control, we wonder less that when the guilty city lay at their feet they should not wholly have reined in their passions than that, at such an hour, they should have given them so little head.[14]

The fire consumed much of Kabul, killed an unknown number of people, and left many more homeless. Then the British flag over Bala Hissar palace was lowered, and on the 11th of October, 1842, the British began their final withdrawal from Afghanistan, taking with them the remnants of the royal family they had installed: the sons and relatives of Shah Shuja, including the brother he had blinded, the onetime king Shah Zeman.

Pollock and Nott enjoyed a hero's welcome back in India: guns were fired and parades were organized to fete them. Lord Auckland had been replaced by this time, and the new governor general issued a new proclamation from Simla, which began with an artful use of the passive voice to explain what had happened:

> The government of India directed its army to pass the Indus in order to expel from Afghanistan a chief believed to be hostile to British interests and to replace upon his throne a sovereign represented to be friendly to those interests and popular with his former subjects.[15]

The document pointedly failed to specify who had done all this "believing" and "representing." Actually, the proclamation goes on to suggest, just the opposite turned out to be true! The old king wasn't hostile, the

replacement king wasn't popular. Therefore, in line with its enduring policies, the British government undertook to restore Dost Mohammed to
his throne. After all, the proclamation concludes:

> To force a sovereign upon a reluctant people would be as inconsistent
> with the policies as it is with the principles of the British Government.
> . . . The Governor General will willingly recognize any government
> approved by the Afghans themselves.[16]

6

The Second Coming of Dost Mohammed

DOST MOHAMMED THE GREAT RETURNED TO KABUL IN TRIUMPH. HE had outwitted the British by outwaiting them. While he bided his time in captivity, his loyal Afghan subjects had hammered the British, and now this proud and undefeated people welcomed their sovereign back with songs and flowers—at least, that's the story I imbibed when I was in school in Afghanistan.

There are some problems with this narrative, however. First of all, before he came back to Afghanistan, Dost Mohammed met with the British governor general and signed exactly the same deal that Shah Shuja had signed much earlier and the same one Dost Mohammed had been eager to sign before the war. He promised never to permit an emissary from Russia or Persia to come to his capital and never to deal with any foreign nation except Britain. If anyone outside his country had a complaint to lodge or a request to make of the king of Afghanistan, he would be referred to Calcutta.[1]

Dost Mohammed also agreed to relinquish his claim to three of the five major cities of Afghanistan: he would have Kabul as his capital and rule only the territories directly north of this city as far as the Amu River (which put Mazar-i-Sharif inside his domains) and south of Kabul beyond the city of Jalalabad but not as far as Peshawar. Kandahar and Herat would remain autonomous provinces ruled by rival members of his clan.

Peshawar would remain in Sikh hands. Dost Mohammed no doubt gnashed his teeth, but he signed off on Britain's demands.

Why? Because in exchange for these concessions, the British agreed to let "the Dost" rule his truncated territory without any interference. They would not station any envoys in Kabul: they would trust the Afghan king. Most important of all, they agreed to pay Dost Mohammed an annual subsidy. In short, you can't exactly say the British lost the war. They came out of it with everything they had demanded going in, and they got what they really wanted: a buffer state to block Russian expansion. What's more, they left Afghanistan divided into three parts likely to stay busy fighting one another instead of marching south to threaten India. Plus, they kept Peshawar out of Afghan hands, which was important because Peshawar was in the plains east of the Khyber Pass, an excellent base for marching into India.

The British disaster had initially left Kabul in the hands of a coalition of chiefs dominated by Dost Mohammed's son, the military hero Wazir Akbar Khan, now the idol of the Afghan masses. At the close of the war, a coterie of tribal chieftains had urged Wazir Akbar Khan to accept the crown. No other man was fit to rule, they said. Akbar turned them down. He was a dutiful son, not a usurper; deposing his own father would be unthinkable. It was true that sons had deposed their fathers sometimes in history, but it wasn't going to happen here in Afghanistan, not to this gigantic father.

The Afghan historian Ghobar suggests that the Afghans lost an opportunity here.[2] The British were in disarray; Ranjit Singh was getting old; the people of his kingdom were gravitating toward an alliance with their Afghan kin in order to stay out of British clutches. A true Afghan nationalist could have built a powerful state and annexed the lost provinces along the Indus River from Kashmir to Sind. Had he done so, a big chunk of "Pakistan" would now be part of Afghanistan. Certainly, the tough-minded revolutionaries who had beaten the British wanted to call the nation to this task. But the insurgents put their faith in their leaders, and their leaders looked to Wazir Akbar Khan, and Wazir Akbar Khan deferred to his father.

And this father no sooner had his throne back, than he moved swiftly to eliminate every leading figure in the rebellion against the British. Amin of Logar, a relentless opponent of foreign intervention, the man who had offered Wazir Akbar Khan the crown, was imprisoned below the fortress-palace of Bala Hissar and lived the last fifteen years of his life in that dungeon.[3]

Mohammed Shah Ghilzai, who had so intimidated the British, they simply called him The Enemy, was a sovereign lord with his own fortress-mansion in Kabul. One day, Dost Mohammed's men swooped down on him and carried him and his whole family away to a remote region in the mountains southeast of Kabul, where they lived in isolated domestic exile.

Another of the Afghans' most feared war chiefs, Sultan Ahmad, was banished to Kandahar. After a few years Kandahar didn't seem far enough, and so, with the agreement of his Kandahar cousins, the amir ordered this dangerous fellow to keep moving, move on west. Sultan Ahmad ended up in Iran. The Dost had not seen the last of him, but that story comes later.

For now, one by one, everyone who had risen to prominence during the First Anglo-Afghan War was stripped of lands, banned from office, banished to a foreign land, imprisoned, or executed. The amir may have given up Kandahar, Herat, and Peshawar, but, in the truncated territory he could call his own, he brooked no rivals.

Dost Mohammed was undoubtedly a big personality. He fought well enough when he had to, but he didn't specialize in war. He specialized in political craft—in this realm he was a brilliant, cold-blooded realist. He slipped out of Kabul just ahead of the British invasion not because he was a coward but because he was a canny survivor: he figured his best play right then was to stay alive and wait for an opening. When the opening came (after the war) he accepted a reduced country not because he was satisfied with a smaller realm but because he still saw biding his time and watching for openings as his best way forward.

In the meantime, how was he to govern the domains that were his by treaty? The Dost was still a tribal chieftain, not a national ruler in the modern sense. He never had a parliament, or a real cabinet, or any administrators to speak of. On a day-to-day basis, his government was largely in the hands of a single assistant called the shah aghassi, who was a cross between a valet and a prime minister. (In European monarchies, a similar figure was known as the lord chamberlain.)[4]

Then again, the Dost didn't need much of a bureaucracy because his government didn't do much governing. That is, it didn't "provide services" or perform most of the duties we commonly associate with government today.

There was no government police force, for example; villages and tribes provided their own security. Education too had nothing to do with the government; it was provided by the mullahs, the lowest level of Islamic clerics. The government had nothing to do with training or appointing mullahs. They emerged out of the population at large, spontaneously, you might say. In most cases, boys who wanted to be mullahs attached themselves to existing mullahs, learned to read from those mullahs, learned about Islam from them, and hung around the mosque helping their mullah/imam do anything that needed to be done, at first perhaps performing only menial chores—sweeping floors, refilling water cisterns, and so on; but gradually, as they gained the imam's approval, working their way up to more responsible duties until, eventually, a day came when someone needed a mullah, and the older one wasn't available, so they went to his apprentice and from then on people increasingly saw the apprentice as a mullah too; and so he was one.

There was no secular court system except for the personal judgments of the king and his officers. The jirgas settled most local conflicts, and they were formed locally by the people involved. Individuals who had some dispute that didn't involve the community paid a small, negotiated fee to a mullah to hear their case. Beyond the village level, the law was dispensed by higher clerics who made their rulings on the basis of the Shari'a, the Islamic code of jurisprudence. These judges needed no government ratification. They emerged from the population at large by a process that the clerical establishment, an autonomous social force, managed and controlled.

The king did provide protection against outside forces such as marauding bands from the lawless central Asian steppes or armies out of Persia. He did provide some security by stamping out highwaymen, keeping the roads open, and quelling rebellions that might flare into open wars. The government did enforce honest weights and measures in the markets, and it enforced some laws in the cities, and the king's army was the final force in any really big dispute.

But the army mainly kept the king's authority fresh so that he could collect taxes, most of which he spent to pay said armies and to support a royal lifestyle. That lifestyle did involve some major construction projects such as bridge building and road repair to facilitate military maneuvering and the refurbishing of important shrines and construction of new mosques to increase the king's fame. Public works such as these provided some employment, but the majority of Afghans needed no John Kennedy to tell them they should ask not what their king could do for them but rather what they could do for their king.

Still, Dost Mohammed Khan needed loyal governors in every province to make sure no one rebelled against his kingship. In the first portion of his reign, the part before the British invasion, he had appointed his brothers as his governors—but they were too much on a level with him. In the second part of his reign, he turned to his sons. The Pushtoons have a proverb: Within the tribe you'd better have a big clan; within the clan you'd better have a lot of brothers; among the brothers you'd better have the most sons. I don't know whether Dost Mohammed had the most sons, but he was surely a contender. His fourteen wives gave him fifty-six children. (Within a hundred years, more than seven thousand men could reportedly trace their descent directly back to Dost Mohammed.)[5]

In his own lifetime, the fortunate Dost Mohammed had enough sons to supply all the governors he needed. He made his eldest the governor of Badakhshan, the next one governor of Balkh, another the governor of Hazarajat, and so on. Each son was responsible for defending his own portion of his father's territory. Each son had to muster and maintain whatever military forces he needed to do that job. Each son therefore had the authority to collect taxes from the people of his province to pay his own warriors. This made each provincial governor a sort of semiautonomous duke, but Dost Mohammed knew how to rein in his sons and keep them obedient to his will. He had to bargain with the British, he had to dance a wary dance with the Russians, he had to accept limitations on his rule imposed by the great outside powers, but over his sons he could exercise absolute authority.[6] Afghanistan was not so much a nation as a family business, and it was not so much ruled by the Mohammedzais as *owned* by them.

The most prominent son got no province of his own, however. This was the famous, dashing, much-admired Wazir Akbar Khan. Dost Mohammed declared this son his heir and kept him close, kept him in Kabul; he was too valuable to waste on any single province. He was needed at his father's side to advise him on matters pertaining to the entire kingdom. Besides, there was no telling when a king might need a charismatic military genius like Akbar to command a campaign for him.

Wazir Akbar Khan did have a major campaign in mind. He wanted to conquer Peshawar and from there, perhaps, all of Sind, not to mention Kashmir—in short the youngster wanted to reconstruct Ahmad Shah's entire empire. But the British knew what territories could be conquered from Peshawar. They wanted to keep it out of Afghan hands for precisely that reason. Dost Mohammed would not violate the agreement he had signed with the British, so he would have none of the campaign his son envisioned.

At one point, a tribal uprising flared in a province south of Kabul, and the king dispatched Akbar to put it down. When Akbar approached the gates of the provincial capital, the rebels came out to greet him. "We're not rebelling against *you*," they said, "nor even against your father. We just want to take back Peshawar. Lead us into battle, Wazir Akbar Khan!"

Akbar wrote to his father begging him to reconsider. The people wanted war, he told the great man. "Command me, sir."[7]

Dost Mohammed sent back a stern letter forbidding his son to attack Peshawar and ordering him back to Kabul. He had an important assignment for him up north. The obedient son returned, received his orders, and headed off. Halfway to Balkh, he fell ill, probably of malaria. The king dispatched his personal physician to his son's sickbed, an Indian doctor who specialized in "Greek medicine." This was a treatment system based on the theory that every illness stemmed from an imbalance among four mystical substances in the body associated with air, earth, fire, and water. The balance could be restored with purges, poultices, leeches, and herbs known only to experts, of whom this physician was one. He treated Wazir Akbar Khan with an herb that would normally have been toxic, but that in this case—well, in this case, unfortunately, it also proved toxic. The doctor expressed his sincere regret: God made the decisions in the end. And so Wazir Akbar Khan died on the road not of the illness he had contracted but from the treatment he received. He was buried in Mazar-i-Sharif and Dost Mohammed had nothing further to gain or to fear from his heroically outsized son.

The death of Wazir Akbar Khan didn't cripple the amir's administration. Dost Mohammed had enough sons left to govern all his provinces and more sons to spare. Here, the term *provinces* should not be taken too literally. Even the outside borders of the country were a matter of opinion; the borders within it remained ambiguous too. There were, however, a number of distinct regions. The highlands of central Afghanistan were known as Hazarajat, "the land of the Hazaras," because they were inhabited by the recognizably Mongolian ethnic group, the Hazaras. Another region further north was called Balkh, because it had once been dominated by the oldest city in Afghanistan, the metropolis of Balkh, devastated by the Mongols in the thirteenth century. There were also Badakhshan, Maimana, Qataghan, Logar, Nangarhar, and other areas that registered as geographically distinct for one reason or another and that I will, for convenience, simply call provinces.

In 1855, the autonomous Kandahar/Helmand region was divided among fourteen feudal lords, all of whom were one another's brothers, cousins, and uncles. All therefore had families in the city of Kandahar itself. Each was constantly coveting the lands of another, and, whenever a dispute broke out, it sparked ruinous fighting among related families in the city. Finally the warring lords convened a jirga and decided they could not work out a peace among themselves: they needed a stronger hand. They sent a message to Amir Dost Mohammed Khan offering to accept him as their king if he would guarantee their property rights and keep the peace. In his treaty with the British, Dost Mohammed had agreed not to attack Kandahar; but this would not be an attack. He had received an invitation. Dost Mohammed accepted the petition and thus regained one of the three major cities he had given up without violating his treaty with the British.[8]

In 1857, a regiment of Indian soldiers had turned their guns on their own British officers, igniting the Great Indian Mutiny, which threatened to drive the British out of India. Dost Mohammed's advisors hectored him to go for Peshawar now. This was the moment, they said: Ranjit Singh had just died, the Sikhs were weak, and the British had their backs to the wall. Dost Mohammed refused to renege on his treaty with the British. This was the time, all right, but not for attacking Peshawar. He seemed alone among Afghans of his time in recognizing that attacking Peshawar was a waste of blood and treasure. The British could not fight the Afghans west of the Khyber, but, in the plains east of the Khyber, they had every advantage. If an Afghan king took Peshawar while the British were distracted, they would take it back as soon as they subdued the mutiny. *Not* attacking Peshawar was an Afghan king's real ace in the hole, because if he *didn't* attack it, he always *might*. Dost Mohammed used the Great Mutiny as an opportunity to secretly renegotiate his deal with the British. He agreed not to attack Peshawar, if the British would let him take Herat back by force—someday. Strapped to a barrel, the British accepted his terms. The Dost put the agreement in his pocket and waited for "someday" to arrive.

In 1861, Sultan Ahmad, the rebel leader Dost Mohammed had driven into exile fifteen years earlier, stormed back out of Iran and took possession of Herat. He declared himself better qualified than Dost Mohammed to be king of all the Afghans. He felt pretty sure of himself because Iran was backing him and Russia tacitly approved of his ambitions. He thought the British had already forced Dost Mohammed to relinquish Herat, and so they surely would not help him now.

Sultan Ahmad didn't realize the rules had changed. When Dost Mohammed led his army to Herat, the British raised no objection. In fact, they had enough power in Iran now to forbid the king of *that* country to "interfere with Afghanistan's domestic affairs." What's more, Russian approval did not translate into guns and money. It was just idle talk, it turned out. Sultan Ahmad found himself stranded and abandoned.

The siege began in 1862 and dragged on into the following year. The curious thing is, the combatants in this war (as in many Afghan wars) were closely related to each other. Sultan Ahmad was Dost Mohammed's son-in-law. At the height of the siege, the woman who was the one man's daughter and the other man's wife passed away, and all hostilities were suspended so that both men could attend her funeral and take part in the mourning ceremonies.[9] Then Dost Mohammed left the city and the siege continued.

Finally, Sultan Ahmad died of stress and distress, and Dost Mohammed took back Herat. How triumphant he must have felt on that April day as he rode through the gates. How thrilling it must have been for him to look back on his long career: born the youngest of twenty-one sons, his prospects dim, rising to mastery during the civil wars only to lose his country to the British, followed however by his return as if from the dead, and then his slow, crafty reconstruction of his realm.

Now his long quest had ended, and he had won: his triangle of a country had one continuous border enclosing the whole territory of modern-day Afghanistan, and he was king of every person in that territory, from the meanest peasant to the grandest khan. Except for the loss of Peshawar, he could die a happy man. And die is what he did. Immediately after taking Herat, Dost Mohammed fell ill, and six weeks later at the age of seventy, "the Great Amir" was lowered into his grave.

7

Eight or Ten Good Years

UNLIKE MOST OF HIS PREDECESSORS, DOST MOHAMMED GROOMED A successor. Well before his death, he named his third son, Sher Ali, as his heir and brought the young man with him to the siege of Herat. Sher Ali was at his father's bedside when the great man died. The troops acclaimed this son as the new amir, and, after fighting his many brothers for nine years—even losing his throne for a moment during that period—he secured his power at last and established a degree of stability, whereupon he resumed his father's project: the attempt to forge a coherent nation impervious to outside powers and ruled by a single government.

In 1863, when Sher Ali first came to the throne, a striking figure worked at his court, a mercurial, mysterious man named Jamaluddin-i-Afghan. It is difficult to say what exactly Jamaluddin was. A teacher? An orator? A political philosopher? A reformist? A revolutionary? He did teach, he did give speeches, he did elaborate political theories, and, in the course of his career, he certainly inspired revolutionary movements all over the Muslim world; but he wrote no books to speak of, created no systematic philosophy, founded no schools, and built no political party. His goals seemed to shift as he moved. In feudal Afghanistan, he sought a strong central government. In Iran and Turkey, which had strong central governments, he urged people to topple their rulers. In Egypt and India, which were under European control, he promoted nationalism. In North Africa, which Europeans had divided into arbitrary national units with senseless borders, he preached pan-Islamic unity superseding nationalism, and he did the same in central Asian Turkestan, which the Russians had divided into separate states.

Jamaluddin's family had lands around Asadabad, a town in the rugged mountains northeast of Kabul. They were distantly related to the royals, but some dispute forced them into exile in Iran for a while.[1] There they settled in a town that was also called Asadabad. As a result, some Iranians now believe this fellow called himself Jamaluddin-i-*Afghan* to disguise the fact that he was really Iranian and that he presented himself as a Sunni Muslim to disguise the fact that he was really Shi'a. Whatever the truth might be, he certainly started his *career* in Kabul, at the court of Dost Mohammed, tutoring the princes, one of whom was Sher Ali.

Shortly after Sher Ali succeeded to the throne, Jamaluddin sat down with the new king, so recently his student, and gave him a step-by-step written program for the modernization of Afghanistan, a detailed plan for developing Afghanistan into a world power. Then, without explanation, Jamaluddin said goodbye, left Afghanistan and spent the rest of his life restlessly roaming the Islamic world, rousing the rabble and afflicting the comfortable. He never returned, but long after his death his body was shipped back to Kabul for burial on the campus of Kabul University.

Sher Ali couldn't follow Jamaluddin's directives until he had defeated his brothers, which took him until 1868, but, as soon as he had secured stability, he launched the program. It planted the seed of a second Afghanistan that took shape and grew like a separate organism inside the original one.

First on the agenda: establish a postal system for the country, with a central office in Kabul and branch offices in the major provincial towns and cities. Theoretically, any Afghan could now write to any Afghan, provided both lived near a big town and provided one could write and the other could read. The letter might take months to reach its target, but Sher Ali's post office was nonetheless a first step toward weaving the country's disparate threads into a single fabric.

Next, the new king made some crucial adjustments to the tax laws that improved the climate for private enterprise. The new laws enabled entrepreneurs to invest money in commercial and protoindustrial ventures, which allowed a few men to gain wealth and power from business acumen rather than from land ownership, which was a first step toward moving past feudalism.

Previous kings had ruled without any official cabinet, employing their kinfolks and close relatives as their functionaries. Sher Ali put together a formal government with a cabinet that included a prime minister, a treasurer, a head clerk, and ministers for such concerns as foreign affairs, internal affairs, and war. The cabinet was selected in the harem, where Sher Ali's wife Mirmon Ayesha presided over the process.[2] This king also created a commission of twelve learned men to study issues confronting the government and the country and give him disinterested advice. It was the faint beginnings of what would develop into a whole class in Afghan society, later dubbed the technocracy.

Sher Ali convened a standing jirga that was an incipient parliament, though its function was purely advisory. It consisted of two thousand representatives from all parts of the country, who met for the first time in 1865. The first question the king put to them had to do with a brother who was raising rebellion. What should he do about this brother? he asked. "Crush him," the parliament cried out, and with their imprimatur Sher Ali marched on Kandahar, called his brother out to battle, and defeated him.[3]

Sher Ali's career suggests he had some mettle in him, but you wouldn't know it from his pictures. Photography had just been invented, so this is the first Afghan king of whom we have photos. They show a solemn, curious man with a full beard, pursed lips, a curved nose, and eyes steeped in a combination of rumination and speculation. He looks sort of melancholy. On his head he wears a tall *karakul* cap that resembles an upsidedown beehive but looks rather more stylish than it sounds.

He cuts a figure that would not have looked out of place in some crowded little clock-making shop in Eastern Europe. Had he not been king of Afghanistan, he probably would have been tinkering with machines and puttering about with odd devices somewhere. Indeed, in the ten years of peace he managed to eke out, he imported various tools and machines from the outside world and tinkered with them in his palace. One such device was a lithographic press, which he installed at his palace of Bala Hissar. He used it to publish the country's first newspaper, a sixteen-page tabloid called the *Sun*, as well as pamphlets on subjects he found interesting, especially military matters, some of which he turned into manuals for distribution to his army officers.[4]

Sher Ali built up a national professional army of fifty-six thousand soldiers.[5] He got it into his head that soldiers should look like the ones in pictures of Western wars. No longer would he tolerate draftees going into battle wearing their own clothes. No more baggy trousers and turbans! The king designed and issued uniforms to his soldiers so that they would all look alike and would all look like the troops of European nations. So the king ensconced in the capital now had an army that *looked* different from the tribal warriors who had served the kings of the past. The tribal warriors still existed, though, since these were not professional soldiers but simply tribesmen who picked up arms when arms were necessary—the country now had two different sets of warriors, one the government's, one the people's (or perhaps, simply, the people).

Quite a few Afghans had gone to India to serve in the British armies. Sher Ali lured some of them back to drill his troops and teach them how to march in rows and pivot on command and present arms and all the other pretty martial maneuvers armies practice when they're not fighting. Sher Ali built the first armaments factories in Kabul so that someday he would be able to arm his own troops without aid from foreign nations. The next time some great power decided to treat this sovereign country as its own back yard (thought Sher Ali) Afghanistan would be ready.

The king ordered that his troops be domiciled not in the cities, rubbing elbows with everyday citizens (with whom they sometimes clashed), but in separate garrisons. In fact, Sher Ali started building a whole new military city called Sherpoor, north of Kabul, a project that employed six thousand laborers, a thousand carpenters, and numerous skilled artisans for five years.[6] But the city was never completed, because in the late 1870s the British and Russians began making trouble again, trouble that brought this brief chapter of the Afghan story to a close.

8

Interrupted Again

BY 1878, CONTENTIONS AMONG THE GREAT POWERS OF EUROPE HAD entered a new phase. Prussia's kaiser Wilhelm I had an "iron chancellor," Otto Von Bismarck, who welded the many German-speaking fragments of central Europe into a single state. The new nation-state of Germany altered the enduring competition among Britain, France, and Russia. Bismarck proclaimed that the great issues of the day could not be settled by speeches but only by "blood and iron." France was his immediate target, and, when one looks at the French president of that time, Louis-Napoleon III, with his moustache waxed to sharp peaks extending past either side of his face, it's hard to avoid seeing a pompous blowhard who wouldn't last long once speechifying gave way to blood and iron.

And so it was. Bismarck tricked the French fool into declaring war on him, thundered across the border, crushed the country with laughable ease, and took the key provinces of Alsace and Lorraine, which were rich in iron ore, a key ingredient of industrialization. The acquisition of those provinces made Germany an instant contender for world power. Bismarck and his kaiser then began looking around the world to see what territories were left for a latecomer to colonize.

The fall of France, however, gave Britain a chance to swell even stronger than before. The British Empire then covered 23 percent of the world's land surface. Counting colonized subjects, the British government ruled about a quarter of the people on Earth.[1] The island itself had only

2 percent of the world's population but 45 percent of the world's industry. Britain consumed five times as much energy as the United States and 155 times as much as Russia.[2] Britain's global domination dwarfed that of any previous power in history. But the rise of Germany looked like a possible challenge to Britain's dominion.

The rise of Germany also created fresh consternation in Russia, which was still huge, primitive, and without ready access to an ocean port, and therefore still hobbled in the global rush for colonies. Two decades earlier, Russia had lost the Crimean War. The subsequent treaty had blocked Russian expansion into the eroding Ottoman Empire and had clipped its naval power even in the Black Sea. Now Russia was fighting back. It was re-establishing its Black Sea ports, and, if it couldn't move into the Balkans, well then, it would push its frontiers further east, the traditional direction of Russian expansion. The Ottoman Empire was going into its real death throes, and European powers were jockeying to pick up the territories breaking off of it. In the Levant, the lands bordering the eastern edge of the Mediterranean, this competition was called the Eastern Question. In central Asia, east of the Caucuses, the Great Game was on again.

In 1865, Russian troops took the city of Tashkent. Two years later, Russia captured the famous old city of Bukhara. The next year it occupied Samarkand. In 1873, Russia forced the khan of Khiva to accept "Russian protection," an imperialist euphemism for "nice little country you got here, what a shame if something was to happen to it." Three years later Russia annexed the adjacent khanate of Khokand. Its power now extended to the very banks of the Amu River. Only Afghanistan stood between the Russian juggernaut and the pugnacious British in India. It was a bad place for a little country to be situated.

When Sher Ali secured control of Afghanistan, William Gladstone's Liberal Party was in power in Great Britain. The Liberals were a probusiness party, rather like America's nineteenth-century Republicans. They were wary of foreign adventures that might cause turmoil, because turmoil was bad for business. When it came to colonial affairs, their attitude was, if it ain't broke, don't fix it. In the decades since Auckland's Folly, an ambiguously autonomous Afghanistan had served British interests well enough. Gladstone thought it best to stick with the status quo there, and his governor general of India Lord Northbrook agreed.

But the election of 1874 brought to power Benjamin Disraeli's conservatives, an upper-class party that was trying to expand its appeal to the working class. Banging the drum for militaristic adventures abroad for the greater glory of empire and queen looked like a way to rally such voters. Disraeli's government replaced Lord Northbrook with Lord Lytton, who definitely favored a "Forward Policy," like Auckland.

Disraeli and his group decided that a neutral buffer state between the Indus and Oxus wasn't good enough. The independent attitude of King Sher Ali worried them. They doubted that, when push came to shove, Sher Ali would be able to keep the Russians out of his country. The czar was looking too aggressive. Better to get a firm hold of Afghanistan at once, was Disraeli's position, before the Russians turned it into one more of their protectorates. The new chapter of the Forward Policy began, therefore, with a move designed to let Sher Ali know who was boss. Sher Ali had a favorite son named Abdullah, whom he had named his heir. He had another son Yaqub, whom he disliked, perhaps because Yaqub had organized a revolt against his father. Sher Ali had put Yaqub in prison.

Imagine Sher Ali's dismay when he received a missive from Lord Lytton ordering him to disinherit Abdullah and name Yaqub as his successor. Why the British preferred one son to the other, they didn't say. Perhaps they had talked privately with Yaqub and liked the way his mind worked.

The missive also warned the Afghan king not to look to the Russians for help because, as Lytton wrote, "we can pour an army into your country before a single Russian soldier can arrive to help you." Sher Ali was told that, if he was friendly, the British could protect him from any czar; if he was unfriendly, the British could break him "as a reed."[3] The letter ended by telling Sher Ali an envoy was coming to talk about these matters.

Sher Ali didn't like the substance or the tone of these directives. He let a period of insulting silence pass, then informed the British that he preferred to name his own heir, thank you, and suggested that instead of receiving an envoy *from* them, he would send one *to* them. Any issues that needed sorting out could be discussed in Calcutta.

When Sher Ali's man arrived in the capital of the Raj, what transpired wasn't a discussion. Britain delivered its terms: British agents *would* be stationed in Kabul. Britain *would* control the borders of Afghanistan. British citizens *would* have free reign to enter the country at will and go anywhere in it that they pleased. British citizens would be subject to British laws, not Afghan ones. British businessmen would be free to cut deals with anyone in the country without government interference. If Sher Ali would concede these few points, the British would let him name his own heir, pay him and his heir handsome subsidies, and supply Afghanistan with all the military aid and advisors the country needed to hold the Russian Bear at bay.

When the amir read these terms, he flew into a rage. Then he sat down and dictated a letter, the gist of which was: No. Unlike his crafty father, this intemperate amir told the British he would defend Afghan sovereignty to the last man. Unfortunately, by then, Russian troops were massing along his northern border. Even as Sher Ali was telling the British they couldn't enter his country, a Russian "diplomatic" delegation was crossing the Amu River without permission, headed for Kabul. Sher Ali sent frantic messages telling them to halt, turn back, they were not invited, they must not come to Kabul. The Russian team ignored these messages. They just kept coming. They came right into the city. They took rooms, unpacked their suitcases, and knocked on the palace door. They were here to make friends, they said.

Tragedy took that moment to strike the amir's household. His favorite son, his chosen heir, his beloved Abdullah, died of some sudden illness. The whole court went into mourning. The amir, a man of strong and tender feelings, took the loss especially hard. He let court business go untended for days while he holed up in his private chambers, steeping in grief. When next he was seen, his eyes were red from weeping. And it was then that another letter arrived from Lord Lytton. Sher Ali should prepare to receive a British mission in Kabul at once. Sher Ali ordered his border forces not to let the British in. When a small detachment of British diplomats and its military escort arrived at the Afghan border, the commander of the border fortress there blocked them from proceeding. "If it weren't for the fact that I have known some of you as friends in the past," he said, "I would shoot you right now."[4]

The British delegation turned back, deeply offended. Lord Lytton wrote an apoplectic letter to the amir of Afghanistan, demanding an apology, then waited for a response. The silence was deafening. It was then that Lytton began massing his forces. In the First Anglo-Afghan

War, India had sent one army of about twenty-five thousand troops. From that disaster they took a lesson: one army was not enough. This time, they prepared three, each about as big as the single army they had sent in earlier.

Sher Ali was in agony. The Russians had come, the British were coming, his heir was dead, and he had no one to entrust his kingdom to except Yaqub, the hateful son who had rebelled. He decided to ask the Russians to help him against the British. But he had to let Yaqub out of prison and put him in charge of the country while he went north to seek an audience with the czar—he had no choice: the British armies were already pushing into the Khyber Pass, the Bolan Pass, and the Kurram Valley. Afghan forces had blocked them at all three entry points, but for how long?

When Sher Ali reached the Amu River, the czar's men wouldn't let him cross. For political reasons much bigger than Afghanistan, the czar had decided this was not the time to confront the British head-on. He ignored Sher Ali's pleas and kept him penned up in his own country, and it was then that this tragic king just gave up. He took to his bed with a fever. The doctors urged him to eat, keep up his strength, but he would not touch food or water. His leg had been hurt during his journey, but he refused medical attention. The wound turned gangrenous, and he turned down all treatment. Within weeks, at the age of fifty-four, the amiable Sher Ali was dead.

His son Yaqub succeeded him, and his actions strongly suggest that the fix was already in. Yaqub ordered Afghan troops to stand down and let the British march into the country peacefully. He himself went south to meet them in a little town called Gundamak. There, Amir Yaqub Khan and the British high command worked out a treaty of "friendship." The Gundamak Treaty gave the British a big swath of southern and southeastern Afghanistan and accepted a permanent British mission in Kabul. Everything the British had demanded of Sher Ali, they got from his son Yaqub.

A British "diplomatic" mission made its way to Kabul, headed by an envoy named Neville Chamberlain. Yes, he was an ancestor of that later Neville Chamberlain who, as prime minister of Great Britain in the 1930s, signed the infamous Munich Pact with Hitler. Accompanying this earlier Chamberlain was Britain's political plenipotentiary, a gentleman named Louis Napoleon Cavagnari, who was part French, part Irish, a smidgen Italian, and all patriotic British subject. He had a full beard and a scholarly look, but he also had a pompous bearing reminiscent of his namesake, the fallen president of France. Cavagnari had carried out numerous missions on the frontier, felt he had the savvy to "handle" Pushtoons, and boasted that he understood them. Pushtoons could be controlled, he told his associates, if one met them with courtesy but firm resolve. When they got pugnacious, one had to exhibit unflinching military courage because that's what impressed Pushtoons. Cavagnari felt he possessed the requisite courage.

When John Lawrence, another officer with frontier experience, heard about Cavagnari's mission and his self-congratulating bombast, he said, "They will all be murdered—every single one of them."[5]

Cavagnari and his team entered Kabul on elephants with gilded *howdahs* (the sedan that fits onto the back of an elephant). They waved to the crowds lining the streets as if they were entering the city to applause. The crowds didn't wave back. The amir made a proclamation designed to palliate his people and inspire a festive mood. He promised to celebrate the arrival of these honored British guests by reducing taxes and paying his soldiers all the back pay they were owed. The population continued to glower. They'd believe it when they saw it.

The British delegation took up residence in a compound at the foot of Bala Hissar. Like the cantonments that had proved so indefensible forty years ago, this compound was flanked by high hills from which an enemy could shoot right down into the yard, but Cavagnari and his team didn't worry. They believed they would not need to defend their compound because this time the Afghans had invited them into the city.

Certainly, if the king was any measure, the Afghans were happy to host the British. Amir Yaqub Khan could not have been more hospitable. He invited the diplomats and high officers of the British mission to feast at Bala Hissar day after day, and, when they weren't being entertained at the palace, they were invited to the compounds of other Afghan aristocrats linked to the amir, his relatives, and his courtiers. One of Cavagnari's team wrote home dazzled: the amir insisted on feeding British troops at his own government's expense, he reported. The amir even sent grooms to tend to the Englishmen's horses. He was such a good chap, really! "But the people are rather fanatical," he added, sounding a note of caution, "not yet accustomed to our presence."[6]

Meanwhile a dispute had arisen between the king and his army. He owed his troops money and could not pay them, despite his promise. He explained that funds were short just now; they needed to be patient. But the soldiers saw money flowing like water to entertain the British and began to murmur discontented words. Soon, it wasn't just the soldiers. Common citizens were turning out on the streets to curse the king and his guests. Cavagnari didn't worry, because he knew all about Pushtoons. "Dogs that bark don't bite," said he.[7]

Cavagnari did notice that Amir Yaqub Khan's authority seemed weak among his people, and this worried him a little. On the plus side, however, he could promise his superiors in Calcutta that this king would stick to his agreements—as if commanding the obedience of a king had some value, even if the king could not command the obedience of his people.

On September 2nd of that year, 1879, Cavagnari wrote to the government of India to say, "All is well with the Kabul embassy."[8] It was an eerie echo of the letter Macnaghten had written to a friend in India thirty-eight years earlier to declare that all is quiet in Afghanistan "from Dan to Beersheba." Just months after writing those words, Macnaghten was dead; Cavagnari was dead one day after writing this letter.

The trouble began when an Afghan general told some surly soldiers to go talk to Cavagnari about their back pay: "He has plenty of money." The troops made their way to the British residency. When the gates were not opened to them, they broke them open and stormed inside. There, they began grabbing horses, saddles, anything they could get their hands on. If they weren't going to get cash, they were determined to take what they were owed in kind. By this time, thousands of Kabul commoners had joined the troops in the looting. Their hostility to the British had come to a boil and they wanted to make a statement.

Somehow, Cavagnari got a message off to the king, informing him of the emergency and demanding he do something. Yaqub, up there in his palace, tore at his hair and wept. He told the messenger to go back and tell Cavagnari he was trying, he was trying; but what could a man do?

Knowing that no help would be coming, Cavagnari climbed onto the roof of the residency to make a personal appeal to the crowd. He was determined to display the cool courage that Pushtoons supposedly found so impressive. No one was impressed. Cavagnari then ordered his troops to fire. Big mistake. The mob surrounding the residency had the British trapped inside with no way to get out and nowhere to hide. That small contingent of British diplomats and troops fought desperately but uselessly. Within a few hours the Afghans overwhelmed and killed them all.

The British fought with astonishing courage, right to the end, according to British historian Maud Diver and others, although—since no one got out—I'm not sure how this fact came to be known. When news of the massacre reached the palace, Amir Yaqub's mullah reported feeling a chill in the air, as if a shadow had fallen over the city. "I knew then that the British were coming."[9]

And of course they were. The three armies checked by the Afghans earlier had entered the country, thanks to Amir Yaqub's submissive capitulation, and one of them marched quickly to Kabul, led by the wiry Irishman Frederick Roberts, a man of resolute chin, huge whiskers, and stern eyes. Roberts was a no-nonsense military martinet who demanded absolute discipline from his men and demanded no less of himself, for which reason he commanded the passionate loyalty of his troops, who knew him affectionately as "Bobs."

Then again, Bobs's reputation may have risen in retrospect from the heroic stature he gained in the eyes of his countrymen during this, the Second Anglo-Afghan War. Considerable numbers of tribal warriors had gathered around Kabul by the time Roberts arrived, but he broke through them, entered the city, and swiftly took control.

An awkward problem then arose. What to do with the king? Could he be allowed to keep the throne? Credible rumors said he had been making secret deals with the Afghan chieftains even while professing loyalty to the British. He might even have conspired in the murder of Cavagnari. Was it enough to slap his hand and say, "Bad puppet!" What good was such a bad puppet to anyone?

Yaqub himself resolved the awkwardness. He came to Roberts and begged to be relieved of his royal duties. "You have seen my people—who could rule over them? I would rather cut grass in the British camp than to be Amir of Afghanistan."[10] He was excused, therefore, and sent to India to live on a British pension, a standard fate, it seems, for ex-kings of Afghanistan. The Union Jack was hoisted over Bala Hissar, for, until another puppet could be found, the British would have to rule Afghanistan directly.

Now the punishments began. The residents of Kabul had lashed out against the British, so all of them were fined. The officials of Yaqub's government had, at the very least, failed to protect their guests, so they were put in prison. Suspected troublemakers throughout the city were rounded up and hanged until corpses swinging from public gallows could be seen in every part of the capital. British troops fanned into the countryside and destroyed forts and burned down villages to force the surrender of tribal chieftains suspected of conspiring with or at least supporting the rebels.

At least one British officer felt uneasy about this strategy. "It exasperates the Afghans and does not funk them," mused Colonel Macgregor. "In fact, we are thoroughly hated and not enough feared."[11]

He was quite correct: the Afghans were more angry than intimidated. Clerics across the countryside, anyone with the slightest claim to religious authority, began to preach that Islam was under attack by infidels and that Afghans had a duty to rise up and defend the faith. One of them was an ancient mullah known as Mushk-i-Alam—"Perfume of the Universe"—who had fought the British in the First Anglo-Afghan War. He was there in the Hindu Kush passes when the British force and all its camp followers were wiped out, and he was not a young man even then. Now he was about ninety years old and could no longer walk, but his followers carried him from village to village in his bed, and everywhere they set him down he gave fiery speeches calling rural Afghans to action. "The Farangis eat pigs!" he thundered. Pigs' flesh is utterly prohibited in Islam. For many Muslims, even the idea of touching it is repulsive. His listeners shuddered with disgust and went home to find their guns.

That fine European-style army that Sher Ali had built, all those salaried fighting men in identical uniforms who were so good at marching in unison and pivoting on cue, proved useless. That force was vanquished quickly and it vanished. What the British faced now were the tribal guerillas: farmers and nomads for whom fighting was not a profession but a way of life. One such commander, Mohammed Jan, roamed the land with twenty thousand men.[12] Villagers fed him and funneled information to him so he could attack the British whenever he had the advantage and slip away into the hills when he didn't.

And, although his was the biggest force, it was only one of many. The British routed these Afghan armies in almost every pitched engagement, but the routed forces melted away, leaving no one to sign a treaty with. Once, an officer named Massey was ambushed, and Roberts had to save him, whereupon Roberts was trapped too. He fought like a mad dog against the forces besieging him, knowing that reinforcements were on their way from Jalalabad. Once they arrived, the rebels would be sorry. The reinforcements did arrive on a cold night, only to find that the vast Afghan force had disappeared. The men had simply gone home. After one year of fighting and over a dozen major battlefield victories, the British had won jurisdiction of every patch of Afghan territory their guns could· cover—but not one inch more.

By January 1880, the government of India was wringing its hands. It wasn't that the Afghans were unbeatable. The British were beating them regularly. It was rather that beating them didn't stop them from continuing to fight. Britain could win battles but could not gain ground in a war that had turned into a money pit, swallowing up British India's resources, with no end in sight. British officials in India began to discuss a new policy. How about giving Afghanistan back to the Mohammedzais but broken into many pieces, with each piece going to a different royal cousin? The British could then pull out and let Russia wade into the civil war they would leave behind.

That summer, however, one of Sher Ali's sons, a man named Ayub, erupted out of Herat with eight thousand soldiers. On July 27, 1880, he met the British at Maiwand, a plain just west of Kandahar, and eviscerated their army of twenty thousand. In Britain, *Maiwand* became a synonym for Afghan savagery. In the West more generally, it is known as the battle in which the fictional Dr. Watson was wounded, just before he started rooming with a detective named Sherlock Holmes at 221B Baker Street.

In Afghanistan, as you might expect, the battle of Maiwand became a thrilling symbol of national pride, famous for an apocryphal anecdote: in the heat of the bloodshed, the story goes, as the Afghan line was starting to give way, a seventeen-year-old woman named Malalai grabbed the bloodied banner of her people, raised it high, and shamed the men into rallying. Malalai was killed, but the charge she sparked succeeded, and

Malalai became Afghanistan's iconic heroine, its Joan of Arc. Later, the first girl's school in Afghanistan was named after her.

All this fanfare about Maiwand is curious, however, because the famous Lord Roberts (infamous among Afghans) hurried west from Kabul as soon as he heard about the battle, scattered Ayub's army, and then took the crucial city of Kandahar. The battle of Maiwand may have been a decisive victory for the Afghans, but in military terms it was only one part of a larger engagement, which the Afghans decisively lost.

Then again, both Maiwand and Kandahar were parts of an even larger drama, the Second Anglo-Afghan War, and it's tough to say who won that one. Ayub earned the fervid admiration of Afghans for defeating the British at Maiwand but made no further mark in Afghan history, for, while he was basking in his glory, a cousin of his marched into Kabul. This cousin Abdu'Rahman, soon to be known as the Iron Amir, had gone into exile in the lands north of Afghanistan with his father in the 1860s, at the height of Sher Ali's reign. Once the war started, he came back.

The British took one look at Abdu'Rahman and saw the Mohammedzai of their dreams. Here was a man tough enough to control the Afghans but canny enough to do business with the British. He was one of the many grandsons of Dost Mohammed the Great, which meant his blood was royal and his claim to the throne as good as anyone's. The British let him enter Kabul unopposed and sat down to cut a deal with him. When the smoke cleared, they were handing him the country.

Of course, they had the usual conditions: he mustn't let any Russians into Afghanistan, mustn't deal with any foreign nations except through Britain, and so on. Abdu'Rahman signed off on all of it. He just wanted the British gone.

He did have some conditions of his own, however. The most important one was this: the British were to give him a free hand to do exactly as he wished within his borders. They were not to interfere. The British said sure, why not, why should they care? The deal was cut, and, with a big sigh of relief, the British withdrew their troops. It's hard to say, therefore, who won this war. Both sides got something; both paid dearly for what they got. In any case, the consolidation of Afghanistan into a country, the story the British had so rudely interrupted, could now resume.

PART II: ONE COUNTRY, TWO WORLDS

When Afghanistan acquired its modern name, it was not a country but a territory. Its borders were a matter of opinion. Its inhabitants were people of various ethnic groups divided into clans and tribes, sharing a religion, a culture, and a way of life, but little else. The king was merely the highest chieftain of a confederation, with little impact on his subjects' daily lives. He ruled his nominal realm but did not really govern it.

Rival chieftains were constantly battling for supremacy, but the outcome of these small wars didn't matter much to most people: whoever won or lost, their lives would go on unchanged. When strong kings did emerge, they applied themselves to military campaigns to expand their territory, expansion being the main business of an Afghan king.

The British were game changers. When they came into the picture, Afghans encountered a monolithic cultural Other. As individuals, the British and Afghans could interact amiably enough, but, as two cultures, they had no propensity to merge. When the British invaded the country, they remained as distinct from Afghans as oil poured into a jar of water. Afghan resistance to the British reflected not the political policy of the rulers but the visceral reaction of the Afghan masses to these aliens in their midst. Fighting the British made Afghans aware that they did in fact all have something in common: they were all not-British.

By the time the British withdrew, the fundamental project of Afghan rulers had changed. From this time forth, they stopped trying to build far-flung empires and started trying to mark off what they definitely "owned" and eliminating would-be mini-sovereigns within their fence. Dost Mohammed and

his sons made good progress toward this goal. By 1879, Afghanistan had defi-
nite borders and a single capital, the city of Kabul. No longer would Kanda-
har, Herat, or Mazar-i-Sharif serve as city-state seats of power for rivals to the
Afghan throne.

The coalescence of an Afghan state alarmed the British and helped push
them into a second invasion, but, once again, by toppling the Afghan monarch
in Kabul, the British managed only to unleash the unruly energy of Afghan
tribal society. Again, therefore, the British were forced to pull out—not because
they were defeated in battle but because they couldn't govern the Afghans. And
again, the British had stirred up a sense of shared identity among Afghans
while reinforcing the centrifugal tendencies that kept them fragmented. When
a new Afghan strongman took the throne, he understood that firming up the
borders and restoring the primacy of Kabul would not be enough. He would
have to create a government pervasive enough to enter and control the daily
life of the entire population. But how could any king assert day-to-day authority
over a people who honored only the dictates of religion, custom, culture, tribe,
clan, village, and family? This was the problem that preoccupied Afghan
rulers over the next half century, a quest that divided Afghanistan into two
cultural worlds.

9

A Time of
Blood and Iron

THE BRITISH LEFT A VERY BIG MAN IN CHARGE. ABDU'RAHMAN WAS CAST
in the same mold as the fiercest of the conquerors who had burst out of
this region in centuries past and was probably the equal of Ahmad Shah
Baba. In another era, he might have built another of those ramshackle
empires that stretched from Iran to Delhi and that fragmented soon after
his death.

But Abdu'Rahman could do no bursting out. Global powers confined
him within his borders. And since he couldn't conquer widely, he set his
cap to conquering deeply, turning his ferocity inward, upon Afghanistan
itself. He tried to transform this universe of tiny independent feudal parts
and autonomous village republics into a single nation-state.

The man who carried out this project was among the toughest figures
ever to stride across the Afghan stage. Even as a boy, he was a scary fellow,
this grandson of Dost Mohammed's. His own father had governed Balkh,
a major province in northern Afghanistan. In his childhood, therefore,
the boy who would be king luxuriated in a provincial version of the royal
court. In that province, his family held absolute power and he enjoyed
every privilege.

One day, at the age of twelve or thirteen, he wanted to see if his small-
caliber gun was powerful enough to kill a man, so he shot his servant. The
man died, the teenager laughed. The murder was so flagrant his father had

no choice but to punish the boy by putting him in prison. But any fellow who can kill a man just to see if his gun works is going to prove useful to someone: his father released him from prison after a year and, by the time he was seventeen, made him one of his major commanders. Later his father rebelled against Sher Ali but lost the contest. When he went into exile north of the Amu River, Abdu'Rahman went into exile with him. The onetime prince and future king lived in poverty for a few years, making a living as best he could buying and selling ancient artifacts and archeological arcana he found floating about in the markets—a warrior scraping by as an antiquities dealer. He lived on a quarter of the money he made and saved the rest for a rainy day—the day he would storm Afghanistan.[1]

In 1893, thirteen years after taking over from the British, this Iron Amir would meet with a British delegation from India to formalize the agreements hammered out so hastily at the start of his reign. The British nominated General Frederick Roberts to head up their delegation, but Abdu'Rahman curtly told them to send someone else: Roberts personified the second British invasion of Afghanistan and was too hated by Afghans for any Afghan king, even an "iron amir," to make a deal with. So the British replaced him with Mortimer Durand, foreign minister to the Raj.[2]

Abdu'Rahman came to the meeting with no advisors, no tribal leaders, and no representatives of his people. He sat down with Durand, one on one. The British diplomat proposed a southern border for Afghanistan, and Abdu'Rahman accepted it. The agreement the two men made at that meeting continues to cause trouble to this day, because Durand drew an arbitrary line on the map, which ran right through lands traditionally occupied by the Pushtoons, a line that corresponded to no geographical feature on the ground. When you're there, you can't tell where it is unless someone tells you. Villages on both sides of this so-called Durand Line are inhabited by members of the same tribes. People on one side of the line have cousins on the other side, and vice versa. How did Durand decide where to draw this line? By calculating how far forward into Afghan territory the British could push without getting pushed back. The Durand Line marks the line of scrimmage at a particular moment. As such, it is sure to be a place of enduring conflict. It froze into place Afghan resentment about losing Peshawar, turning that problem into a permanent political fact.

The Durand Line

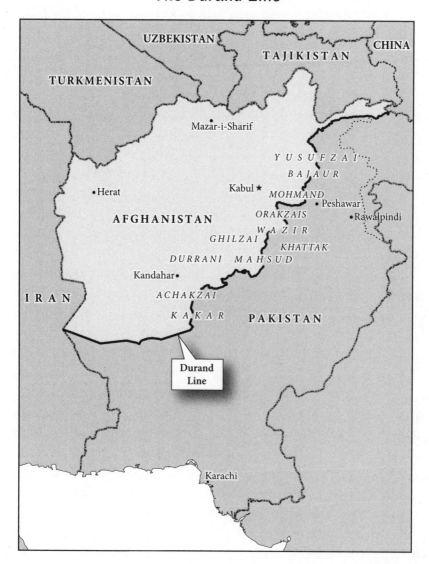

In order to achieve his ultimate goal, however, Abdu'Rahman needed a definite territory within which to reign supreme, so he accepted the Durand Line. Anything to keep the rest of the world out. Once the border was finalized, the amir basically closed it. After that, few Afghans were permitted to travel abroad and few visitors were allowed inside. The amir's government controlled even what artifacts, items, and information came in. To sever his country even more effectively from the outside world, he decreed that no railroads be built within its borders. By isolating Afghanistan, he cut it off from modern advances but secured a free hand to carry out his plan.

Before he could launch his grand scheme, he had a few things to take care of. First on the agenda was Ayub, the hero of Maiwand. This guy was too popular with the Afghan people! He would have to be eliminated. Abdu'Rahman took to the field and defeated him decisively. One down.

Another cousin raised his head. Ishaq wasn't a military hero like Ayub, but he governed a large province in the north and governed it well, dispensing justice with compassion, which made him popular. He too would have to go. Abdu'Rahman took to the field, and Ishaq, never much of a military man, fled the country. Two down. Next?

Next, the whole Mangal tribe revolted. Abdu'Rahman crushed them. Then the Ghilzai tribes revolted. Abdu'Rahman crushed them. In fact, Abdu'Rahman fought forty tribal wars during his reign and won them all. Mere victory wasn't enough for him, though. To make sure his vanquished subjects never rebuilt their power, he launched a policy that the Assyrians had pursued three millennia earlier and that Stalin would try a few decades later. He moved whole populations around the country to separate them from natural allies and plop them down among people whom they didn't trust and who didn't trust them. Entire tribes of Pushtoons were sent from south to north; thousands of families were forced to move from the northern steppes to areas south of Kabul. This autocratic program did have a salutary side effect: it shuffled the separate peoples of Afghanistan together, encouraging their integration into a single polity.

For most kings, fighting and winning forty wars in twenty-one years would pretty much define the reign; how much time would there be to get anything else done? For Amir Abdu'Rahman, the tribal wars were the tip of the iceberg. Even as he was subduing the Pushtoon tribes, the amir was massively reorganizing his country. In the past, Afghanistan had been divided into provinces and districts that more or less matched up to tribal areas. Territory inhabited mostly by one tribe would be one district, for example, and an adjacent territory inhabited mostly by another tribe would be another. The administrative structure of the country reflected the social patchwork. The governor of a district and the main tribal chief of that district would be one and the same. It was easy and it made sense.

Abdu'Rahman went exactly the other way. Not only did he increase the number of provinces and subdivide them into many more districts, he deliberately drew the district lines to cut across tribal territories. A given district governor would thus have families from several different tribes under his jurisdiction, and a tribe that inhabited a single contiguous territory would be divided among two or more districts. Thus, the matrix of governors and subgovernors could not conflate into the matrix of tribes and subtribes. Any particular person answered to the authority of his tribal elders but also to the authority of his district officials. These were two separate, unrelated systems.

The amir then did everything he could to empower his own appointees, whose authority came from the capital, over local tribal chieftains, whose authority came from the grass roots. After all, no matter how much power his governors garnered, he could still fire or reassign them. He could not do this with the khans and other tribal elders.

Then again, there was always a chance that an official appointed to some provincial office would build an independent power base, especially if the amir didn't keep a close watch on him. And how many officials could one amir watch closely? Well, quite a few, actually, if he had an effective spy network, so the amir built an intelligence service second to none, and this became a permanent feature of Afghan politics, continuing to the present day.

Thanks to his spies, the amir was able to disgrace and demote his governors whenever he deemed it necessary. He also regularly ruined his court officials, reducing them to nobodies. Typically, he would call a targeted official to court, claiming that someone had accused him of corruption. The official had to bring his books along and prove publicly, right then and there, that he had not misused the king's funds or done anything wrong. No one was ever able to produce books so clean that some discrepancy could not be found. As soon as a missing number, arithmetical error, or other glitch was discovered, the official was dismissed, his property confiscated, and his reputation ruined. He was lucky if he kept his freedom. In fact, not infrequently, the disgraced official was lucky if he kept his life. This happened so routinely that once, when the amir named an old friend of his to a prestigious office, the man heaped his possessions onto a cart and had them hauled to the palace.

"What's the meaning of this?" the amir frowned

"Your excellency," said the fellow, "I know that once you appoint a man to a high position, his destiny is to lose everything he owns within a few years. I'm trying to save time by turning over my property now."[3] As a token of their friendship, the amir did not have the man killed.

The amir kept a large establishment of bureaucrats at his court, many of whom started out as *ghulam bachas*, "slave boys," although the word *slave* here has the special meaning it acquired in Muslim societies over the course of centuries. These were boys taken from their families in their infancy and raised and educated at court under the guidance of the amir. They were molded into a privileged class of skilled officeholders who ran the country but had no support network of their own, only the amir's approval. In Afghanistan, the most favored of these were called *amir-zadas*, "the amir's children." Later the title was abbreviated to *mirza*.

Abdu'Rahman had a legion of mirzas. He put them in his cabinet and gave them command of his armies. Not only did he allow them to enjoy lives of luxury and grace but he insisted on it, for they represented his grandeur and, therefore, everywhere they went, they must be seen in the finest garments, riding the most magnificent horses. The trouble was, young men steeped in so much privilege tended to get big ideas. The amir was always on the lookout for plots that his pampered mirzas might be concocting. His favorite wife Halima, nicknamed Bobo Gul, once asked him why he didn't just kill the ones he didn't trust.

"It wouldn't be practical," he replied. "I don't trust any of them."[4]

Halima was not only the Iron Amir's favorite wife but something of a co-ruler, a formidable personality in her own right. People said the whole world was afraid of Abdu'Rahman, but he was afraid only of Bobo Gul. Like her husband a direct descendant of Dost Mohammed, she went on diplomatic missions for the amir, negotiating with tribal chieftains and rival commanders. Her maids were trained in the use of guns, and she had her own cavalry of bodyguards, the core of which were women warriors.[5]

Like his uncle Sher Ali, Amir Abdu'Rahman decided the nation needed a professional army. Tribal levies were fine for fighting foreign in-

vaders, but a king needed troops loyal only to him in order to fight . . .
well, his own people. Within three years of taking power, the Iron Amir
had built an army of forty-three thousand paid troops. By 1887, he had
grown this to sixty thousand. By 1890 he had over a hundred thousand
men in arms, including infantry, cavalry, and artillerymen. Every regiment had its own mullah who contributed to the war effort by preaching
that if the troops fled the field of battle, calamity would befall the Muslim
community, and they would face eternity in hell.[6]

Guns had been a hobby of Abdu'Rahman in his youth (surprise surprise). Once he became amir, guns became his passion. A French engineer
once tried to impress him with a telescope. He pointed the device at the
skies and said, "Look, your highness. Through this instrument, you can
see the moon."

"What good is the moon to me?" the amir growled. "Make that thing
shoot bullets and I might be interested."[7]

The amir armed his troops with guns supplied by the British, but he
also built armament factories in and around Kabul. At the height of his
reign, Afghanistan was producing on average *as many guns as any European
power*, enough to put at least one rifle in the hands of every adult male in
the country.[8] But the king had no intention of putting guns in the hands
of anyone except his own troops.

Even though Abdu'Rahman fought virtually all his wars with his own
Muslim subjects, he proclaimed himself the world's leading Defender of
the Faith. Previous Afghan kings had traced their authority to the will
of their people. Ahmad Shah, for example, based his legitimacy on the
elders' vote at that famous loya jirga. Abdu'Rahman, by contrast, derived
his authority from God, like those seventeenth-century European kings
who asserted a "divine right to rule." By waving an Islamic banner,
Abdu'Rahman could accuse rebels against his rule of defying God.

To bolster his religious claims, Abdu'Rahman enforced the most
rigid orthodox laws and the most conservative of social strictures. He had
muhtasibs, "morality police," who operated out of mosques. They forced
women to keep their faces veiled in public, made sure men prayed at the
appointed times, and flogged anyone they caught eating during Ramadhan. Under instructions from the top, they even punished people for
using foul language in public. By aligning himself with the extreme social

conservatives, Abdu'Rahman positioned himself to the right of the classes he intended to attack and defeat—the elders and the mullahs.

This was his most audacious campaign—going head-to-head with the whole traditional leadership of his country in an effort to substitute his authority for theirs. When I say "elders" I'm talking about all those local chieftains, maliks, khans, and paterfamilias, all those men with a reputation among their own, all those guys who had built prestige among their fellows by proving themselves in action over time, all those myriad local leaders whose authority derived from the people they lived among and dealt with directly. This class was all the harder to break or control because the elders had only local affiliations. They belonged to no larger structure. They could not be defeated by defeating *their* leaders. Each and every one of them had to be defeated separately. This was not a case of going to war with a legal entity or a political entity or even with a legal or political system: this was making war on the culture itself. Conquering the tribes was nothing compared to subduing the country's traditional leadership. To the extent that he succeeded, this was Abdu'Rahman's most astonishing achievement.

Here's how he went about it. He ordered that every village, every town, and every neighborhood in the cities elect one man to represent them in their dealings with the government, a figure called a *kalantar*. The king also fielded thousands of his own officials to deal with these local kalantars, and his local officials were called *kotwals*.

The kalantars' job was not to let the king know what the people wanted. They were charged with collecting taxes, enforcing the king's conservative social laws, and reporting any antigovernment talk they heard, any signs of subversion, any hints of suspicious activity. Whatever they discovered, they had to report to the kotwal. Essentially, the kalantars became part of the king's spy network.

They were also made responsible for keeping records of who lived in their area, where they lived, what they owned, and who their fathers were. Every Afghan was issued a numbered identity card, a *tazkira*, on which this information was recorded. Travel was forbidden except by permission of the authorities. Issuing travel permits was another duty of these people's representatives, but they had to secure approval for each permit from the local kotwal.

The kalantars were put on government salaries, which put a carrot into the system alongside the stick. Kalantars got a reward for doing their jobs well, and that was the carrot; but they if they didn't deliver, if they failed to turn in their neighbors and inform on their kinfolk, they were stripped of their livelihood. That was the stick.

The kalantars had quotas, as did kotwals. If a kalantar didn't turn in enough tax evaders, cheats, liars, thieves, murderers, and assorted wrong-doers, it didn't mean his district was well behaved; it meant he was lax in his duties, and his pay was docked. If a robbery occurred and the culprit was not found, the kalantar himself had to recompense the victim.

The kotwals were on the firing line too. If someone was cheating on his taxes and the kotwal did not discover it, he faced punishment. At the very least, he might be obliged to make up the taxes out of his own pocket, but he might go to prison or worse. Dissidents caught disparaging the king had their lips sewn shut and/or their tongues ripped out. Those caught plotting or carrying out subversion were put in iron cages hung by the wayside and left to starve in public view as a warning. The same punishment was meted out to highwaymen and other common criminals, as a result of which the amir was able to boast to an English diplomat that there was less crime in Afghanistan than in England.[9] During his reign, this was probably true.

Sometimes, men convicted of really heinous crimes, such as plotting against the king, were strapped to the mouths of cannons, which were then fired, blowing their bodies to pieces. (This mode of punishment was pioneered by the British to punish mutineers in India.) Although this was actually a mercifully quick way to go, the image created deep psychological dread. Most dreaded of all, however, was the punishment known as *Siah Chah*—"Black Well." I'll leave the details of that one to the readers' imagination.

The amir also went up against another class that was tough to break: the mullahs and other clerics. Again, the power of this class came from social consensus, habit, and tradition. The king could not subdue them by disrupting their organization—they didn't have one. He couldn't destroy their headquarters or their leaders. They had none. So he attacked them in another way. He put them on his payroll.

He didn't give every self-proclaimed mullah a salary, of course—only the ones who toed the line and convinced the amir's kotwals of their loyalty.

Many mullahs accepted the money because they had no reason to oppose the king: he was not against Islam, he wasn't pushing for any social changes offensive to Afghan culture—in fact he proclaimed himself more Muslim, more adamantly orthodox, than anyone. Many mullahs therefore came over. Why wouldn't they?

Once they started living on government money, the king had them. He could impose conditions, and he did. He declared that mullahs had to prove they really knew their religion (quite a reasonable demand, actually). Government officials traveled all around the country administering a test devised by the amir and his top theologians. Some 90 percent of the country's mullahs flunked. This is not such a surprise: most Afghans had their own very idiosyncratic understanding of religion, a combination of classical legislation, local folkways, customs, and traditions. And even though mullahs (supposedly) knew how to read, books were few and hard to come by.

After proving the ignorance of the mullahs, the amir declared that mullahs must be licensed. No unlicensed mullah could get a salary, and anyone caught carrying out the functions of a mullah without a license could be punished. In his compassion for his people, however, and out of his reverence for God's will, the amir set up religious schools where people could learn what they needed to pass the test. Those who studied at religious seminaries in the capital, which were built and watched over by the amir and his high officials, didn't have to take the test. Their diploma alone got them a license. Diplomas from selected prestigious Islamic universities outside Afghanistan were also accepted as proof of religious competence.

The same methods used to bring the mullahs under government control were used successfully to rope in the higher religious judges and jurisconsults—the qazis and muftis. The amir named one judge the supreme judge and included him in his cabinet as a minister of religious affairs, empowered to rule on the rulings of all other judges. The amir also appointed a commission to sort through the schools of Islamic jurisprudence and pick one and one alone for Afghanistan. Sunni Muslims recognize four schools of jurisprudence, four versions of the Shari'a, as equally orthodox. Though similar in principle, they have myriad differences in detail. The commission chose the Hanafi School of Law as the official legal system for Afghanistan. Rulings derived from this version of the Shari'a superseded rulings based on any other schools.

Some clerics resisted the amir's attempt to control them. Those clerics were exiled, imprisoned, tortured, or killed. The whole time this was going on, the amir continued to proclaim himself the Defender of the Faith and the most Muslim of Muslims, which allowed him to argue that recalcitrant mullahs were resisting him out of ambition and pride, not out of religious principle.

The amir's system depended on countless government employees, all of whom drew salaries: his army, his state mullahs, his spies, the kalantars and kotwals, the provincial governors and officials, the district governors and subgovernors, not to mention the mirzas in the capital—Abdu'Rahman needed more revenue than any previous king had squeezed out of this country. He commenced to tax everything: Afghans now had to pay land taxes, animal taxes, and tree taxes; they had planting taxes and harvesting taxes, income taxes and business taxes, trade taxes and travel taxes. In any commercial transaction, the sellers owed something to the state, and so did the buyers. If you got married—look out: you owed a marriage tax. If you died—well, that too was taxed: your survivors had to pay. He ended up gleaning four times as much revenue in taxes as Amir Sher Ali had gotten in his last years.

The king's insatiable need for revenue made his enormous apparatus of kalantars, kotwals, village enforcers, and spies indispensable. He needed them to make sure everyone was paying the taxes they "owed." And the amir couldn't take the chance that his kotwals would collude with the locals to defraud him, so he built a network of spies to spy on his spies. The various levels of spies found plenty to report, because no matter how hard the king beat down his people, the people kept rising up: they were Afghans.

The spies were only one branch of the amir's dreaded Ministry of Interior. His interior minister Mir Sultan specialized in night arrests. Any unexpected knock on the door after dark made people tremble. No one knew who might be arrested next or who had been arrested already or why they had been arrested or what happened to them. Many people just vanished, disappearances that were called *nam-girak*: "the name taking."

Finally, Mir Sultan had sown so much terror that even the highest court officials including the heir apparent wanted him stopped. And the amir agreed. Mir Sultan had been a valuable instrument, but now he had more value as a scapegoat. One day this architect of terror was called to court to defend himself. The amir told his council of advisors, "This man has killed about 60,000 people and I tell all of you assembled here, I sentenced 15 or 20 of them at most. The rest he killed on his own authority and for his own reasons. Tell me, brothers: what should be done with such a man?"[10]

The advisors knew the answer to that one. Mir Sultan was publicly hanged, and the amir took credit for saving his people from a monster. Everyone was glad to see the last of said monster, but most knew who the real king of terror was. The amir made it pretty obvious with his prisons. He had a dungeon below each of his palaces, and near the heart of Kabul he built Dehmazang prison, capable of holding nine thousand prisoners. The prisons kept proliferating until at one point (according to some reports) the amir had seventy thousand people incarcerated in Kabul—equal to a third of the city's population.[11] Political dissidents, corrupt officials, tax cheats, liars, merchants suspected of dishonesty—old, young, men, women, highborn, and lowborn—no one was exempt.

The most savage of the amir's wars were fought not against other Pushtoon tribes but against other ethnic groups within his borders. The Hazaras—a Persian-speaking Shi'a people of Mongolian descent living in central Afghanistan—had been quite autonomous under previous kings. Their autonomy ended in the Iron Amir's reign. Abdu'Rahman Khan deployed an army of a hundred thousand men in Hazarajat, counting both his own troops and the tribal levies he mustered. The entire Hazara population might not have been much more than 340,000.[12] The Hazaras resisted fiercely, and the war was especially bloody, but, when it was over, Hazara power had been broken. The amir legalized slavery briefly, but only for Hazaras. They could be bought and sold in markets, and it even became customary for aristocratic men to give Hazara children to others of their class, just as a way of saying thank you, please accept this token of my appreciation.

Abdu'Rahman's last major campaign took him to the remote valleys northeast of Kabul, which had long been called Kafiristan, "Land of the Infidels," because the people there practiced an animist religion involving elaborate graves decorated with images carved of wood. The five valleys and the numerous side canyons of Kafiristan were so narrow and rugged that no one had been able to conquer this area since Alexander the Great. Amir Abdu'Rahman conquered it in six months and renamed it Nuristan, "The Land of Light." With that conquest he absorbed the last bit of territory within his borders into his administration, and soon he laced it too with kotwals and government mullahs, like all the rest of his territory.

Ahmad Shah Baba, at his height, had been a superchieftain. Amir Abdu'Rahman Khan was not content to be a tribal chieftain of any size. He set out to change who the king was in Afghan society, which required changing Afghan society itself. By the time he was done, Afghanistan had a central government with a far-flung bureaucracy that could make its power felt in every part of the country and could push its way into the lives of all.

But Abdu'Rahman did not succeed in replacing what was there with something new. He may have wanted to create a single, entire, homogenous, new society, but he ended up creating a second Afghanistan laid over the first. The universe of mullahs, maliks, village republics, tribes, and tribal feudalism with all its khans and feudal princes (sardars) remained the deepest subsoil of the country. Another organism atop that subsoil now began sending shoots down into it: the government and its appendages, centered in Kabul with nerves extending into the cities, and its agents and administrators all over the land, a new social system enmeshed and in competition with the old systems.

This is not to say that each particular person was wholly part of one society or the other. Many people who worked for the central government had relatives in the countryside. Some people born into the universe of feudal village republics made their way to the towns and into the bureaucracy. The duality of Afghan society was uneasily recapitulated in private lives.

In the end the fact remained: Abdu'Rahman's agents could not get down into the heart of the villages. They could not get inside the walls of the family compounds or into the hidden worlds of clan and family privacy, the realm that constitutes the bulk of Afghan life. The Iron Amir set the parameters of a struggle in Afghanistan, between forward-looking change led by a central government and an urban elite, and backward-looking stasis vested in the villages and traditional leaders of the country, a struggle that would have profound consequences not just for Afghanistan itself but for attempts by foreign powers to intervene in the affairs of the country over the next century.

10

Starting Fresh

AMIR ABDU'RAHMAN DIED IN 1901, LEAVING A NATION STUNNED TO quietude like a landscape flattened by a hurricane. His son Habibullah succeeded peacefully to the throne, and oh what a happy king was he! His father had done all the dirty work, and Habibullah was left with nothing to do but enjoy being king.

He was a man of lusty enjoyments. He liked food, and so he grew stout in office. He liked sports, especially riding and hunting, and so he didn't grow medically obese. He liked women, so he took all the wives allowed to him under religious law and then went on to accumulate concubines and more concubines, building a harem that might have seemed normal to Shah Shuja a hundred years ago but that, in these more modern times, struck even his closest courtiers as distasteful. And it wasn't just that he acquired concubines. He had an eye for all women, including other men's wives. He designated Wednesdays as Lady's Night at his court and instructed all his officials to bring their wives and daughters to his entertainments. Once, an official refused. He said he was at his monarch's service without reservation, but his wife was not. The king slapped him silly.[1]

Habibullah could punish anyone he wanted, for any reason or no reason. That's what it means to be an absolute monarch. But he didn't want big things, like his father. Abdu'Rahman had wanted to reshape the nation and bend the course of history to his will, so he eviscerated whole villages, whole tribes, whole ethnic groups, whole sections of the country to attain his desires. Habibullah just wanted toys and pleasures, and he grabbed what he wanted, like a big, spoiled, petulant boy, so overprivileged he couldn't even see his own sense of entitlement. He might slap a man who annoyed him, but he didn't go out of his way to hurt anyone. Why bother? It was so much nicer to sit down to a fine dinner and then go visit the harem.

For the rest of Afghanistan, Habibullah's reign was a time of rest, recovery, and revival. Terrible though his father's twenty-one years had been, his reign had wrought productive changes in the nation. The Iron Amir had solidified Afghanistan as a buffer state that could keep both Russia and Britain at bay. And thanks to those twenty-one years of horror, the country could at least be governed now: the king wasn't standing on quicksand. A strong king might have used these assets to accomplish a great deal, had he been so inclined.

Habibullah wasn't really so inclined. He lacked ambition. And yet, despite this deficit, he did oversee a few accomplishments on his watch in an offhand sort of way. In 1904, his government established the country's first secular secondary school, which was named Habibia after the amir. Afghanistan had plenty of *madrassas*—religious seminaries—but here at Habibia boys studied mathematics, geography, English, and Urdu. Eventually drawing, history, Turkish, and various sciences were added to the curriculum. Out of Habibia School came trickling a new class in Afghanistan, an educated elite equipped to develop and administer a modern country. Amir Sher Ali had commissioned twelve experts to advise him. Afghanistan was now producing lots of experts who might advise a king, should he want advice.

This amir also acquired from the outside world whatever devices caught his fancy. On a visit to India, he saw a telephone, a relatively new invention, so he brought a few to Afghanistan. In 1908 he had lines strung from Kabul to several larger towns. He also established telegraph links among the country's major cities. In 1910, the royal government started building a hydroelectric power station near Kabul. Soon the elite of the capital enjoyed electric lighting for at least part of each evening. Amir Habibullah also bought a car, and a few of his privileged friends and relatives followed suit.[2] Then the amir improved a few roads around Kabul so that he and his buddies would have something to drive on and somewhere to go.

Most of the credit for these developments must go to a financial wizard whom the amir employed, a man named Mohammed Hussein. This fellow was unconnected to the royal clan but was learned in the mysteries of bookkeeping and business math. The amir made the man his *mustaufi*—his head accountant and exchequer. He developed into the king's boon companion and the second most powerful man in the land.[3]

Mustaufi Hussein made it his business to normalize the conquests the king had inherited from his father by bureaucratizing the management of these lands and absorbing the conquered people efficiently into a rational tax system. Accordingly, early in his tenure, Mustaufi Hussein toured Hazarajat, the homeland of the Hazara ethnic group, whom the Iron Amir had crushed so terribly. The Mustaufi went there to calculate what the region could yield in taxes. I know something of this journey because he took along his personal physician, my grandfather Einuddin. During that journey, Einuddin cured a village chieftain somewhere. The chieftain expressed his gratitude by giving my grandfather a Hazara girl—for, although the door had been closed on further enslavement, those already owned could still be bought, sold, traded, or given away. That girl ended up as my grandfather's fourth wife and bore him five sons, one of whom was my father.

Afghanistan was now relatively peaceful and safe (unless you were standing close enough to the amir for him to sock you in a petulant moment). As a consequence, people who had fled the country in Abdu'Rahman's time came filtering back. Among them was a man soon known as the amir's chief counselor, or *musahib*, and his five sons, the brothers *Musahibban*. The eldest of these brothers and the leader of the pack was a grim, trim stick figure with gold-rimmed spectacles named Nadir. All five sons had grown up in British India and had been educated there in the British system. All five were well schooled in courtly graces. All five were tough, quiet fellows who hung together and operated as a unit under Nadir's steely direction. They were related to the amir, but only distantly. The two lines had branched apart in the generation before Dost Mohammed the Great. Now that they were back in Afghanistan, they wormed their way into the king's confidence. Nadir became commander in chief of the amir's armies, while his brothers secured important provincial posts. Their sister Ulya Janab helped secure their position at court by marrying Habibullah. This accomplished woman dressed in European clothes, wrote poetry, and spoke several languages fluently. She was translating from Urdu into Dari a biography of Prophet Mohammed's second successor Omar when she died. It was finished after her death, and her brother published it in 1932.

Another man who came back was Mahmoud Tarzi, the most incendiary of the returning exiles. Tarzi's family had settled in the Ottoman Empire when they left Afghanistan, and, growing up in Turkey, Tarzi had imbibed the heady, revolutionary brew stirred up by the Young Turks, who were not so much a movement as a whole array of movements that shared one theme in common: *enough of the stagnant Muslim past! Let us embrace the future, the new!* Not all of the Young Turks were young, and those who started out young were still calling themselves Young Turks when they grew old. "Young" did not denote their age but their attitude.

Tarzi brought Young-Turk effervescence to Afghanistan, and he too became a fixture at court. His great hero and defining influence was the radical Muslim modernist Jamaluddin-i-Afghan, who had tutored the sons of Dost Mohammed and had written up a modernization program for Amir Sher Ali. Like his hero, Tarzi believed that he could transform the nation by molding the mind of its monarch. Like Jamaluddin, therefore, he entered Afghan history as a teacher: he tutored Amir Habibullah's sons, hoping one of them would end up on the throne. What he taught the kids was much more than reading, writing, and 'rithmetic. He filled their heads with information about the world beyond the borders of Afghanistan and with visionary dreams about the future.

As a boon companion of the king's, Tarzi was close to his exchequer Mustaufi Hussein as well. Hussein's son Khalillulah, who became Afghanistan's foremost modern poet, studied with Tarzi as a child. Seven decades later, thinking back to those days, he remembered how he was playing around in Tarzi's study one day when he came across several books his teacher had translated from French into Dari. Khalilullah started reading the first one and kept reading until he had inhaled all four. The books were *20,000 Leagues Under the Sea, Around the World in Eighty Days, The Mysterious Island*, and *A Voyage to the Sky*, novels by Jules Verne.[4]

Tarzi was not just a translator but a writer. Tarzi is actually a pen name that became a family name. It means "stylist," for this was a literary family, going back to the days of Dost Mohammed. Tarzi was an accomplished poet, but he didn't write the old-fashioned stuff that Rumi and Jami and Hafez and Ansary and other Afghan poets had written. He did use classical forms and follow classical rules of prosody, but his lines were not loaded with images of love and wine nor of moths incinerating themselves in candles as metaphors for mystical immersion in God. Tarzi was a different kind of romantic. He rhapsodized about telegraph lines and vaccines and streets paved with asphalt.[5]

He started the most celebrated newspaper in Afghan history *Seraj-ul-Akhbar*, "Lamplight of the News," in which he published news about the world as well as essays about breakthroughs in science and cultural innovations—about radio waves and weather prediction, the germ theory of disease, the French Revolution and its ideas, constitutions and political philosophies, new discoveries in psychology—the pot brimmed, it overflowed! Soon thereafter, his wife Asma Restya launched Afghanistan's first women's newspaper, which she edited and circulated privately among the urban elite.[6]

Young Afghans coming to maturity in Kabul in the early twentieth century were hungry to hear such ideas, thirsty to learn about the great wide world, ready to leap into the never imagined. Maybe the young always have this sort of energy, but it erupts with special intensity in some places at some times. From all the stories I've heard, Kabul just before and during World War I seems to have been one such place and time. For the young men of Kabul, their city must have felt like the Athens of Pericles's time, the Baghdad of the Abbasid era, the Florence of the Medici, Paris in the Jazz Age. And Tarzi was at the center of it all, the match that lit the flames.

Protégés from among the young aristocrats formed a coterie around Tarzi, and no one drank from the fountain more avidly than the amir's third son Prince Amanullah. Tarzi was the father this firebrand never had: so much so that Amanullah married his daughter, the beautiful and accomplished Soraya, which made Tarzi his father-in-law.

But Tarzi and his followers were not the only movement bubbling at court. The amir's brother Nasrullah personified a different current. Nasrullah had matured into a zealous orthodox Muslim. He disdained his brother's indolence and concupiscence but lived with it. Nasrullah had inherited his father's energy and must sometimes have resented not inheriting the throne, but he lived with it. Nasrullah felt a kinship with all those traditional clerics whom Abdu'Rahman had tried to crush or co-opt. Nasrullah knew they were neither crushed nor co-opted but were still shaping public opinion, still molding the passions of the people out there in the countryside. They were still the ocean; the government and its minions still just the foam on the waves. Nasrullah reached out to the conservative clerics and let the strongest of them know they had a friend at court. They in turn assured him that *he* had friends in the countryside. Nasrullah hated the British on religious grounds and sometimes suggested an Afghan jihad against them. In these last days of Afghan subservience to the British—who still controlled Afghan foreign policy—Nasrullah embodied the most deeply conservative posture.[7]

Nasrullah had no official job title, but he sometimes acted as though he were king. He once remarked casually to a companion that he might set Habibullah aside one day. He didn't do it though, because he didn't have to. He could bide his time. Habibullah's heir apparent, his eldest son Enayatullah, was an easygoing nonentity who didn't look like king material to any of the possible contenders.

The big issue for the court in this era was the Great European War, later known as World War I. Which side should Afghanistan take? Both Nasrullah and Tarzi thought Afghanistan should oppose Britain, Nasrullah for religious reasons and Tarzi out of an anti-imperialist passion.[8] But Habibullah said, no, Afghanistan must declare itself neutral. That was the smart play. Afghanistan was Britain's client and Russia's neighbor: it couldn't side against those powers. On the other hand, a leading member of the Axis group was the Ottoman Empire. Afghanistan could not declare war against the leading Muslim power, still considered by many to be the seat of the Khaliphate (a.k.a. Caliphate): it wouldn't look good to the locals.

Besides, privately, the British knew what neutrality meant. It meant Afghans could fight for Britain by filtering across the Durand Line and joining the "Indian" army. Some seven hundred thousand Indians went to Europe to fight for Britain, one-third of whom were Muslims, and, of those, over 80 percent came from the lands bordering or straddling Afghanistan: in short, many were Afghans.[9] That's a lot of Afghans fighting in World War I. When the war ended, Amir Habibullah claimed some credit for the British victory and suggested that Afghanistan take part in the Paris Peace Conference, but the viceroy called the idea preposterous.[10]

We come now to a mysterious event as riveting as any detective novel. In late February 1919, just after the peace conference began in Paris, Amir Habibullah went on a grand hunting expedition. February is an odd time for such a trip, because the mountains are still choked with snow, but the amir loved adventure. His mustaufi stopped in the city of Jalalabad, but the amir's party went on into the mountains. After the king left (witnesses reported), the mustaufi received a private message that made him pale. Immediately, he wrote a letter to the king and gave it to a messenger. He ordered the messenger to wear black and ride a black horse so as to cut a striking figure that the king would notice. He wanted to make sure the king would read the letter at once. But the king was busy having fun and put the envelope in his pocket unopened.

That night, after feasting on grilled meats and subtle side dishes cooked by the royal chefs, the king retired to his tent, happy and spent. His commander in chief Nadir Khan—the eldest of those five Musahib-ban brothers—was guarding the camp. The king's older brother Nasrullah was in camp too. Guards were posted at each of the four cardinal points around the tent. A fifth man, a Colonel Reza, stood sentry at his very door. Three men went into the tent with the king to carry out his bedtime ritual: two were masseurs to rub his feet, one a storyteller to lull him with fantastic tales.[11]

Once the king began to doze, these three slipped out of the tent; but they had gone only a few paces when they heard a bang. A dark figure burst from the doorway. Colonel Reza grabbed the mystery man's arm but could not make out his features. At that moment, General Nadir Khan and the king's brother Nasrullah came running up, almost as if they had been hovering nearby, waiting for something to happen. In the confusion, the presumptive killer wrenched loose and went running off, never to be seen again. Some would later say the king's brother and his henchman Nadir helped the assassin escape—for assassin he was: when the men went into the tent they found the king lying dead, shot through the heart. The assassin must have gotten into the tent earlier and lain in wait. But how could the amir's security have failed so utterly? Was some high-ranking figure complicit in the crime?

The next day, Nasrullah hastened to Jalalabad and declared himself amir. The king's mild-mannered eldest son stood next to him and pledged his loyalty, giving up the throne just like that. The dead king's second son had left the hunting party a few days earlier, saying he had business in Kabul. Had he gone straight home, he would have been in Kabul when the king was killed, in position for a power play, but he fell ill along the way and stopped in some village to recover. The messenger carrying word of the assassination to the capital must have ridden right past the house where he lay moaning.

When the news broke in the capital, therefore, only the third son was on the spot to take advantage: Prince Amanullah, that modernist firebrand. Amanullah wasted no time seizing the treasury, taking command of the army, and announcing a hefty pay raise to ensure the allegiance of the troops. Then he assembled the city's notables for a passionate speech. Drawing a sword from his scabbard, he swore that "I will not sheath it again until I have brought my father's killer to justice."[12]

That Friday, when Nasrullah went to the mosque in Jalalabad, he was astonished to hear the sermon read in the name of "Amir Amanullah." Moments later, Amanullah's men arrived to arrest him and charge him with complicity in the amir's murder. Amanullah then rounded up his father's top advisers, anyone who might pose a threat to him, and put them on trial. The poet Khalilullah, who was a twelve-year-old boy then, reports that his father was among those called to court for interrogation by Amanullah himself. Witnesses saw Amanullah pull out a letter—presumably the one Mustaufi Hussein had sent the king on the day of his murder. Apparently, in this letter, the mustaufi had said something incriminating. The new king was demanding that he account for his words. The mustaufi shouted back for all to hear, "It was you! You killed your own father!"[13]

Amanullah ordered that the exchequer be dragged into the garden and hanged. A couple of draftees were brought in to do the deed, simple peasants from the north. As one of them fitted the noose around Mustaufi Hussein's neck, his fingers trembled. The once-mighty moneyman scoffed at him. "*I'm* the one who's being hung here. Why are *your* fingers trembling? Do your job, boys: don't flinch. But when you leave here, tell the world you acted on the orders of Amanullah!"[14]

A violent end was not uncommon for Afghan rulers, but most were killed in wars or executed after losing wars. The killing of Habibullah was a murder mystery. Who ordered it? Who plotted it? Who carried it out? No one knows. Early armchair detectives suspected Nadir and Nasrullah. Nasrullah had motive, Nadir had opportunity. Perhaps the two were in cahoots. Then again, although Amanullah made a lot of noise about hunting down his father's killers, the only men he actually moved against were those who had pretensions to the throne, not those whom credible evidence implicated in the murder. Very suspicious.

Naturally, no one voiced suspicions about Amanullah at the time because he was the king. Instead they confined themselves to muttering dark accusations about Nadir. Later, Amanullah fell from power and Nadir became king. After that no one voiced suspicions about Nadir anymore. Instead, many now said Amanullah must have plotted the crime. In short, the mystery got intertwined with the political fortunes of the possible suspects, which is why no one knows whodunit to this day. But that is getting ahead of our story.

11

King of
the Radicals

AFGHANISTAN HAD NEVER SEEN A KING LIKE AMANULLAH. BACK WHEN HE was still just a prince, people said, he used to disguise himself in peasant's garb and roam the bazaars, mingling with the common folks—the story sounds apocryphal, but it has the ring of authenticity to me: it would have been in character.[1] The amirs before Amanullah all had a relationship with the British that didn't jibe with the sentiments of the people. Those royals hobnobbed with the foreigners, took their subsidies, and used their military aid to control their own subjects. Twice, the Afghans had gone to war with Britain, and each time it was the tribes and common folks, not the royals, who had done the successful fighting. The Afghan elite got along with the British; the Afghan street hated them and wanted them gone. On this issue, Amanullah was with the street.

Amanullah's mentor Tarzi, an ardent nationalist, had passed on the virus to his student. Even if the new king had not sincerely longed for his country's independence, he might have used this issue to cement his position. Whatever his motive, in 1919, as soon as he had power, Amanullah declared total independence from Britain. His subjects were dazzled: at last, a king who was not a stooge of the foreigners!

Amanullah declared independence by sending a letter to the viceroy in India announcing that the "independent and free nation of Afghanistan" hoped to build good relations with Great Britain on the basis of treaties mutually beneficial to both, language that implied a dialogue between two equal parties.[2] The British high command had a good laugh over that naïve note and never bothered to answer it.

Another letter from Kabul followed shortly, announcing that Afghanistan was establishing a Foreign Ministry headed by Mahmoud Tarzi. This was a slap. British India was supposed to *be* Afghanistan's foreign ministry. This was the one point the British had demanded of every amir since Dost Mohammed. The government of India decided to deal with the upstart by ignoring him.

A few weeks later, letters went out to the United States, France, Persia, Japan, Turkey and Russia, announcing that Afghanistan now had its own Foreign Ministry. Here was provocation indeed! Yet, even so, the British treated Amanullah like a mouse squeaking behind the woodwork.

Clearly, he had to do something more dramatic. And on April 13, 1919, he got his chance. That day, in Amritsar, India, a British general named Reginald Dyer ordered his troops to shoot into the thick of a crowd of peaceful demonstrators who were calling for Indian independence. The ten-minute fusillade left 379 dead and over 1,200 injured.[3] Amanullah seized the opportunity to declare a jihad against the British. The Pushtoon tribes responded enthusiastically. Disorder erupted throughout India's frontier region. The Third Anglo-Afghan War had begun.

At least it is remembered as the Third Anglo-Afghan War, but it wasn't much of a *war*, really. Amanullah had retained Nadir Khan as his commander in chief, and he sent this general and two others to attack British border posts. Some inconclusive skirmishes were fought, but no territory changed hands.

The British, however, feared that if hostilities dragged on "the tribes might rise." This was the enduring British nightmare: The Tribes Might Rise. They decided to end the war quickly by demonstrating a lethal new weapon of theirs: they sent airplanes over the city of Jalalabad to drop bombs. The terrified population evacuated the city, and Jalalabad turned into a ghost town overnight.

Two British warplanes—unsophisticated biplanes like the one Snoopy is seen flying in the *Peanuts* cartoons—then dropped bombs on Kabul. Few were killed, but I can attest to the psychological impact: forty years later, when my father needed to know his age for some document (which was tough to specify because Afghans do not celebrate birthdays), my grandmother was able to tell him exactly when he was born: it was one year before the British bombed Kabul. She knew because she was nursing him when the explosions erupted.

As soon as the bombs fell, Amanullah wrote to the Indian viceroy. War was no way to settle differences, he said: the British and the Afghans should sit down and talk like civilized people. The British did not bother to reply. In another context, this might have been a frustrating humiliation, but Amanullah was able to use it to his advantage: he had sued for peace and the British had not even answered, which violated the code of Pushtoonwali! What kind of savages were these Farangis? Amanullah had achieved the status of hero by calling for national independence and the status of saint by calling for jihad, and now he acquired the halo of a martyr by calling for peace and being snubbed. His stature in Afghanistan was growing by the day.

At the same time, Nadir set siege to a single British fort on the border not just with the regular troops under his command but with the collaboration of some twelve thousand armed tribesmen from that area.[4] The British laughed about the tribesmen's primitive guns—until Nadir's forces managed to cut off the fort's water supply.

Suddenly, the British realized something rather bad was happening. The news got worse: anti-British fever was spreading among the cross-border Afghans. This was the nightmare coming true: The Tribes *Were* Rising. Did the government of India really want to pile its plate high with tribal troubles now, in 1919, when Britain was still reeling from the costs of World War I and trying to regroup? It wasn't Afghan military valor but the larger circumstances of world history that led the British to notice Amanullah's letter finally. They agreed to meet his delegates at the city of Rawalpindi and discuss terms.

So ended the Third Anglo-Afghan War—a war that consisted of a few skirmishes, a handful of casualties, and four or five small bombs dropped on two cities. It wasn't much, but the British figured it was enough, for it had brought the Afghans to their senses. They were begging for terms. In London, officials discussed what terms to impose on them. Some favored taking direct control of the country, but the Paris Peace Conference had just ended, and Woodrow Wilson's fourteen points were still hovering over the Western world. Talk of "self-determination" and the rights of "small nationalities" filled the air. Taking over Afghanistan would not look cool. If it were done, it would have to be done in a "veiled" manner.[5] Such were the thoughts the British brought to Rawalpindi.

The Afghan delegation strutted into the peace talks with a swagger as if they didn't realize they had lost the war. Hamilton Grant, head of the British delegation, led with a number of calculated insults, but Ali Ahmad, head of the Afghan delegation, deflected them suavely. He was by turns charming, disingenuous, conciliatory, offended, aggressive, and diplomatic. The talks lasted the entire summer. Over those months, Ali Ahmad maneuvered the British into meeting Amanullah's bottom line: independence in his foreign policy. The final stroke came in the last days of negotiations, when Ali Ahmad asked that the document refer to Amanullah as "His Majesty" and not simply as "the Amir." Grant refused. That honorific, he said, belonged exclusively to King George, but he offered a compromise. How about dropping all reference to monarchs and letting this be recorded as a treaty between "the Illustrious British Government" and the "Independent Government of Afghanistan." Grant thought he had finessed something, whereas actually he had given away the store. All previous British treaties had been with an individual amir, not with an enduring state. As soon as one king died, all promises were moot. This treaty was with a country, no matter who ruled it—and it used the phrase "independent government."

More importantly, Grant supplied Ali Ahmad with a separate letter affirming that the British government relinquished all control of Afghanistan's foreign policy and recognized it as a sovereign state. "Liberty is a new toy to the Afghan Government," Grant explained in a letter to his superiors back home, "and they are very jealous and excited about it. . . . Later on, if we handle them well, they will come to us to mend their toy when it gets chipped or broken They want the shadow of external freedom and don't really worry about its substance."[6]

The laughing stopped when Amanullah announced Afghan independence at a major mosque in Kabul with the British envoy on one side of him and the *Russian* representative on the other—a Bolshevik. The British realized he might be serious about this new toy of his. The final treaty between the two countries was not signed until November 21, 1921, but by then Amanullah had signed trade protocols and friendship treaties with various states including Japan, France, Italy, and Turkey.

Only one country spurned the Afghans: the United States. The Afghan delegation came to New York in 1922, but as it happened a ludicrous adventurer hit town at the same time: an old woman named "Princess" Fatima Sultana, who was descended from Shah Shuja. She came festooned in jewels and looking like every New Yorker's image of a Theda Bera–style exotic from the mysterious East. Her jewels included one particularly large diamond she called the Darya-i-Noor (River of Light). She was traveling with a rascal who called himself the Crown Prince of Egypt—they were characters straight out of Mark Twain and belonged on a raft floating down the Mississippi.

To make matters worse, these two con artists fell victim themselves to an American con artist named Weymouth, who convinced them he was with the Department of the Navy and said he would present Fatima to the president of the United States—he had his eye on that diamond. The New York press didn't know which was the real diplomatic delegation from Afghanistan, and they picked the one they found more entertaining: Princess Fatima and her entourage. Every day, the papers ran stories featuring her and her diamonds. By then, Secretary of State Charles Evans Hughes had heard from Britain that Afghanistan was still part of the British Empire, not a sovereign country at all. So the real Afghan delegation went home with nothing. The Princess Fatima lost her diamond to Weymouth, ran out on her hotel bill, and got deported in disgrace.

Despite the American slight, the independence of Afghanistan became a fait accompli. Amanullah gained what his predecessors had made bombastic speeches about, and he did it with diplomacy and negotiation, not war. Amanullah then had more political capital in the bank than most rulers ever enjoy. His people loved him, and he loved them back. He made a habit of calling the notables of the city together in the evenings at a great assembly hall and chatting with them about the golden possibilities that lay ahead for Afghanistan. He toured the country and held public meetings in Kandahar and other cities, where he lectured to the common crowds. Educate your children, he told them. The future lies within their reach. If your children will only learn to read, write, and study, Afghanistan will have airplanes and electric lights and roads. Educate your wives too, he preached. A country can't progress without contributions from its women. And treat your wives well, he lectured: do as the Prophet did. The Prophet said all people are equal, men and women. Take his words to heart, Amanullah counseled his subjects.

He was the most democratic of absolute monarchs, and if that's an oxymoron, so be it. He met his people face-to-face, shook hands with them, and heard their pleas. Once, on a journey to the southern border, he insisted on meeting with the laborers working on a road that was being constructed there through difficult terrain, and he embraced these men of the lowest social class and thanked them for their service. He went to all these places without bodyguards, the usual filter between king and people, which all previous amirs had considered indispensable. "The nation is my bodyguard," he said.

Back in Kabul, he and his wife Soraya, Tarzi's well-educated daughter, hosted elegant parties. While Amanullah dazzled the men with his visions, Soraya gathered the wives together and made similarly inspirational speeches to them. The royal couple seemed to see themselves as great teachers, shepherding their people toward the light, except that nothing about their attitude was religious. They were avatars of the secular approach to life, the approach that had made the West so powerful.

12

King's Law Versus God's Law

IN 1923, AMANULLAH PRESENTED THE NATION WITH A DOCUMENT HE had been working on since he took office. He called it the *Nizamnama*, "the Book of Order." It was a new legal code he had invented by himself, taken partly from the code Ataturk was promulgating for Turkey, which was adapted from Swiss, French, and Italian codes. Merely creating such a code was a brash act in Afghanistan, for the clerics believed that men could not make laws. That privilege belonged to God alone, and God had already given humanity the laws men must follow: the Shari'a. No man could substitute his own laws for the Shari'a.

Amanullah didn't call his code an alternative to the Shari'a. He simply didn't mention the Shari'a. The specific provisions of the Nizamnama were just as revolutionary as the mere fact of the king creating his own alternative to the Shari'a. Some of his edicts were exhilarating, but some made people uneasy.

Amanullah's code banned torture, even by the government; forbade forced entry into any private home, even by the government; and gave every citizen the right to bring charges of corruption against any government official—and those who didn't get redress for their complaints at lower levels could take their petition right on up to the king. His code banned slavery too. So far, so good.

But his code also guaranteed freedom of religion in Afghanistan, which made the clerics squint. What did the king mean by "freedom"?

Surely he didn't mean Muslims could convert freely to another faith if they so desired: that went directly against the Shari'a. But what did he mean then, if not that? Was he giving his subjects the right to interpret the Qur'an and the Prophet's sayings for themselves? Even that struck directly at the power of the country's most entrenched establishment, its clerics.

The code went on to outlaw underage marriage. Girls were forbidden to marry until they were eighteen, men till they were twenty-two. Then there was the bride price: in Afghanistan men who wanted to marry a girl customarily paid that girl's family a sum of money negotiated by the men of the two families. Afghan modernists felt this amounted to fathers selling their daughters for profit. Amanullah's code did not forbid the bride price but set an upper limit on it of twenty-nine rupees. Brides had been going for 10,000 rupees.[1]

And then there was purdah—the requirement that women be veiled from men outside their own family. Afghanistan observed the strictest purdah in the world. Afghan women who went out in public had to wear a bag-like garment called a *chad'ri* or burqa over their bodies, which covered them from head to toe, leaving only a tiny patch of mesh for them to look through. Amanullah's code said no law could require the burqa. Women could wear one if they wanted, but no one could force them to wear one, not even their husbands. This was truly radical stuff.

And, while he was at it, the king had some recommendations. Yes, technically, Islam allowed a man to have up to four wives, but only if he could treat them equally, which in practice was impossible for any man except the Prophet; so really the Qur'an was discouraging polygamy, so the king declared. He himself had only one wife, and one, he suggested, was enough for any man.*

There was more. The Nizamnama prohibited shoemakers from making the old-fashioned Punjabi style shoes that curled up at the toes, the norm for most Afghan men. Henceforth, Afghan shoemakers could only make Western-style shoes. Men with beards could not work for the government. They had to be clean shaven. Government officials could not

---

* Amanullah failed to mention his first wife, whom he had not divorced: an arranged marriage.

come to work in the traditional native outfit of turban, long shirt, and baggy trousers. All who worked for the government would have to wear suits and ties and hats with brims.

The Nizamnama hit the society like a fertilizer bomb, but Amanullah and his queen didn't worry. They took the attitude that Afghans would learn: all they needed were schools. So Amanullah began building schools all over the country, and not just for boys. In the new Afghanistan, girls would be educated too. The first schools were not coeducational, but that was coming. The country already had one government high school, the one built by Habibullah. Amanullah added three more. Each of the four high schools taught a foreign language, and, in the upper grades, the scientific subjects were taught in a European language: English at Habibia and Ghazi, German at Nejat, and French at Istiqlal. Boys who graduated from these schools would be equipped to go to universities in Germany, France, England, and America to learn the skills needed to implement the king and queen's vision for a new Afghanistan.

Nadir Khan and his brothers saw both disaster and opportunity in this program. Nadir had spearheaded the military aspect of the war for independence, at which time he had built strong links to tribal leaders in the south. He wanted to disassociate himself from this mad rush to transform Afghan society, and thus avoid squandering the popular support he enjoyed in the countryside. Nadir was too calculating to voice his disapproval out loud, because Amanullah was still the king, but he sought out private meetings with British officials to assure them of his admiration for Britain. He said that Amanullah's revolutionary enthusiasm probably reflected Soviet influence and that he himself favored a strong and friendly relationship with Great Britain. Hint hint. Then he got himself a diplomatic posting to Paris and settled down to observe events from a safe distance.

Amanullah's program came right out of Tarzi's teachings, but his methods made even his mentor nervous. Tarzi counseled his son-in-law the king to slow down, make changes one at a time, give the people time to adjust. Amanullah and Soraya paid no attention. They were like teenagers. To them, old man Tarzi might have had some good ideas in his day, but he was a relic now. Amanullah did take one piece of Tarzi's advice to heart. Tarzi told him to learn from Ataturk. The father of modern Turkey built invincible military strength before launching his reforms. Tarzi advised his son-in-law not to let reforms get ahead of military preparedness.

On this point, Amanullah decided that his father-in-law might be right, so he revived his grandfather's policy of *hasht-nafari* or "every eighth man," which meant that the king's officials would go out and draft every eighth man they encountered.

Amanullah had finally gone too far. Outside the cities, religious leaders were already preaching that the king had become an infidel. Now, they said, he was trying to create an army to enforce his infidel will. He would come into men's homes and rip the veils off their women and God only knew what else. In 1924, a tribal rebellion erupted near the Durand Line. Amanullah defeated these rebels, because his army had superior weapons and he still had considerable tribal support.[2] After his victory, however, Amanullah faced a dilemma.

His dilemma had to do with the most eminent religious personalities in Afghanistan, a set of brothers popularly known as the Hazrats of Shor Bazaar, "the Revered Ones of Hubbub Market." *Hazrat*, a title accorded only to the most highly regarded of religious men, implied learning and scholarship, but it also connoted mystical power and charisma. The Hazrats of Shor Bazaar didn't just have "followers." They had devotees by the thousands.

The Hazrats of Shor Bazaar belonged to a family known as the Mujaddedis, "the Newcomers." They had started out as strong supporters of Amanullah. The eldest of them had placed the royal turban on Amanullah's head and declared him king on that day in the mosque in 1919. But the eldest brother had died just as the rebellion was starting, and his younger brother Sher Agha Mujaddedi had lost enthusiasm for the amir, for he opposed the reforms. He may in fact have helped incite the rebellion.

Amanullah could not arrest Sher Agha, because this was not some isolated mullah preaching in the mountains. This was a national religious personality in a country that took religion more seriously than it took anything else. Sher Agha was so respected he could not even be insulted, much less be accused of criminal treason, even by the king. So Amanullah merely met with the Hazrat and suggested he might be more comfortable in another country. Sher Agha took the hint and moved to India, settling in the vicinity of a town called Deoband.

An ominous choice. Deoband had a famous religious university from which had sprung a revivalist movement called Deobandism. For several generations now, graduates of the Deobandi school had been circulating among Muslims of India, preaching that Islam must be restored to its original form, the form practiced in Mecca and Medina in the seventh century. Theirs was not merely a religious movement but a political program. The Deobandis were asserting that, because Islam provided a comprehensive template for society, Muslims had a duty to help create a state guided only by the Shari'a, a state in which there was no law but God's law.

Toward this end, they said, Muslims must cleanse themselves of infidel ways, such as those exemplified by the European imperialist colonizers. They must return to the pristine ways of the prophet and his companions. You might suppose that radicals of this stripe would have no truck with the infidel British; but the Deobandis, at least in this period, were more concerned with their own backsliding brethren, especially Muslim modernists. They were ready to make deals with the British to combat this "near enemy" (as Osama Bin Laden would later term secular Muslims), confident that, once they had beaten the near enemy, they could take on the further foe. Amanullah personified everything the Deobandis abhorred, and the Deobandis represented everything Amanullah was fighting.

During the rebellion, in order to secure the help of the tribal elders, Amanullah had been forced to cancel his reform program. After the rebellion, he went right back to implementing his Nizamnama. And while Amanullah was proceeding with his reforms, Sher Agha Mujaddedi was keeping in close touch with his friends and allies in Afghanistan. Deobandi agents were traveling back and forth across the Durand Line, carrying messages and reports. Clerics and tribal powers throughout the countryside, taking inspiration and direction from the exiled Hazrat, agitated against the king. He's become a *kafir*, they whispered. He's become an infidel. Afghan conspiracy theorists believe the British secretly incited, promoted, and funded this corrosive campaign.

In 1927, Amanullah decided to do what no Afghan king had ever done. Even with all this whispering unrest in his country, he decided to visit Europe. He left his country in the hands of a regent and traveled through India as a private citizen to Bombay. There, he and Queen Soraya boarded a boat bound for Egypt. En route, Soraya exchanged her heavy

Afghan veil for a piece of cloth that covered only the lower half of her face. When she stepped ashore in Cairo wearing this veil, the paparazzi snapped her picture.

The king and queen of Afghanistan drew considerable crowds in Egypt, for here was the giant killer, the only Muslim monarch ever to back down a European colonial power and achieve complete independence for his country. The excitement in Egypt attracted press coverage in Europe, and a buzz began.

But the events in Egypt made news in the east as well. When Amanullah visited the thousand-year-old Al-Azhar University, the heart of the Islamic intellectual universe, alma mater of the greatest Muslim theologians, scholars, and sages of all time, he didn't wear traditional Muslim garb. He came decked out in a dove gray Western-style suit and prayed in the mosque in a top hat instead of a turban. The professors frowned; the clerics bit their lips. Amanullah's opponents in Afghanistan rubbed their hands gleefully.

From Egypt the couple went to Italy, where some reporters felt Amanullah outclassed their own King Victor Emmanuel in sophisticated grace. As for Soraya, she now let the public see her face, and the public fell in love. The press played up the royal couple from Afghanistan as the fairy-tale prince and princess. The government of Italy went out of its way to prove it could host such a couple in suitable style. The photographers kept snapping pictures.

From Italy, the king and queen moved on to France. There, even more fervid crowds turned out, for their celebrity had preceded them. By no means would the French allow the Italians to outclass them! The president of France himself came to the train station to greet the royal couple. When Soraya stepped onto the platform, he bowed low, took her hand, and gallantly pressed his lips to it. Photographers caught the moment.

The French press went into a swoon. "Soraya," they noted, sounded like *sourire*, the French word for "smile." The queen came to state dinners clothed in exquisite Parisian couture, and oh how well she carried it off! She eschewed the short skirts then in fashion (this was the flapper era), but the evening gowns she wore to state dinner left her shoulders bare, and the little veil she was wearing now, covering only the lower half of her face, was just a film of transparent gauze. She achieved a look delightful to the French, simultaneously exotic and sophisticated, modern and mysterious.

By the time Amanullah and Soraya got to Germany, they were greeted like rock stars. Germany could not hope to match Italy and France for style, and their German hosts floundered a bit, trying to figure out what to serve guests who didn't drink beer or eat pork sausages. But they did the best that money could buy: the government tried to close the gap with gifts and trade deals and offers of economic aid. Amanullah accepted several aircraft, a promise of some transport trucks, and a bunch of industrial machinery, including everything he needed to set up a soap factory, not to mention a trade agreement with a private Germany company, which offered to buy 830,000 rupees worth of Afghan lapis lazuli each year for the next three years.[3]

The whole tour transcended politics—or perhaps "transcended" is not the right word. It wasn't really politics but entertainment. This is easy to see, looking back from a time when hard news has largely given way to entertainment and titillation: Amanullah and Soraya sold newspapers. As soon as they were gone, the press would dig up a new story and they would be forgotten. But Amanullah and Soraya didn't realize that. They only knew that every nation they visited, even Britain, competed to impress them. Everywhere he went, Amanullah picked up gifts and aid offers. How could he not begin to think that even in his most arrogant moments he may have underestimated himself?

The whole time the royal couple was basking in the adoration of European audiences, however, the photographers were taking pictures of them; and those pictures were being published in European magazines, and those magazines were making their way to India, and from there the Deobandis and the Hazrats' agents were taking them into Afghanistan.

Photographs of Queen Soraya with her bare shoulders passed from hand to hand in those mountains. Old bearded and be-turbaned men gawked and clucked at pictures of their beautiful queen sitting half naked at tables with foreign men, half her face exposed, the other half covered only by a filmy little strip of gauze designed, clearly, not to hide her features but to enhance them for the decadent pleasure of lustful viewers. And here was the queen offering her hand for some man to kiss—*to kiss!* And with her husband standing *right there!* What was Amanullah thinking?

What kind of man would put his wife on display like this? Was he a king or a pimp?

Then came the news about the soap-making machinery he had gotten in Germany, the soap factory he was planning to build in Kabul. His enemies in the hills of Afghanistan knew what that was all about. He was planning to make soap out of Muslim corpses. In fact, rumors said, he was planning to kill old people and boil them down and use the tallow to make soap—and then he intended to sell the soap to Hindus and Europeans. (New versions of this urban legend continue to crop up still.)

Amanullah's final European stop was Moscow. The Soviet government faced a dilemma. They felt the pressure not to be outdone by capitalist countries in their display of hospitality, but how could a dictatorship of the proletariat put pomp and circumstance into hosting a king? Fortunately, there was an escape clause. Lenin himself had hailed Amanullah as a brother when he launched his reforms and had called him one of Asia's progressive leaders, so perhaps it would not violate the correct line to fuss over him a little. Amanullah was taken in hand by lesser officials in the Soviet foreign ministry; when they drove the royals from one public function to another, thousands of Soviet citizens lined the streets to cheer. Here, as in Germany, the banquets could not be quite as glamorous as those in Paris, but the Russians did discuss trade deals and military aid with Amanullah. On the other side of the continent, British officials gnashed their teeth.

It was then that Nadir Khan, living in semiexile in France, sought out the British consul in Nice just to remind the British government he still existed, still had friends in Afghanistan, and wanted to be helpful in any way he could—and by the way, had he mentioned how he appreciated all that the British had done for Afghanistan?

———

AMANULLAH CAME BACK TO AFGHANISTAN THROUGH IRAN. FEW MEN had ever been so full of themselves as he was by then. He drove himself across the border with his queen sitting next to him. Soraya was veiled again, but just barely. The first city the royal couple passed through was

Herat. There, Amanullah gathered the eminent men of the city and told them about his great trip with childlike excitement. He assured them that Herat would someday be like Paris, but first the old stuff had to be cleared away. He derided the religious shrine called Gazurgah, burial place of eleventh-century Sufi poet Khwadja Abdullah Ansary, a place of sanctuary so sacred that people who sought refuge there were safe from harm so long as they stayed on the grounds: no king, no warlord, and no government had ever dared drag people from that place. Amanullah called that stuff a bunch of superstitious nonsense. He vowed to level the shrine, sweep away the rubble, and have something useful built in its place, a hospital per-haps.[4] (*Or a soap factory?*)

Already, however, he was sinking into gloom. Europe had been so wondrous, and his own country seemed so hopelessly backward to him now. By the time he reached Kandahar, he was angry. The whole city turned out to greet a man they considered their native son, but he lashed them with a savage lecture, telling them they oppressed their women, they were lazy and ignorant, and they would never improve their prospects un-less they buckled down, worked hard, and changed their way of life—that is, stopped acting like Afghans and started acting like Europeans.

The project of transforming Afghan society took on a manic urgency. The royal couple was evidently living in a dream. They hosted a ball, for example, at which the guests were expected to dress like courtiers in the court of Louis XVI. Amanullah had built some public parks and de-clared them no-burqa zones. One day, when he encountered a woman in a burqa there, he made her remove it, and he set fire to it. She had to go home exposed.[5]

That fall, Amanullah let it be known that he was done compromising with his people. The laws listed in his Nizamnama would go into effect and would be implemented full force. Beards were outlawed. Native dress? Anyone caught wearing a turban in Kabul would be fined. Schools? Com-pulsory! For girls as well as boys! And the schools would be coeducational. What's more, over a hundred men would be sent to Europe to study at universities, and there would be no religious test, only academic qualifi-cation. Ten girls would go abroad as well—only to Turkey and only to study midwifery, but that was merely the beginning. The king invited the leading women of his city to a special audience and told them that if any man tried to take a second wife, he hoped the first wife would shoot him. Amanullah said he would supply the weapon himself.

In October, Amanullah gathered some six hundred notables of the city and delivered a monumental lecture that stretched over five days. He set up a gallery so that Soraya and a selected array of women could attend the lecture as well. The climactic moment came when he told the notables that religion did not require any veil at all for women: none! As he made that declaration, Queen Soraya stood up in the gallery and dramatically ripped off her own light veil—whereupon a number of other women took their courage in both hands and removed their shrouds as well.[6]

13

Things Fall Apart

MEANWHILE, THERE WAS NEW TROUBLE NORTH OF KABUL. IN A DISTRICT called Kohistan (Mountain Land), a colorful Tajik bandit was making a name for himself. People called him Bachey Saqao, or "the Water Carrier's Son." A water carrier was the humblest of street vendors, a peddler who sold water out of a goatskin bag (Rudyard Kipling's Gunga Din was a *saqao.*) The bandit from Mountain Land was indeed a mountain of a man, famed and feared for his strength. Once, in Peshawar, a big iron safe was stolen from a house, and the police immediately suspected Saqao, because who else could carry away something so heavy?

Saqao was not a common thug but a swashbuckling trickster. Many Zorro-like stories circulated about his foiling of the police. Once, the cops had him cornered in a house, but he set fire to it and escaped in the smoky confusion.[1] Many saw him as a Robin Hood figure, because he robbed the rich—moneylenders, merchants, and especially government officials working for the Mohammedzai aristocracy—and distributed the money to poor villagers in his home district (including himself).[2]

He worked solo at first but soon accumulated a band, and his band grew into a small army. His popular appeal and his powerful little force transformed him from a highwayman to a political menace, especially since he declared himself staunchly loyal to the Muslim clerics of the land, who were fighting the infidel in Kabul.

After he sacked a government convoy and made off with a sizable sum, Amanullah had to take him seriously enough to open negotiations with him. The bandit was flattered that the king would negotiate with *him* and even more flattered when Amanullah offered to make him a general. He was ready to sign on the dotted line (except that he couldn't read or write).

Meanwhile a seemingly more serious problem had erupted. The powerful Shinwari tribe south of Kabul had set siege to the city of Jalalabad in the late months of 1928, cutting it off from the outside world. They took control of the roads leading in and out of the city, halting shipments of goods between Kabul and Peshawar. Here was the anti-Amanullah uprising that had been brewing for so long. The king decided to respond quickly and with overwhelming force, so he sent virtually all his troops south to battle the Shinwari.

Then he made a grievous mistake. He telephoned the provincial official in charge of negotiating with Bachey Saqao, and the two men had a good laugh about the ignorant highwayman who thought the king of Afghanistan was actually going to make him a general. What a fool! Little did the king and his official know the joke was on them: they were talking on a party line, and the "ignorant bandit" had friends in the telephone office who were letting him listen in on another line. When the phone call ended, the bandit called his troops together and announced that they were going to Kabul.[3]

Ordinarily, a gang of several hundred bandits could not have taken the biggest city in Afghanistan. The very idea was ridiculous. At this moment, however, the city happened to be unprotected because Amanullah could not recall his army: the telephone and telegraph lines had all been cut.

The road into Kabul went past the military college. Most of the students and teachers had fled, but eighteen cadets (including my then-teenaged uncle Muzafaruddin) stayed behind and, by running from window to window firing guns, fooled Saqao into thinking there was an army stationed in the college, ready to ambush him. The ruse didn't work for long, but it made the bandit and his army pause, gaining Amanullah enough time to get his pregnant wife, his pregnant sister, his children, and members of his close family on a plane to the temporary safety of Kandahar.

By then Saqao had renewed his assault on Kabul. Amanullah put a bounty on his head, but when he woke up the next morning, he found the city plastered with posters announcing Saqao's offer of an even larger bounty for *the king's* head: a menacing sign that the Son of the Water Carrier had a following, even in the city.

Just then, an ultimatum arrived from the rebels in the south. They made all the usual demands of the social conservatives—purdah must be restored, government interference in marriage must stop, taxes must be lowered, the Shari'a must be reinstated as the only law of the land, and so on—but they also included some devastating new demands, aimed at the king personally: if Amanullah wanted to keep his crown, he would have to divorce Soraya, put his father-in-law in prison, and banish the Tarzi family from Afghanistan.

They also included one final curious demand: the king must expel all foreign legations from Afghan soil except Great Britain. Some Amanullah supporters have pointed to that plank ever since as evidence that Great Britain engineered the overthrow of their amir as part of the never-ending Great Game. According to this theory, the Pushtoon tribes, the Deobandi activists, the Hazrats of Shor Bazaar—all were stooges manipulated by the puppet master in London.

Britain has denied this charge, and private correspondence among British officials of that time supports British protestations: clearly the uprising caught the British by surprise, and they had no idea how to deal with it. But there is one final suspicious circumstance, which has kept the conspiracy theories alive. T. E. Lawrence was in Peshawar at this time under the assumed name of T. E. Shaw. This was the famous British intelligence agent known as Lawrence of Arabia, who engineered the Arab Revolt against the Ottomans during World War I. His business in Peshawar might well have been unconnected to the troubles in Afghanistan, but what his business *was* in Peshawar remains unknown.

In any case, the ultimatum from the tribes crushed Amanullah's spirit. He was down to no supporters in Kabul except his private guard, and even them he couldn't trust—and this was the man who had once said, "The nation is my bodyguard." On that winter day of 1929, he attempted a tragic capitulation. He went out in the snow, clad not in Western clothes nor in traditional garb nor in his royal robes but in the drab gray uniform of a common foot soldier. He found a platform for ornamental plants on a city street, climbed up onto the pedestal, and gave a pathetic speech to random citizens passing by, renouncing everything he had been fighting for. He would cancel education for girls, he said. He would shut all schools except the religious schools. He would appoint mullahs to his cabinet, repeal his Nizamnama, and declare the Shari'a the law of the land. As for monogamy—he was mistaken about that one too. Polygamy was a good thing. And to prove he meant what he said, he went back to his palace and married a nineteen-year-old girl living there, his cousin Aliah.

It did no good. Saqao kept up his attacks. In mid-January 1929, the king took flight, driving west in his Rolls Royce. He tried to make a stand at Ghazni, at Kandahar, and at Herat, but no one rallied to his banner. Finally he, his father-in-law, and Queen Soraya drove right out of the country. Tarzi went back to Turkey. Amanullah and Soraya ended up in Italy, where their friend King Victor Emmanuel gave them refuge. They left Afghanistan with no money and had no job skills—openings for "king" being few in Europe just then—so Amanullah ended up making furniture for a living, and a meager living it was. When he died in 1960, thirty-one years after losing the throne, in exile and in poverty, not a single announcement appeared in Afghanistan.

Back in Kabul, Saqao and his peasant army swarmed into the royal palace in the heart of the city. Apocryphal stories have them gawking at the rich furnishings and appropriating chamber pots for use as soup tureens. Supposedly they ate the fruit they saw lying about and tried to spit the seeds out the windows and were surprised to see them bounce back—for they had never seen glass window panes before. Such at least were the anecdotes circulated by the sophisticates of Kabul about the peasants who had conquered them.[4]

Sher Agha Mujaddedi, the religious titan behind the rebellion, was still in India. Events had taken him by surprise. His younger brother Gul Agha was on the spot and figured he could claim the crown. He met with Bachey Saqao, thanked him for his service, and as the new amir of Afghanistan promised him a fine reward.

Saqao begged to differ. *He* was going to be the new amir of Afghanistan. He thanked the Hazrats for *their* service and promised them honorable positions in *his* new administration. On the day of his coronation, Kabul learned that his real name was Habibullah—the same as Amanullah's father. To distinguish him from the first Habibullah, he was called Habibullah Kalakani, a reference to his home village of Kalakan.

This new amir might have been a decent enough person. He was sharp, he had a robust sense of humor, and he was unpretentious. He did not use the money he had gained from banditry to separate himself from the common people or set himself up as a fancy warlord. He told the people of Kabul quite frankly that he would need their help, because he could not read or write. He appointed a few of the former elite to his cabinet. He assured the British legation they were in no danger: his quarrel had never been with them.[5]

As king, however, the poor man was in over his head. He moved to cement his popularity in the simplest way he could think of: he abolished all taxes except the charity levy approved by the Shari'a. Where he came from, that's what everyone wanted of the government: no taxes! Soon enough he realized he needed revenue from somewhere, so he tried to squeeze it out of the useless bloodsuckers who lived off the people. Where he came from, everyone knew who those were: rich merchants, money-lenders, and government officials. He left the actual revenue collection to his equally unlettered right-hand man, who invented new ways to torture, terrorize, and kill. These methods generated some revenue, but not as much as the new king had expected or needed.[6]

Meanwhile the new amir promulgated his own program of social legislation, and it was the mirror image of Amanullah's reforms. He abolished education for girls. He made the burqa/chad'ri obligatory. Women were prohibited from going out in public without a male escort, even in chad'ris. By law, men now had to sport full beards, and any man caught wearing Western clothes or a hat instead of a turban would be fined, beaten, or both.

From January to October of 1929, the Son of the Water Carrier tried to rule Afghanistan. He met every demand in the tribal ultimatum delivered to Amanullah. He wrapped himself as tightly as he could in the mantle of religion. None of that mattered once he was king. What did matter suddenly were his ethnicity and his class. He was a Tajik, not a Pushtoon; and he was the son of a water carrier, the lowest class of coolie, not the scion of some noble line. The Pushtoon tribal powers looked at him and felt humiliated.

The moment was ripe for Afghanistan's own Machiavelli to make his move. Shortly after the fall of Amanullah, Nadir Khan, the eldest of the

Brothers Musahibban, left Paris and headed east, arriving in Peshawar with all the fanfare of Lenin arriving in Finland Station. His brothers gathered to him there. Over the next few months, Nadir made contact with the tribal chieftains he knew from the war against the British in 1919. He evoked those memories in a way that cast himself and not Amanullah as the man who had gained independence for Afghanistan, a masterful rewriting of historical narrative. Nadir was the very man the tribes had been looking for: a strong *conservative* military hero who had good relations with the British and had royal blood going back to the days of Dost Mohammed Khan.

The Musahibban brothers converged on Kabul at the head of tribal armies, rousted Saqao easily, coaxed him into negotiations, grabbed him as soon as he came close enough, and hanged him in the courtyard of the royal palace. End of that story.

Nadir then called a loya jirga like the one that had ratified Ahmad Shah. He told the elders he had come to Afghanistan not to make himself king but to save the country from ruin. Amanullah's few supporters hoped this meant he would restore Amanullah, but Nadir did not even mention the deposed king's name. He said he would pledge loyalty to whomever the nation chose.

At that—spontaneously it seems—voices rang from many parts of the hall, calling on Nadir to accept the crown. Twice he blushed and refused the honor—but the third time he said he would bow to the will of the nation and with humble reluctance take on the heavy burden of being the country's absolute lord and master.[7]

So it was that at the close of 1929, just two weeks before the stock market crash in New York launched the Great Depression in the West, a new era began for Afghanistan.

PART III: KABUL RULES

Abdu'Rahman's twenty-one-year reign proved to be a turning point for Afghanistan. He finalized his country's borders, but, more importantly, he cut a deal with the British that kept outside powers at bay. With the breathing space thus gained, he set to work forging a single nation controlled entirely and directly by him, from Kabul. What he created, however, was a second Afghanistan to compete with the first. The amir's Afghanistan was a matrix of cities, provinces, districts, governors, mayors, supervisors, bureaucrats, administrators, technicians, state-paid clerics, a huge spy system, and a national army. Beneath this web, the old Afghanistan continued to live and breathe, an organic network of peasants and feudal lords, tribal leaders and grassroots religious clerics, nomads and nomad chieftains, self-governing village republics and tribal guerilla armies.

No sooner had these two societies grown distinct, they commenced to diverge. The urban elite of Kabul, which had dealings with the outside world, absorbed cultural elements from the West—ideas, fashions, dreams. Among them an ambition was born to open up Afghanistan to the new sciences, new technologies, and new thinking that had made the West so powerful and thereby secure for Afghans the same prosperity, wealth, comforts, and conveniences enjoyed by Western societies.

But the other Afghanistan—that rural world of village republics, feudal lords, tribal chieftains, and conservative clerics—resisted the pull. Isolated from outside cultural influences, they nursed the antipathy that had formed toward the British and their culture, and they jealously embraced the old values and the luxury of being left alone to practice their own ways. A cultural tug-of-war developed between Kabul and the old Afghanistan. It pulled the country increasingly further in each direction, as first one side then the other gained the upper hand. For many Afghans, Amanullah's reforms marked a swing to the most shocking extreme. Yet the backlash that brought Bachey Saqao to power left the country traumatized and frightened. Once order had been restored, the new dynasty had its work cut out: the contradictions of Afghan society had not been resolved. Western powers still loomed over the country, the ruling class still aspired to move Afghanistan into the modern world, and the old Afghanistan still threatened to erupt violently if anything they valued changed. Steering the country through these rocks became the fundamental project of Afghan rulers over the next half century, a quest that promoted the dominance of Kabul.

14

After the Storm

AT FIRST, NADIR LOOKED LIKE A GRIM REPLAY OF THE DREADED IRON Amir. He declared himself the champion of old Afghanistan. He vowed to preserve traditional tribal society and defend the religion that gave it unity and purpose. His rhetoric led clerics and feudal landlords to suppose that he would stamp out every vestige of Amanullah's reforms. His first rulings sent women back into the lockbox and deployed religious police to patrol the streets, as in the days of Abdu'Rahman. Nadir confirmed the property of feudal landlords and declared the Hanafi version of the Shari'a the law of the land: no ruling could supersede it, no code compete with it.[1]

Actually, despite appearances, Nadir and his brothers were modernizers. Their ultimate vision for Afghanistan was not so different from Amanullah's. They just had a different idea of how to get there. The key word for them was caution. Change would come, but it would be deliberate, slow, and closely managed. The Musahibban had taken a lesson from Amanullah's career. They understood that the hundreds of thousands of traditional leaders still wielded decisive clout in Afghanistan. The rural, feudal world was still the dog, the cities just the tail. They decided to treat the clerics and elders as partners—while undercutting their power.

Nadir didn't do very much of this himself. He reigned for only four years. He had to devote the bulk of those years just to securing his throne. Amanullah still had followers, some of whom hated Nadir as a usurper and a British stooge. The Charkhi family had been especially close to Amanullah and seemed to pose the greatest threat, so Nadir destroyed them with a ruthless brutality not seen since the days of Abdu'Rahman. He had their patriarchs arrested and executed on no charges; he had the top member of the family beaten to death while he looked on.[2]

Amanullah's loyalists struck back. An Afghan student assassinated the king's brother in Germany. Six months later, Nadir attended a high-school awards ceremony for academic high achievers. One of the boys was my father, then in tenth grade. Another was a boy raised in a Charkhi household. My father and this kid played soccer together after school, and that week the boy had bragged that he would soon make some shots that would be remembered in history. My father assumed he meant soccer shots on goal. The next day, at the ceremony, when the king arrived, my father witnessed this boy stepping out of the line to shoot Nadir dead. The king's three surviving brothers retaliated by executing all the adult male Charkhis and putting all the women and children of the family in prison.[3] It sounds bad, and it was worse than it sounds, but by 1934 the struggle had ended, and Afghanistan settled into the grim quietude usually described euphemistically as "stability."

Immediately after Nadir's assassination, something unprecedented happened—or rather, didn't happen. The late king's surviving relatives did *not* tear the country apart in a savage internecine power struggle. The tribes did *not* rise, the other ethnic groups did *not* try to break away. Instead, Nadir's brothers installed his nineteen-year-old son Zahir Shah on the throne, and they all pledged fealty to him. The eldest of the brothers took over as prime minister and did the actual ruling. The other brothers took the key cabinet posts: defense and foreign affairs. The next tier down of relatives and close associates got the next tier down of government positions. The real ruler of the country for the next forty-four years was not an individual but a family that operated like a well-oiled collective machine. From time to time, one prime minister would step down and another member of the ruling family take his place, but, if these changes reflected backstage power struggles, it wasn't obvious from the outside. As far as the public could tell, the Family made decisions by consensus in private councils and showed a seamless front to the world.

Zahir Shah was a figurehead, yes, but a vital one, a vital piece of a governing collective. With him at the prow, his subjects could feel they were ruled by an embodiment of Afghan grace. Holding power entailed killing

and breaking and torturing, and all these horrors were done, but the public did not associate them with the king, who became instead something
of a beloved figure. He was always seen in an impeccable suit or a perfectly
tailored military uniform. If a photograph of him in traditional native
garb existed, I never saw it. His portrait appeared on the wall of every public office and on the frontispiece of every grade school textbook, but, once
he reached the vigorously mature age of thirty-five or so, the portrait
stopped aging. The real man went gray, lost hair, and got wrinkles, but
his image stayed forever young.

Once in a while, over the next forty years, some tribe revolted, and
on those occasions, the Family showed its teeth. Early on, it built an army
no single power in the country could match. More importantly, when one
tribe revolted, other tribes still sided with the royal government, because
the Musahibban were not simply tyrants but masterful politicians who
understood the nuances of Afghan culture and used diplomacy as much
as force to hold the country together. Once in a while, a dissident, drawing inspiration from the heady days of Amanullah, fired a critical salvo at
the government, but he vanished quickly into some secret dungeon, for
the Musahibban revived Abdu'Rahman's network of spies and his secret
police system, and they had no compunction about using it ruthlessly
when they felt the need.

For the most part, the Family's combination of repressive brutality,
cultural grace, and domestic diplomacy kept Afghanistan remarkably calm
for the remainder of the thirties, throughout the forties and fifties, and
deep into the sixties.

In the countryside during these decades, life went back to the older
version of normal, the one predating the upheavals of the Amanullah era.
The government still collected taxes and stationed its officials in every
district, but they left the rural power structure out there more or less
undisturbed and gave every appearance of respecting the elders and rever-
ing the clerics and honoring the autonomy of the tribes. They also let the
nomads roam freely along their old circuits, making a mockery of borders.

Above all, the government renounced any jurisdiction over the internal affairs of families. Every man's home was his castle—such was the official attitude. Fathers who wanted to betroth their infant sons to their
cousins' unborn daughters and have the match consummated as soon as

the girl hit pubescence could do so: who was the government to say no? Guys who wanted to drink whiskey within the walls of their own compounds could do so, as long as they didn't smell of liquor in public. Their own families might sanction them, but what they did at home was no business of the government's. In short, the new dynasty not only respected but enforced the separation between the public and private worlds that was traditional in Afghan culture.

The Musahibban monarchy was a tyranny, no doubt about it, but a tyranny in service to Western-oriented development. The government kept a firm grip on the levers of repression and gave every reassurance to the hidebound masses and their ultraconservative leaders, yet right from the start it was taking baby steps toward changing the country into a modern nation.

Just before his death, Nadir had a constitution written. It was an extremely conservative document that gave absolute control to the royal family and legalized the power of clerics and big landowners, but it *was* a constitution and it planted the idea, at least, that even kings were governed by some framework of law.

Nadir also established a parliament of sorts, the *Shura-i Milli* or National Council. Some members of this body were appointed by the Family, others were the Family's chosen candidates, "elected" without opposition in their districts. The parliament's function was only to give government decisions its (rubber) stamp of approval, but at least it planted the outer form of democracy, a shell that could be filled in later (and was).

The royal family shut down most of Amanullah's schools but slowly opened them again. The number of students dropped from a high of eighty-three thousand in Amanullah's days to a little over forty-five thousand during Nadir's reign,[4] but at least the royal family nurtured the *idea* of modern education as a good thing. It's true that students in those government schools studied Qur'an, Qur'anic recitation, theology, and Arabic grammar—which undercut any complaints the clerics might have lodged—but they also studied mathematics, physics, chemistry, biology, European languages, geography, drawing, and world history—a complete secular curriculum.

The Family even established a few primary schools for girls. When those excited no blowback, one of them was allowed to grow into a girls'

high school called Malalai in honor of the heroine of the battle of Maiwand. There, the daughters of aristocratic families studied side by side
with girls from less distinguished families. When Malalai set off no cata-
clysm, a second girls' high school, Zarghuna, was opened, and after that
came more.

These schools incubated the leaders of a women's movement in Afghanistan, which would grow and flourish over the next four decades—
leaders such as Kobra Noorzai, who became the first Afghan woman to
achieve cabinet rank when she was appointed minister of health in 1965.
Another star student was Massouma Esmatey who later wrote a landmark
book *The Position and Role of Afghan Women in Afghan Society* and at one
point served as minister of education.

The Family resumed Amanullah's policy of sending four or five of the
best and brightest boys from Kabul's high schools to European and American universities each year. No one mentioned that Amanullah had pioneered this practice.

My uncle Najmuddin was in the second of these groups to go abroad.
He attended Tufts University and became a dentist; but when he returned
to Afghanistan and set up a practice, royals and aristocrats insisted on
being seen whenever they pleased without appointment, which so offended my uncle that he shut down his practice and retired. Eventually,
in order that its investment in his education not be entirely wasted, the
government put him on retainer as an advisor to the Ministry of Education, and in this role he wrote textbooks for the government schools and
helped translate the *Encyclopedia Britannica* into Farsi and Pushto.

Another student sent abroad in the early thirties was a disgruntled
Tajik intellectual named Hammad Anwar. He married an American
woman and brought her back to Afghanistan with him. She insisted on
appearing in public whenever she wanted and refused to wear a chad'ri,
which put her husband on such a collision course with the royal family
that finally, for their own safety, these two slipped out of the country and
never came back: another scholarship wasted.[5]

Nadir's assassination alarmed the royal family so much, they suspended the scholarship program for a few years, but in 1937 the five top
graduates from each of the city's high schools were again sent abroad, to
Germany, France, Great Britain, and the United States depending on

which foreign language they had studied. My father graduated from Habibia that year, so he and four of his classmates were sent to America. The prime minister warned the boys not to get mixed up with any foreign women, but my father broke the injunction and married my mother in Chicago. The government canceled his scholarship and called him home, but she came with him and spent the next twenty years in Afghanistan. Two of the other four also ended up marrying American girlfriends, and a third married an Indian woman studying in America. They all returned to Afghanistan with their foreign wives. The government decided to overlook the disruptions set off by these marriages, and so their husbands stuck around, entered government service, and contributed to the development of the country. By relaxing its restrictions on marriage between Afghans and foreigners, the government was able to get some benefits out of its scholarship program, and the country took another small step toward joining the twentieth-century world at large.

In 1932, with help from the French, Afghanistan established a medical school, the first germ of Kabul University. Later in the decade, students coming back from abroad formed new faculties—a college of engineering, a college of science, and so on. My father headed up the College of Literature and taught courses in psychology and education, his areas of graduate study. Slowly, Kabul University grew into a full-fledged academic institution.

From the government's point of view, the secondary schools were not just an instrument for producing an educated workforce but a mechanism for creating national unity. Every kid in every school had to study Pushto because the Family declared Pushto the national language, even though more than half the citizens could not speak it. Pushto was chosen because it was the (original) language of the ruling clan and because it helped the Family cement its ties to the powerful rural tribes of the south and southeast, who spoke only Pushto. The elite members of the royal clan grew up in Dari-speaking Kabul, so many of them no longer spoke Pushto themselves and had to learn it in school. The constitution listed Dari as a second national language—as a sop to the fact that this was the language the greatest number of Afghans actually shared.

Amanullah had established a national holiday at the end of summer called *Jeshyn-i-Istiqlal*, "the Festival of Independence." The Family revived

Jeshyn as yet another instrument for building a sense of nationhood. They turned it into a weeklong holiday centered around government-sponsored entertainments, the biggest of which were held in Kabul. Afghans from all parts of the country made the pilgrimage to the capital each August for the excitement and merrymaking of Jeshyn. Everywhere they went on the festival grounds, alongside posters of King Zahir Shah, they saw pictures of his father Nadir Shah, peering out through round spectacles, the image of a prim, stern scholar: the man who won independence for Afghanistan, the father of his country, the national hero. Amanullah was never mentioned, and his image was not seen anywhere. It was as if he had never existed, even though he was still alive somewhere in Italy, making furniture. Slowly, slowly, he vanished from the country's collective memory.

Amanullah had launched a radio station; the Family now put Radio Kabul back into service, and it began to broadcast music and propaganda (represented as news) to every Afghan who could acquire a radio. Even rural Afghans were proud to have something so modern as a radio station. No one mentioned that Amanullah had founded this institution. It was a credit to the new dynasty.

Under Habibullah and Amanullah, a few capitalist entrepreneurs had emerged; under Nadir and his brothers, the strongest of these swelled to enormous size. Abdul Majid Zabuli, who had started as a cotton merchant, now became a cotton magnate. He secured monopolies of the trade in edible oil and of state transportation and soon accumulated enough capital to establish his own bank, which made private industrial development possible. During the forties, Afghan entrepreneurs built factories to process cotton, make textiles, and the like. It's true that all the new industries were heavily controlled by the government; and that, in order to start a business, one needed permits; and to get the permits, one needed connections; and to activate those connections, one needed to cut members of the royal clan in for a share of the profits—yes, all of that was true, but at least a trickle of industrial development did begin.

Habib Tarzi, the first Afghan ambassador to the United States, presented his credentials to President Truman in 1946, and Afghanistan joined the United Nations as well. That same year, Tarzi visited a San Francisco–based engineering and construction firm, Morrison Knudson, the company that had spearheaded the building of Hoover Dam across the Colorado River. He met with them to propose an audacious project.

Afghanistan was flush with cash at that moment. During World War II, by sticking to a dogged neutrality, it had been able to sell its products to all sides. Afghan nuts, fruits, and foodstuffs had flowed to India to supply the troops. Karakul lambskins had sold blazingly well in the United States, in part because this was the fur used to line bomber flight jackets. The belligerent countries paid with cash because they had nothing to export, their economies being directed entirely toward war. As a result, Afghanistan had sold a great deal and bought very little and thus had come out of the war in a good position to go shopping.

The Family had a plan for spending that cash. The country's biggest river flowed through its flattest landscape, and they thought that if the waters of the Helmand could be used to irrigate the barren flatland, that desert could be made to bloom. California had done just such a thing by building Hoover Dam and using the Colorado River to irrigate the Imperial Valley, turning a desert into a fertile farming region.

Now Tarzi wanted to know if Morrison Knudson would consider building a couple of dams and a network of canals in Afghanistan for $10 million. Morrison Knudson said they would give it a go. The San Francisco construction company and the central Asian nation formed a joint company, Morrison Knudson Afghanistan (MKA). American engineers, Filipino construction technicians, and Afghan administrators moved to the Helmand Valley to get started. The Afghan government built two small towns called Chainjeer and Lashkargah to house them.

In that period just after World War II, optimism permeated Kabul and urban Afghanistan in general. Great changes lay ahead: what changes, no one knew, but the hated British had lost their entire empire, and the world's two mightiest powers, the Soviet Union and the United States, had formed an alliance to vanquish Hitler. With two such powers working together, an age of world peace and prosperity would surely now begin, and Afghanistan might be part of it all.

To suit these happy times, the Family decided to change its stripes. Prime Minister Hashim, a grim figure, stepped down and his kinder, gentler brother Shah Mahmoud took the helm. The substitution of one brother for another took place without a ripple of trouble. This was not a coup nor even a regime change; it was a public relations move: the Family decided to show the nation a different face.

The new prime minister lifted restrictions on free speech, released a host of political prisoners, and sponsored elections for a new parliament—and not just as a rubber stamp. The Family would still appoint members of the Upper House but there would also be a lower house whose members would be chosen by the people in authentic, fair, free elections. That was the theory anyway.

The new parliament met for the first time in 1949. Some of its members were bearded, be-turbaned conservatives, but forty or fifty of them belonged to a burgeoning class of Western-oriented modernists. Some of these were liberal intellectuals who took the royal family at its word about Parliament having real powers and responsibilities. They summoned members of the cabinet before the Lower House to explain the budget. They posed challenging questions on sensitive topics such as corruption and nepotism. The cabinet ministers were all relatives or associates of the king himself and did not appreciate disrespectful questions from hoi polloi upstarts.

Meanwhile, liberal intellectuals were launching private publications in which they spoke freely. The Family got nervous. When it said "freedom of speech," it meant people should feel free to praise the Family in whatever way they wanted. Besides, in these new publications, the Family saw the seeds of dangerous political parties and hints of worrisome political ambitions.

Meanwhile, by 1953, the Helmand Valley project was running into trouble. Every job was taking too long and costing too much. Every piece of equipment needed for the project had to be brought in from abroad. Getting the equipment to the work sites proved difficult because no roads existed to those places, so roads had to be built before the project could proceed, and where would that money come from? The original $10 million was nearly spent with little to show for it. And the American experts were having trouble coordinating with the Afghan administrators: they were arguing over areas of jurisdiction. The disorder in the Helmand Valley seemed to mirror the growing political anarchy in the capital. Finally, the Family decided to make another 180-degree turn. Kinder-gentler had not worked; tough-and-disciplined might be the way to go after all. Shah Mahmoud's Afghan spring turned out to have been false.

The new approach required another change of faces. This time, the Family made a generational change as well. The fathers and uncles had run their course; it was time to give the sons a chance. The younger generation of the Family featured one obvious candidate for power—the king himself. Zahir was no longer a boy but a man. Unfortunately, he could not do what the Family needed done. For nearly twenty years, he had served as his country's emblematic gracious gentleman. If Zahir Shah were suddenly to become a strongman, cracking down on critics and putting dissidents in prison, who would be the gracious gentleman? No, the king had to keep doing his job: appreciating fine music, commissioning art, going hunting—all of which probably suited his temperament better in any case. The baton, or perhaps I should say the club, did not therefore pass to him but to his first cousins Sardar Daoud and Sardar Na'eem.

These two brothers had been educated in France. Their uncle Hashim Khan had started grooming them for power the moment they had come home. Na'eem had been processed through a series of diplomatic and economic posts, Daoud through a series of military and political appointments. Now, like a wrestling tag team, they split the job of running the country.

Na'eem was a lanky man with a long face and an aquiline nose. He looked good in Western clothes and sounded good discussing fine food, classical music, and the great poetry of East and West. Beneath his conversational gifts lived a tough and clever politician. His elegance and diplomatic cunning equipped him to deal with the great powers of the outside world that were always looming over Afghanistan, leaning into its space. He became the country's foreign minister.

Daoud was a stocky man with thick lips, heavy eyebrows and a bald, bullet-shaped head. Later in life, he affected tinted glasses, which completed his resemblance to Telly Savalas. He looked like an enforcer, and he was one. As minister of interior he dealt with the world inside Afghanistan, a tougher job than dealing with the whole rest of the planet. Also, as minister of defense, he commanded the military. Also, as prime minister, he ran the whole show.

The king was still there too, wafting above both brothers, waving graciously to the crowds from the backseat of his Rolls Royce convertible.

The new men at the top, the two brothers, brought the first era of good feelings to an end. They disbanded the liberal Parliament of 1949.

The national assemblymen who had dared to call the king's relatives in for questioning lost their jobs. The private publications that had sprouted under the previous prime minister were shut down. The liberal intellectuals who had called too stridently for secular reforms went to prison. Kabul University professor Mohammed Ghobar, whose book *Afghanistan in the Course of History* gave an unvarnished account of the country's past and painted a harsh picture of the ruling clan, did hard time in a tiny town in the southwestern desert, under guard by a local lord related to the royals: the Afghan version of exile to Siberia.[6] Some people simply disappeared, which raised the specter of Abdu'Rahman's darkest days.

But the triumvirate of Daoud, Na'eem, and Zahir Shah wanted more than power; they wanted to change things. They were men of the world who had seen how people lived beyond the borders of Afghanistan. Absolute power was great, but power over what? Over anonymous peasants, feudal lords, nomadic herders, and religious "scholars," some of whom could barely read? They ruled a nation that could hardly produce a pin much less an automobile. They wanted to rule a rich and developed country.

Though ruthlessly authoritarian, the top man Daoud was a genuine modernist as well. In the fifties and sixties, the "developing world" was full of such strongman-modernists. Shah Reza Pahlevi of Iran and Egypt's Gemal Abdul Nasser were just two of many examples. In his youth, Daoud was even associated with a Young Turks–style group of activists called *Wikh-i-Zalmayan*, "Awakened Youth," which embraced a hodgepodge of modernist-nationalist ideas along the lines of: development is good, education is necessary, obsolete customs should be abandoned, women should be liberated, foreign influence should be resisted, Afghanistan must be for Afghans, hurray for native industries, and so on. Now that he had command, Daoud intended to push the development part of this program to the max.[7]

Financing the development was a problem, however. How could a population of herders and subsistence farmers supply the necessary money? They couldn't. The answer to this problem lay outside the country's borders, in the struggle gathering force around Afghanistan—for this region was becoming a key arena of the Cold War, the global power struggle that dominated the late twentieth century.

15

Nonaligned
Nation

THE COLD WAR BEGAN BEFORE THE HOT WAR ENDED. IN THE LATE stages of World War II, as the Allies realized they were almost certainly going to win, they began jockeying for postwar position. Roosevelt and Stalin met in Tehran and then at Yalta to hammer out a framework for the postwar era, but it was already too late to forestall what was coming. American and British forces were pushing into Germany from the west, Stalin's forces from the east. By the time the armies met in Berlin, Stalin had all of Eastern Europe under his thumb. He set up a string of satellite states stretching from Bulgaria to the Baltic Sea, raising fears in the West that Stalin might do what Hitler had attempted: conquer the world. Western fears intensified in 1949 when Communist insurgents took over China, for at that time Mao Tse-tung was widely considered an obedient factotum of the Kremlin. Yet the United States and its allies could not go to war to stop the Soviets because both sides had nuclear bombs and would soon have thermonuclear weapons, which were capable of ending human life on earth.

Harry Truman, America's first postwar president, formulated a response to the sudden expansion of Communist power, the policy called containment. The United States and its allies would quarantine Soviet influence by surrounding it with a chain of nations hostile to Communism and friendly to the Western European allies. To this end, US diplomats cobbled together a number of military alliances. In the west, there was the

North Atlantic Treaty Organization (NATO). In the east, there was the (weaker) Southeast Asian Treaty Organization (SEATO). And between the two, there were the Baghdad Pact nations, soon renamed the Central Treaty Organization (CENTO), which included Turkey and Iraq as members. The brand-new nation of Pakistan joined both CENTO and SEATO, which made it a crucial link in the chain. With Pakistan closing the gap, SEATO, CENTO, NATO, and east Asian allies of the United States such as Japan formed an almost continuous fence around the Communist bloc.[1]

Not every country belonged to one of the two blocs, however. India emerged from British rule as an independent nation led by the Congress Party, which displayed unsettling independence. India's president Jawaharlal Nehru raised the idea of nonaligned nations forming a third bloc, a notion that developed into a movement. The leaders of such nonaligned countries as India, Sri Lanka, and Indonesia perceived that neutrality gave them leverage with both the Communist and non-Communist sides. Afghanistan embraced nonalignment with a passion.

The Cold War had some hot spots, to be sure. In Korea, Vietnam, and other parts of the "Third World" violent struggles between Communist and anti-Communist forces served as proxy wars between the Soviets and the Americans.[2] But the Cold War also featured a "peaceful" struggle for influence in various "nonaligned" countries, where each side tried to crowd the other out of the picture. These nonaligned countries became arenas for covert spy craft, propaganda wars, influence peddling, and— dueling aid packages.

Nowhere did this competition rage more intensely than in Afghanistan. Here was a nonaligned chip situated precisely at the line of scrimmage. There were three ways Afghanistan might go. It might tip into the Soviet camp; it might be coaxed all the way into the "Free World" camp; or it might remain neutral. Which of the three would happen? The answer mattered for the same age-old reasons: location, location, and location. Afghanistan neighbored Pakistan, and Pakistan linked CENTO and SEATO. If the Soviets took Afghanistan, they might use it as a platform for taking Pakistan. If they took Pakistan, they would have punched a hole in the containment fence. The United States could not, therefore, let Afghanistan "turn Communist."

Strategically, the United States was in the same position as nineteenth-century Britain: it needed to control Afghanistan in order to deny the big power in the north a platform from which to attack India (or at least the part of India that was now called Pakistan). When Daoud and Na'eem gazed out at the great wide world, what they saw in this Cold War competition was opportunity.

American influence in Afghanistan was inextricably tied to the success of the Helmand Valley project, because this was the most ambitious, costly, and visible development project ever undertaken in Afghanistan. If it failed, America looked bad. As it happened, the credibility of the central government in Kabul was also bound up in this project. Here in the Helmand Valley, then, Afghan and American interests converged. The dynamics of the Afghan story dovetailed with those of the Cold War drama.

As soon as Daoud took charge of the country, he created a new agency called the Helmand Valley Authority (HVA) to take the project across the finish line. (It was modeled after the Tennessee Valley Authority, or TVA.) The original $10 million had run out, but the United States now pumped in twice that amount in new funding. Daoud put together a management team headed by my father's buddy Dr. Abdul Kayeum, one of the five Habibia high school graduates who were sent to study in America in 1938. My father came aboard as Kayeum's deputy, and several dozen other Western-educated Afghans were appointed to the remaining posts.

On the American side, the Helmand Valley became a project of the International Cooperation Agency, soon renamed the Agency for International Development or AID, American's main instrument for using development aid to promote Cold War goals. American engineers, geologists, soil scientists, and the like came to southwestern Afghanistan to work with Afghan administrators. The president of HVA was elevated to the rank of a cabinet minister. The nerve center of the Helmand Valley Authority, the little government-built town of Lashkargah came to be known (by Afghans) as "Little America." Surrounded though it was by the most conservative traditional forces in the country, the most deeply entrenched of the Durrani and Ghilzai Pushtoon tribes, Lashkargah featured houses without surrounding walls—very un-Afghan. It had a swimming pool, a clubhouse, a modern hospital, and a government school, where selected children from villages throughout the region were brought to get educated in secular subjects (although religion remained in the curriculum as well).

The core of the project consisted of two huge dams, one on the Helmand and one on its chief tributary, the Arghandab River. Downstream from these dams a network of canals was extended into the desert, equipped with locks and mechanized sluices and other technical marvels. These canals carried irrigation water not to existing fields (of which there were few) but to new government-run "experimental" farms, where Afghan tribesmen learned to use tractors and chemical fertilizers to grow novel crops with seeds imported from America.

At strategic spots in this canal network, government-built model towns popped up like mushrooms, towns such as Nadi Ali and Marjah, featuring neat blocks of bungalows with thick walls and domed roofs to keep in the cool—very necessary in this blistering climate. The houses had modern plumbing and electricity, each one had a small garden, and between the houses ran well-graded gravel roads.

Nomads who migrated through this land seasonally were stopped by government officials and convinced to settle in the model towns and to take up farming. Each family was given a plot of irrigated land within one or two days walk of their house.

And that was not all. The two massive American-built dams were retrofitted with hydroelectric plants, capable of generating enough electricity to serve the whole southwestern quarter of the country, including the big city of Kandahar.

The 1,740-foot-long Arghandab dam was situated fairly close to Kandahar, but the other dam, the one on the Helmand itself, was built far upstream in the mountains, at a place called Kajakai. When first completed, it was one of the most massive earth dams in the world. A thirty-two-mile reservoir formed behind it.[3] A few miles downstream from the dam, on a steep slope high above the river, MKA built a cute village to house its engineers and technicians. The sturdy little houses were made of stone and concrete, far more durable than anything the locals had, and the whole town looked like a charming resort village in Italy. Each of the hundred or so houses had one or two bedrooms and a kitchen equipped with modern appliances and a spare bit of Western-style furniture—beds, couches, chairs, tables, and such.

Once the dam was built, all the experts went home, and no one lived at Kajakai except an Italian couple, Mr. and Mrs. Corriega. He was an engineer, left behind to look after the hydroelectric facilities. Since this normally entailed nothing more than going down to the dam once a day and checking the gauges, he had plenty of spare time to putter about the village doing arts and crafts projects. He was a superb metalworker, so he fitted every house in Kajakai with filigrees of wrought iron railing and other enhancements. Every street ended up with decorative lampposts, all of them different. Mr. Corriega painstakingly collected tons of pebbles of different colors, sorted them by shape and size, and used them to pave the sidewalks and walkways with floral and geometric patterns rendered in green, red, black, white, and others colors of stone. When he ran out of ways to beautify his village, he built a scale model of a luxury ocean liner, accurate down to the quarter-inch deck chairs and the portholes through which one could see tiny beds and miniature armoires.

No one ever saw this eccentric masterpiece except for the few Afghan HVA officials who made the five- or six-hour journey from Lashkargah once a year with their families to spend the three-day holiday of Eid at Kajakai. The other 362 days, the Corriegas lived in a ghost town.

And what of the Afghan villagers who lived in the vicinity? What did they think about the three-hundred-foot-high wall of stones and dirt suddenly blocking their river? As far as I can tell, nobody ever asked them.

———

AMERICAN AID TO AFGHANISTAN DISMAYED THE SOVIETS, ESPECIALLY because the Soviets had gotten in first. In 1950, they had signed a barter agreement to trade oil and gas for Afghan cotton and wool. Two years later Stalin's government inked a deal to provide Afghanistan with cement. They hoped and assumed that with these aid packages they had bought Afghanistan.

Faithless Afghanistan would not stay bought. In 1953, just as Stalin died, Afghanistan changed hands too: Daoud stepped up, and right after that fresh US aid poured in for the Helmand Valley project. No way were the Soviets going to take that lying down. Even amid the disarray that followed Stalin's death, the Soviets pressed new largesse upon Afghan ruler Sardar Daoud. They agreed to build a gigantic bakery (called Silo) in Kabul and to fund a big expansion of textile factories in the north.*

It wasn't enough, however, because by this time the Western powers had permeated deeply into the educational system of Afghanistan. French, German, and American teachers were developing curricula for Kabul high schools, and Afghan students were learning their languages. There was no Russian language high school, no one was studying Russian, and very few Russian-language publications could be found in Afghanistan. Meanwhile Kabul University was forming partnerships with American schools such as Columbia and the Universities of Wyoming, Colorado, and Indiana. Professors from these and other schools were coming to Afghanistan to teach. An ever-growing stream of Afghan students was going to America to study agricultural technology, engineering, medicine, public administration, and other fields. Education is culture, and culture is ideology. The Soviets were spending more money than the Americans and yet were losing Afghan hearts and minds.

In 1955, therefore, Nikita Khrushchev, winner of the post-Stalin succession struggle, visited Kabul. The government rolled out the red carpet for him, and spectators lined the streets to gawk. A few Afghans associated with the conservative religious establishment glowered at this welcome for a man who took pride in being an atheist. A young activist named Subghatullah Mujaddedi tried to organize demonstrations against Khrushchev, but he was tossed into prison and kept there until the Soviet premier was safely out of town. Subghatullah was related to those Hazrats of Shor Bazaar, the revered religious brothers who had helped topple Amanullah. Subghatullah would play a profound role in Afghan politics later, but in 1955 the authorities regarded him as little more than a naïve nuisance. While he was cooling his heels in prison, Khrushchev was in the palace signing an agreement with Daoud to provide an unprecedented $100 million for infrastructure projects.

The United States countered by brokering a deal to build the country a national airline, Ariana, which would be partly owned by Pan Am.

---

* Silo was a boondoggle at first because it produced bagels mostly, and Afghans far preferred their own slipper-shaped whole wheat flatbread. But tastes change, and today Silo is still a working bakery.

Daoud then asked America for military aid as well, but here the dynamics of the Cold War conflicted with those of the Afghan story. Afghanistan and Pakistan were hostile neighbors for reasons that went all the way back to the days of Dost Mohammed, but America and Pakistan were close allies for reasons that went deep into the strategic considerations of the Cold War: by connecting CENTO and SEATO, Pakistan formed a vital link in the containment fence. So the United States said no to Daoud on weapons, because giving military aid to Afghanistan would have ruffled feathers in Pakistan and damaged that alliance.

The Soviets seized upon the opening. They put together a military aid package that provided Daoud with tanks, MiGs, jet bombers, helicopters, and enough small arms to equip an army of one hundred thousand men. They also built for him a large military airbase at Bagram, just north of Kabul, plus two other airbases in the north of the country.

The United States did what it could to counter these Soviet moves. Not only did they fund improvements in Kabul's airport, but they started building a brand-new international airport at Kandahar, projected to be one of the biggest in the world. American development experts hoped it would emerge as a refueling station for long-distance cargo planes, which would make Afghanistan a prosperous hub for international commerce, a role this area had enjoyed in older centuries, when cities such as Balkh served as nexuses for overland caravans. The airport had runways equipped to handle airplanes much bigger than any that existed at the time (but perfect for the big American military aircraft that use that airport today).

The Soviet Union answered by dispatching swarms of geologists and engineers into the country to prospect for oil and natural gas. They found significant deposits of gas in the north and built pipelines to transport it to power stations serving northern Afghan cities, to fuel factories the Soviets had helped Afghans build up there, and to carry the gas into Soviet central Asia. The Soviets also installed more than six hundred miles of telephone and telegraph lines.

They were so alarmingly generous to Afghanistan that in 1959 Eisenhower felt it worth his while to visit Kabul, another huge event for Afghans, although many were a little taken aback to see Eisenhower shaking hands with the Afghan businessman Abdul Majid Zabuli as if a mere multimillionaire ranked just as high as distant relatives of members of the royal family. Eisenhower's visit produced more millions of dollars' worth of American grants and loans to Afghanistan and launched another major infrastructure project, a paved road from Kabul to Kandahar, complete with all the bridges needed to traverse the numerous streams and rivers along the way.

When it came to roads, however, America was already playing catch-up. The Soviets were building an even more crucial and ambitious highway from Kabul to the country's northern border, which included the two-mile-long Salang Tunnel through the mountains at their highest point, gouged through solid rock at an elevation of 11,100 feet, the highest tunnel in the world. This was a road so stoutly overbuilt it could support the weight of tanks—in fact of tanks bigger than any that Afghanistan possessed (but perfect for the tanks the Soviets would send down that highway twenty years later). In fact, from the midfifties to the late sixties, dueling Soviet and American aid packages constructed over twelve hundred miles of superb paved roads through some of the planet's most difficult terrain, completing in the end a great circle of highways connecting all of Afghanistan's major cities.[4] Daoud and Na'eem must have loved the Cold War!

16

Development, No Brakes

AS ALL THIS INFRASTRUCTURE WAS GOING IN, THE FAMILY WAS PUSHING ahead on the social and cultural fronts as well. The toughest challenge they faced was emancipating Afghan women and opening avenues for them to claim an equal share in the life of their society. This was the rock upon which Amanullah had foundered. This was the issue on which Nadir had made the most drastic concessions.

This, however, was an issue that Daoud confronted head-on and finessed masterfully. He began by testing the water with small moves. Around 1957, Radio Kabul began broadcasting music featuring women singers and employed women to read the news occasionally. The government did not disapprove, which could be taken as approval. Or not, if backtracking was required. But no riots resulted, so apparently the conservatives felt women could be heard, as long as they weren't seen. Later that year, Daoud let a delegation of Afghan women travel to the Asian Women's Conference in Ceylon. Then in 1958, forty girls, wearing chad'ris, were allowed to work alongside men at a government pottery factory, after the government had secured letters of consent from their parents. No bloodshed broke out.

Then came the thunderclap. In August 1959, on the second day of the festival of Jeshyn, the royal family appeared in their usual box to observe the usual military parade—but with one unusual difference. The women were not wearing chad'ris. They were sitting there with bare naked faces. Anyone in the crowd could look up and see the features of Queen Humaira and Princess Bilqis. Anyone could see Prime Minister Daoud's wife Zamina Begum. To get an inkling of how shocking this was to Afghans, imagine the First Lady attending the president's State of the Union speech topless. The Family had issued no announcement about this impending move nor passed any law. They simply did it.

The religious establishment responded at once. A group of the country's most powerful conservative clerics signed a letter to Prime Minister Daoud expressing shock and warning the ruler of the country to get back behind the lines laid down by the Shari'a. Daoud wrote back to say he was most anxious to follow the Shari'a to the letter. He just couldn't find the passage in the Qur'an or in any of the Prophet's sayings that mandated the chad'ri. No doubt this reflected his lack of theological sophistication. He begged the scholars to come to the capital and show him the relevant passages. And they came. They brought their books. They pored through them, fulminating and fuming. In the end they could not offer any indisputable scriptural support for the veiling practices traditional to Afghan society.

Thereupon Daoud declared that the women of the royal family would no longer wear chad'ris. No one else had to follow suit. The Family was not trying to tell any other Afghan man how the women in his family should dress. Every family could do what they felt was right. But the royal family was going to follow the letter of the Islamic law as the religious scholars had explained it: no chad'ri.

A number of courageous commoners soon followed suit. One was Kobra Noorzai, who went about her work as an inspector of girls schools without a veil. Another was Massouma Esmatey-Wardak, principal of the Zarghuna school for girls. Lacking the protection of royal power and prestige, these women really took their lives in their hands, but it was their assertion of an Afghan woman's right to a place in the public realm that made the royal family's policy real.

Everyone braced for riots. None broke out. On this issue, the Family had gambled and won. And although the government was careful to assert that it was not forcing anyone to do anything, government officials felt pressure to set an example by allowing their women to go out in public unveiled. Later that year, girls started attending the government high school in Lashkargah (the first of them being my sister Rebecca). Coeducation had come to Afghanistan! What's more, the girls came to school without chad'ris, although they did wear a somber uniform, a black dress with long sleeves, black stockings, and white headscarf. In 1978, TV news coverage of Iran's Islamic Revolution showed Iranian women activists dressed in this type of outfit. My American friends saw that image and clucked at the oppression Khomeini's revolution was imposing on Iranian women. I could not help remembering how, in Afghanistan, less than twenty years earlier, women who dressed that way in public were making a shocking revolutionary gesture of feminist emancipation.

It was a daring move but done with the least possible fanfare. When all was said and done, the Family had taken only the slightest step toward liberating women from gender-based disempowerment. They did not outlaw the chad'ri. They imposed no law barring men from lording it over women. They did not forbid men to marry four wives or extort big sums of money in exchange for marrying their preteen daughters to rich old men. They did not link the chad'ri initiative to any broader program. Had they done so, they might have lit a brushfire.

But against the millimeter of a step they did take, only a brief backlash broke out. A Kandahar street gang called the Barefoot Boys (*Paylucha*) concocted a plot to murder all unveiled women and all foreign workers in the region—of whom there were quite a few, this being the heart of the US-supported Helmand Valley Project. Daoud got wind of the plot, put tanks on the streets, and crushed the uprising before sundown. No further protests broke out, probably because Afghan society was ready for this amount of change. The idea of mullahs and street gangsters conspiring to commit mass murder in reaction to *this* iota of social evolution earned public disapproval. Daoud had thus maneuvered the conservatives into blowing their own credibility on the women's issue.

And even though the steps the Family took were so slight, they opened a door through which came more change. In the next five years, the status of Afghan women went through five centuries of evolution. Girls began attending the university. The graduates began working as teachers, nurses, and even doctors. Women started working in government offices, factories, and private commercial establishments. Ariana Airlines routinely employed women as flight attendants. Radio Kabul regularly exposed Afghan men to women's voices, singing or reading "the news." As transistor radios proliferated, people in towns and cities all over Afghanistan became accustomed to hearing the voices of women to whom they were not related, an unfamiliar experience for Afghan men.

Kabul acquired some half-dozen movie theaters by 1963, three of which showed American and European films. The rest showed Indian films, the genre that has come to be known as Bollywood. And even though Bollywood films are notoriously chaste—no one kisses—they still showed women's faces, women singing, women wearing costumes tight enough to reveal the shapes of their bodies, women dancing in these "tight" outfits. Movie theaters opened in other big cities as well.

Thus did the Family exploit Cold War competition among the global powers not only to fund economic and technological development in Afghanistan but also to push for progressive social change in its wake. All this change created a challenge for the Family, however, a challenge inherent to absolute monarchies undergoing modernization. Dynastic rulers with absolute power prefer to fill all key positions with members of their own families for security reasons, but modernization produces a huge industrial and bureaucratic apparatus that needs innumerable well-educated people to keep it going, an apparatus so huge that eventually no single family can staff all its key positions. So the dynasty has to go outside its circle of relatives and recruit the most talented of its other subjects to handle some jobs.

The need for educated experts cycled an ever-growing number of Afghans through European and American universities and back into Afghan society. The Family tried to put them in charge of carrying out development work while keeping political power out of their hands, but it was hopeless. Managers, technicians, bureaucrats, and administrators have de facto power, whether or not it is legally enfranchised. Afghan teachers, technicians, and financial experts accumulated until they far outnumbered the royal family and its associated tribal aristocracy. They burgeoned into a whole new class, a technocracy powerful enough to challenge the dynasty.

The Family feared the technocrats but also needed them, because the country couldn't go on forever as one family against all other Afghans, a few thousand against millions. Avenues had to be created to allow broader—not universal, perhaps, but broader—political participation. A selected group of nonroyal Afghans would have to acquire a stake in developing the country. Members of the technocracy were the obvious candidates to form this extended elite.

Meanwhile, disjunctions emerged between the Afghan story and the Cold War drama. The Durand Line—that old burr!—generated much of the trouble. Ever since the days of Dost Mohammed, the Pushtoon "street" had wanted the king to go reconquer Peshawar and take back the lost provinces. Other ethnic groups didn't care, but their feelings didn't matter, because the king was always a Pushtoon. To appease his own ethnic base, therefore, every Afghan king since Dost Mohammed had been obliged to at least pay lip service to the dream of reuniting all Pushtoons under one big national umbrella. On the other hand, to keep his throne, every Afghan king had been forced to accept the eastern border imposed by the British, because every king had needed the money, guns, and protection of the greatest great power dominating the country at that moment.

In 1947, a tremendous development was changing the rubrics of this story dramatically. India's long struggle for independence had come to a head, and the British were pulling out of the subcontinent. In the course of that long struggle, a Muslim independence movement had split away from the mainstream campaign led by Gandhi's Congress Party. This nationalist movement led by the Muslim League demanded a separate state for Muslims. The British dealt with the contention by endorsing a partition of the subcontinent into two separate states: India, a secular state with a Hindu majority; and Pakistan, an explicitly Muslim country that would provide a haven for the Muslims of the subcontinent.

The creation of Pakistan reopened an old question: what about the Pushtoons on the eastern side of the Durand Line? Had the time come for Afghans to include their brethren within their borders and absorb their lost lands back into Afghanistan? The British acknowledged that an issue existed and held a referendum in the Pushtoon-inhabited portion of their territory, asking people to choose which state they preferred to join—Pakistan or India?

Really? Pakistan or *India*?

Yes, really. Those were the only options on the table. Most voters sighed and voted to join Muslim Pakistan. Some boycotted the referendum altogether, as their way of saying, "Neither." A sizable number didn't want to join any state. They wanted to form an independent country of their own, called Pushtoonistan. How would Afghanistan and Pushtoonistan be related? Would they form a federation? Would one eventually become an autonomous province of the other? . . .

No one talked about it. In 1947, the Afghan government simply found it politic to blare support for Pushtoonistan without getting into specifics. Afghanistan opposed recognition of Pakistani statehood in the United Nations until "the Pushtoonistan issue" was "resolved." When Pakistan came into existence anyway, the Afghan government continued to support a Pushtoon secessionist movement in the new country.

The leader of that movement, Khan Abdul Ghaffar Khan, was a singular pacifist known as the Frontier Gandhi. The Afghan government let him live in Kabul and use Radio Kabul to broadcast passionate speeches into Pakistan.[1] Pakistan retaliated by setting up "Radio Free Afghanistan" in Quetta and beaming propaganda across the border, urging tribes on the Afghan side to break away and join *their* brethren in the east.

Despite the nonviolent ideals of the Frontier Gandhi, these propaganda spats led to real-life skirmishes. Actual bullets were fired into actual flesh. Scattered casualties occurred. Pakistan closed the border briefly two or three times just to dramatize the leverage it had over a landlocked nation.

As it happened, Daoud took charge in just this period. Daoud was an ardent Pushtoon nationalist. Even if he hadn't been, he probably would have embraced this cause because Pushtoon nationalists were his base, and, even in an absolute monarchy, politicians have to cater to their base. Daoud therefore began to talk the toughest anti-Pakistan Pushtoonism ever heard.

But it was also in this period that he asked the United States for military aid and got turned down. America needed the hundred million people of Pakistan more than it needed the twelve million of Afghanistan. US policymakers worried that this Pushtoonistan ruckus could jeopardize the very existence of their ally, the hodgepodge nation that was Pakistan. After all, the new country was already divided into two noncontiguous parts. East Pakistan would soon break away to become Bangladesh. Kashmir had been claimed by India. If Pushtoonistan formed, part of Sind might go with it, and Baluchistan might split away as well. Pakistan would

Pushtoonistan

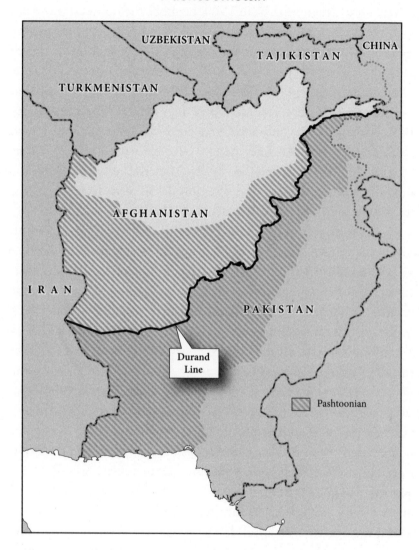

be reduced to just the Punjab, and how long could that ministate survive? And even if it did survive, what good would a tiny Punjab do as the link between SEATO and CENTO or as the sole regional counterweight to left-leaning, nonaligned India? No, the United States could not afford to abandon Pakistan, not on this issue nor any other. American diplomats therefore tried to convince Daoud to accept the Durand Line.

Daoud could not let go of the Pushtoonistan idea but could not make headway on it either. Finally, in 1960, he made the dumbest move of his career. He decided to put pressure on Pakistan by closing the border between the two countries from the Afghan side. As soon as he did this, trade stalled. Nomads bunched up on both sides of a border they could no longer cross. Daoud's Folly emptied the shelves of Afghan bazaars. Around the world observers scratched their heads. Why would a land-locked country close its only access to a port? How was this "putting pressure on Pakistan"? It was like saying, "Give me what I want or I'll hold my breath till I turn blue and die." In Pakistan, the authorities smiled and waited. An alarmed United States removed 150 of its technical advisors from Afghanistan and urged Daoud to quit being such a child.

Daoud wouldn't budge. Dictators with unlimited powers seem to have a hard time saying "I'm sorry." Instead, Daoud looked to the Soviet Union to bail him out. The Soviets obliged. Before the border closure, trucks had been moving a thousand tons of Afghan grapes to Karachi every day. Now the Soviet Union airlifted a few hundred tons north each day. Rumor has it they didn't even want the grapes. They grew their own and couldn't afford to let the imported fruit compete with theirs, so they threw the Afghan grapes into the Aral Sea.[2] The main thing was to build Afghan dependency. In short, Daoud's Folly looked like it would tip Afghanistan into the Soviet camp, and there wasn't a damned thing the United States could do about it.

The Family did not have to stand for it, though. Nonalignment was the policy, and, if Daoud made nonalignment difficult, it was Daoud that would have to go, not the policy. So it was that in 1963 a really stupendous event occurred. King Zahir Shah asked Daoud to step down. He thanked his dear cousin for all his patriotic services and wished him a happy retirement but announced that he, the king himself, was going to take over at last.

17

The
Democracy
Era

EVERYTHING ABOUT THIS TRANSITION WAS REMARKABLE. FIRST OF ALL, Daoud stepped down voluntarily. What strongman relinquishes power voluntarily at a time when he controls the army, the police, the intelligence service, and the spy system that spies on the intelligence service? I can't think of another example. When I was growing up in Afghanistan, I can tell you that Daoud visited my nightmares: I assure you, this was a scary man. Looking back, though, I have to say, he had a greatness about him too. He proved it by the way he managed the unveiling of women, and he showed it again when he left office peacefully instead of resisting and plunging his country into bloodshed, although his main motive may have been to spare not his country but his family. Undoubtedly, there was family politicking, backroom deals, and unpublicized pressures that led to his resignation, but, just as certainly, with the instruments at his command, Daoud had a choice and he chose to step down.

Next came an even more remarkable event. The king decided to weaken himself and his family. He ordered a new constitution written that would limit his powers and give more control to his people. When has anything like that ever happened?*

---

* Amanullah doesn't count: he was a populist but did not officially relinquish one drop of royal authority.

At first, everyone was dreadfully suspicious, of course. People said this was just a replay of Shah Mahmoud's false Afghan spring. Censorship would be lifted and elections held to smoke out potential rebels. Once new leaders had shown themselves, their heads would be cut off and things would go back to the way they were.

People were wrong. The king meant what he said. Not only did he ask Daoud to resign, he asked his whole cabinet to resign. He appointed a leading member of the technocracy as prime minister, and, with the king's approval, he established a new cabinet, not one member of which belonged to the royal family and of whom two were not even Pushtoons. The times they were indeed a-changing.

Prominent political prisoners saw their cell doors open. Members of the Charkhi family, men and women who had grown up in prison, came walking out onto public streets, blinking at daylight they had thought they would never see again. The historian Ghobar returned from ten years of domestic exile and took up his old job at Kabul University.

With the king's approval, the new prime minister and his cabinet appointed a committee of learned men to write a new constitution—a real one this time. The seven members of the committee included my eccentric uncle Najmuddin, a dentist who never practiced his profession. An advisory board that consulted with the committee included a handful of activist women such as Massouma Esmatey-Wardak, Kobra Noorzai, and Shafiqa Ziaie, who was later appointed a cabinet minister without portfolio—that is, she participated in cabinet meetings and government decision making without having a specific department to run. It took the committee a little over a year to come up with a draft and several months to get it ratified, but the final document rocked Afghanistan.

The new constitution established a real parliament and declared that its members would be chosen in real elections and its duties would consist of real legislation.

It circumscribed the power of the king explicitly, transforming him into a ceremonial monarch like Queen Elizabeth.

And then there was the most astonishing plank of them all—Article 24.

Article 24 stated that no member of the royal family and no close blood relative of the king could hold any position of cabinet rank or above nor serve as a member of Parliament nor serve as a justice of the Supreme Court nor belong to any political party.

Wow!

Even as I write this, I am flabbergasted. When has something like *this* ever happened? Don't cite the United States of America: the king was across an ocean when the American colonies were developing into small democracies, and they still had to fight an eight-year war to pry his clutches loose from their lives. The French Revolution does not count either. Yes, France went from extreme absolutism to extreme democracy in a flash, but it took a bloody revolution and a reign of terror to get it done. In Afghanistan, the change happened overnight, instigated by the newly disempowered elite.

All of Kabul walked around in a daze, waiting for the bubble to pop, waiting for Daoud to loom up suddenly swinging his ax. It didn't happen. Daoud was living in Kabul but living the quiet life of a retired gentleman, merely observing events and discussing them privately with his friends, making no public pronouncements. The cabinet of commoners got to work. Elections took place smoothly, and four of the winners were women. A parliament convened. A few intellectuals began tentatively to publish newspapers and no one shut them down, so more publications sprang up.

The border between Pakistan and Afghanistan opened and goods flowed again. The shelves of the bazaars filled up with products from around the world—not just regional goods but Dutch chocolates, French perfumes, pasta from Italy, corned beef from Tanganyika, and canned sardines from Norway, as well as Swiss watches, French fountain pens, German cameras, English bicycles, and American records.[1]

Diplomatically, this velvet revolution of 1963 put Afghanistan back where it needed to be—right between the Communist and Capitalist blocs, sturdily nonaligned, open to flirtation from both sides, and willing to accept whatever gifts were offered.

And plenty were offered. The Germans built an entire modern campus for Kabul University. The Soviets built a housing development of sixty apartment buildings equipped with modern plumbing, electricity, and appliances, a development complete with shaded walkways, stores, and recreational facilities. Tall buildings reared up—a bank . . . then a modern, international hotel . . . then a department store. . . . The big cities got fleets of modern buses, courtesy of the country's Cold War suitors. All the streets of Kabul except the ones in *Shari Kuhna* (Old Town) got paved, and many of the streets got sidewalks. Donkeys and camel caravans stopped coming into the city so much; they gave way to trucks and automobiles. Enormous hydroelectric plants went up on the country's major rivers. They lit up Kabul with a vengeance—lit up wedding palaces where clamorous galas took place every night, lit up modern, Western-style restaurants and cafés that sprouted along main thoroughfares. Bookstores and record stores opened downtown. Teahouses proliferated, and so did ice cream shops and kebab houses. On fine days, the city's burgeoning middle class—members of that new technocracy—drove to nearby pleasure spots such as the little resort town of Paghman, or to Qargha Reservoir, which featured a large patio café overlooking the water.

Afghanistan's great end-of-summer celebration of independence, the festival known as Jeshyn, already the country's single biggest public event, now grew even more splendid. Every year, the government strung lights for blocks and blocks around the fairgrounds where the main celebrations took place.

The festival featured a game of *buzkashi*, the country's national sport, a brutal equestrian contest in which teams of horseman wrestle to gain possession of a goat carcass and drag it across a goal line. Unlike the buzkashi of old, the players in these games were organized into teams representing provinces. Jeshyn also featured massive hours-long firework displays over the lake in the middle of the fairgrounds. The various government ministries sponsored open-air tea gardens where bands played music and the crowds could listen for free to famous singers such as the semiclassical crooner Sarahang or the pop star Ahmad Zahir, master of the electrified accordion, a man who made girls swoon with love songs whose lyrics were written by classic Persian poets from hundreds of years ago. And there were exhibit halls dedicated to the works of modern Afghan painters, who favored realistic landscapes with a slightly fauvist flavor.

More importantly, Jeshyn offered up a trade expo, a venue for Cold War plumage competition. Various countries set up pavilions and displayed their goods. Afghans streamed through these buildings, peering in awe at material marvels made in the United States, France, Czechoslovakia, Poland, China, the Soviet Union—motorcycles and radios, electric egg beaters, ice cream makers, record players, and machine-made fashion items from hats to boots . . . the list went on and on.

In the several theaters situated on festival grounds, Afghan audiences could enjoy such acts as Duke Ellington and his band, flown in from America, or the Chinese opera from Peking, or the Moscow Circus, with its trapeze artists and its jugglers and high-wire acts. "Choose me! Choose me!" sang dazzling artists from both sides in the Cold War contest. "Choose our side, our side!"

Money and technical aid kept pouring in to develop the road system. By the end of the 1960s, a traveler could drive from the Pakistan border through Kabul to the Soviet border in one long day, passing through the Soviet-built Salang Tunnel.

Plenty of foreigners swelled the population of Kabul now. There were Russian and other Eastern-bloc families living rather squalidly, crowded into apartments or small houses, sometimes two or three families to a dwelling, and they could be seen shopping for local goods in the bazaars, elbow to elbow with local Afghans.

Plenty of Americans and Western Europeans could be seen in Kabul too, although, like the British of the nineteenth century, they lived in compounds sequestered from Afghans, and they shopped in commissaries stocked with goods flown in from their own countries. By the midsixties, however, Peace Corps volunteers were flocking into the country. They lived and worked more closely with Afghans and not just in Kabul but in outlying towns, teaching, nursing, or helping out with agricultural projects. These young men and women brought little technical expertise to the field; what they brought were their American faces and their affability. This alone contributed to international understanding (and to the American cause in the Cold War contest).

By 1967, the sixties revolution was sweeping the world, and hippies were starting to stream through Afghanistan. Typically, these new nomads began their trek in Europe, came across Iran, and then traveled through Herat, to Kandahar, to Kabul, and then on to India. The hippies liked what they found in Afghanistan. The hash was good and the people unbelievably mellow. Afghans had strict social regulations for themselves, but their standards for others were remarkably live and let live, at least in the beginning. (This had long been true: Alexander Burnes remarked on it when he traveled through the country in the 1830s.)

What many Afghans along the hippie route saw in this new surge of tourists was economic opportunity. Men with business acumen soon realized that American and European hippies didn't actually want to hang out in real bazaars smoking dope with real Afghans. In Afghanistan, hashish had long been legal but disreputable. Anyone could smoke it, but those who did were day laborers, off-duty truck drivers, and ruffians. Folks with (upper) class drank booze (even though—or perhaps *because*—it was forbidden by religion). Afghan entrepreneurs therefore scoped out the romantic dream that brought the hippies in and constructed that dream for them. They established hotels and set up clubs where Western hippies could get a controlled experience of their imagined Afghanistan.[2] To make sure the experience would be pleasant, they screened out the riffraff. More respectable Afghans, however—educated Afghans, Afghans with connections—could get into these dope clubs. Of course the hippies liked Afghanistan. What was not to like? But just as the Peace Corps volunteers gave Afghanistan an image of the West, so did the hippies. This didn't trouble Afghans much when the hippies were a trickle, but once they turned into a torrent, the image wore on Afghan sensibilities.

By 1969, the social fabric of urban Afghanistan was undergoing rapid, drastic change, particularly in Kabul. The high schools were pouring out graduates, both girls and boys, and women were going to the university in great numbers. Because most of these women were enrolling in the Teachers College and in the College of Medicine, the number of women physicians and teachers in the country escalated dramatically.

Boys and girls who rubbed elbows in classrooms started dating discreetly. It wasn't that anyone asked anyone out—please! It wasn't like *that* yet. Rather, boys and girls would drop hints about where they'd be and then make sure to be there and thus to see each other in a public context. As a result, boys and girls began to choose each other and then push their families into "arranging" for them to get married. These love marriages led to weddings attended by two crowds of people who were strangers to each other—the families of the bride and of the groom respectively, setting up another venue for unrelated boys and girls to meet as individuals, take a shine to each other, and arrange their own marriages.

Meanwhile, in the big city of Kabul, women were beginning to appear in public showing not just their faces but their arms, their legs, even cleavage. Afghan girls of the elite technocratic class were beginning to cotton to Western fashions. They were wearing miniskirts and low cut blouses. Nightclubs were popping up, which served beer and wine and whiskey—and not just to foreigners. Afghans were drinking and making no bones about it. That quaint Italian engineer from Kajakai, Mr. Corriega, had moved to Kabul, and there he was bottling his own brand of wine. Culturally, then, Western Europe and America were winning Afghanistan hands down. Rock and roll, blue jeans, miniskirts—the capital had it all. But on the political and diplomatic fronts, the American and European bloc was losing ground. The Helmand Valley had turned into more of a liability than an advertisement. No one, it seems, had done adequate soil studies before the dams went in. The new irrigation drew salt to the surface, which made much of it impossible to farm: nothing would grow in it.

Also, no one had studied the social consequences of building these dams and irrigation canals, no one had polled the villagers who would be affected, and no one had explained the project to them. Anthropologist Louis Dupree wrote that just after the Arghandab Dam was completed, he found villagers living just twenty miles from the dam who had no idea it was there.[3]

Some time after the Kajakai Dam was completed, my father traveled by Land Rover over roadless terrain to isolated villages far downstream from the dam on some official HVA business or other. In one place, he said, the villagers who came out to greet him asked after the health of King Amanullah. Amanullah had been deposed more than thirty years earlier, but these villagers hadn't heard the news yet. They too knew nothing about the Kajakai Dam upstream from them. They only knew that the river had stopped behaving in its usual way. Now, a great deal of extra water came down at certain times of the year. The villagers' own ancient water-management systems could not handle these inexplicable new water patterns. Their fields flooded and their productivity dropped. They were in trouble and hungry.

What's more, the sudden mystifying change in the river had disrupted the intricate social traditions that had evolved around water management. Villages looked to respected figures known as *mirabs*, "water directors," to organize irrigation-related work and adjudicate water disputes. The eerie changes in the river had overwhelmed the mirab in this village, and his authority had suffered. From this erosion of authority a host of subtler consequences had rippled.

Meanwhile, the model towns were not really working. The government had settled people of different ethnic groups in many of these towns, and the different groups had not worked out ways to reconcile their customs. Conflicts had resulted, and some of the inhabitants of the new towns had gotten fed up and moved away to resume their old nomadic ways.

In the newly irrigated areas, local folks had been moved off their farms to make room for the big experimental farm projects. Later, some of them wanted to come back, but the government would not let them. Resentments were building up.

As for the Kandahar Airport, that whole idea had come to nothing. The airport had been built to accommodate propeller planes, but it was completed just as prop planes were becoming obsolete and jet flight was taking off. And, since the fuel pumps at the Kandahar airport did not work properly, long-distance air traffic did not end up choosing the Kandahar airport as a refueling station, so there it sat in the desert: huge, modern, and empty.

Some of the development projects were completed successfully, but their benefits did not reach the villages, only the larger towns. One day's walk in any direction from any of those marvelous modern highways brought one to villages that didn't know what electricity was. People in these villages had never heard the term "Cold War." As for the changes wrought in the cities, they knew only what other villagers had reported, and these were often distorted by the disapproval of the reporters.

The old Afghanistan, which Abdu'Rahman had tried to crush, the one that had toppled Amanullah, was still out there, and most Afghans still belonged to it; but it was more disconnected than ever from the urban Afghanistan that the Kabul government and its technocracy inhabited and administered.

18

Rise of the Left

AFTER TURNING TO THE SOVIET UNION FOR MILITARY AID, DAOUD had started sending Afghans to Russia and Eastern Europe for military training. By the early sixties, as hundreds of Afghans were coming back from Western universities, well trained to handle administrative and technical jobs, hundreds of other Afghans were coming back from Communist countries, well equipped to move into the ranks of the military. Those who had studied military sciences in Communist countries often acquired a Marxist-Leninist framework through which to understand Afghanistan and their own lives. Marxist ideology told them that Afghanistan was a feudal country in transition to prerevolutionary industrialism. It told the young officers that they, an enlightened vanguard, cleansed of all that heaven and hell nonsense, were destined to build a paradise here in Afghanistan right now—a worker's paradise.

From the military, these ideas spread into Kabul University. From Kabul University, graduates who moved into teaching introduced Communist ideology into the secondary schools. Many university graduates ended up teaching in government schools in the provinces because there weren't enough jobs in the capital to absorb them all; young military officers were posted all over the country as well. Through them, proto-Communist ideas filtered into a thin stratum of provincial Afghan society. In Kabul, a handful of dissident intellectuals began to meet quietly in small study groups to educate themselves in Marxism-Leninism. These groups typically numbered no more than ten or twelve members, and, when the Parliamentary era began, there were no more than several dozen of them in all, but the ideas were there, percolating.

In 1965, thirty men from a number of Marxist study circles got together at the home of journalist Nur Mohammed Taraki, who had gained some notice in the Soviet Union for his didactic novels and short stories about Afghan workers and peasants. Born into a poor Ghilzai Pushtoon family himself, he had made his way through government schools and into the technocracy, even clocking a short stint as an aide at the Afghan Embassy in America. One of his novels had been translated into Russian, and the Soviets had hailed him as "the Afghan Maxim Gorky." Most of the men at the meeting were recent university graduates, and Taraki established his dominance in this assembly because he alone was a white-haired older man, and, in Afghan society, age counts.

He failed to impress one man at the meeting, however. Babrak Karmal may have lacked Taraki's white hair, but at thirty-six years of age, he was halfway to elderhood himself. Karmal had some prestige among the radicals of Kabul because, in his student days, he had organized a number of antigovernment rallies, which finally earned him a prestigious four-year prison sentence. It was there in Daoud's dank cells that his fellow inmates, dissident intellectuals all, introduced him to Marxism. After his release, Babrak returned to the university and got a law degree, but, at the same time, as a charismatic older student with a glamorous prison record, he acquired a following among his younger peers. In 1965, he was no longer a student but still had lots of connections among student activists on the left.

Before the night was out, the thirty men at the meeting had decided to form a political party and contest the upcoming parliamentary elections. They called themselves the People's Democratic Party of Afghanistan, or PDPA. On that night, the men in the room were not just the leaders of the party but also (the bulk of) its members. About half of them hailed from rural Pushtoon families: they were boys drawn out of the old Afghanistan and into the new by government schools. The rest came from privileged urban backgrounds. Taraki embodied the first group: his father was a shepherd and his recent ancestors were nomads. Babrak Karmal embodied the second group. His father was a general and a good friend of Prime Minister Daoud's.

In the parliamentary elections, virtually all of Karmal's group won seats. Virtually none of Taraki's group did. Still, the PDPA now had representation in the country's new legislative body. But when this Parliament began its deliberations, students from the university crowded into the spectators' gallery and staged one of those demonstrations that give student activists a bad name. They booed the newly elected parliamentarians for not having produced full democracy yet, drowned out their speeches, and charged them with corruption and nepotism. They demanded that the prime minister and cabinet appointed by the king one year earlier resign or be dismissed. Apparently, the PDPA had organized the demonstration. In the middle of the shouting, one member of Parliament rose dramatically in the hall. It was Karmal, in shirt sleeves, dressed down, looking like a student. The demonstrators fell silent, giving Babrak Karmal an aura of command. He delivered an impassioned speech about the country's troubles and the suffering of its peasant masses, which had even some of his enemies weeping. Once he sat down, the shouting rose up again, and Parliament had to adjourn.[1]

The students kept disrupting the parliamentary proceedings day after day until at last security guards cleared them out of the building. They continued to demonstrate on the streets outside, and their numbers swelled as other students heard about the excitement and flocked in to be a part of this historic moment, whatever it was about.

On October 25, 1965, some authority ordered the police to disperse the crowd. Three shots were fired, three bodies fell. Two were students, one a bystander. You might suppose that in a country where political violence had claimed so many lives, three more would go unnoticed, but you would be wrong. These three victims became a cause célèbre. The day went down in Afghan history. In the Afghan calendar, it was *Sehum-i-Aqrab*, "the third of (the month of) Aqrab," and over the next decade Sehum-i-Aqrab came to denote not just a calendar date, but a movement.

In 1965, the demonstrations turned into a strike that shut down the university. The students took a petition to the vice rector (who happened to be my father), demanding that the person who gave the fatal order to fire on the students be identified and punished. They warned that if their demand was not met, they would shut down the university for the rest of the year.

The demonstrations had already forced the first prime minister to resign. His replacement Hashim Maiwandwal accepted the petition he was given and promised to investigate. Eventually, one obscure university teacher was charged with some ambiguous misdemeanor, but in reality nothing came of the investigation. Street gossip said the king's cousin General Abdul Wali, commander of the Kabul garrison, had given the order to shoot; if so, it's no wonder the investigation went nowhere. Some blamed the minister of interior Abdul Kayeum who resigned his post and went into exile, in a sense taking responsibility for the deed whether or not he was actually responsible for it.

To this day, no one knows who really ordered the shootings, and in truth, it probably doesn't matter. Something like this was bound to happen in the tinderbox that was Kabul. The events of that October day merely caused coals already smoldering to burst into flames. Every year after that for the next decade, students poured into the streets on the Third of Aqrab to demonstrate and disrupt.

————

IN MOST OF THE WORLD AT THIS TIME, "STUDENT ACTIVIST" AUTOMATICALLY meant "leftist" or at least "liberal." In Kabul, the two terms were not synonymous: here, an equally vociferous and disruptive number of campus activists were radical Islamists. A number of theology professors at the university incited and led them. Professor Burhanuddin Rabbani was one. Abdul Rasool Sayyaf was another. Both men had earned their degrees from Egypt's famous Islamic seminary, Al-Azhar University. Just as the military students brought back Communist ideas from Russia, these theology students brought back Muslim Brotherhood ideas from Egypt. They embraced the Brotherhood doctrine of a universal Khaliphate and of the need to cleanse Islam of Western ideas such as democracy and humanism. They embraced, too, the Brotherhood vision of building a state based exclusively on the Shari'a.

Among their student followers, two firebrands stood out: Ahmad Shah Massoud, an ethnic Tajik, and Gulbuddin Hekmatyar, a Ghilzai Pushtoon. Hekmatyar cut a particularly menacing figure. He (allegedly) started out as a Communist but swung to the other extreme with a vengeance. He and his cohorts protested social change in Kabul by stalking unveiled women on campus and throwing acid into their faces.[2]

In short, the student activists of Afghanistan were polarized from the start. What's more, neither extreme had a single, unified leadership. Both Right and Left splintered into many factions, reflecting underlying ethnic, tribal, and personal conflicts; and even the splinters were riven by rivalries, which generated further splinters. The PDPA was founded in 1965, with thirty members. Two years later it had grown to—thirty-five members. Then Taraki and Karmal had a falling out—you could see it coming. After that, the PDPA consisted of two factions, each with a little more than a dozen members. Each faction published a newspaper that not only reviled the government and the monarchists but the other faction. Taraki's newspaper, and therefore his party, was called *Khalq* (The Masses). Khalq more or less became the Marxist-Leninist party of the rural Ghilzai Pushtoons. Karmal's newspaper called itself *Parcham* (Banner). Parcham became the name of the Marxist-Leninist party of the detribalized urban technocratic elite. (Some mockingly called it The Royal Communist Party of Afghanistan.) Neither Khalq nor Parcham could hold together. Even tinier leftist groups split off from each of them, identified with even more particular ethnic groups, subtribes, or "leaders."[3]

Ominously enough, throughout this decade of the "new democracy," Daoud was inviting carefully selected leftists to his house for private discussions, sounding them out on their affiliations, loyalties, and ideas, and building a network of new alliances in the old Afghan way. It was natural for the former strongman to seek friends and allies among the younger officers of the military, many of whom belonged to the Parcham Party ("The Royal Communist Party of Afghanistan"), and it was not improbable for them to rally to Daoud, for it was his policies that had sent them to the Soviet Union to be trained and educated—and radicalized. As the 1960s came to a close, Kabul was boiling with energy. The hippies were flowing through, music was thundering from nightclubs and private parties, factories were growing, workers were proliferating, and schools were sprouting.

Students were incessantly shutting down their schools over academic demands like easier grading. Workers were agitating for change and shutting down their factories over issues like higher wages and shorter hours. In the summer of 1968, Afghanistan saw fifteen major student strikes and twenty-five industrial strikes. Meanwhile, junior officers in the military were muttering about "the revolution." Islamist students in the university and in the mosques were fulminating about the apocalypse—it was the best of times, it was the worst of times. The vitality of Kabul overwhelmed the senses, but trouble lurked behind the merrymaking; and the whole time—still!—a few hours walk from any major highway or government outpost, the other Afghanistan, the universe of village republics and nomads, of mullahs, maliks, and khans, rumbled along on its own course.

In 1973, the inevitable ax fell. The king went on a vacation to Italy, and his cousin Daoud executed a quick, nearly bloodless coup. It was probably a coup-by-arrangement: at least one of the king's Rolls Royces was sent to him in Italy, which is a nice coup if you can get it. The core royal family had probably decided that anarchy was the biggest threat to the country and had to be staunched. Daoud had long been preparing for this day. Once he deposed the king, he declared himself the country's first president. Many would say that real presidents don't appoint themselves, but hey, political development is a slow process; America wasn't built in a day. "King" sounded too old fashioned now. "President" had a more modern ring to it.

Daoud used the Parcham Party to come back to power, but he himself was no Communist. As soon as he felt safely powerful, Daoud began to undermine his leftist allies, demoting some, promoting others to irrelevance, and sending a great many abroad as harmless ambassadors. He kept talking about the everlasting friendship between Afghanistan and Russia but started cultivating relations with America's regional allies. He met with Zulfiqar Ali Bhutto, the Berkeley-educated president of Pakistan who wore suits from Savile Row. He met with Reza Shah, America's ironman in Iran. The three leaders talked about organizing a regional trade alliance—Afghanistan, Iran, and Pakistan. They pondered a collective security pact. They discussed building a railroad linking the three countries. The Soviet Union looked upon these talks from afar, and alarm bells began to sound.

Even as he was defanging his leftist allies, Daoud made sure to neutralize all danger from the Right. When leading Islamists such as Rabbani, Ahmad Shah Massoud, Gulbuddin Hekmatyar, and a number of others tried to stage a revolt, Daoud crushed it and the Islamists fled to Pakistan.

Daoud was still a tough guy. He could still defeat his political enemies with guns and prison cells and the new torture equipment he ordered from Germany upon resuming power,[4] but he couldn't hold the society together with these instruments; he couldn't keep the fabric from tattering. He could not stop students from striking or keep workers on the job. In April 1978, two unknown gunmen assassinated a popular leftist leader, Mir Akbar Khyber, and his death triggered days of massive demonstrations in Kabul. This time, Daoud decided, he would do something decisive—something that sent a message. In one swift swoop, he arrested all the leftist leaders he knew about, especially those belonging to Khalq—but he wasn't swift enough. Just before being hauled away, one high-up Khalqi, a smooth operator named Hafizullah Amin, managed to send his young son out with a message to the underground cadre of his party, telling them to launch the coup. Apparently, the party had worked out a plan long ago and was merely waiting for the right moment to carry it out.

A day or two later, one of Daoud's tank commanders came to him with worrisome news. He had heard rumors of some conspiracy in the works—something big. The attempt would be made on April 27. He asked permission to load his tanks with live ammo and advised Daoud to station them around the Arg, the royal palace in downtown Kabul, on the morning of the 27th—just in case.

The 27th dawned bright and clear. All morning, the streets remained quiet. The minutes ticked by. Had it been a false alarm? At twelve noon, a cannon boomed from a nearby hilltop—no cause for concern. That cannon was fired every day at noon, to mark the hour. The people of Kabul set their watches by it. This time, however, minutes after the cannon sounded, the tank turrets swung around until their guns were pointing toward the palace. Only then did Daoud realize why his tank commander knew about a conspiracy in the works. He was in on it: he belonged to Khalq, secretly.

Daoud retreated deeper into his besieged palace. There he called his family and associates together and told all who wanted to leave to do so now. They should take this chance to survive if they could: he would think no less of them. No one left.

Outside, the guns began to thunder. Some two thousand elite bodyguards manned the palace grounds, and they fought ferociously, but planes came flying in low, strafing the yard. Later, some people said the planes had come from Tashkent, not from Afghanistan's own Bagram military airfield, which would have tied the Soviets directly to the coup, but as far as I know, no proof of this has ever been produced. In any case, the guards in the courtyard were all killed. The Khalqis moved in and engaged Daoud and his family in hand-to-hand combat. Daoud went down with a gun in his hand. Between eighteen and thirty members of his family were killed with him. In his heyday, Daoud had inspired such dread that, once the palace was taken, a small group of Khalq cadre quickly, secretively loaded his corpse into a covered truck and drove it away for burial in some unmarked location. They never revealed where they had buried Daoud. Indeed, the party never named the men who had done the burying. That's how much they feared Daoud. Thirty years later, however, one of those men still remembered the spot, and he led some officials to Daoud's bones, which were dug up and reburied—but that happened much later. On April 27, 1978, Daoud, his whole family, and his two thousand bodyguards went to their graves, and the House of Dost Mohammed came to an end.

19

Change
by Decree

THE PEOPLE'S DEMOCRATIC PARTY OF AFGHANISTAN WAS NOW IN charge—theoretically. In practice, it faced the same challenge as Dost Mohammed: somehow it had to consolidate a power in Kabul that could dominate the countryside and hold the outside world at bay. In the days after the coup, PDPA militias began hunting down surviving members of the royal family throughout the city. Royals and royal relatives who could escape the country did so. On Radio Kabul, a little-known PDPA functionary announced that "the revolutionary council" was in control. Much of the country wondered what the hell a revolutionary council was. Later, on the radio, Afghans learned that air force lieutenant Abdul Qadir was in command. Most said, "Lieutenant who?" The coup had been so sudden, even the winners didn't know who exactly had won. It took a few days to sort it all out.

In the end, journalist Nur Mohammed Taraki emerged as president, party leader, chief of this, and head of that—in short, proud possessor of all the titles that mattered. Coup captain Hafizullah Amin, who had once been the principal of the Teachers' College, emerged as his number two.

The cabinet consisted entirely of PDPA members, divided more or less equally among Khalq and Parcham faction honchos. Khalq had the dominant posts, however, and soon got rid of the Parcham. Comrade Karmal was sent to Eastern Europe as an ambassador. In the streets of

Kabul, Khalq and Parcham cadre fought occasional Wild West–style gun battles, but Parcham was on the run and Khalq soon reigned supreme.

The PDPA had matured underground, and, though some of its members went public when Parcham helped Daoud gain power, much of the party's membership remained secret. After the coup, therefore, few knew who was and wasn't in the party, including other party members.

But, as the PDPA gained confidence, even its lower-ranking members began to flex their muscles. Throughout government offices, supervisors began to encounter eerie episodes of disrespect, disobedience, or mockery from random subordinates. Army officers began to realize that a whole alternative command structure existed in which corporals might outrank colonels. No one knew whom to trust or what could be said in front of whom: the safer course was just to shut up. Fear clamped over the city, then, as a hitherto invisible organism laced throughout the technocracy began to rise like a kraken into daylight: the PDPA. All these years, the various factions and splinter branches of the PDPA had been formulating "programs" in their clandestine sessions. Khalq therefore had a complete array of policies to enact—without having had one minute of experience actually enacting policies. It began issuing decrees based on "scientific" Marxist theories.

In theory, many of its decrees were progressive, even noble. For example, they improved the status of women. Early decrees banned the domination of daughters by fathers and wives by husbands, outlawed the bride price, and forbade underage marriages—the same measures Amanullah had tried to promulgate. The new regime decreed that literacy classes be established for women and mandated 270 days of paid maternity leave to new mothers.

Measures like these touched only people in the cities; in fact, for the most part, they affected only Kabul—which is not surprising since the PDPA was composed of disaffected members of the salaried urban technocracy, not of peasants still living the rural life. Because the people of the villages were not immediately affected, they took a wait-and-see attitude. Then the regime passed decrees aimed at *their* lives. One decree canceled all debts of peasants to landlords and outlawed high-interest loans secured by land. You can see why this one sounded noble. Big landowners had long been binding their local poor, their relatives, and dependents to serf-like servitude by lending them money on predatory terms. They practiced what amounted to radical usury, despite the Islamic injunction against charging interest, by using elaborate schemes to circumvent the letter of the religious law—and did so with the collusion of the clerics. Small farmers who had trouble making loan payments were gradually losing their lands to big landowners. The PDPA regime thought that canceling debts would wipe out this evil at one stroke, like an ax severing a head.[1]

The trouble was, poor villagers often borrowed money for one of two purposes: young men did it to finance marriages; families did it to finance funerals. When the regime abruptly canceled debts, landowners and rich merchants simply stopped lending money to anyone for any purpose. Suddenly, young men could not afford to get married unless they were rich, so sexual and emotional frustration built up.

Also, suddenly, only the rich could afford lavish funerals. When the patriarch of a poor or even a middling well-to-do family died, his survivors could afford to host only a scant turnout of mourners and could serve them only humiliatingly meager fare, which made them feel ashamed and dishonored.[2] The PDPA wiped out social mechanisms tradition had created to meet crucial needs of a traditional society without providing new institutions to meet those needs. When things started to go wrong, the feudal lords had no trouble convincing the penniless poor that the regime was attacking their interests, their lives.

Another decree set an upper limit for land ownership. No one could own more than sixty hectares (148 acres). In its first year, the regime took some eight hundred thousand acres of land away from big landlords and divided it up among 132,000 poor families. They also announced a plan to organize one million families into forty-five hundred farming cooperatives over the next year.[3] These decrees magnified manyfold the mistakes American-educated administrators of the Helmand Valley had made when they forced nomads of different ethnicities to work together in model towns. The PDPA planners thought they could supersede the sense of group identity derived from tribe and village (and the cooperation it enabled) with an artificial new unit they had created by bureaucratic fiat: the "cooperative."

In this arid country, however, land is useless without water, and managing water requires intricate cooperation. Over the centuries, rural

Afghanistan had developed a low-tech but effective water management infrastructure of wells and ditches and *kahrezes*, or underground canals, which required a corresponding network of social roles supported by tribal values and interlaced with religious and folk traditions.

The Communist regime's new rules tossed a Molotov cocktail into this delicate apparatus. In Afghanistan, most big landowners were not disconnected city magnates sucking revenue from distant estates (although a few of those did exist). Most were local chieftains who controlled large tracts of land that the whole local population in some sense saw as "theirs." When these large tracts were broken up into parcels, they were distributed among hundreds of individual families who had no established social mechanisms for working together and thus could not muster the cooperation needed to manage their water collectively. The redistribution of land set families against families in a competition for water that resulted, finally, in no one getting as much water as they needed. My cousin Mazar, who was living in Afghanistan at the time, told me that small farmers were coming to the city to complain to the government that in the new arrangements their plots were receiving as little as thirty *seconds* of water a day. Land that had recently fed all the inhabitants of an area (albeit unequally) could not now sustain *any* of the families living on it. All were equal now, but starving.

To cap the growing dispute of all against all, beneficiaries of the redistribution had to cope with a sense of guilt for accepting land seized from people whom custom and religion told them were its "rightful owners." For many rural people, therefore, land reform meant crop failure, quarrelling, and a greater chance of going to hell. Add sexual frustration and shame to the mix and you can see why trouble began to bubble in the provinces, a rage that needed no ideological explanation, for, by their own strictly material standards, the PDPA was producing disaster.

The Khalq regime kept plodding doggedly into this disaster because it analyzed Afghan society strictly in terms of class warfare. It assumed it would prevail in this war because it was siding with the many against the few. As a rule, however, Afghan peasants didn't see their life in terms of class interests. They saw their world layered and compartmentalized by ethnic, tribal, and religious factors. Peasants were often the poor relations of wealthy local khans. Even leaving blood ties out of account, rich and poor were commonly bound together by mutual obligations and ties embedded in centuries of family history, personal interactions, and emotions. The very word khan derives, some say, from *distar-khwan*, or tablecloth: a khan was someone who laid out feasts for others.[4]

In Afghanistan, Hemingway's answer to Fitzgerald really held water: sure, the rich were different—they were richer. Religion taught peasant sharecroppers to accept their lot; culture ensured that their lot would be ameliorated by the generosity of their "betters." Peasants derived some satisfaction from being part of something bigger—a tribe. I've heard clerks in corporations say "we" when they mean the corporation, taking pride in the dynamism of the business that employs them. How much more powerful that sentiment of loyalty must be when the belonging stems not merely from a paycheck every two weeks and a bonus at Christmas but from reciprocal memories of funerals and weddings and Ramadhan fasting and Eid festivals going back generations.

No law said khans had to feed their poor relations (and many didn't), but custom decreed that munificence gave them prestige, and their dependents counted on that custom-driven generosity and were loath to alienate their khans lest it leave them out in the cold. Land reformers told the poorest in these structures to never mind, squander the goodwill of the khan, incur his hatred and enmity by using the land taken from him—and not to worry about it, because they wouldn't need his generosity; the government would see to it.

Then there were the nomads, who still numbered 12–15 percent of the people.[5] They didn't think of class as the factor that separated them from settled farmers and city folk. And what could *class interest* mean *within* a nomadic clan? What could it possibly mean between one nomadic clan and another?

Wherever land was under tribal control, chiefs had tribal interests in the routes they used for smuggling, in the subsidies they had extracted from the government since Dost Mohammed's day, and in the guns they used proudly to defend themselves against neighboring tribes. Were these people going to let themselves be absorbed into a framework defined by class interests?

And although every village and clan had deeply rooted institutions for quasi-democratic decision making within the clan or village, few had any experience of democratic decision making between villages or across tribal lines. The regime was inviting them into a framework where affiliations would be based on policies rather than blood, history, and personal connections. It had no chance of working.

A FUNCTIONAL GOVERNMENT IN KABUL MIGHT HAVE TAKEN STEPS TO stem the tide of woe, but the government in Kabul was the Keystone Kops of revolutionary juntas. It would have been comical had it not led to such epic tragedy.

As soon as the Soviet-oriented Marxist-Leninist Khalq eliminated the Soviet-oriented Marxist-Leninist Parcham, it set to work eliminating those whose ideology was next closest to its own. It went after the Maoists. It went after other minor leftist parties. When it first came to power, the new regime made an ostentatious gesture of releasing political prisoners but only, it turned out, because they needed the cells for their own political prisoners.

By most accounts, the coup took even the Soviets by surprise—sure they had hoped for some such outcome someday—but this was almost too soon! Oh well, they made the best of it by sending "advisors" in to help the new regime. Gradually, about five thousand of these technical and military advisors accumulated in Kabul, enough to provide every important government official and every key military commander with a personal Soviet advisor of his very own.

The KGB helped the Khalq Party set up the single most indispensable branch of government for a tender young regime just finding its way—a secret police force. The intelligence service set up at this time kept changing its name as ruling cliques rose and fell, but finally it came to be known as KhAD, a name that still sends shivers up and down Afghan spines.

While Khalq was herding its enemies, rivals, friends, and distant acquaintances into prison by the thousands, it was doing what it could to win the love and respect of the people. Mainly, this entailed instructing the masses on the greatness of Comrade Nur Mohammed Taraki. Gigantic posters of him appeared all over Kabul, identified by such honorifics as "the Genius of the East" and "the Great Teacher."[6] Taraki's childhood home near Ghazni was turned into a shrine, decorated with red flags and colored lights. Here, visitors could see the bed he slept in as a child and the humble utensils he used to eat his simple meals.

Taraki's pre-coup home in a middle-class neighborhood of Kabul became a museum. (He himself moved into one of the former royal palaces.) In his old home, his desk went on display and his ink bottle and the pen he used to jot his great thoughts and his shoes and his boxer shorts and the chair upon which he liked to sit and think. Guides were on hand to explain to visitors the mighty insights that had occurred to him on that very chair! The Afghan Writers Union was directed to study the Great Teacher's novels and short stories and to model their own style after his sentimental novels, which were thinly fictionalized didactic tracts.[7]

Curiously, Taraki himself was not responsible for this florid campaign. His second-in-command, Hafizullah Amin, concocted and carried it out. For each title he assigned to Taraki, Amin gave himself a corresponding honorific. If Taraki was the Great Teacher, Amin was his Faithful Student. In one of his more colorful literary flourishes, Amin compared himself and Taraki to a fingernail and a finger, the one embedded in the other's flesh, inseparable.

Even more curiously, the two men had no such relationship whatsoever. Amin was a ruthless, cunning, well-educated political manipulator who exercised real power. Taraki was a dull-witted, self-educated buffoon who functioned as a mere token of that power. Amin didn't have sole control of that token; he was one of several men wrestling to possess it. Taraki was not so much a leader as a piece of furniture upon which others were competing to sit.

Amin had the edge because he had the biggest list of contacts, knew where all the bodies were buried, and had the best head for organization. It was he who had extended Khalq recruitment into the army until his faction had a deeper penetration of the armed forces than Parcham. Most importantly, on April 27, when all the other PDPA leaders had been arrested, it was Amin who acted decisively to launch the attacks that toppled Daoud. Without his leadership, they would all be dead.

There was, however, one asset Amin did not possess: the trust and affection of the Soviets. They wished another Afghan Communist had carried out the coup—ideally Karmal, but, if not him, at least Taraki. Perhaps they believed the rumors that Amin was a CIA agent. In Afghanistan, which may well be the world capital of conspiracy theory, hardly anyone was ever not suspected of being a CIA agent, but in Amin's case there was some basis for the rumors. When he was a student in the United States in the midsixties, he headed up the Afghan Student Association. In 1967, *Ramparts* magazine published an expose revealing that the CIA was funneling money to the Afghan Student Association through a quasi-governmental aid organization called the Asia Foundation.

The rumors were probably false,[8] but Amin did pose a problem because he didn't want to be absorbed into the Soviet camp as a wholly owned subsidiary. He envisioned carving out some autonomy for himself and his country. He hoped to make Afghanistan like Yugoslavia or at least Albania: a hard-line Communist state, but nonaligned. This objective the Soviets found unacceptable.

The conflict between Amin and the Soviets might explain the strange events that took place February 14, 1979, nine months after the Communist coup. On that Valentine's Day, a group of armed men kidnapped American ambassador Adolph Dubs. Yes, America still had an embassy in Kabul at this time. Surprisingly, perhaps, America still hoped to retain some influence in Afghanistan. Amin's nonalignment ambition fanned this hope. The kidnappers allegedly belonged to a Maoist splinter party that Afghans characterized as *chupi-i-chup*, "left-of-left." (There were quite a number of these "left-of-left" groups, most too tiny to be called "parties.") The kidnappers were allegedly trying to get their leader released from a PDPA prison, but, if that had really been their goal, why kidnap the *American* ambassador? The Americans had no pull with the PDPA. Why not the *Soviet* ambassador, a hostage who would really have put some pressure on a regime acting as a proxy for the Soviets?

Furthermore, instead of whisking their victim away to a hidden location and issuing demands from that safe spot—as any normal kidnapper would have done—they took him to the biggest, best-known, and most centrally located *hotel* in Kabul—to the Kabul Hotel, in fact, where diplomats and foreign journalists stayed, the one location in which the government's security apparatus was already established, the one place from which the kidnappers could not possibly escape, no matter what the outcome of their adventure. A strange decision.

American embassy personnel begged the Communist authorities in Kabul to let them negotiate with the kidnappers. They knew how to wear down such hostage takers with talk. They felt sure they could get the ambassador out safely. The regime—on the advice of a KGB agent in Kabul—said no: the Afghan government would take care of this. And they took care of it all right. They sent a strike team into the room guns blazing, killing all the kidnappers and Dubs as well. Problem solved. In mere minutes.

Predictably, the United States closed its embassy, pulled out all its personnel, and cut off diplomatic relations with Afghanistan. Thus ended Amin's dream of autonomy. The regime had no choice now but to rely totally on Soviet aid and protection. The mysterious Adolph Dubs affair inched Afghanistan closer to becoming one more Soviet Socialist Republic.

The following month, a bunch of rebels kidnapped and killed nine Soviet advisors in the city of Herat. Immediately, planes took off from Dushanbe, the capital of Soviet Tajikistan, and bombed Herat, reducing a third of the city to rubble and killing, by most accounts, as many as twenty-five thousand people. (The Soviets and some leftist writers of the time claimed the number was closer to eight hundred.)[9]

Whatever the body count, the Soviets implausibly denied any connection to the massacre. Hafizullah Amin, by contrast, saw an opportunity to build his reputation as an intimidating enforcer, so he insisted *he* had ordered the destruction of Herat. In Peshawar, a number of Islamist Afghan exiles went through a parallel exercise. Professor Rabbani, late of Kabul University, claimed *he* had instigated the uprising that drew such a horrific government response, but his rival Subghatullah Mujaddedi protested that no, no, he was the one—he had organized the rebellion that led to such destruction. At both ends of the political spectrum, people were competing to claim credit for carnage.

Meanwhile, radical Islamism was making the whole region less and less hospitable for a Communist regime in Afghanistan. Unlike the coup in Afghanistan, the upheaval in neighboring Iran was a real revolution: the fall of the Shah and the advent of Ayatollah Khomeini in 1978 signaled a real sea change. Radical Islam was on the march in Pakistan as well. There, in 1977, Bhutto tried to steal an election, but his fraud gave the country's reactionary religious parties the power to rally outrage. Massive demonstrations toppled Bhutto, and an Islamist general, Zia al-Haq, seized power. Zia and his allies put Bhutto on trial, found him guilty and shocked the world by hanging him, thus ending the secular-modernist experiment in Pakistan.

Afghan Islamists who had been active in Kabul before the coup were all living in Pakistan at this point. Pakistan's new president saw them as an opportunity. Perhaps, by aiding these rebels, Pakistan might weaken its truculent neighbor.

Inside Afghanistan, new insurgencies kept bubbling up in rural areas such as Nuristan. Taraki and Amin kept "requesting" more and more military aid from the Soviets, and soon it wasn't just advisors the Soviets were sending in, but whole battalions, whole airborne divisions.

Even so, PDPA control kept deteriorating. The Soviets blamed the breakdown on Amin. From the Soviet perspective, this man combined the worst of three characteristics: First, he was a ruthless bully whose tactics were inciting hatred of Communism. Second, he was an incompetent commander who couldn't manage the rebellion he was inciting. Third, he wouldn't take orders. Even stupid Taraki would make a better head of state. In the late summer of 1979, Taraki went to Cuba to attend a socialist conference. On his way home, he was told to stop in Moscow for a chat. At the Kremlin, the Great Teacher was told to assassinate Amin the moment he returned to Kabul—simply gun him down at the airport as he approached the plane. Taraki's entourage included Amin's chief spy, and although the Teacher's aides had all been excluded from the meeting with Kremlin leaders, Amin's spy had slipped a listening device into Taraki's pocket. He knew all about Taraki's assignment.

Before he left Moscow, Taraki sent word to four of his cronies in Kabul, ordering them to kill Amin at the airport. When Taraki's plane reached Kabul, however, it didn't land. It just circled and circled. Down below, the four men tasked with killing Amin—the so-called Gang of Four—looked around and realized they didn't recognize any of the airport personnel. All the usual workers had been replaced by Amin's gunmen. The Gang of Four realized it was they who might be gunned down if they tried anything. Then, just as Taraki's plane finally came in for a landing, Amin drove up in a white Volkswagen, blandly greeted his four deadly rivals, and arrogantly strolled out to meet Taraki. As the two shook hands, Amin nodded toward the Gang of Four and told his supposed boss, "Get rid of them."

The plot had been foiled. What to do? Taraki and his Gang of Four met and fulminated. They *had* to kill Amin now, or they would be in trouble with the Soviets. Finally they came up with a plan. Taraki would invite Amin to lunch. Before he arrived, the Gang of Four would strap a time-bomb to the toilet in the palace. When Amin went in to use the facilities, they would lock the door—boom! Ha!

But Amin was too wily to fall for the old exploding-toilet trick. He arrived two hours early for the lunch. The Gang of Four were away, getting the timing device for their bomb. The Great Teacher was standing at the top of the stairs with two guards. When he saw his Faithful Student walk through the doors and start up the stairs, he ordered his guards to open fire. They killed Amin's sidekick instantly, but Amin rolled down the steps, pulling his own sidearm as he fell, and fired back as he ran out to his car, bullets zinging past his ears.

After escaping with his life, the Faithful Student collected his men and returned to the palace. Taraki was never seen in public again. According to government newspapers, he fell ill. Three weeks later, a four-line item in the state newspaper announced that the Great Teacher had resigned all his party positions and died of natural causes. Henceforth, his Faithful Student would be shouldering his duties.[10]

As the Soviets had feared, Amin took immediate steps to reduce his dependence on the Soviet Union. He put diplomatic feelers out to several other nonaligned powers, hoping to broaden his connections to the outside world. At the same time, he stepped up police activity, repression, torture, and air strikes inside his country to make sure that even if he lost Soviet support he would be able to hold onto his country. Of course this repression only inflamed the opposition.

The Soviets wrung their hands. With Amin at the helm, the whole situation was going to hell. If the PDPA lost its grip entirely, America might move in with a vengeance, especially since the Shah of Iran had fallen in 1978, and America was no doubt looking for a replacement ally in the region. In Soviet circles, some were saying it might be best to take direct action, just as the Soviet Union had done in Hungary in 1956 and in Czechoslovakia in 1968.

That October, a top Russian general and some sixty high-level officers visited Afghanistan. They didn't mention that they were on a reconnaissance trip. They toured the country, studying the terrain to see if an invasion might be feasible. Even after the reconnaissance, the General Staff wasn't sure. This was a dicey moment to be contemplating drastic action. Brezhnev still gripped the country with an iron fist, but the arm attached to that fist had corroded, and the brain directing that arm had begun to wander and stammer. In short, Brezhnev was old and sick. By the following year, he would be virtually incapacitated, and, for the next two years after that, the Soviet Union would have a figurehead at the helm while behind the scenes faceless bureaucrats in black greatcoats and sable caps struggled for power. Was this a good time to invade another country, even a small, primitive country like Afghanistan?

According to a document prepared by the Russian General Staff, the decision to invade was not finalized until thirteen days before the invasion began.[11] At that point, scattered units were sent to Tajikistan to muster near the border. Reserves were called up to form a force of eighty thousand, known as the Fortieth Army. Its troops were mostly from the central Asian Soviet republics abutting Afghanistan, because Soviet planners thought the invasion might feel less invasive to Afghans if the face of it were people of their same ethnic group. The Russian General Staff seemed not to take into account the fact that there were many ethnic groups in Afghanistan and that the dominant Pushtoons, who formed the numerical majority, were not even cousins to the Turkish minorities of northern Afghanistan.

The Soviets put a top man at the head of the Fortieth Army: General Ivan Pavlovsky, who had directed the crushing of Czechoslovakia's "Prague Spring" eleven years earlier. Czechoslovakia . . . Afghanistan . . . it was pretty much the same problem, wasn't it? What had worked in Eastern Europe ought to work here: a sudden, overwhelming assault—all potential dissidents stomped flat at once—a few weeks of tanks patrolling the streets—and then . . . as soon as quiet returned—restoration of a Communist order with a competent local fellow in charge—that was the plan.

The Fortieth Army massed along the border in the late weeks of December 1979. The day before Christmas, an airborne division of Soviet troops landed at Bagram airbase near Kabul. The troops zipped quietly to the city, fanned out through the streets, and took control of key military and political installations. At the same time, the rifle battalions of the Fortieth Army were completing a hastily flung up pontoon bridge across the Amu River, the broad ribbon of water marking the northern border of Afghanistan. On December 27, Soviet troops marched across that bridge into Afghanistan. The soldiers in that army didn't know their real mission. They thought they were securing a strip of territory near the border because "bandits" had been disrupting the peace. Once they were inside Afghanistan, they received new orders, to proceed to Kabul on the superb highway the Soviets had constructed two decades earlier.

By December 28, the Soviets were totally in control of the capital. The first troops to land had hurried to the presidential palace. Hafizullah Amin knew this sudden, aggressive thrust by the Soviets did not bode well for him, but he didn't know what to do about it. The masses of rural Afghans outside Kabul hated him and his party, so he couldn't look to them for help. Virtually all the ordinary Afghans throughout the city feared him and despised his People's Democratic Party of Afghanistan, so he couldn't count on their support. Within the PDPA, perhaps half the cadre belonged to the other faction, the Parcham group. They had suffered viciously at the hands of Amin's Khalq and had been sharpening their knives and waiting for this moment. No help there. As for Amin's own group? His own Khalq faction? Well, everybody knew Amin had murdered Nur Mohammed Taraki, and, although many regarded Taraki as a horse's ass, many didn't. Even within his core circle, Amin didn't know whom to trust, and so he was reduced to depending on his Soviet-supplied bodyguards. They were Spetsnaz troops, the Soviet equivalent of Special Forces, men trained in the science of killing. They had their orders already and, with Soviet troops in the city, they hurried to carry out those orders. By the time the main Soviet forces arrived, Amin was dead. Reports on how he died vary. He may have been shot, he may have been suffocated. Either way, he was apparently poisoned first.

The Soviets claimed a group of Afghan conspirators had killed him. They had to say this to defend their claim that they had entered Afghanistan by invitation. Whatever Amin might have been and however he gained power, he *was* the head of the ruling regime when the Soviets arrived. He was the only man in a position to invite the Soviets in. The Soviets could not openly declare that their first move upon entering the country by invitation was to kill their host.

In his place, they installed Babrak Karmal, head of the Parcham faction of the PDPA. Karmal had been living in the Soviet Union before the invasion, having sought refuge there when the struggle between Khalq and Parcham got too hot. The Soviets floated a suggestion that Karmal was the one who had called on them for help. In short, they were "invited" into Afghanistan by a man who wasn't there (until the Soviets brought him in). You have to take your legitimacy where you can find it, I guess.

20

The Soviet Occupation

With Babrak in place, Communist Afghanistan could supposedly start afresh. Job one: to wipe out the rural insurgents. Before the Soviets swept in, these Muslim antigovernment groups, generally known as the Mujahideen—"the ones who conduct jihad"—still operated as conventional forces. They fielded armies that fought pitched gun battles with government troops. Before the Soviets arrived, this made sense because the Mujahideen and the government were not so mismatched. The government was better armed but not *dramatically* better armed than the rebels.

The Soviets, however, brought overwhelming military superiority to the field. Their tanks, jets, and field artillery made quick work of Mujahideen armies massed in the hills. Within weeks—only a bit longer than it had taken to crush Hungary and Czechoslovakia—the Mujahideen as such had been annihilated. Meanwhile, KhAD, the PDPA's secret police, was busy arresting all urban residents suspected of any sort of antigovernment activity, including listening to BBC news broadcasts. Those "dissidents" were hauled into Pul-i-Charkhi, Kabul's main prison, and the nightly executions began.

Then came a shocker. On February 22, all across Kabul, from their rooftops and yards, people began to chant *"Allah-u-Akbar!"* which means "God is Great!" There was nothing the Soviets could do to stop it: the chanting was coming from everywhere. It was happening at night. The city had no searchlights, and the people could not be bombed into silence because the Soviets themselves were living among them.

The Soviets tried to drown out the roar of human voices by firing rockets, but the human voices shouted louder, drowning out the rockets. The sound of a whole city shouting in unison was so loud, nearby villages heard it, and *they* joined in. The Allah-u-Akbar demonstration lasted the whole night through. The cry of Allah-u-Akbar didn't mean all the inhabitants of Kabul and its surrounding villages were religious zealots. They chanted the phrase because it was the most efficient, most universally understood way to express "We are Afghans, we oppose you and your puppets."

From then on, one shocking demonstration followed another. Students from the universities poured into the streets. When the police tried to break them up, the women demonstrators taunted the police, ridiculing their masculinity, putting their own headscarves on the cops in mockery. Instead of brutalizing them, some of the police joined them. Secondary school students then began to stage protests. Finally, even kids in primary school were on the streets, waving signs and shouting. The regime couldn't rely on the regular police, but it had plenty of party thugs to enforce the rule. The young Parcham cadre had no compunctions about shooting women and girls. One demonstration was led by a girl named Naheed, and, when the student marcher next to her went down, Naheed kneeled and took the fallen student in her arms, while still inciting the crowd, only to be shot dead herself at that moment. This made her a martyred hero of the Afghan resistance, like the woman who had rallied the Afghans against the British in the iconic battle of Maiwand: Naheed was the new Malalai.

By this time, the Soviet troops in charge of pacifying the countryside were discovering that defeating and dispersing the Mujahideen armies had not solved their problem. In fact, it had only complicated their task, because now the difficult terrain of Afghanistan, in and around the thousands of villages, was swarming with tiny groups of antigovernment militants, invigorated by the notion that they were fighting to defend Islam against an implacable atheistic enemy. These little forces never numbered more than about a hundred men and most were smaller, down in the twenty-man range.

In fact, who was to say all the "forces" were even as large as twenty? Anti-Soviet rebels didn't have to be part of any organized force. They could operate on impulse as individuals. The Allah-u-Akbar demonstrations in Kabul proved that it was not necessary to have lines of communication or secret meetings or organizational charts for everyone to get on the same page of the same overall enterprise. Rumor and gossip was perfectly equal to the task of permeating the nation with a broad sense of mission and with an intellectually vague but emotionally intense sense of mass intention, an exhilarating sense of a unified "Us" mustering to fight against a massive, evil "Them."

With that mood in the air, any group, from a handful of teenagers to an organized cluster of adult men, could conceive of a mission, plan it themselves, and carry it out. Such missions didn't need to fit in with some larger strategic plan. It was enough to have struck a blow against the hated enemy, and that enemy was easy to identify.

The enemy was easy to identify, because the Soviets looked foreign. Their Communist allies within the country also stood out from the rural natives because they dressed like urban folks, in suits, shirts, and western hats, not in dress-length tunics, baggy trousers, and turbans. Any self-defined volunteer anti-Communist rebel in the most outlying of villages could easily see whose murder would be a noble act of patriotism rather than a crime.

And besides, the enemy was constantly coming around, for the government kept sending teams to the villages to teach the people what Communism was and what the Communist government was going to do for them. These teams tried to organize village councils to govern their local areas and administer Soviet development projects. The Soviets and their client regime assumed that as soon as people quieted down and the development projects began to show results, as soon as the electrical power started to flow, the roads were built, the goods came flowing in, the medical clinics popped up, and people saw their material lives improve, they would understand and embrace the revolution.

But the little groups the government sent around were always composed of several Soviet advisors, one or more members of the dreaded KhAD, a number of officials from the Ministry of Interior (which ran the police and the prisons), a few PDPA cadres, and one or two mullahs and Muslim scholars employed by the government who, to the local people, inevitably looked like lapdogs and window dressing. And because

Afghanistan was an ever more dangerous country for them, these itinerant teams had a few dozen soldiers along for protection.

What the villagers saw coming at them, therefore, was a tense cluster of people from not-around-these-parts, dressed like the hated enemy, accompanied by men-with-guns, pulling into town in armored vehicles, and calling upon the village elders and leaders to muster up for a public lecture, at which quite often the villagers were told that the first thing the government was going to do for them was to educate their women and girls. The government team would then order that the women and girls be brought out so that the best candidates for education could be selected.

The second thing the government was going to do was execute land reform. Who were the big landowners around here? Bring them out too, the officials would say. The big landowners were told: you are stripped of your holdings. Your land is to be divided. The people who worked it for you own the land and you work for them now. Deal with it.

Afghans use a pithy phrase to sum up why men fight wars: *zar, zan, u zameen.* "Gold, women, and land." That's exactly what these foreigners seemed to be after, at least to the villagers they were "educating."

Inevitably, when these government teams pulled into small rural villages and tried to modernize them overnight by fiat, clashes broke out. The villagers lost those clashes, because they lacked the firepower to stand up to the Soviets. So the government education and development teams were often in the position of telling villagers whose men they had just killed, "Bring us your women. We're going to educate them."[1] When the government teams left, it was very easy for Mujahideen agitators to come back in and convince the villagers they should fight to drive these satanic foreigners off Afghan soil and reclaim the lives they used to have.

Meanwhile, Soviet forces fighting these fragmented, ever tinier units of Mujahideen (if they can even be called units) found themselves—incredibly enough—losing this grinding war of grain-scale violence. For one thing, the Mujahideen refused to engage in pitched battles. They fought only when they had some tactical advantage.

A Soviet officer named Major Petrov described one typical encounter. In March 1982, he was assigned to hunt down and kill forty Mujahideen said to be hiding in or near a village called Sherkhankel. He decided to conduct the operation at night with one artillery division and four helicopter gunships. The team pursued figures they thought were Mujahideen down a long straight road between a mud wall and a cement canal. Petrov didn't realize he was being drawn into an ambush. He didn't fear it, in any case, because he thought the Mujahideen had only bolt-action single-shot World War II–era rifles. Suddenly, through holes in the wall came grenades, rockets, and machine gun fire. It took the startled Petrov a few minutes to figure out where the gunfire was coming from and to give his men the command to fire back. By then, the Afghans had sneaked away through those underground irrigation tunnels or kahrezes that laced Afghanistan. There was no one left to fight. The Soviet soldiers were firing a hundred rounds a minute into rocks and dirt.[2] The British could have told them about this kind of war: they'd been there, done that, in 1879–1880.

The Soviets soon discovered that, in this kind of war, their fancy equipment was useless. The terrain was so uncharted they couldn't move their tanks and armored vehicles into most of it. They could patrol the cities but were totally incapacitated in the countryside. They had mobile artillery, but these were too heavy to carry into the mountains, so they had to leave them behind. Their high-speed jets had targeting devices that enabled them to pick off individual enemy soldiers with eerie precision, but these too were useless for they moved too fast to spot, much less shoot, guerillas hidden among the rocks of Afghan canyons. The Soviets deployed their high-tech instruments to detect the Mujahideen; the Mujahideen tuned into the flight patterns of birds, which sense the faintest sounds and slightest disturbances of the air. When the guerillas saw birds rise up from a distant peak, they knew the jets were coming, and they dove into the safety of some convenient cave or crack.[3]

The only military equipment the Soviets found really useful were their big Hind helicopter gunships, which they could fly into the canyons. The 'copters could hover in one spot, and from there gunmen could shoot the guerillas with high-powered artillery as soon as they showed their head. The only trouble was, the guerillas eventually began to acquire Soviet weapons from tanks they had captured and from soldiers they had killed, as well as from allies outside the country dedicated to hurting the Soviets. Once they had machine guns, the Soviets had to hover at least three hundred yards away from any guerillas they spotted, which eliminated some of the advantage the helicopters gave them.

Ultimately, winning battles in canyons and defiles and sparsely inhabited mountains and deserts wasn't going to enable the Soviets and their puppets to govern the country. They had to eliminate the Mujahideen guerillas—not just defeat them in isolated battles but *eliminate* them.

The trouble was, the Mujahideen looked just like other rural Afghans, which was scarcely surprising because most of them were just rural Afghans, not full-time revolutionaries or warriors. When they weren't fighting the Soviets, they were pursuing their usual lives: plowing their fields, grazing their sheep, hatching advantageous marriages, and scheming to one-up their cousins in the next village.

When they killed a few Soviet advisors in a canyon and then melted away, where they melted to was their local village or qala, where they joined their relatives and friends. When a government team came to set up some program, they were part of the crowd listening quietly and acting docile. After the soldiers left, they dug up their buried weapons and killed the representatives the government had left behind.

The government couldn't defeat these Mujahideen by cutting their supply lines to the outside world because most of them *had* no connection to the outside world. Their base was their own home or a home very much like it: a place where people would gladly feed and shelter them because they knew these guys or guys just like them and subscribed completely to their cause.

The Mujahideen thus had no logistical problems themselves and were in excellent shape to inflict logistical damage on the Soviets. They devoted themselves to destroying bridges and blowing up sections of highway so that the Soviets would be unable to truck in supplies. The battle was unequal—the Soviets held the short straw.

At last, Soviet military planners made a fateful decision. They decided to deny the Mujahideen their logistical advantage in the only way that looked feasible to them: they would cut the ties between the people and the guerillas by driving the people out of the countryside. Thus began the most terrible phase of this terrible war, a phase that should never be allowed to fade from the annals of infamy. The Soviets launched a deliberate effort to depopulate rural Afghanistan. They bombed countless villages. Flying over the farmlands, they scattered land mines, which still litter Afghan soil and have made much of the land difficult if not impossible to cultivate. They strafed livestock from the air, cutting them to pieces so that the rural population would no longer be able to feed the guerillas—or (incidentally) themselves, which would force them to move, either to the nearest big city, which the Soviets *could* control with their armored vehicles and artillery, or to the nearest safe country of refuge, which for most meant Pakistan or Iran. The bloodiest year of the war was 1985. By the end of that year, some one million Afghans had been killed and some six million were living in Pakistan or Iran as refugees.

The refugees, however, were not whole families, generally. The horror rained down upon the country aroused a grim resolve among rural Afghans to fight this implacable enemy to their last drop of blood. Men of fighting age moved their families to the refugee camps outside the country and went back inside to keep on fighting. The culture paid a terrible price for this decimation of families, a price that has never been analyzed systematically. Afghan culture is, to be sure, a macho culture. From the earliest age, boys are expected to be tough. They think nothing of taking beatings from their fathers and elder brothers. They learn to laugh off such beatings and even take pride in how hard they've been hit by the people who care about them most. It's all part of becoming a man. It even makes them feel appreciated because heaven help the boy who comes into adulthood a weakling.

But the macho elements of Afghan culture are tempered by many other factors—by the pride Afghan boys take in representing their family and the shame they feel about bringing their families into disrepute, by the solicitude they express as a matter of course toward their elders, by the tenderness so many Afghan men intuitively display toward babies, whom they dandle and kiss without embarrassment, by the almost exaggerated protectiveness they display toward their mothers and wives and sisters, by the demands their culture places on their instincts for charity and the ways in which it honors their impulses toward generosity . . .

At the height of the Soviet occupation, Afghanistan became a country in which the tempering effects on men of living as members of families, clans, and communities dropped away. Millions of men went through years of living solely in the company of other adult men in some of the toughest conditions imaginable. They were members of militias in a land devoid of women, children, and elders. That experience changed the soul of the country, or so it seems to me.

To make matters worse, the Soviets invented a type of land mine designed to look like a toy and thus specifically to attract children. These mines were not strong enough to kill, just strong enough to maim. As a military strategy, the idea was to hurt the families migrating to the refugee camps. A child killed by land mines was buried wherever he or she died, and the family moved on. Children who lost a foot or a hand but survived bogged down their whole family. They would not be abandoned, it would take the man of the group much longer to get his family to refuge before he could go back to the war, and he might not even abandon them once he got them to safety. Viewed purely in scientific terms, these toy-like land mines were an intellectually elegant solution to a military problem.

Many of the mines are still there. Most of the people who planted them are middle-aged men living in some blighted part of the former Soviet Union. And the men who dreamed up this scientific scheme have, for the most part, died of natural causes by now.

PART IV: OLD AFGHANISTAN ERUPTS

Nadir Shah and his family had resumed the project launched by Dost Mohammed, the project that consumed Abdu'Rahman and Amanullah. The Musahibbans moved more cautiously, but they did move relentlessly to consolidate a country governed from an all-powerful center. The ruling elite in Kabul saw development as the key to this project, so they used strategic nonalignment to squeeze resources out of both sides in the Cold War, which they used to build roads, schools, postal services, telecommunications, and other infrastructure. Sure enough, all this development directed from the capital made Kabul not just a city but The City: bigger, stronger, and more culturally dominant than all the other major cities of Afghanistan combined. It also spawned a powerful new class of technocrats that outpaced the old aristocracy, a class whose prestige derived from secular skills and education, not from ancestral religious and tribal affiliations. Kabul became an imperial presence in the Afghan countryside, building institutions that could not help but put pressure on the traditional Afghan way of life. The tug and push between new Kabul and old Afghanistan became a contest between modern ways and traditional ways, internationalism and parochialism, religious law and secular law, Western culture and Islamic culture, urban values and rural values . . . and Nadir Shah's dynasty seemed destined to succeed. Old Afghanistan seemed to be giving ground, losing steam.

Actually, no one was giving ground. The forces pulling the country in opposite directions were only gaining ominous intensity. Their tension generated an appearance of stability only because the two sides were evenly matched: equilibrium was not stability. Something would have to give, and the rising tension guaranteed that, when it did, it would be explosive. Within the urban camp, radicals strained against moderates to push for secular development harder, faster. When Afghan Communists seized power, it wasn't a revolution of the poor against the rich or of peasants against landlords. It was a putsch within the urban elite about how to pursue the long-standing goals of imperial Kabul.

The real conflict wasn't within Kabul, however, but between Kabul and the countryside; and that showdown was yet to come. When the Soviets crashed into the country, they intended to keep the country out of American hands, but they need not have bothered. The emergent Afghan Left may have embraced one side of the bipolar global confrontation between Communism and Capitalism, but their opponents felt no analogous affiliation with the other side. These were not proxies for American interests or ideals. Domestically, they represented old Afghanistan, the one that Abdu'Rahman and his successors stomped but couldn't kill. Ideologically, they were proxies for a new factor in global politics: revolutionary Islamism. In short, the Afghan conflict had little to do with Cold War issues. It was an eruption of unresolved Afghan contentions going back to the days of Amanullah and Bachey Saqao and before. By intervening in this contest, the Soviets shattered all the checks and balances and accommodations Afghans had crafted over the course of the previous 140 years, and they opened the gates to forces that had been repressed for decades by the modernizing project emanating out of Kabul.

21

The
Mujahideen

AFGHANS ARE SAID TO BE A PEOPLE WHO COME TOGETHER AS ONE IN THE face of foreign invaders, but that is a sentimental stereotype. Within one year of the Soviet invasion, over eighty resistance groups were operating out of Peshawar, Pakistan.[1] Some were big, some were small. A tiny fraction of these groups came from the liberal left, a few espoused some form of traditional nationalism, but the overwhelming majority claimed to be fighting under the banner of Islam as Mujahideen, "Defenders of the Faith."

If all these groups were fighting for the same cause against the same enemy, why were there nearly eighty of them instead of just one? Good question. And the answer is, because they coalesced around particular personalities and their allies, not around ideological positions and ideas. Every leader was in competition with every other for command of the whole. Not one was willing to merge with a similar group and accept the authority of *its* leader. Why? Because leadership in Afghan culture still goes back to personal interactions and associated networks of personal connections. This was true in the days of Ahmad Shah Baba. It was still true in 1985—and it was just as true for the Communists as for the Mujahideen.

The eighty-plus groups in Peshawar did not correspond to eighty-plus armies in Afghanistan. Most of the Peshawar groups were stand-alone entities connected only tenuously, if at all, to in-country fighting groups, of which there were not scores but hundreds, perhaps thousands. The connections between groups in Pakistan and those in Afghanistan were based on personal favors and deals between the leaders.

What favors? What deals? Well, the Mujahideen leaders in Peshawar were essentially fund-raisers, competing for money and guns from various sources out there in the wide world. Some groups had major sponsors in Saudi Arabia, others in Iran, and others with Islamist revolutionary parties in Arab North Africa.

And, right from the start, at least a trickle of money and guns was coming from the United States, Britain, and other Western European countries. The Western aid did not flow directly to the Mujahideen but to the Pakistan government, which distributed it among its favorites. For this reason, the various Mujahideen competed ferociously for influence in the Pakistan political establishment.

The agency that handled most of the aid flowing from the West to the Mujahideen was Pakistan's InterServices Intelligence, or ISI. This spy agency theoretically served all the branches of the Pakistan military. It was a small outfit compared to, say, the Pakistan army or air force, but, as the liaison among the various military branches and the one group privy to the secrets of all, ISI was in a unique position to build its power. Now, with Western money flowing through its hands, this agency had its own considerable off-the-shelf budget. And because ISI could disburse the money as it pleased without having to answer for its choices, this secretive nodule within Pakistan's political establishment was able to gain commanding influence among the dangerous Afghan militants on its soil—which made ISI itself the most dangerous gang of all.

The Peshawar-based Mujahideen in turn funneled the money and guns they received to *their* selected in-country commanders, using this aid to build stables of clients among the guerillas, thereby laying the groundwork for the day when they would be competing with one another for power in Kabul. What the Soviets and their puppets faced, in short, was not an entity nor even a movement but a *situation*.

The country the Mujahideen hoped to govern someday was more than fragmented now; it was atomized. Farming and manufacturing had pretty much shut down. Aside from gem smuggling, gun running, and the opium trade, there was hardly any economy. Afghanistan was living on foreign subsidies—the cities on Soviet money, the rural people mainly on money from Arab and Western sources. Much of the Western money didn't get all the way through the pipeline. Much stuck to sticky fingers in ISI, turning that little agency into a state within a state. Some improved the lifestyle of the Afghan fund-raiser–politicians in Peshawar, transforming them into a unique class of their own. What did finally get through to Afghans in the country funded only violence.

Among the Mujahideen in Peshawar, every leader was competing with every other for followers. Since all were theoretically fighting for Islam, none could advance his cause by declaring himself more moderate than the next man. "More moderate" connoted less committed, less pure, less Muslim. In the cauldron of that competition, every leader was under pressure to prove himself *more* Muslim than his rivals. If one said he planned to establish an Islamic state, the next one had to say, "Mine will make his look like an atheist's fleshpot." The structure of the situation kept pushing the Mujahideen toward extremism, and it favored those who were already authentically extremist in their views.

Although much of the aid came through ISI, not all of it did. Iran dealt largely with the country's Shi'as, the biggest group of whom were the Hazaras, the ethnic group crushed by the Iron Amir in the nineteenth century. The Hazaras mounted stiff resistance to the Soviets but were not about to join the Sunni-dominated Mujahideen of Peshawar. The Saudis, too, set up direct channels with some groups, bypassing ISI. Egypt had its clients, and so did India, Pakistan's implacable enemy.

The anti-Soviet war became a proxy for many deadly conflicts in the wider world; those conflicts in turn stoked ethnic, religious, and linguistic divisions among Afghans into hostilities. Non-Afghans sometimes say, "Oh, these people have been fighting one another for a thousand years." Not true. Before the Soviet invasion, the country's various ethnic, linguistic, and religious subgroups were not at war much except during the reign of the Iron Amir. They had learned to accommodate one another and had evolved complex symbiotic interdependencies. Feuds, yes. Inter*tribal* wars, yes, sometimes; but those involved warriors fighting warriors, not armies eviscerating one another's homes, farms, flocks, and families. The Soviet invasion and the Afghan response shattered age-old accommodations among groups and laid the groundwork for savage ethnic wars to come.

The Soviet invasion and the resistance to it also reconfigured the social fabric of the old Afghanistan, the universe of village-republics described in Chapter 2, which was still more or less intact when the Soviet invasion began. In the village-republics of Afghanistan, authority had always belonged to secular "elders"—landowners, tribal chiefs, village maliks. They were partnered with clerics, but clerics had the subordinate role. The elders made the serious decisions because they had the land, wealth, weapons, and will to fight. The clerics' role was to give their decisions sanction.

The war reversed that equation.[2] Now, when the ever more religiously purist Mujahideen looked for partners in the country, they zeroed in on clerics. This class gained unprecedented power at the expense of the secular elders, whose basis for authority all but vanished once the land was scorched, the economy destroyed, and the old tribal structures blown apart by Soviet carpet bombing, which drove so many millions into exile. Also, a whole new class of elite emerged out of this struggle, new men whose power was based on their skill with guns, not on tribal connections, ancestry, and such.

Early on, no one gave the Afghan resistance any chance against the Soviets. A few primitives against the Red Army, what were the odds? Virtually every analyst assumed, however, that if the Afghans were to have any chance, any chance at all, they would have to unite. In fact, the strength of the Afghan resistance lay in its disunity. The same problem that had plagued the British in the nineteenth century plagued the Soviets. It wasn't that the foreign superpower couldn't beat any Afghan force it faced. Seen purely in military terms, those few celebrated Afghan victories against the British—at Maiwand, in the Hindu Kush passes between Kabul and Jalalabad—were trivial. The real problem was that those wars dissolved Afghan society into thousands of fragments, every one of them dead set against the British (and now the Soviets) and so the British (and now the Soviets) had no one to beat that would matter, no one to negotiate with whose acquiescence would enable them to govern.

In the grand scheme of things, of course, the fragmentation hurt the Afghans far more than the Soviets. All the consolidation and development the House of Dost Mohammed had achieved between 1826 and 1978 had been wiped away. Akbar Nowrouz, whose father headed up the parliament in the days of Zahir Shah, once remarked, "It will take us 50 years to get back to where we were 50 years ago."[3]

Among the many Mujahideen leaders, a dozen or so were prominent and two stood out dramatically: Ahmad Shah Massoud and Gulbuddin Hekmatyar. Both were young men who had swashed some buckle as sixties' activists during Zahir Shah's tumultuous final decade.

Massoud was a Tajik from Panjsher and thus belonged to the country's second-biggest but traditionally subordinate ethnic group. His family had moved to Kabul when his father was appointed to some minor post in the technocracy. Massoud went to the French-built school Istiqlal, next to the royal palace where the doomed Daoud made his final stand. Much later, I realized that Massoud must have been at Istiqlal at the same time as I, but he was in the sixth grade when I was in the eleventh, so I didn't notice him. After Istiqlal he entered the Polytechnique Institute, a Soviet-built engineering school, but did not finish because he got distracted by politics.

By the time Massoud started college, he was not just a devout politicized Muslim but one who constantly harangued his classmates for neglecting their religious duties, if he saw them eating during Ramadhan, for example, or playing when it was time to pray. Already, he embodied a departure from the easygoing attitude that had typified the old Afghanistan.[4] He was not just a Muslim but an Islamist.

Massoud was a moderate, however, compared to Gulbuddin Hekmatyar. This rebel started at the military academy and then transferred to Kabul University, but politics distracted him from finishing too. He did take a few engineering courses, which led him to ever afterward call himself "Engineer Gulbuddin." Rumor has it that Hekmatyar started his career as a member of the Marxist PDPA, a rumor he and his followers indignantly deny; and, indeed, whatever he may have flirted with in his youth, there can be no doubt that the adult Hekmatyar has staked his life on representing the most radical Islamist extremism. In 1972, Hekmatyar was sent to prison for murdering another student, a supposed Maoist; a few years later, however, a prime minister hoping to curry favor with the Islamist right set him free, whereupon Hekmatyar fled to the safety of Pakistan.

Massoud belonged to a religious party called *Jamiat-i-Islam*—"Islamic Society"—founded by Kabul University theology professor Burhanuddin Rabbani. Even after Massoud became the best-known Afghan resistance leader in the world, he defined himself as a mere member of that party and deferred to Rabbani as his leader. Hekmatyar started out in Jamiat but soon broke away to form his own organization, eventually called *Hezb-i-Islam* or "Party of Islam." Jamiat (The Society) and Hezb (The Party)—these would be the two most significant players in the years of violence that followed.

In 1975, when Daoud was running the country with a cabinet of Communists, Hekmatyar, Massoud, Rabbani, and other Islamists tried to organize a putsch out of Panjsher. They failed, and all had to flee from Daoud's wrath, to Pakistan. That's where they were living five years later, when the Soviets invaded their country. The moment the tanks crossed the border, these men knew their time had come.

Massoud shot back to his home valley of Panjsher to organize resistance, while Rabbani remained in Pakistan to protect the interests of the Jamiat party. In this one case, the guerilla commander in the country and the politician outside the country really were partners joined at the hip.

Hekmatyar also planted himself in Pakistan and only sporadically went into the country to fight alongside his men. He took lobbying, fundraising, and political organizing as his central duties, but somehow he managed to extend his influence to every corner of Afghanistan.

Massoud had been something of a mediocrity among student activists back in the days of marching and speechifying. He wasn't good at that stuff, which could be why he abdicated political leadership to Rabbani. Once he hit the mountains, however, he found his calling. He was, it turned out, a military genius on the order of Che Guevara and Mao Tsetung. Admirers were soon calling him the Lion of Panjsher (*Panjsher* means "Five Lions"). Not only could he set an ambush and shoot down helicopters, but he had a gift for organizing civil life on the fly, administering his community with a gun in one hand and a stone for a pillow. He organized a system, for example, whereby the people of his valley would hide in the hills during the day when the Russians did their bombing and go down to their fields at night to plow, plant, and take care of other rural chores.

In the early eighties, Massoud cobbled together a supervisory council to coordinate the actions of 130 separate guerilla commanders, but, being a Tajik and given the growing ethnic tensions of this period, Massoud could not build much strength among the majority Pushtoons.[5]

Massoud inspired in his followers a loyalty that bordered on religious reverence. Years later, I talked to his close aide Abdullah Abdullah, and, when I asked Dr. Abdullah what he remembered about Massoud, he fell to reminiscing about the warmth Massoud used to radiate when he came home from a hard day of killing Russians to play with the children. Of such stuff are legends made, and of such legends do later generations craft mythological heroes. The truth, it seems, was far more complicated.

In Hekmatyar, however, Massoud faced a formidable rival with assets of his own. Hekmatyar didn't have Massoud's charisma, and he wasn't much of a guerilla warrior; it wasn't his thing. Hekmatyar was (and apparently remains) a brilliant organizer with superb political savvy. I have a hunch Dost Mohammed was a man like this. While Massoud was inspiring adulation in the mountains, Hekmatyar was busy cultivating friends in the ISI. As a result, as much as three-quarters of the money and guns that ISI disbursed went to Hekmatyar. He used this bounty to build Hezb-i-Islam into a powerful, intertribal (though basically Pushtoon) guerilla network, with fighters all over the country and agents in all the Afghan refugee camps on the Pakistan border, where Afghan boys were growing into grim, emotionally disturbed Afghan men.

As the years wore on, even though Jamiat and Hezb both fought the Soviets and their Afghan puppets ferociously, they also fought each other. In fact, Hekmatyar's group acquired a reputation for attacking other Afghans in the resistance. Once, they almost succeeded in killing Massoud. Everyone knew that a showdown was coming someday between these two men.

22

Cold War Endgame

THE INCENDIARY AFGHAN RESPONSE TO THE SOVIET INVASION, THE apocalyptic revolution in Iran, the fall of Bhutto and the triumph of Islamism in Pakistan, the rise of clandestine, antigovernment, anti-Western, revolutionary Islamist cells and parties throughout the Arab world—all these developments presaged a reconfiguration of global tensions along a new fault line. In the Muslim world, not just thinkers and activists but ordinary people in the bazaars were reframing current history as a contest between Islam and the West.

In the West, by contrast, late into the eighties, political analysts still saw global events in terms of a bipolar confrontation between the Soviet camp and an American-led camp. Both sides had nuclear weapons, so neither could attack the other directly, which locked them into that Cold War competition for influence and sometimes proxy wars within the (so-called) Third World.

In 1980, conventional wisdom in the West saw the Soviet Union verging on victory. The American economy seemed moribund, having managed to combine high inflation, stagnation, and high unemployment, a trifecta that economists had previously deemed impossible. Oil prices had skyrocketed, and US president Jimmy Carter had responded by telling Americans to wear sweaters. The pessimism shrouding America inspired the president to go on TV and tell the nation it was suffering from a malaise.[1]

Meanwhile, Castro was clinging to power in Cuba despite all CIA efforts to destroy him. Leftist Sandinistas had taken control of Nicaragua. Leftist guerillas were fighting hard for El Salvador. In Europe, Soviet power had seemingly crushed the dissident Polish labor union Solidarity. The Soviets had installed a new type of nuclear missile, the SS-20, capable of hitting targets in Western Europe. In the Middle East, America had lost its stoutest ally, the Shah of Iran. To make matters worse, a bunch of student-age Iranian activists had seized the American Embassy and taken fifty-two US diplomats hostage—an unprecedented humiliation for a great power like the United States. Now the Soviets were in Afghanistan. Was there no stopping this juggernaut?

Jimmy Carter responded to the Soviet invasion of Afghanistan with the curious declaration known as the Carter Doctrine. He said the United States would regard any Soviet interference in the Persian Gulf as a threat to America's vital interests and act accordingly. In other words, he conceded Afghanistan and moved the goalposts to the Persian Gulf.

His national security advisor Zbigniew Brzezinski took the view that Afghanistan might well prove to be a quagmire for Russia, draining it of blood and treasure in the same way that Vietnam had sapped the United States. He saw Afghanistan as an opportunity to make the Soviets suffer at little cost and no risk to American lives. Brzezinski was not proposing that the United States help the Afghans win, because the idea of an Afghan victory never seems to have crossed Brzezinski's mind. He only thought America could prolong the war and thus make the inevitable Soviet victory as costly as possible.

In retrospect, it's hard to see why the Soviet Union struck such fear and awe into the hearts of people around the globe in 1980. America might have been wobbling a bit, but the Soviet Empire was in its actual death throes. The government had degenerated into a rust-caked bureaucracy that even its own functionaries despised. Its "command economy" couldn't produce anything but megaweapons and industrial machinery—certainly not the seductive consumer goods that Soviet citizens now knew the "Free World" was enjoying in abundance.

Worst of all, the empire had no animating ideal to compensate for the drab grind of daily life. Communism had fulfilled this function once upon a time, but Communism had lost credibility even in the Communist world, where it now lacked the power to inspire even Communists. Brezhnev was a sick old man, unable to rule but impossible to get rid of. The Soviet political establishment was just waiting for him to die but had no charismatic visionary waiting in the wings to replace him. When Brezhnev did finally expire in 1982, power passed to Yuri Andropov, about whom little was known because, as head of the KGB, it was his business to be little known. Already an ill old man, Andropov died within fifteen months of his ascension, to be succeeded by an even more colorless politburo cog, Konstantin Chernenko, another ill old man who lasted less than a year. This was the country that was, to Western eyes, winning the Cold War and might soon (cue evil laughter) rule the world.

Yet, because the Soviet Union did still project so much menace, Ronald Reagan was able to win the 1980 presidential election by campaigning as a cowboy. He called the Soviet Union "the evil empire."[2] He vowed to stand up to it as his hand-wringing predecessor Jimmy Carter had not done. Afghanistan (and Iran) gave Reagan a decisive cudgel with which to beat Carter about the head and shoulders. Afghanistan served Reagan especially well because it had become a cause célèbre among old-guard anti-Communists on the Right, one of Reagan's key constituencies. Political activists on the Right, who knew little about Islamism (or Islam for that matter), lauded the Afghan Mujahideen as glamorous freedom fighters, seeing them only as anti-Communists.

After the election, Reagan had to back up his macho campaign image with some real action. I don't mean to imply that it had all been for show. Reagan surely meant what he said. To gain advantage in the Cold War, he did not hesitate to use nuclear brinkmanship. He put Pershing missiles in Germany, close enough to bomb Moscow, and grinned amiably at the Soviet squawking that resulted. He threatened to build a defensive shield that would render Soviet nuclear missiles irrelevant. His Strategic Defense Initiative (popularly known as the "Star Wars" defense) jolted nuclear policy experts, for it violated the core formula of Mutual Assured Destruction upon which the Cold War stalemate (and global stability) was based: neither side could afford to use nuclear weapons because it would result in the destruction of both. If the United States achieved immunity from Soviet nuclear attack, the United States could attack the Soviet Union with impunity. If the Soviets saw this outcome as imminent, they might launch a pre-emptive strike. Reagan flashed his avuncular grin and reckoned he'd take that risk.

The Star Wars defense might not have been viable, but the Soviets could not afford to dismiss it. They had to pour enormous sums they could ill afford to develop new nuclear weapons that would keep them in the arms race.

As a gesture of macho strength, however, the Star Wars initiative was a bit abstract, even for those who approved. To really back up his ten-gallon stance, Reagan had to bull up to the line of scrimmage in the real-time US/Soviet confrontations of the day. One such spot was Nicaragua; another was Afghanistan.

For the Reagan administration, Nicaragua was the main item on the agenda. There, the administration promoted right-wing rebels called the Contras, who eventually did bring down the first Sandinista government. The Reagan administration also opened the tap to let guns and money flow a bit more freely to the Mujahideen. It was only a few tens of millions, but it was more than the Carter team had contemplated spending.

As always, all this Cold War pushing and posturing had implications for Afghanistan. In 1985, the Soviet Union finally got a dynamic younger man at the helm, but Mikhail Gorbachev had inherited a sinking ship. Reagan's initiatives had forced the Soviets to risk spending themselves to death. Gorbachev knew he would have to scale back the military and shrink his country's foreign commitments, or the country was doomed. So he launched several policies. One was *perestroika*, which gave the market a role in the Soviet economy. Another was *glasnost*, which allowed Soviet citizens some limited freedom of expression. The West applauded Gorbachev as a heroic reformer.

The Soviet chief also met with Reagan to discuss some way of reducing nuclear tensions, and their conversations led to real progress. Reagan reaped the rewards in domestic acclaim, but Gorbachev won some applause as a peacemaker too (except among right-wing evangelical Christians who saw the birthmark on his forehead as a sign that he was the Antichrist).[3]

Gorbachev probably did deserve some praise, but, for Afghanistan, his advent initially brought untold horror. Gorbachev thought the invasion had been a mistake, and he wanted to get the Afghan albatross off the Soviet neck; but, instead of ordering an immediate and unilateral withdrawal, he told his generals to win the war as quickly as possible by any means necessary. Like Richard Nixon, who had sought "peace with honor"[4] in Vietnam, Gorbachev wanted to get out of Afghanistan with at least the appearance of a victory: he couldn't afford to look weak going into the sensitive nuclear negotiations he had set in motion.

The Soviet military stepped up its bombing and flew more sorties than ever, up and down the narrow valleys of Afghanistan, shooting peasants from their deadly helicopter gunships. The first year of Gorbachev's tenure proved to be the bloodiest, most horrific period of the war in Afghanistan. It was in this year that the Soviet military adopted its genocidal plan to depopulate the Afghan countryside as its strategy for victory. In this year, Soviet carpet bombing laid irreparable waste to that universe of tribal village republics that was the old Afghanistan. It was then that the Afghan refugee population in Pakistan and Iran, already vast, swelled past six million—and Afghanistan *had* only twenty million people when the war began. In an age of refugees, Afghans became the world's largest refugee population. The destruction of Afghanistan did not come at the hands of a mighty superpower at the arrogant height of its power: Afghanistan was destroyed by a dying dragon flailing its spiked tail in its final agony.

With the flames rising ever higher in Afghanistan, elements in the United States defense and intelligence establishments began to glimpse the astonishing possibility of an actual Afghan victory. In Congress, Senator Gordon Humphrey, Congressman Don Ritter, and others lobbied for the Afghan cause. Reagan adopted an advisor for Afghan affairs, an Afghan expatriate educated at the American University of Beirut, Zalmay Khalilzad. Texas congressman Charlie Wilson, who chaired the House Appropriations Committee, embraced the Afghan cause and, together with allies in Congress and the CIA, managed to triple the (secret) US funding for the Mujahideen. What's more, he convinced the Saudis to match whatever the United States contributed. By 1987, the Mujahideen were receiving a billion dollars a year from the United States—almost all of it coming through the ISI pipeline, of course—and that much again from the Saudis.

Then Wilson and his allies happened upon a landmark insight. They figured out exactly what type of weapon the Afghan resistance needed: something the guerillas could hand-carry into the hills and use to shoot down helicopters.

No such weapon existed yet, so Wilson and a self-appointed Afghan task force within the CIA set to work to get it invented. With technical help from the Israelis and logistical help from Egypt, they came up with the surface-to-air missile known as the Stinger, a heat-seeking rocket fired from a long pipe that two men could carry and one man could shoot. It wasn't much, but it was enough.

On September 25, 1986, Hezb-i-Islam commander Abdul Ghaffar (Engineer Abdul Ghaffar, he called himself) fired the first of the Stingers at a Soviet helicopter landing at the Jalalabad airport. The moment it hit its mark, the war was effectively over. A lot of bombs would still fall, a lot of lives would still be lost, but the economics of the thing was decisive. By the summer of 1987, according to ISI reports, Afghans were hitting one or two aircraft a day with these weapons. A Stinger cost less than $40,000 to produce. A helicopter gunship cost more than $10 million. Do the math. The CIA provided the Mujahideen with more than five hundred Stingers, and perhaps as many as twenty-five hundred. (British and Chinese versions of this weapon soon began reaching the Mujahideen as well.)[5] Financially, the doddering Soviet Union simply could not fight a war on such unequal terms—losing $10 million at a pop to guerillas armed with little more than huge shotguns. Gorbachev knew he would have to get his troops out of Afghanistan as soon as possible in any way he could—peace and honor be damned.

The first step was to get rid of Babrak Karmal. His stewardship had been an unmitigated disaster. In his place, the Soviets installed the director of KhAD, Dr. Najibullah, a big brute commonly known as "the Ox" because of his heavily muscled weightlifter's body. Najib had his instructions: he was to quit pushing Communism, negotiate with the Mujahideen, establish a coalition government, and build a broad base of domestic support. If only he could succeed in this, the Soviets would be able to get out with a clear conscience.

Najib tried, he really did. He tried everything he could. He changed the name of KhAD to WAD, but everyone knew it was the same old dreaded secret police. He renamed the PDPA the "Fatherland Party," but no one started singing patriotic anthems. He had a new constitution written declaring Afghanistan an Islamic republic and guaranteeing the freedom of all citizens, but no one believed him. He started building mosques and religious schools. He called for national reconciliation. He offered cabinet positions to selected Mujahideen leaders. He even offered to step down if certain conditions were met.

The plan might have worked—ten years earlier. But in the late eighties, too much blood had flowed under the bridge. The longtime chief of Parcham's secret police was never going to convince Afghans he was a Muslim nationalist interested only in restoring the values of Old Afghanistan. The Mujahideen cleaned their guns and moved closer to the city.

The United Nations had launched peace talks in Geneva near the very beginning of the war. All these years, representatives of various countries had been trudging to Geneva and dutifully talking. In 1987, however, Gorbachev announced that the Soviets would begin withdrawing their troops the following year, come hell or high water in Afghanistan. That year, in Geneva, the Soviets tried to secure some agreements from Pakistan and the United States. They wanted some guarantees about the borders; they wanted the United States to promise it would stop supplying antigovernment forces with military aid; they wanted the world to accept a hands-off-Afghanistan policy. No one was in a mood to concede a thing, and the Soviet Union was in no position to press its points because its dissolution was picking up pace.

In 1988, the first Soviet troops did come home from Afghanistan. All that year the trickle of withdrawal continued; meanwhile, however, from the Soviet and global point of view, bigger things were happening. The Baltic states, Estonia, Latvia, and Lithuania, formed popular fronts to oppose their own local Communist parties. Demonstrations broke out in Armenia, and then in Azerbaijan, and then in Georgia. The collapse of the empire had begun.

In February 1989, Soviet commander Colonel Boris Gromov became the last Soviet soldier to leave Afghanistan when he walked across the Termez Bridge to Uzbekistan. The Soviet withdrawal was complete, but few noticed because by then world attention was fixated on the wave of revolutions sweeping through Eastern Europe. It began when Gorbachev, on a visit to Poland, repudiated the Brezhnev Doctrine and announced a new Soviet policy of noninterference in the affairs of other independent nations. Officially, these included the Soviet satellites in Eastern Europe. In Poland, Solidarity forced elections—and won them.

Hungary then held free parliamentary elections and changed from the People's Republic of Hungary to just plain Republic of Hungary. The grim regime in East Germany tried but failed to stop thousands of its citizens from escaping to the West. Hard-line East German ruler Erich Honecker was deposed, and in November the people of East Berlin began to tear down the wall separating them from the Western half of the city. Symbolically, that moment marked the end of the Cold War and of the Soviet empire. I can't think of another time in history when such a gigantic empire came to an end so abruptly and so decisively. By New Year's Eve 1989, all the Soviet satellites had broken away. In the year that followed, the various republics that formed the core country—the Soviet Union itself—began to declare their independence. When Russia declared its independence in 1991, the end had come: there was nothing left to gain independence *from*.

23

From Horror
to Chaos

THESE DRAMATIC EVENTS LEFT NAJIBULLAH STRANDED AS THE LAST
Communist ruler of Afghanistan. He was still struggling to cobble together a compromise with the Mujahideen, but he was playing poker with
a deck of Crazy Eights. With the Soviets gone, Najib the Ox had no one
to depend on but himself. He did still have the awesome arsenal the Soviets had left behind, and Kabul was a garrison, so he dug in for the next
year and five months, while the guerillas came closing in.

At that moment, as Kabul University economist Dr. Shams pointed
out,[1] Afghanistan had close to 300,000 battle-tested men in arms—perhaps
100,000 in the national army and about 180,000 fighting for the Mujahideen. It also had jet bombers, tanks, heavy artillery, as many as a thousand Stingers[2] still unused, more than one machine gun for every man,
woman, and child, and enough ammo to last for years. Had Najibullah and
the Mujahideen come together to form one unified government, Afghanistan would instantly have become the most powerful state in the region.

There was no chance of that happening, of course. Najibullah fought
like a dog but couldn't keep the wolves at bay. His army defected to his
enemies in chunks. The heaviest hit of all came in April 1992, when one
of his key allies, an Uzbek army officer named Rashid Dostum, joined
forces with Tajik commander Ahmad Shah Massoud. Dostum had started
out as a labor union boss in the days before the Communists took over,

but after the 1978 coup he enlisted in the army and worked his way up the ranks. During those years, he built a disciplined corps of Uzbek soldiers loyal directly to him, an army within the national army. In the last days of the Soviet occupation, he had more than thirty thousand and perhaps as many as fifty thousand men fighting for him (on behalf of the Soviets).[3] His subsequent career shows, however, that he wasn't really a Parchami or a Khalqi, nor did he belong to any other ideological category. He was a two-fisted, hard-drinking nonideological secular pirate of a man whose religion was political realism and whose program was survival.

At this crucial moment in 1992, with Najibullah and the Mujahideen locked into a standoff, Dostum saw his chance to multiply his leverage. When he switched sides, taking his private army with him, it was game, set, and match for the Ox. By the end of April, tens of thousands of guerillas had moved into position on the slopes surrounding Kabul. The city was about to fall—but not to any single group. Those thousands of guerillas in the hills represented no fewer than eleven different armies.

On the evening of April 16, 1992, Massoud called Hekmatyar on a satellite phone. Their conversation was recorded, and a scratchy tape of it is still kicking around on the Internet.[4] Massoud can be heard saying to Hekmatyar, "We should talk. I'm concerned about this Sunday. There might be trouble; because when one side enters, all the other armies and forces will enter too. The chaos that will result, the wreckage that will result—hits and blows among the Mujahideen—I want to lift these concerns by sitting down with you and your followers, let's work out something, establish an acceptable government, and then we'll proceed toward elections. It would be better to take these steps now, instead of getting to the stage where we're settling things by force. It would be better if you would promise me that on this coming Sunday—"

Hekmatyar interrupts. "There won't be any trouble. So long as the situation that develops does not require our men, our followers, our Mujahideen to take action, we probably won't resort to aggression at this time."

"You say no trouble will erupt, but I assure you," says Massoud, "severe trouble will erupt if we don't take some steps. We are not afraid. Everything depends on you and your followers—"

"I've heard your words," Hekmatyar cuts in, "and I have told you my intentions."

"Are you telling me you will certainly attack on Sunday? Should I prepare?"

"Prepare for what?"

"Prepare to defend the people of Kabul, the women of Kabul, the men of Kabul, the young and old of Kabul," Massoud exclaims. "Prepare to defend this cruelly wounded nation, these people who by God every day call for refuge and plead to know what their future holds. I tell you, I take it as my duty to defend these people against every form of attack to the limits of my ability."

Then static comes up and the conversation ends.

The next day, the various armies began filtering into the city. Najibullah and his brother left the royal palace in their chauffeured vehicle, headed for the airport. There, by prior arrangement, a United Nations plane was waiting to fly them to India. But Dostum knew of the plan and locked down the airport. No planes would be leaving that day.

When Najibullah saw the roadblock, he had his chauffeur hang a U-turn and drive him directly to the United Nations headquarters, which granted the men political asylum. The Mujahideen respected this asylum: as long as Najib and his associates stayed in that UN building in the center of the city, they were safe—but only in that building. So there they stayed for the next four years. Their "political asylum" was indistinguishable from prison, except that they could order takeout and get all the Bollywood movies they could watch.

The Mujahideen had cobbled together a loose plan for an Afghan Interim Government (AIG) when they were still in Pakistan. According to this plan, the relatively insignificant Subghatullah Mujaddedi, head of the smallest of the seven main Islamist parties in Peshawar, would start out as president. After two months, he would step down, and Burhanuddin Rabbani would take over for four months. Then he would step down and elections would be held. Ahmad Shah Massoud, whom many in the Western media saw as the face of the resistance, would merely be minister of defense (although this was, of course, *the* key post). Each Peshawar party of any significance would get at least one cabinet position. Hekmatyar, the other major figure, would be prime minister.

Hekmatyar refused the title. "Prime minister" was too small for him. He headed up the biggest party, Hezb-i-Islam, he felt he should head up the whole government, and his sponsor ISI was determined not to let him slip into a junior role, for they had Hekmatyar chalked in as the man through whom Pakistan would take control of Afghanistan. He simply *had* to be the top guy.

After Rabbani took over the presidency, Hekmatyar did grudgingly accept the post of prime minister but still refused to come into the city. If the cabinet had to meet, he insisted that it come to a building just outside the city and meet with *him*.

Almost immediately after the new government was in place, chaos broke out, just as Massoud had predicted; but Massoud, it should be noted, was among the architects of this chaos. He took action when *Hezb-i-Wahdat*, a supergroup representing all the various parties of the Hazara ethnic group, claimed southwestern Kabul, where the Hazaras mostly lived. Massoud would have none of this. He made common cause with Abdul Rasool Sayyaf, an Arab-backed Pushtoon warlord. Sayyaf's army held the territory southwest of the Hazaras. Massoud occupied the territory northeast of them. Between their two armies, Massoud and Sayyaf had the Hazaras in pincers.

But the Hazaras fought back ferociously. The fallout was horrific: looting, rape, and murder rose to a crescendo amid gun battles and bombardment. My cousin Zaheda lived at the western edge of the city when these battles began. She later recounted how a contingent of Hazaras burst into her compound and commandeered it for use as a military post. Zaheda and her family scurried out and made their way to my uncle Asef's house, deeper inside the city, which was abandoned because my uncle had fled to America.

Here, Zaheda told me, things were quiet at first, although one could hear occasional gunfire in the distance. Then it seemed the shots were ringing out a little closer, but it was hard to tell. Then they seemed to be sounding more frequently, but it was hard to judge. Then gunfire was definitely close and constant, but Zaheda and her family could not now leave the compound—it was too dangerous. They should have left then, however, because leaving was still possible. They only realized this later when leaving had become even more dangerous; for, instead of fading away, the battle grew hotter. Bullets were zinging into the yard, shells were coming over the wall—they had to retreat into the house.

But then shells started hitting the windows, and they had to retreat to a windowless storeroom in the deep interior, where they had raw onions and potatoes to eat, but no water. Every night, therefore, under cover of darkness, Zaheda's husband went out to get water from a well in the yard. One night a piece of shrapnel hit him, and he crawled back bleeding. The wound was not critical; Zaheda cauterized it with burning cotton soaked in rubbing alcohol; but that moment tipped her into a freak-out. "If we don't get out of here right now, we're going to die in this house," she said.

So she put on all her jewelry, an Afghan woman's portable wealth, and the family bundled together all the money they had, and as soon as there was a lull in the gunfire, they stepped out of the compound. The street was littered with corpses. At the end of the block, they saw a Hazara teenager with a cigarette in one hand and a machine gun in the other. He would take a puff, fire a few rounds at the hills, take another puff, fire another round. Every time he shot at the slopes, Massoud's forces, dug into the mountain, would fire back.

My cousin yelled to the boy to *please* stop shooting for a few minutes, so they could get away. He shrugged and complied, and they got to the river and made their way along the banks to a safer neighborhood where they knew a man who would take them in.

For people who lived in Kabul between 1992 and 1996, my cousin's experience was typical. News reports record the struggle for that city as a series of battles punctuated by periods of calm, but for residents it might as well have been one continuous stream of carnage: more than sixty thousand people were killed, and perhaps five times that many fled to the countryside, ending up as IDPs or "internally displaced persons," which is what refugees are called when they don't make it out of the country. Rashid Dostum, who kept switching sides and was allied to every other major figure at some point or another, perpetrated some of the bloodiest battles. The Hazaras took a vicious battering but—let's face it—dealt it out just as savagely. Sayyaf, Massoud—all ended up with blood on their hands.

By all accounts, however, the author of the greatest, most inexcusable bloodshed was Engineer Gulbuddin Hekmatyar. As soon as his rival Massoud established himself in Kabul, Hekmatyar dug into a suburb some miles away and, from there, hit the city relentlessly with rockets. In one two-day period (August 10–11, 1992), he fired over a thousand rockets into Kabul. He claimed to be aiming at particular targets, but since he didn't have the technology to aim his rockets precisely, his claim couldn't be true. Also, firing from a stronghold several miles outside the city as he was, he couldn't have known where his bombs were landing, even if he could have aimed them. The rockets came in at the rate of two or three a minute some days, hitting random spots and killing whoever happened to be standing where they landed.

The Soviets had destroyed the Afghan countryside; now Afghans themselves destroyed the cities. The Mujahideen reduced nearly half of Kabul to rubble. Kandahar fragmented into gangland chaos. The civil war took on an ethnic cast, which planted resentments that will be difficult to erase, for, although few remember or even know which particular *person* killed their loved ones, they know and will long remember which *ethnic group* committed the crime.

As the carnage was ripping apart the cities, warlords were fighting to solidify holdings in the countryside. Hundreds carved out tiny semi-sovereign domains of their own. Numerous checkpoints sprouted up on what remained of the roads. At each checkpoint, some local strongman collected tolls from travelers happening by. The few goods that made it into the shops cost more than most people could pay. Poverty became endemic. Starvation loomed. Such was the final legacy of the Soviet invasion of Afghanistan.

24

Out of the Camps

DIRECTLY AFTER THE SOVIET WITHDRAWAL OF 1989, THE UNITED States and its allies might have called their clients together to work out a framework for a stable post-Communist government. There's no telling whether it would have worked, but at least, at that moment, the United States had some leverage with both Pakistan and the Mujahideen.

It was then, however, that Afghanistan dropped off the US foreign policy view screen. Global politics drew US attention elsewhere. Afghanistan had been a Cold War battlefield, and the Cold War was over. It didn't officially end until 1991, but it was over effectively as soon as the Soviet Empire went into its final throes. The fall of the Soviet Empire was the defining political earthquake of the early nineties, whose aftershocks monopolized Western policy and punditry for the bulk of the decade. In 1991, when aides briefed President George H. W. Bush on a new outbreak of fighting in Kabul, he said, "Is that thing still going on?"[1]

Actually, for the United States, the trouble in Afghanistan was just beginning. Crucial ingredients of this trouble started to form during the Afghan-Soviet War. In that period, some 3.5 million Afghans fled to Pakistan and almost that many to Iran. The refugees lived along the border in huge camps such as Shamshatoo near Peshawar and Hazara Town near

Quetta. These camps were invariably situated outside cities to mitigate friction between the refugees and Pakistan's own citizens. The refugees were not allowed to seek jobs because they would be taking employment away from Pakistani citizens. They were not allowed to start businesses because they would be competing with Pakistanis. They were welcome to huddle in the camps, safe from Soviet bombing, but not to build new lives. Food and water were delivered to them, courtesy of the United Nations; the food consisting mainly of oil, flour, sugar, salt, and tea. All the refugees had to do was nothing.

In general, these camps were surrounded by wire-topped fences that made them feel a bit like open-air prisons. Each camp had a gate manned by the Pakistani military. I visited some of these camps in 2002 and was amazed to find them filled with children. Every kid I talked to in the alleys of Nasir Bagh claimed to have ten or twelve siblings. Camp officials told me then that three-quarters of the population was under fifteen years of age. Hundreds of thousands of teenage boys were cooped up in these camps with no outlet for their restless teenage energy and nothing but horror to build memories around.

The boys did, however, have one escape hatch from the boredom. They could go to a madrassa. Hundreds of such schools were built by Pakistani clerics, and they were controlled by Pakistan's powerful right-wing Islamist parties such as *Jamiat-i-Ulama-Islam* (The Society of Muslim Scholars), parties closely connected to ISI. Many of the schools got funding from wealthy Saudi Arabians intent on promoting the doctrines of their country's Wahhabi sect, the most rigidly puritanical, fundamentalist, and politicized Islamic reform movement to come out of the Arab world in the eighteenth century. The Wahhabi establishment was, in turn, intimately connected through marriage and tradition to the ruling elite of Saudi Arabia, and they had been proselytizing vigorously in recent decades—but not among non-Muslims. They weren't interested in converting non-Muslims to Islam; they wanted to convert Muslims to *their* brand of Islam. Official records list more than two thousand of these madrassas in the eighteen districts near the border, with a total enrollment of nearly 220,000 students.[2] No one knows how many more were unlisted.

Afghan boys were welcome to enroll in these schools for free, and they even got room and board, provided they put themselves entirely in the hands of their teachers. Once they entered a madrassa, refugee boys were pretty much cut off from alternative sources of news and information about the world. And their teachers here didn't just teach religion. One official report to the prime minister of Pakistan named about a hundred madrassas that were also teaching combat skills. The actual number was probably higher than the official count.[3]

Mostly, however, what the religious teachers gave their captive audiences was a narrative. They told the wide-eyed refugee boys about a perfection that had existed just once in history, during the lifetime of Prophet Mohammed, at Medina. For one generation, they explained, a whole community had lived in absolute obedience to the laws of God Almighty and that obedience had made them mighty, because God accompanied the original Muslims into every battle, and against God, no force could stand. This was not wild-eyed raving; it's pretty much the standard core of the Muslim narrative. The context was what made it volatile.

Also, in recent years, the Muslim world had been awash with expectations of an apocalyptic battle coming up between God's people and the devil's, and this narrative came to permeate the camps and madrassas. Religious teachers preached that the rebirth of the perfect community would mark the beginning of the battle. Yes, if only some group of Muslims would live as the people of Prophet-guided Medina had lived—by those exact rules, by that code—the world would be saved. Boys who were suffering through the worst childhood on earth were allowed to imagine that it might be *their* destiny to establish the community that would save the world.

There will always be some dispute about the role that the Pakistan government played in all this. They were creating the cadre of the future Taliban, but did they know this? Was Pakistan consciously building an army to send swarming into Afghanistan someday? Public records provide no answer. The deliberate calculations, if any, were made behind closed doors.

One thing is certain. Pakistan had interests to advance in Afghanistan, interests shaped by factors, forces, and considerations beyond Afghanistan itself. Yes, once again, global forces were moving into position to do battle for big prizes, and once again Afghanistan was situated exactly where those forces would come crashing into each other.

IN PRESIDENT CLINTON'S FIRST TERM, HIS SECRETARY OF STATE, WARREN Christopher, never mentioned Afghanistan in his public speeches, not even once.[4] Christopher's diplomatic energies were focused mostly on Eastern Europe, and quite reasonably so; for it was here that the Soviet collapse produced the most violent repercussions. Here, the "stability" forged by Communism unraveled most drastically as nation-states dissolved into warring "nationalities" determined to settle old scores. Serbs fought Croatians, Croatians battled Bosnians, Macedonians Serbians, and Kosovans Macedonians. As each group tried to rid its territory of other groups, the term "ethnic cleansing" entered the lexicon of human shame. No wonder so much of the world's attention focused on Eastern Europe.

But the aftershocks of the Soviet collapse rippled to the eastern frontiers of the former empire with equally momentous implications, although these went more unnoticed at first. The former Soviet Socialist Republics of central Asia—Kazakhstan, Kyrgyzstan, Turkmenistan, Uzbekistan, and Tajikistan—had been joined only uneasily to European Russia. Once Moscow's power evaporated, trace memories of an earlier culture, long submerged by European Communism, began to re-emerge.

All of these countries (except Tajikistan) had been inhabited by Turkish-speaking ethnic groups since ancient times. All (including Tajikistan) had once been an integral part of the Muslim world. When the Soviet Union collapsed, bureaucratic inertia transformed the top Communist officials into newfangled dictators. They didn't rule as Communists anymore, just as strongmen offering their people posters and statues of themselves and national holidays commemorating their own birthdays in place of something, anything, to believe in. No wonder Islam began to rise again here. It was the one indigenous spiritual idea that promised to provide some cohesive social meaning.

And because post-Soviet central Asia was in such cultural flux, it looked like it might be up for grabs politically. Turkey took an interest, for, after all, wasn't a pan-Turkic state stretching from Istanbul to China a plausible vision? Iran's whiskers began to twitch, for, after all, didn't several major empires of classical times include both Iran and the Turkish steppes? Never mind that Persia was a conquered province in those em-pires, and the conquerors were Turks.

Above all, Pakistan saw seductive possibilities in the reconfiguration of central Asia. Throughout its brief history, Pakistan had been a fragile country wedged between a hostile Afghanistan and a hostile India. Central Asia looked like an escape hatch because there as elsewhere Islamism came flowing in as Communism ebbed out, and Islam, as it happened, was the fundamental political and ideological premise of Pakistan, the one theme that provided social cohesion to Pakistan's disparate parts. Also, no matter what Turkey and Iran might feel, ancient trade, traffic, and con-quest through central Asia had flowed just as vigorously north and south as it had east and west. Never mind that the traffic had consisted largely of central Asian horsemen thundering south to sack the cities of the plains. There *was* a historical connection between central Asia and south Asia, and Islam might be the cultural solvent that could meld them into one again.

To Pakistan, this prospect looked especially promising because Sunni Islam was the dominant sect in both central Asia and Pakistan. Iranians by contrast were Shi'as, who had been at odds with Sunnis for fourteen centuries, so they looked to have no real chance of enlarging their influ-ence in central Asia. As for Turkey, it was so far away. If Pakistan could get some trade links going with central Asia, it might build a loose Sunni Muslim co-prosperity sphere directed from Islamabad that would have the power to confront both India and Iran on equal terms. If that hap-pened, Pakistan might end up as the greatest power in the region and the predominant country in the Muslim world!

There was just one problem with this vision: any trade route between Pakistan and central Asia would have to run through Afghanistan. Some-thing would have to be done about Afghanistan.

———

THE SOVIET COLLAPSE WAS NOT THE ONLY FACTOR FRAMING GLOBAL politics in the nineties. Even before the Cold War officially ended, the first salvo had been fired in a new set of wars that political scientist Michael Klare has dubbed "resource wars."

The core resource at issue was petroleum. Oil politics had reared its ugly head in the seventies when the Organization of Arab Petroleum Exporting Countries suddenly cut production in order to punish Western industrial powers for supporting Israel. Their embargo tripled the price of oil in a single year, driving the Western world into a recession. The oil embargo of 1974 sounded a warning: oil was clout. By the time the Cold War ended, the demand for oil had only risen, what with the world population growing by almost a billion people and industrialism spreading throughout the "Third World."[5]

In 1990, Iraqi dictator Saddam Hussein suddenly annexed his neighbor Kuwait, thereby gaining control of the second- or perhaps third-largest oil reserves in the world. Only Saudi Arabia (and possibly Iran) had more. With his armies massed on Kuwait's far borders, Hussein seemed poised to take over Saudi Arabia as well. He certainly had a big enough army.

But Saudi Arabia had an asset of its own: a big friend. US president George Bush declared of Iraq's invasion, "This will not stand." His administration forged a coalition of thirty-eight nations and got United Nations approval for a war. The coalition landed 850,000 troops on Saudi soil to fight Hussein.[6] The war began on January 17, 1991, and lasted forty-two days. The US and its partners hit Iraq with eighty-five thousand[7] tons of bombs, Saddam's army broke like a rotten reed, and his troops—mostly miserable draftees—fled back toward the city of Baghdad, with coalition jets shooting them from the air. The coalition sustained 358 casualties in that war, Iraq as many as 100,000.[8] Bush then declared an abrupt cease-fire that left Saddam Hussein in place.

That (first) Gulf War dramatized what everybody already knew: the world's oil came so predominantly from the Persian Gulf that a handful of countries around this body of water—Iran, Iraq, Saudi Arabia, Kuwait, and a few of the United Arab Emirates—could hold the whole industrialized world hostage. The stability of the world required that oil and gas sources be diversified, and because the competition for oil was sure to grow more desperate as supplies shrank, the major industrial powers had to think strategically about retaining access to whatever new oil was tapped.

In the 1990s, geologists calculated that more than 50 percent of the world's proven petroleum reserves lay in the Persian Gulf region, but that oil was being pumped vigorously and draining fast. The second-greatest known reserves were thought to lie in the Caspian Sea basin, from which oil had hardly been tapped.[9] This region included Turkmenistan, Kazakhstan, and Uzbekistan, the very countries that Pakistan, Iran, and Turkey were eying hungrily. As the Persian Gulf oil diminished, the oil and gas of the Caspian Basin would become ever more precious.

How could the industrialized West take delivery of this oil? There were three options. One: a pipeline could be built directly to Western Europe from the Caspian Basin, but it would have to pass through thousands of miles of the former Soviet Empire, and Russia would certainly impose prohibitive tariffs. Beyond Russia lay strife-torn Eastern Europe, where the pipeline would have to cross many national borders, no doubt incurring fees and duties at every one; and heaven help the world if one of those unstable countries should go up in flames. So option one looked dubious.

Option two: the oil could be piped to ports on the Persian Gulf, which were already set up to ship oil. In that case, however, the pipeline would pass right through Iran, giving *that* country a stranglehold over the future of the industrial world, and this was unacceptable to the United States because Americans still saw Iran as their number one enemy (and vice versa).

That left option three: a pipeline could be run directly from Turkmenistan to Pakistan. From ports like Karachi on the Arabian Sea, tankers could take the oil anywhere in the world. Option three would be the shortest pipeline of the three. The United States certainly favored this option, because Pakistan was a long-standing ally. Pakistan, of course, favored it, not just for economic reasons but because the pipeline would give Pakistan real leverage in world politics. Add the pipeline to the possibility of building a Sunni Muslim entity stretching from Pakistan to Kyrgyzstan, and wow: the future looked exhilarating!

There was just one problem with option three. The pipeline would have to go through Afghanistan.

On the face of it, building a pipeline through explosive, anarchic Afghanistan seemed . . . what's the word I'm searching for? Insane. But after

The Pipeline Proposal

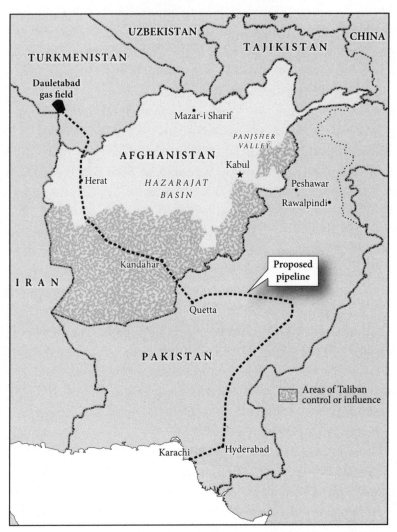

you considered the other options, Afghanistan didn't look so bad. It was just one country, after all. Surely, one country could be tamed, no matter how chaotic it was. Pakistan, in short, had a huge stake in stabilizing and controlling Afghanistan. And ISI had long worked to put the pieces in place to achieve this exact goal. The key to the plan was their factotum Engineer Gulbuddin Hekmatyar. ISI had hoped he would emerge as the undisputed boss of Afghanistan.

Hekmatyar, however, disappointed his sponsors. First of all, he couldn't match up to Massoud as a warrior. He rained death on Kabul but couldn't gain an inch of territory. Also, he couldn't form a coalition government with any of the other Mujahideen leaders. No one trusted him. Even when he negotiated a cease-fire, he himself broke it. Worst of all, he proved unable to win over the masses of Afghan people.

On this score, it must be said, none of the other rebel leaders was doing much better. Every one of them was losing popularity fast. In fact, the Mujahideen as a whole were forfeiting credibility as saviors because wherever they took over they plunged into looting, raping, killing, and fighting one another.

Finally, some movers and shakers in Pakistan began to think ISI was backing the wrong horse. One such figure was Pakistan's interior minister, Major General (Retired) Naseerullah Babar. Even within ISI, some were losing faith. The doubters started looking for an alternative, and their gaze fell upon a little group just then getting organized in the city of Kandahar.

In 1994, these activists were not known as "the Taliban" or as anything else. "Getting organized" might be an exaggeration. They were hardly a group, just a handful of youngsters who had been through the cauldron of the war together and hung around with a slightly older man named Mullah Omar. They revered Omar and helped him carry out audacious actions he sometimes cooked up to protect local people from thugs.

Omar was about thirty years old at this time. He had joined a Hezb-i-Islam splinter group as a teenager and spent most of his adult life fighting. He had lost his left eye fighting the Communists, a badge of pride. After the Soviet withdrawal, he turned his weapons over to a senior commander and entered a madrassa, an Islamic seminary, to get some religious learning. That's when people started calling him "Mullah."

Like many Afghans, Mullah Omar got disillusioned with his former comrades in arms. He began cursing them as traitors to the faith and as criminals under the Shari'a. His daring denunciations won him a following among men his own age or younger, most of whom were or had been students at madrassas. The Arab word for student is *talib*, the plural of which is *taliban*, so this term was not the name of a party or a movement, originally. It merely described what Mullah Omar and his companions were: students.

Legend has it that sometime in the spring of 1994, the Prophet Mohammed appeared to Mullah Omar in a dream, offered him his cloak, and asked him to save the Muslim people. A few days later, the story goes, Omar heard about a particularly horrible crime in his neighborhood: some brutal Mujahid gangster had kidnapped two girls for himself and his men to rape. Mullah Omar told his followers to do something about it, and they did. Not only did they rescue the girls, they hanged the rapist from the gun barrel of his own tank as a warning to evildoers: there was a new sheriff in town.

I say "legend has it" because this story might be apocryphal. I know of no evidence that it was told at the time. This and many similar stories were told later, and often, when the Taliban were developing an image of themselves as incorruptible knights of Islamic piety and disseminating this image to the public—an image that, it must be said, they undoubtedly believed to be true.

Even if the stories were apocryphal, those young men must have been doing something to impress the locals, because they caught the eye of important people in Pakistan. Colonel Imam, ISI's man in Herat, contacted Omar and began to work with him. Pakistan's general consul in Kandahar (also an ISI man) helped out. Pakistan's interior minister, General Naseerullah Babar, looked on approvingly.[10] Pakistan's Frontier Corps (a militia run by the Interior Ministry) began to provide Mullah Omar's boys with military training. By October, they were ready to be tested.

Babar ordered that a convoy of trucks loaded with seductive merchandise enter Afghanistan and attempt to cross it. He wanted to see if the truck could make it all the way through this warlord-infested territory to Turkmenistan. If it could, Pakistan could open a trade route with central Asia, Pakistani products could flow north, and oil could flow south.

Sure enough, near Kandahar, a gang of warlords hijacked the convoy and stole the merchandise. Then—a contingent of two hundred well-armed young men swooped down from the hills, fought a two-day battle with the hijackers, beat the hell out of them, hanged their leaders, and restored the merchandise to its rightful owners.[11] The Taliban had arrived! The fact that some of the fighters spoke Urdu, the lingua franca of Pakistan, was noted at the time but not much discussed. The big story was Mullah Omar and his band of mirthless men. General Babar liked what he saw! He gave the go-ahead for Mullah Omar's Taliban to be developed into a real force, and it was then that the legends about the Taliban began to circulate. And, although they may have been planted by Pakistani spies originally, they soon gained a life of their own.

The legends "went viral" because Mullah Omar's Taliban really did what they claimed they would. They cleared all the "checkpoints" between Kandahar and the border, for example, whereupon merchandise flooded into the bazaars of Kandahar—and at lower prices, too, because the traders no longer had to pay seventy-plus "tolls" between border and bazaar.

Later that month, the Taliban captured an arms depot near the Pakistan border, which supposedly belonged to Hezb-i-Islam. They took it virtually without a fight, gaining some eight hundred truckloads of guns and ammunition.[12] And if you think Pakistan put the arms there and arranged for the Taliban to "capture" it, you must be very cynical.

Within two months, the Taliban had airplanes, automobiles, artillery, tanks, helicopters, sophisticated radio communications, guns, bullets, and money. Pakistan professed amazement at how quickly these plucky youngsters were progressing—and on their own, too—for Pakistan denied having anything to do with creating or arming the Taliban. According to Pakistani spokesmen, the Taliban captured all their materiel from the Mujahideen or acquired it from commanders who joined them.[13] At the same time, Pakistani officials flung open the gates of those Afghan refugee camps and let thousands of recruits pour across the border to join the new force.

In November, the Taliban decided to conquer Kandahar, the country's second-biggest city, and took it with shocking ease, in part because Kandahar was the Afghan city most ravaged by Mujahideen gangsters. Its citizens had been living in fear. They were sick of violence and hated the "holy warriors." They had not turned against Islam or the Shari'a—only against the Mujahideen. They welcomed the Taliban because these young men proclaimed themselves to be true, incorruptible Muslims on a mission from God: to disarm all militias, restore order, and enforce the Shari'a. Common folks believed them because they so fervently longed for a savior to believe in.

The Kandahar victory energized the Taliban, and the boys went campaigning. They took Ghazni, took Wardak, took Logar; they acquired the image of an irresistible force. In September 1995, they reached the country's third-largest city, Herat, which was ruled by the warlord Ismail

Khan, an ally of Ahmad Shah Massoud's. Ismail Khan fled to Iran as soon as he saw the Taliban coming, and so this "Army of God" took Herat without a fight too.

Six months after anyone had heard of them, the Taliban controlled nine of the country's thirty-four provinces. Their growing mystique and the widespread public hatred of the Mujahideen contributed to their success, but they had another asset too: plenty of cash. They simply paid warlords to stop fighting, and, since most of the warlords were only in it for the money, they agreed. Cynics charged that no way could a ragtag band of supposed students have raised so much cash on their own: they must have gotten it from Pakistan. Pakistani officials were shocked to hear such an accusation. And, the thing is, throughout this first year, the Taliban were, in fact, true to their word. Wherever they took over, they did shut down militias, confiscate arms, and introduce a fragile sense of security.

Even as they were conquering western Afghanistan, the Taliban were also pouring east across the landscape in fleets of brand-new all-terrain Toyota pickup trucks that had machine guns bolted to their beds, vehicles that made them fast and deadly, rather like the Mongols' mobile cavalry of centuries past. The Taliban were headed for Kabul now, which was not only the capital but bigger than the next *six* biggest cities combined.

They reached the suburbs in September 1995, around the same time they were conquering Herat. Hekmatyar warned them not to approach his stronghold, or else he'd show them what grown-ups did with guns. Absurdly enough, he also offered to take over their forces and be their boss. Even as he was issuing warnings and tendering offers, his men were defecting to the Taliban in droves. Hekmatyar appealed to his sponsors in Pakistan, only to find they didn't love him anymore. Hekmatyar was forced to swallow his pride and join forces with Massoud (whom he soon betrayed).

The Lion of Panjsher drove the Taliban back from Kabul, dealing this sudden army its first setback. But Mullah Omar simply issued a call for fresh volunteers, and thousands of new recruits came rushing from the madrassas and refugee camps in Pakistan. They had no trouble getting across the border: Pakistani border officials were just glad to be of any assistance. The Taliban set siege to Kabul, and over the next few months their bombardment drove half the remaining population out of the city and into IDP camps.

25

Taliban Versus Mujahideen

In April 1996, as the siege of Kabul was still under way, some thousand rural clerics gathered in Kandahar to acclaim Mullah Omar as the Amir al-Mu'mineen, the "Commander of the Faithful." This was the title adopted by Prophet Mohammed's second successor (also named Omar). By assuming this title, Mullah Omar was equating himself with the most revered religious personalities in the annals of Islamic history. Just in case anyone missed the symbolism, he appeared before the crowd holding up a garment said to be the cloak of the Prophet himself. It was the most precious relic in the main mosque of Kandahar and one that the public rarely saw, but the mosque officials gladly gave it to Mullah Omar now to use for his political purposes.

Mullah Omar was claiming a status beyond that of any mere king. To his followers, he was God's deputy on earth, like the immediate successors of Prophet Mohammed—this man who knew nothing of science, geography, mathematics, or economics, who spoke no language but Pushto, and who quite possibly had never read a newspaper.

The first siege of Kabul failed, but the Taliban tried again in the fall, bringing four hundred new tanks into the fight as well as jet planes, helicopters, and heavy artillery—not bad for an army of schoolboys led by half-educated peasants. Dostum still had his disciplined fifty thousand crack troops, but he decided Kabul was not worth the fight and retired to

the north to build a quasi-autonomous state. By then, defections had reduced Massoud's forces from thirty-five thousand down to a scant ten
thousand.[1] The Taliban surrounded the city in force and strafed it daily.
Finally, Massoud too decided that it was better to run away now and live
to fight another day. He pulled back to his home valley of Panjsher, a
sixty-mile crack in the mountains north of Kabul.

On the morning of September 26, 1996, the people of Kabul woke
up to find bearded young men with kohl-rimmed eyes and bulky, black
turbans patrolling their streets. To the people of Kabul, this did not feel
like a regime change but an occupation. These new conquerors looked
as foreign to them as had the blue-eyed Russians. Mujahideen leaders
such as Massoud, Rabbani, Sayyaf, Hekmatyar, and Mujaddedi were at
least familiar figures from the tumults of the sixties and seventies. People
knew them.

The Taliban, by contrast, were the children of rural Pushtoons from
the southwestern deserts and the mountains straddling the border with
Pakistan. They truly hailed from the "other" Afghanistan, the one
Abdu'Rahman had subdued but had failed to absorb. Long before the current war, a chasm of cultural separation had opened up between these
folks and the sophisticates of Kabul. What's more, most of the young men
and teenagers stalking the streets with machine guns didn't come directly
out of the rural villages of the old Afghanistan. They came out of the
refugee camps. Most had only distorted images or none at all of the traditional Afghan life their parents had enjoyed long ago.[2]

The Taliban espoused the same doctrine as the Mujahideen, only
more so. On every point, they were more literal, more simplistic, more
extreme. In their own view, what they were was more pure. They had no
interest in discussing what was best for Afghanistan because they already
knew what was best: the Shari'a. They were here to enforce the law (as
they understood it) without compromise or deviation. This is what the
bulk of the cadre undoubtedly believed.

On their first day in Kabul, the Taliban lured former Communist
president Najibullah and his brother out of the United Nations compound, tortured them, beat them to death, castrated them, mutilated their
bodies, and hung them from a lamppost in Ariana Square, where they
used the corpses for target practice.

The message was clear: the Taliban did not give a fig about world opinion. But if this was so, how come they took the trouble to lure Najibullah out of United Nations compound? What made these tunnel-visioned fanatics sensitive to the diplomatic consequences of violating the sanctity of the UN? The probable answer: they weren't. Behind the ragtag cadre stood a corps of sophisticated military strategists and tacticians affiliated with the Pakistan government. The scruples in this instance probably belonged to them.[3]

But why would high officials of the Pakistan government be interested in imposing the Taliban's ideas of social order on Afghanistan? Why would they care whether Afghan women wore veils or Afghan boys flew kites? The answer is, they probably didn't. As long as the Taliban served Pakistan's global interests, officials in Islamabad probably didn't care what domestic policies the Taliban pursued. The Great Game was back, and Pakistan had stepped into the shoes once worn by the British.

Conversely, although Mullah Omar's Taliban might have been willing tools of Pakistan with regard to Great Game considerations, they had their own agenda, separate from Pakistan's needs and desires. As soon as the Taliban had the rudiments of a government in place, they announced their program.

Only then did Afghans discover what Taliban-imposed security would cost them. Women were henceforth forbidden to show themselves in public. Women could not work outside their homes or go to school. Women could not leave their compounds unless they were wearing that oppressive head-to-toe covering known as the chad'ri (or burqa). Women could not be on the streets without a male escort. That male escort had to be a husband or a relative close enough to meet the mandate of the Shari'a. Taxis were forbidden to pick up unveiled or unaccompanied women. Shopkeepers could not sell goods to such women. Outside the home, women were to be treated as nonpersons—unless they were showing some skin, any skin, in which case they were to be beaten on the spot.

The criminal penalties listed in the Shari'a were to be enforced exactly as prescribed. Thieves were to have their hands cut off. In specified cases, they must lose their feet as well. Doctors were called away from legitimate patients to carry out these surgeries. Relatives of murder victims were given guns and invited to shoot the murderers, if they were caught.

Women charged with adultery were stoned in public. At least once, this was carried out in the city's main stadium, where crowds had gathered in former times to watch entertainments such as soccer. Long trials were declared a thing of the past. Judgments were to be delivered swiftly, and sentences carried out on the spot.

Music was banned. Movies were banned. Photography was banned. All representational art was banned. Theaters were turned into mosques. Video stores were burned down. Television sets still provided some entertainment—not the shows, the sets themselves: those were set up in the streets, and the cadre shot them to pieces with their machine guns. Anything that smacked of gambling was outlawed. Kite flying was therefore prohibited. Soccer and chess were heavily discouraged, because people *might* place wagers on those games. Afghans enjoyed keeping pigeons and other birds, but those days were over. Pets were banned.

The celebration of any non-Islamic event (such as New Year's or Afghan Independence Day) was criminalized. Everybody, both men and women, had to wear clothing that conformed to the mandates of the Shari'a. The national tribal dress—long shirt, baggy pants, turbans for men, headscarves for women—fit this description. Western clothes did not, so Western clothes were banned. Long hair was banned for men. Beards, by contrast, became mandatory. Anyone caught violating the dress code could be punished. Prayer was mandatory too. Anyone caught not praying at the prescribed times would be punished.

It's worth noting that this program, which sounds so unprecedentedly grim to modern sensibilities, was pretty much precisely the same one Bachey Saqao had imposed after he drove Amanullah out of power. This whole story had happened before.

At least two men were dropped from second-story windows for skipping prayer. Those guilty of minor infractions, such as shaving, could be whipped with a braided cable. The punishments were meted out by minions of a new government agency called the Ministry of Vice and Virtue (it had a longer official name but hardly anyone used it). This ministry had cabinet status equal to such portfolios as foreign affairs and defense. The Iron Amir, Abdu'Rahman, had a department with a similar name, but its work was incidental to the affairs of state. Under the Taliban, by contrast, stamping out "vice" and enforcing "virtue" were the core purpose of the state.

Although the Taliban believed they represented nothing but Islam in its purest form, they were an overwhelmingly Pushtoon party, and their program featured ethnic, racial, and religious hatred directed largely at the Shi'a Hazaras. Early in their tenure, they made sweeps through Hazara neighborhoods, drafting all the men and boys they could catch, to serve as cannon fodder in their campaigns. All who resisted were killed. Never before had the long-suffering Hazaras suffered as they did under the Taliban. What the Taliban carried out against the Hazaras in Afghanistan was exactly the same practice that was called ethnic cleansing elsewhere in the world.

And yet, in those first few months and years, the world turned a blind eye to the Taliban's activities. What kept most of the world neutral was the politics of oil. Indeed, oil was the subnarrative to the whole Taliban drama. Pakistan supported the Taliban from the start because they thought this group could make Afghanistan safe for an oil pipeline. Western oil companies came around to the same idea. As early as 1991, Carlos Bulgheroni, chairman of the smallish Argentinean oil company Bridas, flew into the region seeking to secure the rights to Turkmenistan's oil and gas. He met with President Niyazov, Turkmenistan's eccentric dictator, fielded the first proposal to build a pipeline across Afghanistan, and courted competing Afghan warlords to discuss deals. Bulgheroni actually believed his pipeline would bring peace to Afghanistan.

The power brokers in Pakistan colluded with Bulgheroni, although they had exactly the opposite analysis: peace would bring the pipeline. Peace at any cost came first. Hence, the Taliban.

Bridas executives talked to the Taliban but also to all the other factions in the country. They were hedging their bets. In early 1996, Bulgheroni negotiated a thirty-year deal with the Rabbani government for the right to build his pipeline across Afghanistan. He also got guarantees of protection. Rabbani was guaranteeing something he could not deliver. His government controlled virtually nothing outside of Kabul by then, and it would be driven even from Kabul within the year. Bulgheroni had signed a contract with a ghost.

US oil companies had been skeptical about the pipeline at first, but once the news of Bridas's negotiations got into the wind, the Texas-based oil company Unocal got interested. Unocal executives flew into Turkmenistan to talk to Niyazov, who decided that his deals with Bridas had been premature. He put the Argentinean company on hold while he invited the Unocal people to tell him more.

Unocal brought heavy artillery to the competition with Bridas. They had friends in the Republican Party, including power brokers such as Henry Kissinger and Alexander Haig, as well as Ronald Reagan's erstwhile Afghan advisor Zalmay Khalilzad. Khalilzad, in turn, had an Afghan associate by the name of Hamid Karzai. Khalilzad and Karzai, in concert with their neoconservative allies in Washington, DC, argued that the Taliban deserved US support because they could be a stabilizing force. Khalilzad predicted that the Taliban would develop into a regime much like that of Saudi Arabia, a refreshing contrast to those madmen in Iran.[4] While Bridas was busy negotiating with the Mujahideen, Unocal put its trust in the Taliban.

As soon as Unocal launched its bid, a host of US military, intelligence, and diplomatic officials got involved. They could be helpful because they had links to key figures in the Pakistan government. The US government naturally wanted to help an American company beat out foreign competition for access to Caspian Basin petroleum. To be sure, the American government did have some security concerns. Would American citizens be safe building the pipeline in Afghanistan or working there after it was built? Pakistani officials assured the Americans that the Taliban controlled much of the country and would soon have it all. They were the one force capable of ending the internecine warfare and making Afghanistan safe for business.

This context explains why authorities in the West paid such scant attention to the Taliban's social policies. They took the position that the Afghan government's domestic policies were nobody's business but their own. If the Taliban became a regime like the one in Saudi Arabia, would that be so bad? Americans didn't have to like the Saudi way of life to do business with them. They were rational people. The only real question for America was—could the Taliban really stabilize their country? Khalilzad insisted that they could, and State Department officials figured he should know: he was after all an Afghan.

The United States did not create the Taliban or fund them directly, as some critics later charged. They only kept funding their ally Pakistan, ignoring the fact that Pakistan was nurturing the Taliban. The United States also took Pakistan's advice to stop supporting Massoud and his allies. In fact, the United States tried to ensure that no aid of any kind reached Massoud from any Western source.

MASSOUD, HOWEVER, WAS FAR FROM BEATEN. WHILE THE TALIBAN WERE securing Kabul, Massoud was regrouping in Panjsher. That November 1996, he convened the leaders of many former anti-Soviet groups and formed a coalition called the United Front for the Salvation of Afghanistan, which included the Uzbek warlord Dostum, the Hazara militias of central Afghanistan, the Ismaili Shi'a Tajiks of the northeast, and representatives of virtually all other non-Pushtoon minorities, plus a few Pushtoon "moderates" from the south. It was Afghanistan's first truly multiethnic political entity.

I call it an entity because it was more than a party but less than a government. Ostensibly, this Northern Alliance—as it later came to be called—sought independence for Afghanistan from all foreign powers including Pakistan, and they promised to set up a modernist, multiethnic Islamic state. The alliance could broadcast such a program now because the extremism of the Taliban had created room for a more liberal interpretation of Islam to compete for credibility.

The Northern Alliance chose Rabbani as its president and Massoud as its commander in chief. Rabbani toured neighboring countries seeking military help from anyone but Pakistan, and the aid came flowing in, from Iran, from India, and even from Russia. The Russians contributed because they wanted to block Taliban-style Islamist fundamentalism from spreading to their country. The Iranians worried that Taliban-style hatred of Shi'as would infect the region. India saw Afghanistan as a chip in its struggle with Pakistan.

For the next four-plus years, the Taliban launched one assault after another on the Northern Alliance. They took territory, lost territory, took it back, lost it, and took it again. In the spring of 1997, they captured Mazar-i-Sharif, the major city of the north, and proceeded to massacre the Hazaras of the city. Their learned scholars came along to sanction the ethnic cleansing on the grounds that Hazaras were not Muslims. They opined that killing a Hazara might even help a man get into heaven, so long as it was not the only good deed to his credit.

Pakistan picked this moment to recognize the Taliban as the legitimate government of Afghanistan. Saudi Arabia and United Arab Emirates quickly followed suit. Every other country including the United States (as well as the United Nations) held back, but, in general, attitudes about the Taliban remained ambiguous. In this period, Unocal flew top members of the Taliban's inner council to Dallas to talk about the pipeline. The Taliban opened an office in Washington, DC, to conduct business, and Taliban well-wishers in DC hired a public relations firm to burnish the group's image in America.

26

Al Qaeda

THE MUSLIM WORLD HAD LONG BEEN RIPE FOR REVOLUTIONARY activism, because virtually every Muslim-majority country from Pakistan to Morocco had an authoritarian government propped up by police power. Militant anti-Western sentiment had been rising since the 1970s as the entrenched elites of Muslim countries kept getting guns and money from Western imperialist powers to help them stay entrenched. Development in these countries had widened the gap between haves and have-nots, and, ominously enough, that gap had come to mirror a *cultural* gulf between Westernized elites and the masses they ruled—the same gulf that had begun to open in Afghanistan in Abdu'Rahman's day and had been growing ever since.

During the Cold War, some Muslim malcontents espoused Communism, simply because by doing so they could get aid from the mighty Soviets. But Marxism had never been a good fit for the Islamic world, and, once the Soviet empire was gone, Muslim revolutionaries had nothing to gain from clinging to Communist doctrine. Many now turned to an indigenous revolutionary ideology with deep roots in Muslim soil. This was *Islamism*, a political program derived from Islamic sources. Afghanistan became a nexus for Islamism because its anti-Soviet war of independence attracted so many thousands of Islamist activists from around the Arab world. They came to Afghanistan as radicals; they left as hardened revolutionaries comfortable with violence. These Arab veterans of the Afghan war came to be known as the "Arab Afghans."

One of these Arab Islamists was Osama Bin Laden, the seventeenth of fifty-plus children born to a billionaire Yemeni businessman who had close ties to the Saudi ruling family. Most of the Bin Ladens were high-stepping jetsetters, but Osama went the other way: in reaction to his family's dissolute splendor, he embraced extreme "piety." In the mideighties, he joined the thousands of Arab ideologues flocking to Afghanistan. There he used his wealth to help fund the jihad, which gained him many Afghan friends. He also took part in the fighting, which gained him some respect, although his military exploits were rather more modest than later legends would suggest. Early on, he established a guesthouse in Peshawar for Arab radicals coming to fight in Afghanistan, a base from which they could sally into battle and then come back for a hot shower and a good meal. The guesthouse was known as *al Qaeda*, the Arabic word for "base." In 1988, with the war winding down and the Arab Afghans going home, Bin Laden transferred this name to a new organization he had founded, an organization dedicated to helping Arab radicals overthrow their home countries' regimes.

Bin Laden went home plumped up with self-importance about his exploits in Afghanistan. Saddam Hussein had just invaded Kuwait and had positioned his army on the Saudi border, but Bin Laden told the Saudi government not to worry. He would lead an army of Arab Afghans in a jihad against Hussein. The Saudi government didn't take his offer seriously. They dismissed the hero of the Afghan Jihad and then, as if to rub salt in the wound, asked the United States for help instead. They even let the American-led coalition use Saudi soil as its base. Osama cursed the Saudi royals for all this, and they responded by asking him to leave the country.

Bin Laden moved to Sudan, where he continued to rage against the Saudi royals publicly, which drove them finally to revoke his citizenship. By then he was busy building up al Qaeda and studying the political possibilities of terrorism—that is, of exploiting the very weakness of his group, its very lack of numbers and resources and territory, to wreak terrible carnage on civilians by sneaking individual saboteurs and suicide bombers into "enemy territory." In November 1995, al Qaeda agents tested his method with a bombing at an American compound in the capital of Saudi Arabia that killed several dozen American engineers and support staff.

The CIA now took notice of Bin Laden. They pressured Sudan to do something about this guy, and the Sudanese government reluctantly asked Bin Laden to go somewhere else. In 1996, Bin Laden moved back to the snake pit that Afghanistan had become, but for him it was like alighting in a nest: he was home.

He renewed his friendship with the ISI folks he had gotten to know during the anti-Soviet jihad, and he set to work cultivating the Taliban. Mullah Omar's minions were expanding across Afghanistan just then, and Bin Laden gave them $3 million to help them buy off warlords south of Kabul, which made him one of their favorite Arab Afghans. Five months later, the Taliban took Kabul, a sunny development for Bin Laden, because everything he embraced, the Taliban espoused. Bin Laden pleased Mullah Omar by proclaiming his Afghanistan the world's only true Muslim community.

Warlords allied to the Taliban gave Bin Laden a complex of irrigation tunnels at a place called Tora Bora, near the city of Jalalabad. Bin Laden retrofitted this cave complex into a formidable underground military installation not only with his own money but with covert support from rich Wahhabis around the world. Mullah Omar liked what Bin Laden was doing and gave him more land along the country's southern border, near the border city of Khost. There, Bin Laden built a string of training camps, a West Point of terrorism, so to speak: would-be soldiers for the global jihad came here to learn the same skills taught to US Navy SEALS and Army Rangers.

The Taliban also gave Bin Laden a large compound near the city of Kandahar, a former agricultural co-op called Tarnak Farms. Bin Laden made that place his headquarters. He brought his wives and children to live with him, and it was there that he huddled with his associates to plan his global campaign.

On February 23, 1998, Osama Bin Laden and his cohorts issued an in-your-face statement declaring war on Israel, the United States, and the West. He had published a similar statement two years earlier, but it had gone unnoticed because it was long and rambling; this one was shorter, bolder. He quoted passages from the Qur'an (about fighting unbelievers), laid out a list of grievances against Jews and "Crusaders" (meaning any

Westerner engaged in any project in the Islamic world), and delivered the following edict:

> The ruling to kill the Americans and their allies—civilians and military—is an individual duty for every Muslim who can do it in any country in which it is possible to do it.

Bin Laden called his declaration a fatwa. A fatwa is not, as is commonly thought, an assassination order or a declaration of war. It is a religious ruling about a case not covered by existing precedents. When a novel situation crops up, a religious authority must decide how the Shari'a applies to this situation, a ruling that adds another precedent to the ever-growing body of established (Shari'a) law. Because this is a very serious matter in Islam, only the highest religious authorities may issue fatwas. Was Osama Bin Laden such an authority? Not really. He had no religious training and no standing among mainstream Muslim scholars. He was just a rich man who had fought in a jihad.

Islam has no pope-like figure or clerical hierarchy to formally disqualify anyone from issuing a fatwa. Certification comes, ultimately, from the consensus of the community. If someone says he's issued a fatwa and the Muslim community accepts it as a fatwa, then it is a fatwa. Bin Laden issued his declaration as if he had the authority to do so, and, because he had followers, at least some Muslims accepted the "religious duty" he imposed.

This would probably have been a good moment for US policy makers to step back and develop a broader view of the problem. They might have studied what Jihadism was, where it came from, to whom it appealed, why it appealed to them, and how it had gotten into the culture of Afghanistan and Pakistan. They might have tried to identify religious intellectuals with credibility among Muslims who were offering alternative interpretations worth supporting. They might have explored how Jihadism and its rivals were intertwined with social and political undercurrents in Muslim societies to craft policies that would undercut the seductions of Jihadism far upstream from actual crises. Finally, they might have worked out how to distinguish long-standing local contentions from global arguments and dealt with them separately.

But US policy makers went the other way. They narrowed the scope of their approach, excluding social, political, cultural, and economic factors from consideration to focus tightly on Islamism as a military problem. They also narrowed down their definition of the military problem finally to one man: Osama Bin Laden. By implication, neutralizing him would end the threat.

There was, to be sure, some truth in this simplistic analysis: Bin Laden was a dangerous and determined man. US president Clinton recognized the menace he represented and wanted someone to do something—but who should do it? So many agencies had people dealing with terrorism. Until now they had mostly been concerned with spotting and foiling isolated plots: a hijacking here, a bombing there. A transnational organization of unknown scope declaring war on a state was something new. Whose jurisdiction was it to counter this? The CIA? The Pentagon? The NSC? The FBI? Army intelligence? Naval intelligence? The marines? President Clinton appointed a White House terrorism czar to coordinate all counterterrorism efforts and gave this man, Richard Clarke, cabinet rank. In the end, Clarke only added one more voice to the dissonant clamor about the terrorist threat.

The State Department complicated the matter. Experts such as Deputy Secretary of State Thomas Pickering said that only a Pushtoon from the south could really rule Afghanistan, and the United States must not hitch its wagon to any other star on the Afghan scene. To Pickering, only the Taliban fit the profile, because they were Pushtoons from the south. Hence, the United States had to let them complete their takeover. Whatever was done about Osama Bin Laden, it must not hinder the progress of the Taliban. The State Department was also locked into Pakistan as its indispensable ally in this region. After all, Pakistan had been so good about funneling US aid to the Mujahideen in the 1980s, and, during the Cold War, Pakistan had served America's policy so well by completing the containment fence around Communism. Whatever new trouble was looming here, the United States must partner with Pakistan to combat it. Whatever the United States did about Osama Bin Laden, therefore, must not ruffle Pakistani sensibilities.

Unfortunately, Bin Laden was in bed with the Taliban and under the protection of Pakistan—who were thoroughly intertwined with each other. The question became, how to extract Bin Laden from this tangle without "altering the battlefield." Just when a panoramic engagement was needed, American policy narrowed down to one narrow obsession.

The CIA hatched plans for a "snatch operation." They would swoop in, grab Bin Laden, and lift him out of Afghanistan without leaving a ripple behind. The snatch-op would be easy because everyone knew where Bin Laden lived: at Tarnak Farms, an isolated compound surrounded by nothing but desert and brush. The CIA worked out a plan to drop a thirty-man strike team into that desert one night. The men would creep into the compound through drainage ditches, drag Bin Laden out, stuff him into a helicopter, and fly away.

At the last moment, however, President Clinton got cold feet. Jimmy Carter had tried something very much like this in Iran during the hostage crisis of 1980, and the operation had gone catastrophically wrong because of a dust storm. Carter had never recovered politically. Then too, in a satellite photo of the Tarnak Farms compound, Clinton saw a child's empty swing set, and the worst-case scenario occurred to him: what if the operation failed *and* Bin Laden escaped *and* . . . children were killed? Clinton could not afford the fallout from such a failure. He called the whole thing off.

The CIA was disappointed but put together a new plan. They would kill Bin Laden by bombing one of those training camps at Khost when Osama Bin Laden and his cohorts were there. Again, however, at the last moment, Clinton backed out. He received word that the people in that camp weren't Bin Laden and his associates but the royal family of the United Arab Emirates, who came here every year to do some falcon hunting. The last thing Clinton needed was the flak he'd face if he tried to kill Bin Laden and instead killed the royal family of the UAE. So again he called off the operation. (Carping about Clinton's indecisiveness should be tempered by the fact that he made the right decision: the report was correct, it turned out. The strike would have missed Bin Laden and killed the royal family of a US ally.)

Meanwhile, Bin Laden was plotting his next move. He had sleeper agents around the world, including Africa, and he decided the time had come to wake some of them up. On August 8, 1998, at ten thirty in the morning, al Qaeda operatives blew up a truck behind the American Embassy in Nairobi, Kenya, killing 213 and wounding more than 4,000, of whom 300 later died. The casualties included twelve Americans. Nine minutes later, a truck loaded with explosives drove into the American Embassy in Dar al Salaam, Tanzania, killing eleven Tanzanians and injuring eighty-five.

Crimes like these demanded an immediate and strong response from the American president. Bill Clinton, however, had to react amid a hobbling and quite unrelated domestic crisis. Long before he became president, Clinton and his wife had lost money in some ill-fated Arkansas land deal peddled by the Whitewater Development Corporation. As soon as Clinton became president, his opponents called for an investigation, and Congress appointed a special prosecutor, Ken Starr, to look into the case. He went after the Clintons with the tenacity of Victor Hugo's Inspector Javert. He couldn't define any exact charges related to Whitewater, but during his investigations a woman named Paula Jones filed a lawsuit against the president for sexual harassment dating back to his days as governor.

Her suit was eventually dismissed, but by then Ken Starr had absorbed it into his investigations, and in the Jones testimony he found hints of a recent sexual liaison between President Clinton and a White House intern named Monica Lewinsky. Starr's relentless probing turned up evidence that this intern may in fact have fellated the president in the Oval Office while he was conducting government business. Starr leaked the most lurid details of his findings to the media in the weeks before the Africa bombings, setting all of America abuzz. On the day of the bombing, Monica Lewinsky was testifying to a grand jury about her sex acts with the president. On August 17, Clinton went on TV and admitted his sexual transgressions. From that humiliating TV appearance, he went directly into a secret meeting with his military and intelligence experts to discuss how America should respond to the embassy bombings in Africa. That day he gave an order that was carried out on August 20: the United States fired sixty Tomahawk cruise missiles at the terrorist training camps near Khost and another dozen or so at a chemical plant in Sudan that was said to be manufacturing chemical weapons.

The strike cost $55 million. It didn't kill any important al Qaeda figure. Bin Laden had left the camp just a few hours before the missiles struck, which is no surprise, since Pakistan's prime minister Nawaz Sharif knew about the impending strike the day before it happened. As for the chemical plant in Sudan, al Qaeda propagandists quickly claimed it was actually an aspirin factory. This claim remains disputed, but only perception mattered at the time, and al Qaeda won that battle of perception.

What Clinton got out of his decisive move was ridicule. In America, few potential voters believed he did it to save America from terrorists. Pundits and late-night TV comedians agreed that this was all about the Monica Lewinsky scandal. They referenced the hit movie from the summer before, *Wag the Dog*, in which a fictional US president fakes an invasion of Albania to distract voters from his sexual peccadilloes.

Bin Laden, by contrast, got everything he wanted from the bombings with *his* target constituency: disgruntled Muslims attracted to militant Jihadism and open to recruitment by al Qaeda. His grandiloquent fatwas had served notice that he didn't wish to be categorized with Carlos the Jackal and the Gambini brothers, but with the Clintons and Yeltsins of the world. Now, the only remaining superpower validated his image by hitting him with the sorts of weapons usually reserved for wars between states. And not only did Bin Laden live to tell the tale, but he quickly released a videotape crowing about his triumph. In Pakistan, two flattering biographies of Bin Laden hit the bookstores and turned into immediate best sellers. (In America, nonfiction best seller lists around this time featured a book about Princess Di and another about Monica Lewinsky.)

That fall, Congress began talking about impeaching Clinton for lying about his sex life. The impeachment drama further hampered Clinton's ability to take military action against bin Laden, and, in any case, the military approach had not really worked, so the US government changed tack and decided to ask the Taliban to arrest Bin Laden and turn him over for trial. Such feelers from the United States only pumped up the Taliban's sense of self-importance. They exulted in saying no, Osama Bin Laden was their guest. The code of Pushtoonwali obliged them to protect a guest with their very lives. Besides (they claimed) they had no idea where Bin Laden might be staying.

The United States tried to get some help from Pakistan. Clinton personally appealed to Pakistan's prime minister Nawaz Sharif to capture Bin Laden for the United States. Sharif wheedled that he'd try but couldn't promise anything. He lamented that he didn't have the elite team of highly trained military experts it would take to catch such an elusive terrorist mastermind. Thereupon, the CIA gave Sharif the money, materiel, and consultants he needed to create exactly such a strike force. Once it was operational, the new strike force didn't go after Bin Laden. It went after his enemies. In January 1999, this team was implicated in the murder of the wife and children of Abdul Haq, the most prominent anti-Taliban Pushtoon warlord—quite a setback because Pushtoons who opposed the Taliban were as precious as platinum.

The truth is, Pakistan's top officials were no longer in a position to help the United States, even had they wanted to, because Pakistan no longer controlled the Taliban. When Pakistani military and intelligence officials first began nurturing the Taliban, they were thinking of their own regional and global interests. They wanted a government in Afghanistan through whom they could control Afghanistan's foreign policy. In exchange, they would let the Taliban pursue whatever domestic policies they wanted.

But the Pakistani architects of the Taliban had failed to take a few things into account. They had failed to consider the appeal Talibanism might have to the countless disaffected Muslims in their own country. They had failed to note that the Taliban were not only Islamists but Pushtoon chauvinists and that Pakistan had millions of Pushtoon citizens whose relationship with the Pakistan state had always been contentious. They had failed to predict that these Taliban, these case-hardened, battle-tested, radically religious Pushtoon chauvinists, who were no longer boys but men, had the wherewithal to forge closer links with powerful, potentially rebellious elements of Pakistani society than the country's own ruling military aristocracy could—closer even than top ISI officials. The Taliban had gotten cozy, for example, with Pakistan's radical religious parties, with the smuggling mafias that operated across the Durand Line, with the mosques and madrassas that had so much influence among the conservative, impoverished masses, with the rural clerics who railed and raged against secular values, with bazaar merchants in the border provinces, and with tribal chiefs in areas like Waziristan. And why wouldn't they? They spoke the same language, they shared a culture, and in many cases they were tribally related.

Pakistan sent the Taliban into Afghanistan, but Talibanism came seeping back across the border, disrupting Pakistani society. By 1999,

Pakistan's military and intelligence officials knew they had created a monster, but it was too late. The border between the two countries was vanishing, and Pakistani territory from Karachi to Kashmir was awash in Talibanism. The lower and middle ranks of the army and of ISI were Taliban loyalists just as much as they were Pakistanis. As a result, the top officers of these outfits, especially political appointees, no longer dared order their subordinates to move against the Taliban for fear that the orders would be disobeyed—because if the lower ranks realized they could disobey their superiors with impunity, all bets were off.

27

America Enters the Picture

In America, meanwhile, Clinton's team defeated the impeachment attempt. He would be allowed to finish his term, but the scandal had weakened him, and his anointed successor, Al Gore, had to deal with the electoral consequences. The Democrats desperately needed to shore up the women's vote in the United States. This political imperative made the White House pay heed to a whole new voice about the Taliban. Feminist activists in America had discovered what sort of society the Taliban were creating, and they were appalled. While Clinton was battling his critics for getting a blowjob at work, Radio Shari'a in Kabul was proudly announcing how many hundreds of women had been beaten on the streets each day for letting their hands or faces show in public.

A group called the Feminist Majority began to broadcast information about the Taliban as vigorously as it could. The information added up to a compelling horror story that was true enough in broad outline. Comedian Jay Leno's wife Mavis Leno donated money to the cause. The Feminist Majority circulated an e-mail reporting grim facts about Taliban social policies, and this e-mail, one of the first to go viral, introduced the term "gender apartheid" into the American political conscience.

The efforts of these feminist activists would have been futile had they been aimed at shaming the Taliban into altering their policies. Mullah Omar had total control of his territory and didn't care what American women thought about him. But the feminist activists had targets that did matter. They picketed Unocal's offices in the United States, which sent a warning to Western companies and governments: dealing with the Taliban might cost them. Unocal put its pipeline project on hold (although the company denied they were responding to the picketing). US policy showed traces of change as well. Secretary of State Madeleine Albright made statements critical of the Taliban, and in 1999 the United States supported a United Nations resolution to impose economic sanctions on the Taliban.

To say the Taliban were unmoved would be understating the case. Their policies turned even more virulent. Mullah Omar issued a fatwa that Hindus had to carry yellow identification stickers—reminiscent of the Nazi directive about Jews. In Mazar-i-Sharif, a woman charged with adultery was triumphantly stoned in a sports stadium for a huge audience of men. Mullah Omar also flexed his muscles with a curt message to the prime minister of Pakistan: begin enforcing "Islamic law . . . step by step," he ordered the president of Pakistan, or "there could be instability in your country."

In the central valley of Bamiyan, Taliban soldiers used explosives to destroy the largest sculptures in the world, two ancient standing Buddhas carved into the face of a cliff there over a thousand years ago. Of all their deeds, this one drew the broadest international attention and condemnation, prompting a puzzled Mullah Omar to ask what everybody was crying about. "We're just blowing up stones," he said.[1]

Even as the United States grew less friendly to the Taliban, however, it continued to hold the Northern Alliance at arm's length. The marks against Massoud's group remained unchanged: too many of them were not Pushtoons, and the US State Department was still sure that non-Pushtoons could play no part in ruling Afghanistan. Never mind that Massoud's inner council now included Hamid Karzai, scion of Kandahar's Durrani Pushtoons, who had turned against the Taliban after they assassinated his father. It also included Hajji Qadir, prominent among the Ghilzai Pushtoons of Jalalabad and brother to the famous commander Abdul Haq. (Also included were Uzbek leader Dostum, Hazara leader Karim Khalili, and Herati leader Ismail Khan among others—it was a broad coalition.) America's real objection to Massoud's alliance might have been the support it received from Iran. The friend of America's enemy could only be America's enemy.

Even so, US strategists did see some value in the Northern Alliance. If the Northern Alliance were extinguished, the Taliban would lose all incentive to turn over Bin Laden. As long as they kept fighting, the Taliban might feel some need for outside help. Therefore, the CIA began delivering just enough aid to Massoud's group to keep it alive, though not enough to let it gain ground. The CIA did hint that it would give Massoud more help if he would capture Osama Bin Laden alive and turn him over to America without hurting him.

This was a truly clueless demand. As a practical matter it was asking the impossible, but politically it was even less feasible. Massoud was a Muslim leader, competing for the same hearts and minds as Bin Laden. He could have killed Bin Laden in battle without losing any prestige, but *capturing* Bin Laden at America's behest and turning him over *to the United States* for trial would have marked him as a stooge and lost him all his standing with Afghan Muslims. His cooperation with the United States would thereafter have been worthless to the United States.

Clinton's term was running down and a US presidential election was coming up. Although the Clinton administration may have had tunnel vision with regard to Afghanistan, the Bush team viewed the country and the problems it posed through a blindfold. The Clinton crowd was obsessed with Bin Laden. The Bush crowd scarcely noticed Bin Laden, much less the storm clouds of which he was but a drop. During the presidential election campaign of 2000, when George Bush was asked about the Taliban, he thought the interviewer was asking about a rock band.[2] Bush's foreign policy expert, Condoleezza Rice, dismissed the Taliban as a front for Iran—the Taliban's most implacable regional enemy. As for al Qaeda and its ilk, the Bush team promised to put together a master plan eventually, but it didn't want to fuss about individual threats. "I'm tired of swatting flies," Bush told Rice. Terrorism was important, Secretary of Defense Donald Rumsfeld allowed, but "it isn't tomorrow."[3]

George Bush and his team had other fish to fry. They were neoconservatives with a new global vision. The collapse of the Soviet Union had left a single superpower astride the planet, and American neoconservative intellectuals (originally called neoliberals) argued that the new circumstances gave the United States an opportunity—nay, a mission, even— to reshape the world in its own image. To neoconservatives, this meant establishing electoral democracies wherever possible, promoting American social values, pushing for free-market capitalism around the world, tearing down barriers to free trade, and reducing the ability of governments to regulate private enterprise. Meddling with the economy was the Communist prescription, and look what it got them; now it was time to see what private capital could do when liberated from all restrictions.

As it happened, the decade just ending had also seen a technological revolution so sweeping and sudden, it made the Industrial Revolution look like the Stone Age. Just as the Mujahideen were pulverizing Kabul, the computer and its implications were hitting a tipping point in the industrialized West. Even as the Taliban were marching into Kabul, the PC was making its way into millions of middle-class homes, and e-mail was starting to render postal services obsolete. The cell phone, which didn't even exist in 1989, was evolving into a cassette-sized device that would soon unmoor communication from fixed locations in space. By the time the Taliban got traction dragging Afghanistan back to the seventh century, the Internet was expanding at the speed of thought, and by 2001 anyone with a modem hooked up to the grid anywhere in the world could access a universe of information unparalleled in history.

The new technology and the neoconservative vision dovetailed with a growing trend toward globalization, which meant, among other things, that large corporations could distribute their operations across national borders in whatever ways maximized profits. Because workers in "less developed countries" commanded lower wages, production was moving to places such as China, India, Southeast Asia, and Mexico, while the executive functions of those same enterprises were coalescing in places where life was rendered comfortable by developed infrastructure, such as Western Europe and the United States. Financial and accounting functions, meanwhile, were moving to "sovereign" countries where taxation was light.

Afghanistan provided the starkest contrast to these developments. Along with Somalia and other "failed states," it seemed so irrelevant to these great new developments, it was hardly worth noticing. And yet it was here that the vast disparity between the most and least advanced parts of a rapidly globalizing planet would reach not the tipping point but the ripping point.

The presidential campaign of 2000 deadlocked. At the end of the year, as the two candidates were arguing about "hanging chads," Arab students attending Al Quds mosque in Hamburg, Germany, were drinking in the fulminations of radical Muslim cleric Zammar, a veteran of the Afghan jihad. Four of these students, Mohammed Atta, Ziad Jarrah, Marwan al-Shehhi, and Ramzi Binalshibh, had gone to Afghanistan to meet with top Al Qaeda leaders and present a plan they had conceived: to use hijacked airplanes as suicide bombs. Bin Laden listened with interest.

In the summer of 2001, Ahmad Shah Massoud made his first and only visit out of Afghanistan. He traveled to France, at the request of a Belgian diplomat, to address the European parliament on the danger posed by al Qaeda. There, he told the assembly that Afghanistan was an occupied nation. The Taliban, he said, were a front for yet another foreign invader—Pakistan, this time. He said that the Taliban and al Qaeda had turned the territory they controlled into one gigantic training camp for terrorists whose only aim was to harm the West and that if the West did not help Massoud and his alliance, it would suffer terrible consequences. The delegates applauded politely.

Massoud went home a failure. His alliance had lost most of the country by this time. They had been squeezed into northeastern Afghanistan and were fighting doggedly to survive in even that small pocket. Massoud spent the hot nights remaining of that summer on the roof of his house, reading classical Persian poetry, of which he had hundreds of volumes. His hair had turned gray, his back was in constant, excruciating pain, and his life's work was in a shambles, but he had not given up. The tide, he believed, was turning. Muslims would come to realize the cruelty and ignorance of Talibanist "Islam" and then they would open up to the interpretation that ethical, rational Muslims favored. Someday, he believed, Afghanistan would be a prosperous, modern, educated country whose practice of Islam would provide an example to the world of how just, gentle, and democratic Islam could be. He needed only to get his message out to Muslims around the world to trigger a turning of the tide. He needed to break out of the shell of isolation into which Pakistan, the Taliban, and the United States had cooped him.

He was delighted, therefore, when he received a request from a London-based television station, asking for an interview. The station said they were sending two journalists to film him. A tentative ally of Massoud's, Pushtoon warlord Abdul Rasool Sayyaf, who was much indebted to Saudi money and Wahhabi support, claimed to have vetted the journalists and sent word to Massoud that these two were legitimate. Whether he spoke with nefarious intent or was himself fooled, no one knows.

On September 9, the two "journalists," Karim Touzani and Kasem Bakkali, visited Massoud in his sparsely furnished office. They asked a few questions to disarm suspicion, and then the cameraman activated the bomb hidden in his camera. He himself died in the explosion, Massoud's face was blown away, and his aide, son of the famous poet Khallili, was badly injured. The second "journalist" escaped through a window, but Massoud's men caught him and beat him to death on the spot. Some have seen this killing as suspicious. Why not hold the man for questioning, they ask? Was it because he had some incriminating information about a traitor on Massoud's staff? Was it because some member of his inner circle was actually . . . a CIA agent? . . . Or an ISI agent? . . . Or an al Qaeda operative? . . . Or? . . .

Personally, I laugh at such theories. Here was a man who had penetrated to the heart of Massoud's headquarters and killed the mythic hero in his very home. Of course the killing unleashed a blind rage in his followers, grizzled warriors all. No explanation is needed for the carnage of the next few moments. Had the assassin gotten out alive, a theory would be needed.

Just two days later, as all the world knows, twenty-two men associated with al Qaeda, four of whom had actually trained for this exact mission at one of Osama Bin Laden's camps in Afghanistan that summer, hijacked four civilian jetliners and flew one of them into the Pentagon, two into the World Trade Center, and one into the ground near Pittsburgh, killing some three thousand people total. It was the most horrific single act of terrorism the world had ever seen.

WHEN THE NEWS HIT AFGHANISTAN, SOME UPPER-ECHELON TALIBAN exulted. They didn't know who had done this thing, but it made them glad: America was the enemy and the enemy had been damaged. They never dreamed the deed could blow back on them. After all, Washington was so far away. What could Americans do to Kabul?[4]

Most of Kabul felt differently. Educated Afghans saw America as an overwhelming power, and they didn't have to wait for Bush's speech to know that this juggernaut was coming. Indeed, within days of the mass murders (within hours, according to the New York Times)[5] the United States was on a war footing.

On October 7, 2001, the attack began. Tomahawk cruise missiles fired from ships in the Arabian Sea hit Afghan cities with deadly accuracy. Long-range bombers, British and American, rained destruction upon hapless Afghanistan. Global news stations such as CNN provided continuous reports about the attacks, illustrated with animated graphics. What viewers saw was a stream of arrows arcing from the Arabian Sea to small circles representing the cities of Afghanistan, where explosion icons bloomed repeatedly.

Newscasters fleshed out these images with words, but only English-speakers knew what they were saying. Scores of millions of Muslims watching the broadcasts understood only what they gleaned from the graphics: explosives hitting Afghanistan, boom, boom, boom.

Meanwhile, Osama bin Laden was taping a video of himself speaking from the mouth of a cave, dressed in stately white robes, quoting Koranic verses in a grave voice. This too was broadcast globally. Bin Laden was speaking Arabic, and, because most Muslims don't speak Arabic any more than they speak English, they didn't know what *he* was saying either, but they understood the iconography. He was evoking the most resonant scene in the Muslim imagination, that moment when Prophet Mohammed transformed from an ordinary man into God's personal spokesman. In addition to the military battle, in short, a message-battle raged in the mediasphere. The West won the "ground" war, but bin Laden may have won the first stages of the "air" war, especially if his goal was to provoke a global showdown between Islam and the West and to position himself as a leader in that clash.

After a few weeks, the United States ran out of significant targets to bomb in Afghanistan and switched to a two-pronged new strategy. Prong one: entrust the actual fighting to the Northern Alliance and only provide them with air support. Prong two: put pressure on Pakistan to cut its support for the Taliban.

The pressure consisted of financial and diplomatic measures that had been available to the United States for years. As soon as they were tried, they worked. Without support from Pakistan, the Taliban turned out to be nothing. *With* military support from the West, the Northern Alliance proved unstoppable.

On November 8, Pakistan ordered the Taliban to vacate their consulate in Karachi. Just three nights later, Taliban leaders slipped quietly out of Kabul under cover of night. The next day, the city was without a government. Northern Alliance forces hovered just a few miles outside the city, but US commanders ordered them to stay put until "the international community" (read: the United States) drew up a plan for a new governing authority. Perhaps US policy makers wanted to avoid a repeat of the 1992 debacle. Or perhaps the fix was in: perhaps Pakistan had agreed to support the US intervention only in exchange for assurances that its proxies would remain in control of Afghanistan. In the week before the flight of the Taliban, the media did buzz with speculation based on leaked reports that there were actually two kinds of Taliban—the bad kind who oppressed women and made common cause with the likes of Osama bin Laden, and the good kind who were merely conservative Afghans devoted to their country's traditional Islam.

The Northern Alliance, led now by a rather ramshackle cluster of Massoud's former aides and associates, decided not to wait for the "good Taliban" to dig in. They knew that only by taking possession of the city could they secure any say in the future of the country. If they didn't have Kabul, they would be sidelined. On November 13, therefore, the diverse troops of the many formerly-warring Mujahideen parties marched back into the city they had abandoned five years earlier. This time, no violence broke out. For one thing, Hekmatyar's group was missing from the equation. Kabul welcomed the Mujahideen, the troops behaved themselves, and residents of the city poured into the streets to celebrate. People were downright *euphoric*, and no wonder: everyone thought the war had ended finally: America had come to save the day!

On December 7, just two months after the bombing of Afghanistan began, Mullah Omar and his cohorts fled their real stronghold, which wasn't Kabul but Kandahar. They hightailed it for the Pakistan border, melting into the population as they moved. The last of them disappeared finally into the border belt where most of them had lived as refugee children during the anti-Soviet war.

PART V: THE STRUGGLE RESUMES

On the face of it, when Afghans took up arms to expel the Soviet invaders, they were waging a patriotic war of independence. In reality, the anti-Soviet war mapped onto many preexisting conflicts of Afghan society. The Afghan Communists were not just puppets of the Soviet Union: they were The City. The Mujahedeen were not just anti-Communist "freedom fighters." They were The Country. This war resumed the campaign of conservative Muslims against Amanullah in the 1920s. It resumed the ferocious contention within Afghan culture about the proper role of women in society. It was a war between the secular modernist impulse and the all-governing religion of Islam.

The political dominance of Pushtoons had been a given of Afghan society ever since a Pushtoon warrior founded the country, but the anti-Soviet war reopened that old can of worms. It put the question of power relationships among ethnic groups back on the table. When Ahmad Shah Massoud fought the Communists, he wasn't just fighting against the Soviets but for the Tajiks. The Hazara militias were fighting as Hazaras, the Uzbeks as Uzbeks. The Taliban capture of Kabul marked a triumph for Pushtoons against the other ethnic groups, and, within Pushtoon society, it represented a triumph for the southern Pushtoons of the area straddling the Durand Line over their sophisticated northern rivals, the aristocratic Durannis. With this victory, old Afghanistan looked to have beaten the new one decisively; the rural forces had defeated The City; the emancipation and empowerment of Afghan women had been halted for good; Amanullah's revolutionary reform program was dead at last.

In fact, everything the House of Dost Mohammed had built was in ruins. Kabul was not even the single, unquestioned capital of Afghanistan anymore. Kandahar was the real seat of Taliban power, Herat was in play again, Mazar-i-Sharif was the capital of an independent ministate in the north, and most parts of the country were ruled by autonomous, local warlords. In the south and southeast, even the border was dissolving. Was Afghanistan really a country? For some people, even that question was back on the table.

But when al Qaeda used this territory as its base for attacking the Twin Towers in New York, it drew the United States into the Afghan story. The United States quickly toppled the Taliban, but what did this portend for Afghanistan? Would Kabul stage a comeback? Would the urban elite now come back from exile? Would the old technocracy rise again? Was Afghanistan back on course to becoming a centralized modern nation-state with a democratic, constitutional government? Such were the questions Afghans were facing now.

28

The Bonn Project

THAT DECEMBER THE UNITED NATIONS CONVENED A CONFERENCE IN Germany to hammer out a plan for Afghanistan. It wasn't the usual sort of postwar peace conference, at which winners sit down and dictate their terms to the losers. The losers were not even at the table here. This conference was held to negotiate peace *among the winners*—that contentious array of Afghan factions and forces that had fought the Soviets. The Bonn Conference of December 2001 was, in fact, the meeting that probably should have taken place in 1992, right after the Soviet pullout. It brought together all the key players from that era (except the Communists, who were irrelevant now).

The delegates came to the meeting as individuals but could be sorted into four identifiable groups. There was the Northern Alliance, representing the minority ethnic parties of the north. There was "the Peshawar group," Pushtoon Mujahideen who had operated out of offices in Pakistan. There was "the Cypress group," delegates affiliated with the various groups supported by Iran, including the Hazaras and Heratis like Ismail Khan. Finally there was "the Rome group," the allies, associates, and supporters of former king Zahir Shah. These were the urban elite of prewar Afghanistan, including the educated technocrats who had been living in the West all these years. The Rome group represented the hopes of Afghan expatriates in Europe and the United States; to them, these were the men and women who would take Afghanistan back to the future.

The tribal Pushtoons of the rural south and southeast were excluded from the meeting, because the Taliban had sprung from among them and

American management felt that, if they were given a voice, the Taliban might sneak back into power incognito. The trouble was, the excluded Pushtoons were a key segment of the country's population. Excluding them could not help but expand the existing fissures of Afghan society, such as the rivalry between Ghilzai and Durrani Pushtoons, whose contention went back to the days of Ahmad Shah Baba. Excluding them also mapped onto the festering sore of Afghan history, the Durand Line, which split the territory of the very Afghans who were shut out of Bonn. The exclusion of these Pushtoons also emphasized the chasm between the wealthy cities of the north, especially Kabul, and the impoverished rural tribal south. This exclusion and its consequences would come back to haunt the country.

At the time, however, the delegates at the Bonn Conference went about their work with energy and optimism. "Guided" by the Western powers, they came up with a four-step plan:

1. First they would cobble together an interim government to manage the country for six months.

2. Next, they would convene a loya jirga—a Grand Tribal Assembly—to forge a two-year "transitional government" and elect a good man as its head.

3. Third, during that two-year transition period, a commission of learned Afghans would draft a new constitution.

4. Finally, presidential and parliamentary elections would be held, thereby completing Afghanistan's metamorphosis into a normal parliamentary democracy.

This plan had one telling flaw. It assumed an end point. The delegates at Bonn felt they could mandate presidential and parliamentary elections based on a constitution that had not yet been written because they already knew the constitution would set up a government with an elected president and parliament. The Bonn plan might have been perfect for a country being formed from scratch. Here, however, a story was already in progress, the story of a long-standing struggle between contrary impulses that kept pulling this society in opposite directions, polarities that included city versus countryside, change versus stasis, new versus old, state bureaucracy versus tribal relationships, secular institutions versus religious establishment, national military versus spontaneously self-organized local guerillas, and a central government operating out of Kabul versus an amorphous universe of village-republics without any center, the original Afghanistan versus Abdu'Rahman's Afghanistan. The history of the country was the story of the pendulum swinging back and forth between these camps. In recent decades, each swing of the pendulum had taken the country further in each direction. The Communist regime represented the country's most extreme swing toward an urban centralized state imposing secular authority over all the land; the Taliban regime had been the most extreme swing toward a conservative-religious Afghanistan ruled by clerics turned feudal warlords.

What came out of Bonn was not a plan to reconcile these extremes but a mustering of international support for one side of the struggle. The conferees mapped out a vision of Afghanistan rebuilt as a secular nation around a core of Western values. Many Afghans would sincerely love to see that plan succeed. I include myself in that number. But then, we would: we're products of the modernist impulse in Afghan history. So are most of the Afghans known to most Americans, because we're the ones who made it to the West when the Soviet invasion drove Afghans into exile.

The Bonn plan represented a comeback for the Afghan technocracy and the old Afghan aristocracy. It marked a resumption of the oft-interrupted Afghan project launched by Dost Mohammed, enlarged by Abdu'Rahman, and radicalized by Amanullah. There was never any doubt that the other side would regroup and fight back, because the pendulum has never stopped swinging in Afghanistan, between a temporary victory for one side, followed by a backlash and a temporary victory for the other side.

The Bonn Conference completed its work smoothly. With pronounced and perhaps heavy-handed guidance from the United States, the delegates shaped their interim authority and selected a compromise candidate, Hamid Karzai, to head it up. Karzai was a logical choice for America, even though he had never done much to prove himself a leader of men. He had relatives living in the United States—his brother Mahmoud had built the first significant Afghan restaurants in the United States, including the Helmand of San Francisco, which had won acclaim from

Gourmet Magazine. Karzai was friends with Reagan's Afghan advisor Zalmay Khalilzad and through him had connections to the Republican insiders who had engineered the election of George Bush. He was rumored to have worked for Unocal, the Dallas-based oil company, although the exact relationship remains ambiguous (and Karzai himself denies there ever was one). A worldly sophisticate, Karzai understood the priorities of global business, spoke fluent English, and could be trusted not to sow social discomfort at diplomatic gatherings.

On the other hand, Hamid Karzai had some good, old-fashioned Afghan tribal cred as well. He was a Pushtoon; his father was a khan of the Popalzais, a leading (Durrani) Pushtoon tribe; the Popalzai were a leading clan in Kandahar, the most Pushtoon of Afghan cities. And although the Karzais had supported the Taliban early on, Karzai Senior was assassinated by the Taliban, which made Hamid credible as an opponent of the ousted regime.

It's true that Karzai had no personal following in Afghanistan, but this meant he had no die-hard enemies there either. He had no legendary anti-Soviet military exploits to his credit, but, then, every leader who had distinguished himself in that war had also disgraced himself in that war and its aftermath. With no following, no enemies, and no war crimes marring his résumé, Karzai looked like an ideal man to oversee the building of a new country utterly severed from its past.

The Northern Alliance could not be ignored, however, because they occupied Kabul, so the three key ministries—defense, interior, and foreign affairs—went to Massoud's three chief aides, General Fahim, Younus Qanouni, and the man with the name so nice they gave it to him twice—Dr. Abdullah Abdullah.

The Bonn Conference differed from most peace parlays in another way as well: it began before the fighting ended. In fact it began before the fighting even peaked. As the Afghan delegates were making their way to Germany, US Special Forces and Northern Alliance warriors were attacking the Tora Bora cave complex near Afghanistan's southeastern border. US forces fired incendiary devices into the caves and incinerated everyone inside, but Osama Bin Laden somehow escaped.

In the north, Northern Alliance troops continued to battle hard-core contingents of Arab and Pakistani Jihadis. Hundreds of the latter were captured, but most of them were later killed during an attempted prison break. As many as seven thousand Taliban militants and hard-core al Qaeda operatives were cornered in the north, but the United States allowed Pakistan to airlift the several thousand Arabs and Pakistanis away in Pakistani airplanes before Northern Alliance forces could get to them.[1]

In the south, after Tora Bora, the fighting moved to the valley of Shahikot. Eight soldiers were killed in a helicopter crash there, America's first major casualties. I saw the news on the big-screen satellite TV in a Peshawar guesthouse where I happened to be staying at that moment, a TV that could get fifty or sixty channels, from CNN to Al Jazeera to dozens of local stations that usually broadcast cricket or soccer games. That day all were covering the death of the eight Americans, nonstop.

An Afghan villager who had recently crossed the border was sitting next to me, staring at the TV in awe: "Who were these great generals?" he asked.

"They weren't generals," I told him. "They were regular soldiers."

He was puzzled. "In my village, people are killed every day, sometimes ten or twenty in a single day, and it's never on the news. You must be wrong. These men must have been very important."

At Shahikot, the Taliban fought savagely but went down to utter defeat in a week. On March 18, US general Tommy Franks declared that the major fighting was over and America had won. Contrary to all the "graveyard-of-empires" talk, conquering Afghanistan had been easy. A few thousand troops would remain along the border to "mop up" "Taliban remnants," but the Bonn process could now proceed.

Step two was scheduled for June. Backstage managers had arranged for this step to run smoothly too. Old King Zahir Shah had agreed not to reassert his former authority. In return, ousted president Burhanuddin Rabbani, head of the powerful Northern Alliance, had agreed not to bid for any office. This deal cleared the way for the man who was now widely perceived as a suave international fashion plate, Hamid Karzai, to take charge of the transitional government.

Then came a glitch. In the week before the jirga, one of the king's grandsons gave an interview. He said that *actually*, His Majesty might want to play a more active role after all. The next morning the walls of the city were papered with posters of Rabbani, which sent a chilling message. If the king ran, Rabbani would run, and, if he ran, the streets of Kabul might soon run red with blood in a horrifying replay of 1992. Zalmay Khalilzad swooped in to smooth things over, and he managed it: the king said he'd been misquoted, the posters of Rabbani vanished. The jirga opened on June 11 as scheduled and went smoothly. Very smoothly.

Too smoothly, perhaps. At a real jirga people would have been arguing for days, roaring out speeches, and cutting deals on the perimeters. The outcome would have been unknown at the start, and the group's decision would have represented an actual and hard-won consensus. This jirga was stage-managed to the max, its conclusions preordained. Everybody knew Karzai was America's choice and would win.

For form's sake, two other candidates got listed and gave brief speeches at the podium. One was a woman named Masooda Jalal, a powerful feminist voice who vowed to defend women's rights. She got a few polite votes. The other was the poet Nedai, who told the assembly he would create jobs. He got a few token votes. Later, Nedai said he knew he had no hope of winning but felt that an election with only one candidate didn't look good. He ran for office only to help build democracy per se: quite a gallant gesture, really.

To this day, Afghans wonder why the United States was so determined to squeeze the former king, Zahir Shah, out of the picture, even though he was the only credible countrywide symbol of reconciliation. Dr. Shams, a former economics professor at Kabul University, told me that, if only he had been allowed to run, he would have declared full support for the American intervention and then told the assembly that if elected he would hand all power over to the former king, the man the assembly really wanted. Shams figured his promise would bring him a flood of support that would overwhelm the American plan to install Karzai. His scheme sounded cunning, but he was not even allowed into the tent, much less to the podium. The loya jirga moved swiftly to elect Hamid Karzai, legitimizing his rule by the very same process that had elevated Ahmad Shah Baba to the throne—at least to the extent that Afghans considered this assembly a real loya jirga, but many didn't. The seeds of doubt about America were planted at this first grand council.

Next, Karzai appointed a commission to draft a new constitution, and they completed their task by December 2003. The government called another loya jirga to ratify this document, which was less stage-managed and therefore a bit more messy. One of the most electrifying moments came when Malalai Joya, a young female delegate from a western border province, stood up and denounced the bearded old men surrounding her as warlords and criminals. She said they should be in a docket on trial for war crimes, not seated in a national assembly, discussing the future of the nation. The old guard shouted her down and called her a harlot.

Over the next month, every interest group in the country pushed for alterations in the draft constitution, resulting in a final document that is oddly vague in some places, oddly specific in others. It takes the trouble, for example, to declare ex-king Zahir Shah "the nation's father," a stipulation soon rendered irrelevant by the old man's death. This constitution declares many times that Afghanistan is an Islamic republic and bans any law conflicting with the Shari'a, but it also specifies that men and women are free, that women have equal rights, and that these include the right to vote, work, and get a (free) education, all of which echo the issues of Amanullah's day and tries to finesse them in the same way as he.

The new constitution sets up a parliament with a lower house elected by the people and an upper house appointed by a president, and it limits the president to two consecutive five-year terms—unless, at the end of his second term, he deems it necessary for the good of the country to stay in power, in which case he can.

Both parliament and president can initiate laws, but if parliament doesn't approve of laws issued by the president, he can't enact them—unless he deems it absolutely necessary for the good of the nation, in which case of course he can.

When the new constitution was promulgated, I asked some of my Afghan acquaintances in California what they thought of it. Mustafa Popal, a college administrator in Alameda, answered, "If it gives us ten years of peace, I'll be happy. Ten years is all I ask." A low bar for a constitution, it seems to me.

The real issue for Afghanistan, however, was not whether the constitution would provide adequate mechanisms but whether Afghans would accept a constitution at all. Filmmaker Tamara Gould, in her documentary *A Hell of a Nation*, asks a man on the street what he thinks of the *Qanoon-i Assassi* (Dari for "constitution" but literally "the Fundamental Law"). The man just shakes his head. "Why do we need a fundamental law?" he grins. "We already have a Fundamental Law. It's called the Shari'a." All his buddies hanging around nod and chuckle knowingly at the absurdity of forging a fundamental law for a country that already *has* one!

Still, the Bonn process moved forward well enough at first. In the fall of 2004, the country held a remarkably successful presidential election. Before the election, the United Nations organized teams of Afghans to fan out across the country and register voters. The teams included women who could get inside the rural fortresses and tell the folks inside what elections were all about. My cousin Zaheda, who worked with one such team, found tremendous enthusiasm among rural women. "I'm going to have my husband bring me an armload of ballots, as many as he can carry," one woman told her. "I'm going to spend the whole election day just voting and voting."

In the end, more than 12 million Afghans registered to vote, including 750,000 living in the refugee camps in Pakistan. Considering that Afghanistan has a population of 30 million and that 57 percent of them were underage (eighteen or younger), that 12 million probably represents the bulk of eligible voters. And about three-quarters of the registered voters made it to the polls, numbers that may seem inflated in the United States, where fewer than half of voters cast a ballot, even fewer if it rains; but investigations turned up (relatively) few examples of fraud, and anyone who drove around on that election day could see the long lines that formed at voting places, even women in burqas waiting for hours to exercise their right.

There were eighteen candidates on the final ballot, ranging from the secular Tajik poet Abdul Latif Pedram to the conservative Islamist professor "engineer" Ahmad Shah Ahmadzai. One of the eighteen was physician Masooda Jalal, who opposed Karzai at that first loya jirga. She campaigned on the slogan "This suffering country needs a mother and a doctor, and I am both."

Campaigning was limited, because only Hamid Karzai had the resources to send his team to every part of the country. "Taliban remnants" tried to intimidate potential voters, in one hideous case ambushing a bus and killing all on board who had voting cards in their possession. Even so, more than 9 million people cast ballots on election day. It was heroic.

Most of those voters could not read, so they had no idea who was on the ballot. To alleviate the problem, candidates were allowed to include a graphic or icon next to their picture that conveyed what they stood for. One candidate, for example, wanted voters to know he was a progressive who stood for modern education, so he chose as his icon—a book. Another candidate wanted everyone to know he was a God-fearing conservative who stood foursquare by the Koran and so he chose as his icon—a book.

In short, many who went to the polls that day didn't really cast a ballot for a particular candidate. Their vote expressed support for voting itself. Seen in this light, the election was a big success.

Parliamentary elections held a few months later were more disorderly. More fraud occurred, more violence broke out before, during, and after election day; but in the end a parliament was seated and so, by early 2005, the four-step process mapped out at Bonn had been completed, and even a moderate optimist could believe that Afghanistan was on the verge of takeoff.

TAKEOFF WAS NOT BY ANY MEANS A DONE DEAL, HOWEVER. THE BONN plan was coming to a country devastated by violence and chaos. In the decades of turmoil, the smartest move for any Afghan had been to trust in guns, distrust neighbors, and cluster under the protection of the nearest strongman of familiar ethnicity. The Bonn project could not succeed so long as the country remained in that state of jangled paranoia. From the moment the first loya jirga ended, a race was on between order and chaos. Peace could come only if order won. Order could come only if most people put away their guns and started hatching long-term plans. Most people, however, don't patiently pursue long-term goals unless they believe the future will be stable. No use repairing a house if a bomb is going to land on it tomorrow.

The architects of the new Afghanistan therefore had to restore enough normalcy to make at least a few people believe that the Bonn process was going to work and hence that those who bought in early would be the big winners later. If just a few started trying to establishing credibility as citizens of the new order—by entering schools, acquiring job skills, starting businesses, and so on—the Bonn process would look credible, whereupon others would follow suit, whereupon the Bonn process would start to look inevitable, whereupon waves of people would surge to board the train before it left the station, and society would hit a tipping point toward (the new) order.

Not everyone *wanted* peace and order, however, at least not the kind envisioned at Bonn. If Kabul could impose its authority over every district and village, the country as a whole might see more peace and some people in the country might build fine lives; but at every level of local power, there were people who would lose something: the power struggle delineated in Abdu'Rahman's day was hardly over. Self-appointed rural clerics, tribal chieftains, village maliks raised to power by jirgas—all these would lose the ground they had gained during the chaos. All would see their status sink. And if Western values prevailed down to the level of households, men as a class would lose some of the power they had to lord it over women in their own households. Among the women, uneducated older women who dominated domestic governance would be superseded by younger women comfortable outside the compound, girls who would go to school and who might even contemplate careers in the public realm. Anyone who stood to lose from the Bonn project had a stake in seeing it fail.

Most importantly, there were rootless men roaming the Afghan landscape who had come of age during the chaos. They may have hailed from lower-status families, but, during the war, nothing mattered except how well a man could fight, so the toughest fighters had come to prominence. And, once Afghans had started fighting one another, it wasn't just fighting ability that determined pecking order, because lots of men could fight; when two tough guys went head-to-head, the winner was apt to be the one with the fewest scruples and the greatest appetite for brutality.

The years of war and chaos had thus acted as a filter, sifting out traits such as compassion and refinement and favoring unscrupulous brutes for whom the breakdown of social structures was a boon. The dissolution of families and communities liberated them from the judgments of their culture; the absence of any controlling authority gave them license to operate with impunity. Back when Afghans were still fighting the Soviets, guerilla leaders were called "commanders." After the Soviets left, many came to be known as warlords. Their prevalence sparked the backlash that led to the rise of the Taliban, but, in the end, the Taliban years only sifted out from among the hardest of hard cases those who could attach the honorific of "mullah" to their name. Afghanistan was now brimming with commander-warlord-mullahs. In a society governed by jihadist ideology, their skills would count mightily. They would be heroes. If the Bonn process succeeded, their very strengths would become liabilities, and they might be redefined as criminals. *They* had every stake in preventing the new society from taking shape.

The majority of Afghans were sick of war. Nine million of them said so by going to the polls in 2004. But the architects of the new order faced a harder task than the militant radicals interested in keeping society fragmented, because no single positive accomplishment ignites a prairie fire of belief. It takes an accumulation of good moments. The inauguration of one hospital, the completion of one bridge, the opening of one school, the graduation ceremonies of one class—each adds a drop to the pool of public confidence, but it takes a lot of drops to fill a pool.

By contrast, the bombing of one hospital, the burning down of one school, the destruction of one bridge, the disruption of one graduation ceremony with a suicide bombing triggers a shock that feeds on itself like a scream in an echo chamber. The real thugs needed to deliver only sporadic blasts of horror, knowing that each one would trigger masses of people to grab for guns, bar their windows, and get ready to shoot on sight. As more people behaved this way, behaving this way would become an ever smarter move, until turmoil reached a tipping point. In the race between chaos and order, everything depended on which side reached a tipping point first.

Pakistan still had a stake, too, in preventing an autonomous government from coalescing in Kabul. Talibanism seeping into Pakistan had set off insurgencies directed at the government in Islamabad, with tribal rebels from the Swat Valley to Baluchistan organizing their own militant movements in the name of the Shari'a law and ethnic chauvinism. The Pakistani government had everything to gain from redirecting this insurgent energy back toward Kabul and away from Islamabad, which might be accomplished by sending agents in to commit occasional acts of senseless sabotage.

What's more, the various mafias that operated along the border—the trucking mafia, the drug mafias, the smuggling mafias, the gun-running mafias (overlapping groups, to be sure)—had become thoroughly intertwined with the Talibanism movement, and they were busy building up their own militias. All these forces had their own reasons to block the rise of a new Afghanistan, and they lined up against the central government, the urban culture of Kabul, the war-weary Afghan majority, the expatriate Afghan technocrats, the international community, and the might and money of the United States.

29

Kabul Spring

AT FIRST, THE BONN PROJECT HAD THE MOMENTUM. IN JANUARY 2002, right after the conference ended, representatives from a host of developed countries met in Tokyo to calculate what it would cost to put Afghanistan right. Dizzying numbers were flung about: $10 billion . . . $15 billion . . . $20 billion. . . .

In the United States, President Bush spoke of a "Marshall Plan for Afghanistan." Marshall Plan! Urban Afghans knew about that Truman administration program to help Europe rebuild after World War II. The program spent staggering sums of money, and the spending worked: it revitalized the whole Western European economy. It stemmed the advance of Communism—and incidentally helped enrich America. The success of the Marshall Plan made it seem plausible that America would spend massively to help get Muslim Afghanistan back on its feet: after all, a loyal, prosperous *Muslim* ally at the heart of central Asia could serve America's strategic interests incalculably—and certainly help stem the tide of Jihadism.

By summer, Afghans were buzzing about the Marshall Plan. Everybody was talking about what they were going to do with their share of the money. On the plane from Delhi to Kabul that year, I met a man who said he was going to start a cosmetics factory. Mind you, this was not some Afghan-American suit from Fremont, California, but a shopkeeper who had never been further from his hometown than Delhi. He had a huge black beard and was wearing a traditional knee-length shirt, baggy pants, and a bulky turban. I could easily imagine Reuters using his photo as a stock image for generic stories about the Taliban.

"A cosmetics factory?" I said.

"Yes," he explained. "Now that the Taliban are gone, women are going to be going out, and there will be a huge demand for cosmetics. My cousin is already planning to get rich importing lipstick from Dubai, but I say— why import? We Afghans are perfectly capable of making our own lipstick."

In the village from which my family hails, people were talking about using their portion of the Marshall Plan money to dig artesian wells (a common small-scale business scheme before the war). The drought was entering its seventh year, but, if they could only irrigate their fields, they could produce commercial quantities of the coveted Hosseini grapes that sold so handsomely in Kabul. Why, they'd be rolling in money!

Young Kanishka Nawabi, who had lived in Peshawar during the Taliban years and had worked there for a Swedish-based environmental nonprofit called AREA, Association for Reconstruction and Energy Conservation in Afghanistan, was back in Kabul with a plan to distribute some AREA inventions commercially. One was a portable, water-driven generator that might be marketed to villages not yet hooked up to the grid: virtually every village had, after all, a stream rushing down from the high peaks, or else there wouldn't have been a village in that spot at all. With his device, a village could use its creek to generate enough electricity to power at least a communal town center and still use that same water to irrigate fields downstream. It would be huge! The same group had created a solar heater that could double as a TV satellite dish and another device that extracted fuel-grade methane from cow dung. All were surefire best sellers in rural Afghanistan.

The Tokyo Conference finally decided that the reconstruction of Afghanistan would require $25 billion! Afghan leaders attending the conference didn't push their luck; they asked for only $10 billion. Unfortunately, donor nations at the conference pledged only $3 billion. Never mind: that was still more money than anyone had dreamed possible only one year earlier, and more might yet be pledged.[1]

By midsummer, optimism filled the air of Kabul like the fine silt that filled the constant summer breeze. The exiles were streaming back, all those PhDs and doctors, all those financial experts, administrators, and engineers. There were people like Dr. Sherzai, who came home from Fremont, California, the biggest Afghan community outside Asia, to serve as his country's deputy foreign minister. From Johns Hopkins University came Professor Ashraf Ghani, an eminent political scientist and economist who had once been short-listed to succeed Kofi Annan as secretary-general of the United Nations. He stepped into the role of finance minister. And there were many others.

By the end of the year, however, less than half the amount pledged at Tokyo had come in. Still, for a poor country like Afghanistan, even a billion or two was manna. Expatriates returning from the West began to reclaim their properties in Kabul. Most of their houses were rubble, but the land was still good—they could build on it again. Some returning exiles who had studied architecture and city planning helped the government draw up an urban renewal plan that envisioned sewage pipes, streetlights, electrical lines to every home, a municipal water system, and all the other elements of infrastructure so vital to a great metropolis and so difficult to install once a busy city already exists. It was almost a boon, really, that a third to a half of Kabul had been destroyed during the civil war and that none of it had been rebuilt by the Taliban. In fact, planners decided not to even bother hauling away most of the rubble: they would build a new Kabul north of the ruins, on what had previously been farmers' fields or simply barren desert.

Many Afghans with a modicum of money living in Europe and America returned to Afghanistan to carry out idealistic development projects of their own. There was Mohammed Khan Kharoti, for example, a longtime resident of Portland, Oregon, who graduated from the same school I had attended in Lashkargah. He was the child of one of those nomad families who were settled in the model town of Nadi Ali by the government of that time. He had acquired expertise in medical technology and was making a good living in America, but he began journeying back to his hometown to build the Green Village Schools. Actually, he'd founded these schools in Taliban times, with the consent of local Taliban officials, who had even allowed some girls to be educated there, so long as Kharoti promised to do his work quietly. Now, he didn't have to be surreptitious about his project anymore. Green Village Schools prospered and attracted donations and drew volunteers from abroad.

In Khost, the town near the Pakistan border where Bin Laden and al Qaeda had sunk such deep roots, Ghafar Lakanwal, a onetime Communist official who had defected from that government in the eighties and had been working as a community organizer in Minneapolis, built a school funded by American donors but supported by the local population in Khost. Lakanwal's school, too, educated both boys and girls. He insisted on it as a condition for building the school. Lakanwal had grown up near Khost, in one of those rural fortress/village communities that had only a few hundred inhabitants, the typical rural configuration of so much of Afghanistan. He wanted to give something back.

Other countries also began building schools. In early 2003, I attended a fund-raiser organized by a group associated with the Iranian filmmaker Makhmalbaf, which had ambitious plans to construct scores of private schools in Afghanistan. It wasn't clear to me where the schools would get their operating budget once they were built, and only later did I wonder what the curriculum would be and who would develop it. One thing was certain: these schools would educate girls as well as boys. In the aftermath of the Taliban's notorious gender policies, this was the one thing everybody was sure of: every new enterprise planned for Afghanistan would function as an instrument for liberating and empowering Afghan women.

Kabul University had never quite closed, but in Taliban times the clerics had reduced it to little more than a stunted madrassa. And, even before that, the Communists had compromised the academic integrity of the university by twining Marxist-Leninist doctrine into many courses. But now Kabul University became a full-fledged four-year university again, back on the road to academic respectability. By fall, the campus teemed with several thousand students, and already, I was told, about 40 percent of them were women. And the university didn't just offer programs in technical, medical, and scientific fields but also in cultural disciplines such as literature, history, and the arts. When I visited the art college, I saw some students creating meticulous, nonrepresentational Islamic art, but others were painting or sculpting portraits, landscapes, and other figurative subjects that the Taliban would have found offensively pagan.

Music burst out in the cities. Some people still had transistor radios from the old days and others acquired new ones now. Kabul Radio—dubbed Shari'a Radio in Taliban times—reclaimed its old name and began to broadcast popular tunes once more. Previously unheard-of pop singers came to instant prominence. I was particularly taken with singer Dil Agha's merry song "Kabul Jan" (Kabul Dearest), a raucous celebration of his native city.

Old music was heard again too—songs by the revered Ahmad Zahir for example—since it turned out that just about everybody still had cassette tapes hidden away from the old days. In Taliban times, they had listened to their tapes secretly, after dark, with the curtains drawn and the volume turned down low. Now they broke them out and blasted their music in public. In the streets, one saw people with Walkman-type players and earphones plugged into their ears, bobbing their heads and bopping as they strolled along.

Both old and new music came flowing in from Pakistan, where some of the refugees had never stopped recording. In the heart of Kabul, near the river, at the very site of the Grand Bazaar that the British had burned down 161 years earlier, a labyrinthine covered market sprang up, with scores of stalls that vended audio- and videotapes. Arnold Schwarzenegger movies were popular, but the hottest video of them all was the James Cameron blockbuster *Titanic*. In fact, shopkeepers built stalls down in the riverbed of the Kabul River (the river had gone bone dry during the long drought that ended in 2002), and this came to be called the Titanic Bazaar (because if the river were running as in olden times, the shops would all have been underwater).

The national theater, Kabul Nindari, opened up again. In the 1960s and '70s, Kabul Nindari used to mount original Afghan plays during Jeshyn, the celebration that was banned by the Taliban for commemorating a secular event, Afghan independence from the British. Gul Makai Shah, who had acted on the Kabul Nindari stage as a girl, came back from exile as a middle-aged woman to revive the theater as its director. She recruited actors and scripts and, over the next few years, produced dozens of new plays and delivered over two hundred performances.[2] A children's vaudeville-type circus began touring the country, and another troupe hit the road with a Dari version of Shakespeare's *Love's Labour's Lost* set in modern Afghanistan.

The Asia Foundation funded a poignant project of the Afghan Media and Cultural Center, which resulted in a film called *Afghanistan Unveiled*.

Fourteen young Afghan women were taught how to use video cameras and were trained as video journalists. The young women then journeyed to various parts of the country, urban and rural, to interview women. The resulting film was fascinating both for the documentary footage the girls got and for the dramatic story of the girls' own lives unfolding. The women's world recorded by these young women had been inaccessible to male filmmakers even in pre-Taliban times because Afghan families simply don't let male strangers into the private portions of their homes; so these lives had been unseen by any public, even in the liberal era. What's more, the young videographers had all come of age in Taliban times. They themselves had hardly ever set foot outside their own compounds and didn't know what the street looked like one block over from their own. Now they were having the revelatory adventure of a lifetime, traveling to places as far away as Herat, Mazar-i-Sharif, and Khost, talking to strangers, finding out about their fellow Afghans, and in the process—it's plain from their commentary—finding out about themselves.[3]

In the late 1960s, a fledgling film industry had been born in Kabul. A government institute, Kabul Films, had built a library of movies relevant to Afghanistan. Only about forty of them (mostly shorts and documentaries) were made in the country. The civil wars had strangled the industry in its cradle, and then the Taliban in their last days sent an official to the institute to demolish its collection. He burned about two thousand films and destroyed all the filmmaking equipment he could find. He didn't know, however, that the institute's employees had hidden one thousand films and some production equipment behind a false wall.[4] Now, with the Taliban gone, they took down that false wall. Kabul Films rebuilt its production facilities with money from Japan. Expatriates such as USC film school graduate Yama Rahimi flew in from California to teach a summer film class at Kabul University to forty eager students.

At this time, Siddiq Barmaq, former director of Kabul Films, began working on his powerful narrative feature *Osama*—which has nothing to do with Osama bin Laden: the title character is a young girl who masquerades as a boy named Osama during the Taliban era in order to survive; her ruse is discovered and she is absorbed into the harem of a Taliban-connected mullah as one more of his chattel. The film garnered broad acclaim and won awards at international film festivals, paving the way for other productions, such as Horace Shansab's *Zoleikha's Secret*, filmed entirely in Afghanistan and shown to considerable applause at film festivals around the world.

The majestic Buddhas of Bamiyan had been destroyed by the Taliban, but several Kabul University professors now proposed that one of them be reconstructed—and the other left shattered as a solemn memorial to the tragedy that had befallen Afghan culture. The plan was controversial, but even as people were debating its pros and cons, an Afghan archeologist living in France, Professor Zemaryalai Tarzi, announced his belief that an even bigger *reclining* Buddha lay somewhere beneath the earth of this valley. His theory was based on a study of old travelers' texts, which suggested that the "sleeping Buddha" might be as much as three times larger than the largest of the standing Buddhas. Every summer after that, Tarzi led a team of excavators to Bamiyan to search for the sleeping Buddha. (Lately, the quest has been on hold because of fears that, if it were unearthed in this still-volatile era, new barbarians might destroy this treasure too.)

The Kabul Museum was a dramatic story in itself. In 1978, this was known as one of the world's finest small museums. It had a rich collection of art from the country's Gandharan period, when Buddhist influences mixed with Greek aesthetics to generate a Greco-Buddhist style found nowhere else in the world. But in the Communist era, Soviet and Afghan government officials had pilfered items from the museum and sold them into the international black market. After the Soviet withdrawal, the wars of Kabul had damaged the museum building. In the late nineties, the Taliban had hammered the remaining Greco-Buddhist statues into rubble. Now, museum officials set the rubble of each sculpture on a pedestal and above each pile of rubble hung a picture of the work as it once had looked: the museum became a testament to the cultural barbarity of the Taliban.

Then came the most astonishing announcement. In April 2004, museum director Omara Massoudi revealed that fifteen years earlier, foreseeing the troubles that were coming, he and a few associates had hidden more than twenty thousand of the museum's most precious artifacts in a secret vault. Archeologists from around the world gathered to watch him open that vault. It was practically like the discovery of King Tut's tomb except televised. Several hundred items from that breathtaking collection later toured the world as a show called The Gold of Afghanistan.

The fact that many of the artifacts are made from gold and silver and are studded with precious and semiprecious stones is the least of their fascination. The collection reflects the culture of this region from 2200 BC to about 100 CE, a span of more than two millennia. Here, in and around Afghanistan it turns out, someone was producing sophisticated bowls and flasks of gold and silver at the same time that the last pharaohs of Egypt's Old Kingdom were building pyramids and Sargon of Akkad was forging the first great Mesopotamian empire. From the Bactrian city of Al Khanum, built around 300 BC, a host of Greek items were recovered, such as a bronze Hercules and a silver plaque depicting the nature goddess Cybele riding a Persian chariot.

Nomads roaming northern Afghanistan at the time of Christ had their own workshops where they made refined artworks that combined influences from Persia, Greece, Rome, China, India, and Siberia: diadems encrusted with turquoise, a portable gold crown that folds for convenient storage, thin gold slippers worn by a nomad princess.

The show included amazing artifacts excavated from two sealed rooms found at Bagram. Originally, archeologists thought the rooms must have housed some king's treasures. Now, they know those were commercial warehouses where some merchant stored the items he was buying and selling: flasks of blown glass from Roman Egypt, bronze statues from Syria, Chinese lacquer, Indian ivory sculptures, pendants depicting Greek myths, plaques recounting the life of Buddha, and complex sculptures of big-breasted mother goddesses intertwined with dancing Hindu gods. Journalism professor Joel Brinkley recently described Afghans as the most brutal and primitive people on Earth and casually asserted that "Afghans are like wolf spiders. They eat their young."[5] When one stands before these artifacts and reflects on the risks that Massoudi and his aides took to protect and preserve them, one can't help but find Brinkley's racist utterance particularly loathsome. The horrors seen in Afghanistan recently were not spawned by a genetic resemblance between Afghans and wolf spiders but by decades of catastrophic tragedy. Now, however, the dark ages seemed to have ended. Afghans were poised to embark upon another epoch of civilized achievement. Or were they?

THE MARSHALL PLAN FOR AFGHANISTAN NEVER MATERIALIZED, unfortunately. The thousands of Afghans with small-scale schemes never got the starter money they needed to ignite their dreams. It was private enterprise on a larger scale that took off with a vengeance. Many of the returning exiles had enough money, savvy, and connections to raise capital for such enterprises as banks and cell phone companies and TV stations. A country that never fully made it into the industrial age looked like it was about to proceed directly to the postindustrial age. A place that never had railroads would now have air service to every city—this was the promise. A place that never had much in the way of telephone landlines would jump directly into the age of the cell phone. A place that never managed to get a truly national postal system working would have the Internet now, and everyone would acquire an e-mail address.

In the world at large, multinational corporations and international agencies were rendering national borders ambiguous; in Afghanistan, a place that never completely coalesced into a nation-state, the first post-national society seemed to be emerging, a territory in which private companies headquartered in China, Russia, Turkey, India, Iran, Holland, Australia, Germany, Canada and elsewhere would shape everyday life, and government would be an afterthought, shriveled to irrelevance, for it would scarcely be needed once untrammeled private enterprise really felt its oats.

30

The Persistence
of Trouble

STILL NO ONE COULD KID THEMSELVES: THE URBAN ARCHITECTS OF A NEW
Afghanistan faced daunting problems. Take, for example, the refugees—
by whom I mean those poor, mostly rural Afghans who, when they fled
the Afghan holocaust, got only as far as camps in Pakistan and Iran. (I re-
serve the term *exile* for educated Afghans who had the resources and skills
to make it to developed countries and establish new lives.) In 2002,
Afghans constituted the world's biggest refugee population, the Cambo-
dians being a distant second. Many of those six million refugees now
wanted to come home, and host countries were pushing them to go.

But home to what? Many of these folks had eked out a living as
herders, but they couldn't go back to herding; their flocks had mostly been
slaughtered by Soviet gunners and the rest they had lost when they fled.

Fruits and nuts had been big commercial crops for Afghan farmers in
the old days. Afghan grapes had once supplied over 10 percent of the
world's raisins including most of those found in Raisin Bran.[1] The country
had also earned cash from figs, pomegranates, pears, almonds, walnuts,
mulberries, melons, and the like. But Pakistan produced many of these
same fruits and nuts, and during the wars Pakistanis had paid cash for
Afghan bare root fruit trees, especially pistachios. Afghan orchards had
gone unplanted and neglected. Now, even if farmers were to plant new
trees, they would take years to mature.

Of course, Afghans had harvested other crops such as wheat and cotton in the old days, but they lacked seeds, and irrigating their desert soil would be difficult now—not just due to the drought the country was going through but also because the old underground irrigation canals had been destroyed. Some had silted up, some had been bombed, and many had been converted into guerilla hideouts. (When you hear about Afghans living in caves, the "caves" in question are often these underground irrigation tunnels retrofitted with concrete for military use.)

Besides, their fields were filled with land mines. No country on earth had more of these pernicious devices. A land mine costs about $3 to plant and about $1,000 to remove.[2] Rural Afghans didn't have the sophisticated equipment they needed to remove the mines safely. They simply had to crawl over their fields on their hands and knees, looking for the dust-colored triggers. If they missed one and crawled over it, they would be crippled or dead. Children were still losing limbs to land mines every day, and farmers had to clear a lot of acres to make a living growing wheat. Too many. It just wasn't feasible.

Many of the refugees therefore didn't go back to their original homes. They went to the cities to look for jobs. Jobs being scarce, many ended up as homeless squatters living in the shells of abandoned ruins. The returning families were preponderantly made up of widows and orphans. The widows roamed the streets in their blue burqas, begging for change, and anyone who looked like he or she had money was well advised to keep moving so as not to be mobbed by these burqa-clad beggars. The children roamed the streets scavenging cans to sell as scrap metal and discarded shoes to sell for leather and anything else of value they could sort from piles of trash.

Into these cities crowded with homeless female beggars and packs of parentless children came the exiles from the west. They had the skills needed to rebuild the country, and they felt equipped to undertake the job, but there were problems inherent to projects in which upper-echelon managers who had lived abroad in safety and comfort were directing workers who had lived in Afghanistan all along and had suffered through the horrors of those years. The latter began to call the former "dog washers," a jesting suggestion that, in the West, the exiles had made their living washing dogs for rich folks. (Dogs are considered unclean by Muslims.)

It was a way of saying, "We stayed, we suffered, but we never bowed our heads; you went abroad and prospered but you lost your honor kowtowing to infidels."

Liberal peace activists in the West regarded education and reconstruction as the answers to all the ills of Afghanistan, the moral alternative to military force. Perhaps this idea held water in 2002, for, at that moment, the prospects for an Afghan renaissance looked rosy. The country was bursting with entrepreneurial energy, everyone had a project in mind, and microlending on a grand scale might have made all the difference.

By microlending, I mean foreign funders doling out loans and grants for small projects proposed by enterprising Afghan individuals and groups and letting those Afghans design and run the projects as they deemed fit—deep wells, lipstick-making workshops, whatever. For example, a group called Afghans-4-Tomorrow developed a hand-operated device it is distributing in rural areas, a device that compresses agricultural waste—sticks, stems, wheat stubble, and the like—into bricks of long-burning fuel. In a country virtually denuded of firewood, such a project is manna, especially since individual families that own these devices can use them to produce home heating fuel commercially.

Microlending to projects like this would have meant that instead of spending $1 billion on three projects, the international community would have given $5,000 apiece to half a million projects. In 2002, when a single dollar equaled 45,000 afghanis, $5,000 would have gone a long way. Much of the money disbursed in this manner would no doubt have been "wasted." Some would have been stolen, and many of the projects would probably have failed, but manageably small sums would have percolated into the local economy even through the failed projects—and at least some of the money would have done some direct good, because Afghans' ideas of what to fix and how to fix it would have come out of their own actual lives and would have drawn upon technologies with which they were familiar.

There was never any realistic chance of this happening. For one thing, no infrastructure existed for disbursing the money this way, no army of grant officers that could be fielded quickly. Besides, this approach would have required that donors pay out vast sums with no control over how the money was spent and with no direct benefit to themselves, and no funder was going to do that. Finally, most potential donors, including the deepest and purest of idealists, didn't want to see mere restoration in Afghanistan; they wanted to see transformation. So when reconstruction money came pouring in, as it did eventually from countries around the globe, it came in huge chunks for grand projects planned abroad and designed to produce a national metamorphosis.

The US contribution got off to a slow start because the party in power had a conflicted attitude about helping any ruined nation recover its social and economic infrastructure. As a candidate campaigning for the presidency, George Bush had railed against "nation building" and had vowed that *he* would never do any of it if he were elected. It was natural, then, for his administration to treat the intervention in Afghanistan as a purely military mission. The aim had been to topple the Taliban and kill Osama bin Laden, nothing more. Afghanistan might be hurting, but fixing it wasn't America's job—so went one strain of thinking in the Bush administration.

For the rest of that year and into the next, the bulk of American spending in Afghanistan went to the 5,200 troops still stationed in the far southeast and south, near the Pakistan border. Their mission was quite specific. They were to "mop up" the last of the "Taliban remnants" and come home as soon as that job was done. Securing the rest of the country was turned over to the International Security Assistance Force, or ISAF, staffed by nations such as Turkey and Germany (and soon run by NATO).

But the run-up to the intervention in Afghanistan made a quick in-and-out impractical. For one thing, every war needs public support. Public support requires righteous passion. Anger about 9/11 provided plenty of passion but didn't fully satisfy the requirement that the passion be noble. The women's issue was co-opted to meet this need. Officially the war may have been fought to punish terrorists, but sentimentally it was fought to rescue Afghan women from Afghan men. Never mind that the situation of Afghan women was embedded in the culture, which only Afghans could transform. Now that the war was over, it was necessary that the lot of Afghan women at least look improved before American troops left the country. Otherwise—Osama bin Laden having escaped—the whole thing would have been for naught.

Also, just months after the United States intervened in Afghanistan and before the fighting ended there, the Bush administration started beating the drum for another war, a war to topple Iraqi dictator Saddam Hussein. This new war was sold on the core neoconservative doctrine that America could spread democracy and promote happiness by taking aggressive military action against tyrannies. So the United States sent a hundred thousand troops into Iraq, supported by forty-seven thousand from Great Britain and twenty-seven thousand from the "Coalition of the Willing," a ragtag lineup of thirty-six other countries (including Iceland, which contributed two). Hussein proved easy to topple, but the democracy, prosperity, and happiness that were supposed to follow proved elusive.

By mid-2003, Iraq looked like a failed initiative, and that failure made a happy outcome in Afghanistan all the more crucial. Originally the Bush administration seemed to think Afghanistan would straighten out on its own, but by the end of 2003 it was coming to terms with the probability that the United States might have to do some nation building to ensure that women be liberated and empowered, that democracy take root, and that Afghanistan end up stable and prosperous.

In 2002–2003, America spent some $35 billion on military operations and war-related costs in Afghanistan.[3] It budgeted nearly $800 million for humanitarian and emergency aid, and less than a tenth of that, about $64 million, on long-term reconstruction projects. The following year, funding for reconstruction and development projects began to climb.[4] By then, money was also beginning to pour in from many other countries. Some was spent directly by government agencies of the donor nations. Most went through private firms hired by governments or through nongovernmental organizations (NGOs), which are private organizations funded by public grants and private donations—analogous to what, within America, are called nonprofit corporations. The NGOs ranged from private charities such as Roots for Peace (an organization dedicated to removing land mines) to long-established giants such as the Asia Foundation, which has been doing development work in Asia since the early days of the Cold War, largely to support US foreign policy goals. Many NGOs, especially those staffed by Afghans and run locally, did truly vital work against great odds. Still, by 2003, more than three hundred outside NGOs had some ten thousand employees living and working in Kabul, and, as of 2006, that number had climbed above sixteen hundred.[5]

In fact, 77 percent of the reconstruction money spent in Afghanistan bypassed the Afghan government entirely, according to a study done in 2009: it went through NGOs, private corporations, or foreign government agencies without ever passing through Afghan government ministries.[6] Whatever benefits these billions of dollars may have conferred (and some conferred a lot), they did nothing to build the government's authority within the country. To many Afghans these projects made their government look like a hapless bystander.

Some projects planned on the other side of the world might have been sound in theory, but on the ground they looked like they were carried out for somebody else's benefit, and, because some were executed hastily (to provide markers of success ahead of the re-election campaigns that both Bush and Karzai would be facing in 2004), they were carried out incompetently.

A road linking Sar-e-Pul to Shiberghan, two provinces in northern Afghanistan, offers a striking example. The road was a good idea; it cut travel time between busy provincial cities, a wonderful impetus for trade. The trouble was, people living along the road did not have occasion to visit the cities frequently, and many did not own cars or trucks. When they did go to a city, they usually traveled on foot, with donkeys carrying their goods, so the better road didn't cut their travel time by all that much. The new road was certainly better than the dirt tracks the villagers had built and maintained themselves over the decades. Those tracks were ruts filled with dust in the summer and mud after the rains started.

The American road was built on a raised stone substructure to keep it dry, but the surveys done so hastily failed to take the slope of the landscape into account along the entire length of the road. In some places, the high, impermeable berm acted as a dam. The road didn't have culverts in the necessary places, so the water collected into pools on the uphill side. Villagers worried that the water would soften the soil enough to make their cob huts collapse. Some villagers went out with picks, therefore, and cut channels in the road to serve as drains, which defeated the whole purpose of the road, because automobile traffic could not cross even one such improvised ditch. The police caught and arrested the villagers who had done this destructive deed.[7] The road did thus create an interaction between the rural folk and the government, but not one that made *the* government feel like *their* government.

The biggest, most heroic reconstruction project attempted by the Americans in the early days was to rebuild the road between Kabul and Kandahar, the country's two main cities. No one could impeach the argument for this project, which cut travel time between these cities by two-thirds. It proved extremely expensive, however, and, as with many construction projects carried out in Afghanistan by American technical experts and with American funding, much of the money was spent in America. That's because infrastructure projects of this sort had to gain approval in Congress, and the legislators voting for it had a responsibility to their constituents. If their votes didn't bring jobs and money to their districts, they were not likely to get re-elected. So development projects earmarked for Afghanistan were structured to ensure that the necessary supplies and equipment were purchased in America or paid in salary to US technical experts whenever possible.[8]

Afghanistan didn't have the technical experts needed to plan projects like the Kabul-Kandahar road. This part of the job was farmed out to consulting firms in America, who farmed out portions of their tasks to subcontractors, who farmed out parts of it to sub-subcontractors, and so on down. Typically, then, as much as sixty-six cents out of every dollar allocated for development work in Afghanistan was banked in the United States. This was not corruption. It was democracy. To Afghans at the other end of the pipeline, however, it looked a lot like the practices that in Afghanistan were universally labeled corruption.

Still, let's be honest: by Afghan standards, a huge sum of money did make it to Afghanistan. Some of this, however, was paid to foreign technical experts working on-site. These professionals demanded at least as much money to work in Afghanistan as they would have made working in the private sector at home, which is reasonable. Why else would they go to this distant and dangerous place? In fact, because the work entailed real risks, professionals of the highest caliber could only be recruited with offers of better money than they could have made at home. So engineers and technical consultants working on a project like the Kabul-Kandahar road could expect to earn at least $100,000 a year and as much as

$200,000. Plus, they certainly could not be asked to do this work unprotected, and Afghan police were ill equipped to provide such security, both their competence and their loyalty being uncertain. So, private construction companies such as the Louis Berger Group procured crack bodyguards from private security firms such as Blackwater and Global Security. These aces commonly made $1,000 a day, ranging up toward $250,000 a year per person.

Most of the American experts working in Afghanistan didn't even speak Dari, the lingua franca of Afghanistan, much less Pushto, the major language of most areas in which America was doing civil reconstruction work, so they needed their own translators, ideally ones who could act as cultural interpreters. Translators had to speak English just as fluently as the local languages, so expatriate Afghans were hired by private contracting firms, the neoconservatives' preferred avenue of aid delivery, to supply translators/interpreters to the big construction companies as well as to NGOs, government agencies, and the US military.

I was amazed when a recruiter for one such firm called me out of the blue one day to offer me, sight unseen, a job over the phone. I said I didn't speak Pushto, which I knew to be the language really needed, but the recruiter told me not to worry. "Your Pushto is good enough." Since the only sentence I know how to say in Pushto is "I don't speak Pushto," I doubted her assurance.

She urged me not to decide, however, until I had heard the offer: the job would pay a little over $200,000 a year, 80 percent of it tax free, all benefits and travel included, and no expenses to speak of, because I would be fed and lodged by (in this case) the US army. Quite a number of my friends and relatives have said yes to this type of offer, so I know it wasn't exceptional.

Finally, when a technical expert with his bodyguard and interpreter went into the countryside, he generally traveled in an armored vehicle priced around $100,000. In short, one unit of technical expertise roaming the Afghan landscape represented nearly $1 million on the hoof.[9] Meanwhile, locals hired to do the physical labor were paid on the local scale of forty to seventy dollars a week. So million-dollar units were managing the work of people breaking rocks for five to ten dollars a day. That's a prescription for trouble.

Then again, ten dollars a day was more than many of these workers would have made if the road project had not come through their district. Once the road was extended into the next district, they would be laid off, and people in the next district would get jobs. So local people working on the road had an incentive to go out each night and sabotage the work they'd done each day, with some confidence that the sabotage would be blamed on "the Taliban." No wonder the highway was expensive to build.

Even though so many of the dollars allocated for Afghan development were siphoned off before the funds even left the donor countries, torrents of money did end up flooding local markets. Because it was overwhelmingly out of proportion to the domestic economy, it had unintended consequences. Even the NGOs contributed to this syndrome. Many had branch offices in Kabul operating from headquarters in foreign countries. Their staff members may have been true idealists with the best interests of the country at heart, and many made less money than they could have earned in the profit sector at home, but, still, they did get salaries commensurate with the low end of the pay scale in their home countries. And some were, in fact, compensated more handsomely, which was only natural, since they were risking their lives to vaccinate children in a place where doctors were getting killed for vaccinating children. And of course many foreigners came to Afghanistan to work not for NGOs but for private companies intent on profit.

The bottom line was that Kabul filled up with foreigners who had cash in their pockets and little to spend it on. These folks could pay whatever was asked for any local product or service. They didn't have to haggle, and haggling would indeed have seemed tasteless, given their wealth relative to the general populace of this ruined country. So any Afghan with a house or an office to rent to foreigners could name his own price. Consequently, rent on top properties soared. Philanthropist James Ritchie (who takes an interest in helping Afghanistan because he lived in Kabul as a child when his parents were doing development aid work there) opened an office in Kabul just after the fall of the Taliban. He rented it for $200 a month. By the time I spoke to him, five years later, the rent on that space had climbed to $3,000 a month.[10]

When rents went up for foreigners, rents went up for everybody. And when rents went up, so did the price of real estate. Kabul properties began to sell at near-California prices. With inflation in the housing sector came inflation in other sectors. Extravagant demand meant some consumers were willing to pay reckless premiums to get what they wanted—pay whatever to get it now! get it fresh! hot! the best!—which drove up the price of shoes, bread, and other common items not just for foreigners and the nouveau riche Afghans living on their runoff but for everyone.

All this new cash floating around didn't come from any basic change in the domestic economy. It wasn't generated by new businesses, rising trade, or increased productivity in the domestic economy, so it didn't correlate to a general rise in incomes. Only Afghans working for NGOs, international companies, and foreign governments could get a cut of this cash dropping out of the sky. This is why men with medical degrees shut down their clinics and went to work driving cars for foreigners: they could make more money as chauffeurs than as doctors.

Many of the city's inhabitants, however, were living in the old economy at the old salary scales. Teachers, cops, and civil servants were making somewhere between thirty and fifty dollars a month. Even high-level government officials were getting salaries in the mere hundreds of dollars a month, not thousands. Afghans operating private businesses catering strictly to locals might earn even less than cops and teachers, unless their business involved smuggling.

The disparity between the old and new economies, fueled by the influx of outside money (and of drug money) began to strain the Afghan social fabric. Small-scale "lunch-pail" corruption turned endemic. Postal clerks routinely sold ten-afghani stamps for twenty afghanis and pocketed the difference.[11] After all, they had to make a living too. Cops who came upon the scene of an accident fined everybody they could catch including witnesses, bystanders, gawkers, and random people passing by, regardless of involvement. Bureaucrats in charge of processing any kind of paperwork had one power above all, the power to slow things down, and they were certainly going to exercise that power unless they got a tip, more commonly known as a bribe. What else could they do? They had to get to work every morning just like everyone else, and gas cost four dollars a gallon in Afghanistan just as it did in other countries.

31

Drugs and Corruption

MEANWHILE, OUT IN THE COUNTRYSIDE, FARMERS FOUND A SOLUTION TO their problems. They could grow opium. Opium had many advantages over other crops. For one thing, it was drought resistant. You could grow it just about anywhere that was warm enough, even without any irrigation system to speak of. Second, opium sap could be stored for years without any loss of potency, making it immune to the vagaries of the market. Third, once processed into heroin, it was light and easily transportable. Fourth, it sold for so much more than wheat or grapes that farmers didn't have to risk their own lives or their children's clearing many acres of land mines. They could grow enough opium on small plots to support their families.

It's true that cultivating commercial quantities of opium takes special expertise, but Afghans had this know-how. The Taliban regime had gotten much of its revenue by taxing opium farmers, so they had worked to raise production, in part by sending "consultants" out to teach farmers how to grow opium, how to score the bulbs to let the sap weep out, and how to glean and process the precious gum. They also sent enforcers out to make recalcitrant farmers switch to opium from other crops. The program worked so well that by 1999 Afghan opium had flooded world markets, the Taliban had a glut in their warehouses, and the price of opium crashed. At that point, the Taliban banned opium farming to bring prices back up, exactly the way oil-exporting countries cut production to control the price of oil (giving rise to an enduring but mistaken myth that the

Taliban were at least against narcotics).[1] The Taliban restricted the harvest in their last years, but Afghan farmers had not unlearned the skills the Taliban had taught them.

Moving this illegal product to market requires special skills too. But here again Afghans were equipped, for smuggling was a familiar business in these parts. In earlier decades, smugglers used to sneak bricks of gold from the Middle East to China and automobiles from Dubai to Pakistan, evading the tariffs governments and their corrupt agents would have levied at each border. Skills developed for smuggling gold could easily be applied to smuggling narcotics.

Every industry needs appropriate workers in order to flourish. Digital technology bloomed in California's Silicon Valley because schools like Stanford and Berkeley were pouring out computer engineers, the category of skilled worker most needed by that industry. What illegal drug-smuggling enterprises require above all else is experienced gunfighters, and, in this type of workforce, Afghanistan led the world. A quarter century of war had spawned a generation of men who were expert at little else, and with the wars winding down these experts needed jobs. If the narcotics industry had not opened up, they would have resorted to robbery to keep body and soul together. In a sense, then, opium farming actually promoted peace.

It also generated income. The industry quickly acquired a hierarchical structure. At the bottom of the pyramid were the opium farmers—the peasants. They could support their families but remained poor. The smugglers who transported the goods to markets in Iran and Pakistan and later to central Asia (whence it could be shipped to Russia) were professionals: they could get downright rich before they got dead. Even they, however, soon found themselves working for clever, sophisticated men who had the skills needed to organize complex enterprises, administer far-flung corps of workers, and keep track of finances. These new lords made their homes in Herat and Kandahar and Kabul, where they used their drug profits to invest in other enterprises, often legal ones, such as airlines, telecommunications, banks, trucking, construction, and real estate—yes, I know I mentioned all these same sectors when I spoke of the exiled elite coming back to Afghanistan, and I don't mean to suggest that the old exiles were the new drug lords. I only mean to say that in booming Kabul everything got sort of intertwined. Certainly, the money did.

In short, the neoconservative vision of a country rebuilt by private entrepreneurs unrestricted by petty regulations was working: Afghanistan was growing! The money was great! Everybody was happy, except for the poor, who were legion, and the drug addicts, whose numbers skyrocketed to at least a million in Afghanistan and far more than that in Iran and later spread throughout the central Asian republics of the north and on through Russia and eventually into Turkey and then Europe. And of course, as the industry became more profitable, the stakes went up. Drug militias began fighting for routes and territory. Innocent bystanders got killed. Also, because drugs were still technically illegal, the wealthy drug mobsters had to budget some money to buy off the government officials and police officers whose job it was to block their activities. The narcotics industry thus became one more factor in the corrupting of all government operations from top cabinet ministers to lowliest border guards.

Iran, the chief victim of the Afghan drug trade, stationed some hundred thousand troops on this border and built a six-hundred-mile fence between the two countries to keep out Afghan drug smugglers; but the smugglers just bought off the guards with cash and/or drugs. Iranian soldiers posted on the border to stem the flow of narcotics ended up colluding in the trade or getting addicted to narcotics themselves. Drugs came to permeate Afghanistan, and its social fabric changed accordingly.[2] This social fabric, which was already weakened by pervasive small-time corruption, took even worse hits from big-time corruption and from charges and countercharges of corruption. Consider the case of Ibrahim Adel, whose job it was as minister of mines to negotiate with foreign firms for the rights to Afghanistan's minerals. In 2008, his office awarded the copper concession to a Chinese company for $3.5 billion. The *Washington Post* reported that he took a $30 million kickback in exchange for giving that contract to the Chinese company. The accusation came from an unnamed US official who cited a military intelligence report, according to which the money changed hands in a Dubai hotel room. Adel denies the charge and was never indicted or tried, but, by the time the allegations surfaced, Karzai had replaced him.

Adel had originally been appointed to privatize the government-owned Ghori cement factory. He imposed an interesting last-moment condition on companies bidding for the contract. They had to show they were serious by delivering $25 million in cash to the ministry. The only firm able to come up with that much moolah on such short notice was the Afghan Investment Company, owned by Mahmoud Karzai, the president's brother. Flanked by hired gunmen, Mahmoud Karzai took the money to the ministry in a cardboard box and placed it on the minister's desk in person.[3] His company won the bid and contracted to raise the plant's cement production from forty thousand tons a year to three million.[4]

How did Mahmoud Karzai come up with that much cash? Well, he borrowed it from the country's biggest private bank, of which he happened to be a shareholder. Kabul Bank was launched by two financial swashbucklers, Sher Khan Farnood and Khalilullah Ferozi. Farnood, who was born dirt-poor, went to school in Moscow during the Soviet occupation. In the nineties, he roamed the world as a high-stakes poker player, earning more than $600,000. His deputy Ferozi had once worked for Ahmad Shah Massoud, selling gems and using the profits to print millions of dollars' worth of Afghan currency to fund Massoud's military campaign. Massoud ditched him upon discovering that he was also printing currency for the Taliban.

How could two such characters build a bank with $1 billion-plus in assets?

Well, they had the skills best suited to the moment and the circumstances. They could form personal links with people who were politically connected. They loaned Mahmoud Karzai $6 million, which he used to buy a share of the bank, a loan he then paid off with his share of the bank's profits. Another prominent shareholder was Abdul Haseen, half brother of General Fahim, the country's vice president. Fahim took over as commander in chief of the Northern Alliance after Massoud's assassination; he was one of that handful of men who could not be denied a powerful post in the new government after the American intervention.

Fahim used his position to get his brother Haseen started on the road to wealth. First, he helped Haseen secure contracts to pour concrete for the new NATO base and for the US Embassy renovations. Haseen used these profits to build a high-rise mall housing a cluster of jewelry stores on a prime patch of downtown real estate that his brother acquired for a song. Nothing illegal in this: the guy who owned the property could sell it for as much (or as little) as he wanted. Apparently, he felt it was worth taking a loss to build a relationship. Haseen used the profits from the mall to start several more businesses, including a private security firm that scored rich contracts protecting foreign government officials and CIA bases. Haseen also acquired a share of Kabul Bank. As a shareholder, he borrowed more than $100 million from the bank not just to finance further business ventures but also to speculate in Dubai real estate.

Some Kabul Bank shareholders also owned shares in Pamir Airlines, which was founded by alleged drug lord Hajji Zabi Shekhani. Another private airline, KAM, was established by the godson of Uzbek commander Abdul Rashid Dostum. Both airlines competed with the venerable national airline Ariana, whose chairman Dr. Nadir Atash moved to privatize the airline and was then shocked—shocked!—to discover that most of the shares were acquired by top government officials and their cronies in the business community.[5] Atash later came under fire from an anticorruption commission run by another returning exile, Zabiullah Asmatey, who was assigned to investigate charges that Atash had pocketed $6 million on a deal to buy airplanes from Boeing. Nothing was proven, no charges were filed, and Atash fled the country to write a book accusing his accusers of corruption. Anticorruption crusader Asmatey briefly took charge of Ariana Airlines, before dying suddenly of unknown causes. In 2011, a new attorney general issued arrest warrants for Atash and two of his associates.[6]

The attorney general in office when Atash fled was Abdul Jaber Sabet, later fired for grossly corrupt practices himself. (Later still, the poor guy was kidnapped, and, at this writing, his whereabouts remain unknown.) Sabet worked for the US government radio station Voice of America after 9/11. He visited Guantanamo to inspect the facilities and came back with a very favorable report, whereupon US and British officials pressed Karzai to appoint him attorney general of Afghanistan because, they said, he was a "crime fighter's crime fighter." Once in office, Sabet used his prosecutorial powers to undermine business rivals by going after them on charges of—you guessed it: corruption. During Sabet's tenure, contraband trafficking out of Kabul Airport allegedly skyrocketed. In the end, rumor had it, Kabul Bank officials were smuggling up to $10 million worth of raw currency out of Kabul every *day* on Pamir Airways, but the crime fighter's crime fighter was too busy fighting crime to notice. Sabet arrived in Kabul a relatively poor man, but, after his stint as attorney general, he had enough money to develop a prime housing site in Kabul's poshest neighborhood.[7] I have to smile when I hear that the State Department has recently brought in some experts to teach Afghans how to network.[8] It seems to me that Afghans are already pretty good at networking.

Meanwhile, another of the Afghan president's brothers, Ahmad Wali Karzai, had grown huge in Kandahar. He headed up only the provincial council, but everyone in Kandahar knew he also controlled the police and gave orders to the mayor. Anyone who wanted a project approved came to him because, if he didn't broker it, the thing would not get done. The CIA paid Ahmad Wali Karzai to recruit a paramilitary force to patrol Kandahar and its environs. This was something they wanted to do, and to get it done they had to go to the go-to guy. Ahmad Wali Karzai was such a well-known power broker that allegedly even the most dangerous of drug lords curried favor with him.[9]

I say "allegedly" because much was alleged about Ahmad Wali Karzai, and nothing was proven. When he was finally assassinated in late 2011, the killing was ascribed to some private quarrel: it was a crime of passion, not of politics or drugs. In fact, the key figures in this emerging corruptocracy (to coin a term) were not warlords but power brokers.

Some ambiguity shrouds the word *corruption* in this context. From Ahmad Wali Karzai to the minister of mines, most of these power brokers were simply doing business the way it's done in these parts, and the way it is emphatically *not* done in the West. Patronage is built on personal relationships, civil service on impersonal abstractions.

The very statement "carried $25 million in cash in a cardboard box" sounds criminal. And in 2010, when the media discovered that Hamid Karzai—the president himself!—had been receiving monthly payments totaling millions—in cash—euros—from Iran . . . an uproar erupted.[10] Media commentary kept circling obsessively back to the *way* the payments were made: in plastic bags, brought to Kabul by a Karzai associate as *carry-on baggage*! In the United States only a criminal would do such a thing. Actually, not even a criminal would do it because it's so risky and so foolish; but it's not, when you come right down to it, illegal. In devastated Afghanistan, not so long ago (and perhaps still), carrying your cash around in a box with armed men protecting you was probably safer and *less* foolish than putting it in a bank.

The big-time corruption in Afghanistan has mostly consisted of nepotism in various forms. People have used their positions to enrich their kinfolk and close friends. In Afghan culture, however, helping one's kin is not only legal, it's honorable. In fact, it's an obligation. If you're an Afghan, you can damn well count on your own family standing with you, against whatever outsiders might be coming. Who are you going to help if not your own family—some stranger? Have you no shame? Every family that has come to prominence in the new Afghanistan has therefore done its best to place at least one of its own in government to help others of the family make their way. That's what the government is *for*. Just a few generations back, when most Afghans were tribal nomads or poor villagers living in a harsh environment on the edge of survival, an ethos that said you do not, in any circumstances, abandon your kin was essential. Bring that ethos forward into an urban landscape through which billions of dollars are flowing into a ruined country, and it's not such a good thing. Combine that ethos with the neoconservative doctrine that the public good is best served by people vigorously pursuing private profit, and you have the phenomenon commonly referred to as monumental corruption.

American neoconservatives, of course, did not envision free enterprise happening in a state of nature. There had to be rules. Laws were laid down, and everyone was supposed to operate within those parameters. The idea was, if private entrepreneurs were free to compete by any legal means in pursuit of their own interests, the process would weed out the incompetents and let the best and smartest thrive and rise and run things.

Under those ground rules, however, when two business competitors went head-to-head, and both were smart and both were well educated and both had funding, the one who played closest to the line of legality was apt to win. They were not necessarily criminals, just folks willing to take the chance that they were doing something illegal, willing to gamble that they would not be charged or that the charges wouldn't stick. The system attracted and rewarded risk-taking gamblers like the men who founded Kabul Bank: a high-stakes poker player and a gem smuggler willing to counterfeit money for both sides in a war. Most of these gamblers have been right so far. Lots of anticorruption commissions have been formed, but few government officials have been charged or tried or convicted of any crimes. Add the rise of the corruptocracy to the things that went wrong with reconstruction.

32

Talibanism

OUTSIDE THE CITIES, SEEDS OF TROUBLE WERE GERMINATING IN THE SOIL from the start, but the widespread optimism sparked by the American intervention created an environment hostile to violence at first, so these seeds germinated in quiet secrecy. Christoph Reuter and Borhan Younus tell the story of Mullah Farooq, a former madrassa student—hence, technically, a Talib—who lived in a rural part of Ghazni province. He was angry about the ousting of the Taliban and wanted to do something dramatic, something to show the world his people were not dead, were still fighting, and would fight to the last drop of their blood. In late 2002, he went to his friend Abdul Ahad, a more experienced commander, and proposed that they cook up some violence. "No," said Ahad. "It's too early . . . The people would not follow us yet." The time was not ripe because "the people"—the masses of Afghans—still had high hopes that America would improve their lives.[1]

So Ahad and Farooq waited for things to go downhill, and downhill they went. The failures of reconstruction were only one part of it. The month after that first loya jirga in the summer of 2002, US warplanes flying over Helmand Province mistook a wedding party for a band of insurgents because the men in the party were firing rifles into the air, as is the festive custom at weddings in that area. The warplanes strafed the wedding party, killing 47 civilians, including women and children, and wounding another 117. Upon discovering the error, US officials in Kabul tendered profuse apologies. The episode left a bad impression, and yet, at the time, I heard people in Kabul saying they understood that the situation was chaotic and mistakes happen. They were willing to forgive the Americans so long as they learned from their error and never repeated it.

By the end of the year, however, US violence in Afghanistan was, from the Afghan point of view, being institutionalized. The United States took over the big Soviet-built airbase at Bagram, just north of Kabul, and converted it into an impregnable fortress that no random Afghan could approach, much less enter. The few Afghans who got a glimpse inside reported that an entire ready-made American city had gone up within Bagram, complete with nightclubs, cinemas, restaurants, and shops (a gross exaggeration). Soldiers and private contractors from many countries lived and worked there, and the base therefore cost millions to sustain, but the spending had no impact on the economy of the surrounding area because everything the inhabitants of Bagram used or consumed was airlifted directly from some foreign country. The beef served in the mess halls, for example, came from Australia. And there were even rumors of pork.

At Bagram, the United States set up a detention center whose dark reputation quickly came to rival that of Guantanamo. US Special Forces and intelligence agents brought Afghans suspected of involvement in terrorism to this detention center, the biggest in the region, for interrogation by specialists. The specialists were not all US military personnel; they included private contractors hired by the US government. Sometimes the United States admitted they had swept up some innocent individual mistakenly, and these detainees were released—but not necessarily before they had been "interrogated." Those who went into Bagram and came out to tell the tale reported that people were beaten in there or chained, hooded, and made to stand for several days and nights on a box. One man, a taxi driver believed to be innocent of any connection to the Taliban, was beaten to death, apparently because the specialists interrogating him got a kick out of hearing him shout "Wakh! Allah!" each time he was dealt a blow.[2] These reports mingled with similar stories seeping out of Guantanamo and spread a sense of horror among Afghans.

The Karzai government moved rapidly to establish an Afghan National Army (ANA) and an Afghan National Police (ANP) force, and this was obviously the right thing to do: the alternative would have been instant chaos. But "rapidly" meant giving guns and authority to thousands of unvetted men and sending them into the field with a vague directive to stop evildoers. Inevitably, many of these new security forces behaved as if their guns and badges entitled them to special privileges. One day, for example, an army officer working for the national intelligence service came to a fabric merchant, Abdul Karim of Ghazni, to buy some cloth. He demanded a deep discount, the merchant refused him, and the officer then accused Abdul Karim of fronting for al Qaeda and took him to prison. There the poor man was beaten. He got out, finally, by paying 10,000 rupees, but the whole debacle took him away from his shop for a year, by which time his business was all but ruined.[3]

The cloth merchant's case was not special. Episodes like this became routine. To make matters worse, the army and police forces were staffed disproportionately by Tajiks and Uzbeks, because those ethnic groups dominated the victorious Northern Alliance. Although they hailed from the north, they were stationed mostly in the south, because that's where the unrest was thought to be, and those areas were predominantly Pushtoon. So Tajiks and Uzbeks were given state authority and sent with guns to impose order on restive, defeated Pushtoons, which did not help promote a single, unified Afghan society.

As resentment built up, every story about the depredations of the new regime grew legs and wings. People coming back from Kabul reported seeing empty liquor bottles littering the streets. One mullah in a rural area west of Kabul built a fiery Friday sermon around reports of boys and girls in the capital having casual public sex and of public indifference to the outrage. This, he said, was what Kabul had come to: it was "a piece of Europe" now. Rumors began to circulate that the Americans were raping old men in Bagram. Such outlandish stories were easy for rural Afghans to believe because by this time many had seen or heard about the photos taken at the Abu Ghraib prison in Iraq, one of which showed a female American prison guard walking a naked Muslim man on a leash like a dog and another a pile of Muslim men forced to lie naked on top of each other, heaped up like cordwood.

In August 2003, Mullah Farooq and his associates decided the grass was dry enough, the time had come to light a match. Did they attack a military convoy? No. A US base camp? No. A government installation? No: they killed two relief workers employed by the Red Crescent Society (a Muslim version of the Red Cross). Broad outrage greeted this horror, but the outrage only served Mullah Farooq's cause. He wasn't out to win any popularity contests. He wanted to make himself known. What mattered was not how much disapproval his act incurred but how many people heard about it. The murders put him and his little group on the map. People now knew there was something to fear in their own neighborhood.

A few months later, in the fall of 2003, two men on motorbikes shot and killed a French relief worker, twenty-nine-year-old Bettina Goislard, who was there on a UN project to resettle fifty thousand displaced persons (internal Afghan refugees). Her work could hardly have been more charitable or more cherished. The infuriated locals caught the killers, beat them, and turned them over to the government for trial. You might suppose this reaction would have led Mullah Farooq and his group to reconsider their strategy. But no: they perceived—quite correctly—that any stretch of days going by with no traumatizing events served the cause of the Kabul government and its foreign sponsors. Any frightening act of brutality, no matter who committed it, undermined public confidence in a positive future and weakened civil authority. Chaos was the intermediate stage needed to discourage and drive out the foreigners, before the insurgents could reimpose law and order—their law, their order.

The United States, NATO, and the Karzai government contributed in a sense to Farooq's cause. One month after the assassination of Bettina Goislard, a NATO air strike destroyed a building thought to house a suspected Taliban leader. Instead it killed nine children and some random guy who had nothing to do with the Taliban. This action engendered the same revulsion as the killing of Goislard and fueled a sense of moral equivalency: the Taliban were killing innocent charity workers; the United States and its allies were killing innocent children. What was the difference?

When the United States killed civilians by mistake, it admitted its error and compensated the families of the victims, but the compensation itself became a problematic practice. The thing is, US defense personnel knew that in Afghanistan, among Pushtoon tribes, murder cases were sometimes settled by the murderer's family working out a payment to the victim's family. This may have led all too easily (I suspect) to the notion that compensation for wrongful death was a business transaction. I met one earnest young analyst at a training session in Washington, DC, who told me what the standard payment was for such cases in Iraq—he'd studied up—and he wanted to know what "the going price" was in Afghanistan.

But payment for wrongful death is not a "going price" kind of deal. It's part of a complex network of social mechanisms that regulate tribal interactions. This particular mechanism provides an escape clause from the endless blood feuds set in motion by another social mechanism, the deeply felt obligation to avenge injuries to one's kin. Each settlement is a complex negotiation among personalities within a cultural setting. From the US point of view, the payments must have settled the matter because they were accepted. In fact, the payments may have only complicated the resentments people felt about their kin being killed by a foreign power in their own land.

In July 2004, Afghan police stumbled upon a private prison in a residential neighborhood of Kabul set up by Jack Idema, a former Special Forces operative "gone rogue." He was working with a partner, Brent Bennet, and a third man, Edward Caraballo, who was there to film their exploits. When busted, they were holding eight Afghan men captive in their house of horror. Three were strapped to a ceiling by their feet, hanging upside down. Idema and Bennet had been "interrogating" their prisoners for days. God knows what information they expected to get. The United States disavowed any connection to Idema, but the disavowals had begun a week or two before the private prison was discovered, suggesting that some US officials may already have known what Idema was up to. (Of course, it's also possible that they simply found him weird and unsavory.)[4]

The Karzai government was trying hard to establish a normal administration in places like Andar, the rural district that Mullah Farooq called home. It appointed governors for the various districts, it staffed up the police forces, and it established municipal centers and courts to dispense government functions. Various NGOs came into Andar and similar areas to restore water supply systems, build health clinics, and provide other improvements that people desperately needed and wanted.

But the new insurgents honed a strategy to blunt the good these development efforts might have done. They didn't hurl themselves directly at the Karzai government or the foreign forces. They attacked carefully chosen individuals, one at time, like wolves picking off strays. Sometimes these were government officials; more often, they were just people who had cooperated with the government or expressed a willingness to embrace the new order. The government might muster troops to defend an area or a town or a district or even a building. But one policeman? One clerk? Hardly. Which left the targeted individual swinging in the breeze.

Take the case of Abdul Hakim, who worked with the police in Ghazni. He didn't have an important job, just some obscure position connected to the police department. Mullah Farooq sent letters warning him to quit his job. He also slapped "night posters" on his walls describing what would happen if he didn't quit. Hakim stood firm. Then one day his oldest son was coming home on leave from the army, and unknown assailants killed him within sight of his father's door. A few weeks later, Abdul Hakim's younger son was "arrested"—that is, kidnapped—and "tried" as an American spy. He was found guilty and executed. Abdul Hakim got the message.[5]

When a private construction company tried to build a road through Mullah Farooq's district, his men sabotaged the project repeatedly. Farooq let it be known that he wasn't against a road; he was just against outsiders working in his district without his permission. NGOs and private companies realized they could save themselves a lot of grief simply by getting in touch with Mullah Farooq before they came to his area and securing his approval. It cost them nothing and ensured that they would be able to do their work safely, so why not? But when outsiders sought Mullah Farooq's permission to work in his district, they tended to validate him as the ruler of that little district.

Mullah Farooq was not important. He was just one man and his reach was limited. Within a couple of years of the American intervention, however, hundreds of Mullah Farooqs were sprouting in Afghanistan. They were autonomous players acting on their own initiative—but then again they weren't. They had kin who knew people who knew the kin of others like themselves. They formed connections with these others, came to cooperative arrangements, and made agreements. Gradually, the multitude of Mullah Farooqs coalesced into networks directed by bigger figures whose leadership was the sort familiar to these parts, a leadership based on prestige acquired through traditional channels and built on reciprocal obligations deriving from many years of favors done and hardships shared as well as tribal and familial links.

One of the biggest networks operated in the southeast under the direction of Jalaluddin Haqqani, a prominent figure from the days of the Mujahideen. In the 1980s this man had received large shipments of money and arms from the CIA to help him fight the Soviets. In the first Mujahideen government, he had served as minister of justice (alongside Hamid Karzai, who was a deputy foreign minister in that same cabinet). After the Taliban were overthrown, Haqqani declared himself a member of the Taliban and began fighting Western forces. He pronounced Mullah Omar his spiritual commander in chief and claimed that Omar had appointed him military commander for the whole southeast region. His son Siraj, a famously ruthless advocate of suicide bombings and beheadings, served as his second-in-command.

Gulbuddin Hekmatyar, that most grizzled survivor of the old days, came back too, from Iran, where he'd been in hiding. Hekmatyar had been the main darling of the CIA and of ISI in the old days, but now he too declared that he had joined the Taliban. In practice, this meant reactivating his old Hezb-i-Islam organization. Hekmatyar didn't dominate any single region the way Haqqani dominated the southeast, but Hekmatyar had national reach. He established "islands" of control throughout the country, in other people's territories. He was a player again.

Mullah Omar, along with the high honchos of his regime, had regrouped in Quetta, a city just east of the Afghan border, and set up a *shura*—a council. Supposedly, Mullah Omar was still in charge of the whole insurgency, although he never appeared in public. His pronouncements came through spokesmen; and, since the spokesmen sometimes contradicted one another, there was no telling whether they really spoke for Omar or just for themselves. To remedy the problem, Mullah Omar named two men his official spokesmen—but he did so through spokesmen. The two men were named Zabiullah Mujahid and Dr. Hanif. Henceforth, only their statements would have the amir's imprimatur.[6] But these men communicated with the media only by phone from undisclosed locations, and no one knew what *they* looked like either, so they might have been many men using the same two names. If so, there was no telling which of their statements authentically came from Mullah Omar.

None of this really mattered because Mullah Omar wasn't an actual operational leader so much as an idea. If he had interacted with real people, directing the insurgency in person, he might have commanded the obedience of many, but he would surely have made some enemies as well. Nobody can please everybody. By staying out of sight and issuing only grand, thematic directives, he became a mythological figure that each person could fashion into the leader he wanted. People bitterly in conflict with each other could thus both claim Mullah Omar as their spiritual leader. After all, doing so didn't commit them to any specific course of action.

Whatever its overall authority, the Quetta Shura supposedly directed insurgent operations throughout southern Afghanistan. I say "supposedly" because the shura's actual administrative control is debatable. On the ground, whole networks of insurgents claimed to be acting under the direction of the Quetta Shura but seemed pretty autonomous in practice. At times these networks worked together, but at times they competed for control of drug routes and such.

One network leader, Mullah Akhtar Osmani, collected taxes for the Taliban as part of his massive smuggling operation. He was killed by a NATO air strike in 2007, possibly because his whereabouts were leaked to NATO by another network leader, the notorious Mullah Dadullah, whose ferocity so frightened even his friends and associates, they called him "the Butcher" (a reference to his predilection for chopping off heads with an ax). Dadullah reportedly directed several hundred subcommanders (each with his own semiautonomous group), but Dadullah himself was killed by British Special Forces, possibly after his movements were leaked to NATO by rival drug lords within the Quetta Shura.[7] His brother Mansur inherited the network, but he was captured by Pakistani agents, allegedly at the behest of Mullah Baradur, who held high rank in the Quetta Shura, possibly even the number two position. (Mullah Baradur himself was arrested by ISI in February 2010, but may have been released nine months later.)

The media frequently ascribed acts of violence in Afghanistan to "the Taliban." The charge was misleading, I think, to the extent that it implied a single organization with an established hierarchy. Perhaps, in 1996, when the Taliban first swept southern Afghanistan, they were an organization loosely answering to this description. But, after the American intervention, a new insurgency best described as "Talibanist" gradually took shape. Today, the term "Taliban" casually lumps together all sorts of figures from drug-mafia captains to local religious zealots to foreign Jihadist radicals to former honchos of the Mujahideen movement that fought the Soviets.

Tom Coghlan of the *London Times* provides an illustration. On June 18, 2006, a car carrying associates of a Karzai government official, Amir Dado, was attacked near Kandahar, and Dado's brother was killed. Thereupon, a wave of violence swept the district, and by the end of the day more than forty of Amir Dado's relatives had been killed. Was this a Taliban operation?

Well, sort of. Amir Dado had been a brutal warlord before the Taliban took over, one of those criminals whose depredations had fueled the rise of the Taliban in the first place. After the American intervention, he was among the many warlords who reasserted themselves. Too weak to oppose them all, the Karzai government expediently appointed some of them to official posts in areas where they held power anyway.

Dado was also a member of a tribe that had long been locked into a struggle for dominance with two other local tribes, a feud that dated back to ancient times. In recent days, the struggle among these tribes had evolved into a fight for control of the local drug trade. Amir Dado's tribe gained advantages from his having a position in the Karzai government, a fact resented by the rival tribes.[8]

So, when anti-Dado gun battles spread across the area that day, it *was* partly a popular uprising: locals hated Amir Dado from the old days. It was also in part a localist uprising against the central government and also in part an episode in a long-standing feud among three tribes and also in part a battle over drugs and money. But also, in part, it was a blow struck by the Pakistan-based Quetta Shura, in their campaign to reassert their control of Kandahar. So it's accurate to "trace" this battle to "the Taliban," but the significance of doing so dissolves once one deconstructs the term "Taliban."

Antigovernment violence gathered force throughout 2005, but in this period the government also made progress. An elected president began his first term. An elected parliament went to work. New companies sprang up in Kabul. Elegant guesthouses opened for business in many cities. Five-star hotels like the sophisticated Serena went up in Kabul, providing classy accommodations for the international businesspeople flocking to Afghanistan from all parts of the world. In cities such as Kabul, Mazar-i-Sharif, and Herat, the foreign community could dine out and not just on Afghan fare such as kebabs and palow but cuisines ranging from Thai to Italian. In 2005, an American fellow who had just come back from Kabul told me Afghanistan was much better now: "You can buy beer on the street," he gushed. In Kabul shoppers could visit a mall that looked not so different from malls in Santa Monica, and, in the posh neighborhood of Wazir Akbar Khan, foreigners could buy groceries at a Western-style supermarket.

Consultants to the Kabul ministries began to sort through the tangled archives of land ownership in the country. They organized and digitized these records to facilitate the exiles' reclamation of their properties, for, over the years, each change of government had given a whole new set of officials a chance to seize desirable houses and falsify documents to support their claims of ownership.

Kabul University added branches of learning and institutes devoted to particular academic topics. An Afghanistan research center began to collect and digitize historical documents, which they are now putting on the Internet, making them available to scholars anywhere in the world. A new private university was launched in Kabul, and it was not cheap, but there were Afghans who could now afford not-cheap.

The constitution had promised freedom of the press, and, despite a few well-publicized incidents of attempted censorship, the media flourished. Private newspapers, magazines, and radio stations were born. One family of exiles returning from Australia established the eminent TOLO (Sunrise) TV station. Then came Ariana TV, and Shamshad, and numerous local stations, not to mention dozens of independent radio stations.

And of course exiles, NGOs, foreign governments, and the Afghan government continued to push for schools and more schools and still more schools, in all the cities, in all the towns, and in the rural areas as well. Everyone agreed that education was the key. To quote a woman who approached me at a meeting in Los Angeles in 2002, shortly after the events of 9/11, "If only we could *teach* those Afghans." When I asked her what she thought we should teach those Afghans, she wrung her hands and lamented, "Just . . . *everything*!"

33

The
Tipping Point

At least to the end of 2005, then, in the race to a tipping point, chaos and order were running neck and neck. Bridges were bombed, clinics sabotaged, innocents murdered; but also, bridges were built, cell phones proliferated, new schools opened up, and even remote villages began to participate in national elections. In 2006, chaos began to inch ahead. On this point, casual observers and policy experts seem to agree: 2006 marked a turning point. And, for the Talibanist insurgency, schools turned out to be the key: 2006 was the year of school burning.

Many people speak of schools as if they are a neutral good. Surely, the thinking goes, all parents want their children to get educated, but such thinking also assumes that there is universal agreement on what *educated* means. Schools are an instrument for transmitting ideas; when a war of ideas is under way, building a school is an act of war. In Afghanistan, when good-hearted, well-intentioned people built schools in rural areas roamed by smoldering insurgents, they were putting undefended structures in a war zone and filling them with the softest of targets: children. In 2006, the Talibanist insurgents realized what an opportunity this afforded.

Perhaps they had not dared to attack schools before this time for fear of crossing a line that would seriously, permanently alienate them from the people they hoped one day to rule. Between 2002 and 2005, however, a propaganda war softened the field. In that period, relentless propaganda from the Quetta Shura and from the Pakistan madrassas created what might be called "education anxiety." Parents who were themselves illiterate were told that, if they sent their children to schools endorsed by the West, their kids would turn against Islam. The propaganda referenced what had happened in the sixties and seventies to rural children who had gone to government schools: they had turned into Communists, climbed into Soviet warplanes, and come back to bomb their own villages, their own families. Now (said the propagandists) the very people who were littering the streets of Kabul with half-empty whiskey bottles and selling hard pornography in the bazaars and teaching girls to walk around half-naked in public and airlifting mountains of pork into Bagram were demanding that they be allowed to "teach the children."

Into the anxiety stirred up by this campaign, the Talibanists launched their attacks. In mid-December 2005, they killed a teacher at the gates of his school in Helmand Province. The following month, they beheaded a high school teacher in Zabul Province. That month, they burned down schools in Kandahar, Helmand, and Laghman Provinces. In the months that followed, more teachers were brutalized, and more schools were attacked, burned down, or badly damaged.[1] At Ghaffar Lakanwal's school in Khost, for example, insurgents piled all the desks in one room and set them ablaze. In Nadi Ali, Kharoti's Green Village Schools came under siege. By the end of the year, more than two hundred schools across southern and southeastern Afghanistan had closed: parents, it seemed, just weren't willing to put their children on the front lines.

The school attacks began to drain away that aroma of hope. Suddenly, the future looked bloody again. Insurgent violence spiked in the south, along the whole border between Afghanistan and Pakistan. In 2007, Helmand province clocked 751 violent outbreaks, from assaults to murders to jailbreaks.

If that year was bad, the next was worse. The attitudes driving the insurgency spread like a flesh-eating infection. By "attitudes" I mean the generalized sense that attacking anyone associated with the foreign project in Afghanistan was laudable—government officials, US personnel, NATO personnel, UN personnel, NGO staff, relief workers, what have you.

The Talibanist campaign began to acquire a structure. Ideologues and "shuras" outside the country emanated an ideology that acted as a solvent and a cement, giving the heterogeneous "movement" a sense of solidarity and making it possible for men of diverse backgrounds and ethnicities, scattered across a landscape, in no direct communication with one another, to form a uniform sense of who they were and what they were fighting for. This sense was all the easier to evoke because it came out of traditional, tribal Islam, the deeply familiar social system of rural Afghanistan and the one set of ideas on which the rural masses mostly agreed, whatever their differences.

Network heads like Haqqani, Mansur, Hekmatyar, and Mullah Toor (the Black Mullah) mapped out grand military schemes that required coordination among many commanders and their networks. These leaders coordinated with counterparts in Pakistan, where similar networks of Talibanist insurgents were taking shape (to the extent that an amoeba can be said to take a shape), networks like the one led by Beitullah Mehsud and his family in the Swat Valley. The network heads secured financing, managed money, and distributed arms.

Below them emerged a layer of operational commanders in the field, professional militants and full-time hit men whose sole occupation was insurgency. These men moved from village to village, getting food and shelter from the villagers, striking targets of opportunity, and retreating to Pakistan to recuperate and get fresh weapons.

The full-time insurgents had a far larger pool of part-timers to call upon in any locale, fighters who operated only in their home district. When they weren't fighting, these men were farming or doing other standard rural chores. They fought only when they and their friends concocted some scheme or when they got the call from some respected authority like the Quetta Shura to help out an operation in their district.

The insurgency depended almost entirely on murders, assassinations, and small-scale hit-and-run attacks. This style of warfare neutralized the advantages enjoyed by an enemy with more troops, more money, more weapons, and better technology. Talibanists did sometimes attack police stations and other defended locations, and for such operations they could convene as many as one hundred part-time fighters on two or three days' notice. Even then, however, after launching a surprise attack, they typically fought for only a few hours and then dispersed, before NATO air support could arrive.[2] Once they slipped away, they became indistinguishable from the general populace—in part because most of them *were* the general populace. The Soviets, in their time, had faced exactly the same problem. And the British before them.

By 2008, "the Taliban" were designating certain of their commanders "officials" of a shadow government. Men were appointed shadow mayors of towns, shadow police chiefs, shadow directors of districts, shadow governors of whole provinces. It's not clear that these shadow administrators did any actual administering. The mere fact that the insurgency had officials gave it the feel of a mature alternative to the Bonn project—as if a new government was ready to step in and start running things the moment Karzai and his foreign friends were driven out.

Most importantly, "the Taliban" developed an alternative to the government judicial system.[3] Talibanist mobile courts began to roam the landscape (like the assizes of old England). They weren't directed from above—they didn't have to be. These courts were based on a judicial system that already existed. It had been developed over the course of fifteen centuries. The laws were very specific, they were already on the books, and the books were innumerable. All those who could lay claim to some scholarly prestige—and that was just about anyone whose name included such honorifics as mawlawi, mufti, or qazi—could assert authority to dispense justice in accordance with the Shari'a. For that matter, anyone titled mullah could do the same, even though *mullah* does not technically denote sufficient scholarship to legislate or judge. In a pinch, even someone known to be a *hajji* (which only means the person has made the pilgrimage to Mecca at least once) could call himself qualified to dispense justice. If the people accepted his judgments, then he had the authority he claimed, because that's how Islam works at the ground level. Not that all these judges actually knew the Shari'a. What they knew were the embedded judgments and customs of the people among whom they lived.

In areas affected by the insurgency, people with disputes to settle had a choice, therefore. They could go to the nearest government court, where they might have to pay a bribe to have their case heard and where the size of the bribe would probably determine the outcome, or they could wait for a mobile Taliban court to come to their district and take their case to that panel of judges.

Rural people began to seek adjudication increasingly from Taliban courts not just because they might be killed (by insurgents) if they went to the government court but also because, even in the most uncorrupted government court, the judgment would be based on a code of law that contradicted the customs, mores, entrenched power relationships, and deepest prejudices of the people seeking judgment. For example, if a man had given a distant relative a quantity of opium in exchange for his twelve-year-old daughter and then the relative had sold the opium for cash but failed to turn over the girl because the girl herself objected—well, a Taliban judge would understand the plaintiff's grievance; an honest, upstanding government judge, by contrast, acting in accordance with enlightened laws promulgated at the capital, might say, "You sold your daughter to this guy? In exchange for opium?!! Forget who's got the grievance, you're *both* going to jail!"

The insurgency poisoned life in the countryside. In 2007, when the UN tried to do a survey of attitudes toward the government in Paktika, a province abutting the Pakistan border, its researchers could not even get into many districts.

The war came creeping into the cities too. Suicide bombers hit a sugar factory in the industrial city of Baglan, killing seventy-five people. In January 2008, four gunmen wrapped in explosives attacked the Serena Hotel and killed a guard before two of them were killed and the other two captured. The death toll was not dramatic, but the target! The Serena was the hotel of choice for international businesspeople in Kabul. One month later, suicide bombers in Kandahar blew themselves up in a crowd of spectators watching a dogfight and killed about a hundred people. That July, someone drove a car bomb into the Indian Embassy and killed fifty-eight people, most of them local Afghans. The media speculated that the Taliban were responsible. As I said before, well, duh.

By this time, the Taliban had come a long way toward establishing a revenue system based on a 10 percent tax collected on all profits, especially from farmers. The only agricultural product worth discussing at this point was opium, and, in the leading opium-growing areas, this product had gone through a bizarre metamorphosis. It was no longer just a crop that people sold for money. Opium had turned *into* money. People were using it as a currency, to pay for even trivial consumer goods such as clothes and groceries.[4] Opium went through this transformation because it had every quality a substance needs to function as currency. It was (for all practical purposes) imperishable, it was precisely quantifiable, it was universally negotiable, and the supply was limited: the only way to have opium was to produce it or be involved in the economic system within which it was traded. Like any good currency, therefore, opium brought (some) stability and order to economic interactivity.

With a system of taxation in place, a network of shadow administrators, a rapidly developing (mobile) court system, and (a simulacrum of) a currency of its own, the Taliban could plausibly claim to be functioning as an alternative to the Karzai government, at least in the provinces. I say "claim" because they had no obvious mechanisms in place to actually run a country. What they did have, pretty certainly, was the power to make Afghanistan ungovernable.

The Talibanist insurgency thus came to present the same challenge to NATO and the United States as the Mujahideen insurgency had posed for the Soviet Union in the 1980s and as Afghan tribesmen had posed for Britain in the Anglo-Afghan war of a century earlier. The British gave up on trying to defeat the insurgency of their time and simply pulled out of Afghanistan the moment they found someone to whom they could hand the reins, a man tough enough to dominate the country yet canny enough to act as Britain's partner on international, strategic matters. America would be wise to do the same if it could only find a man like Abdu'Rahman, but no one on the Afghan political scene right now seems to fit that description.

34

Obama's Surges

WHEN BARACK OBAMA WAS CAMPAIGNING FOR THE PRESIDENCY IN 2008, he kept saying he would withdraw American troops from Iraq and send them to Afghanistan. I know that many people who voted for him took this saber-rattling as a rhetorical attempt to look just as tough on terrorism as his opponent. They assumed that if he won he would start wrapping up all of America's foreign military involvements.

They were mistaken: apparently Obama meant what he said. He came to office with four clear insights, and he meant to act on them. His first insight: Afghanistan mattered more than Iraq; his second, Afghanistan was not just a cleanup operation but a real shooting war; his third, the United States and its allies were losing this war; and, finally, America had to get out of this place but without letting the house catch fire on its way out, or else the whole neighborhood might go up in flames.

Obama was the first US president to take official if muted note of Pakistan's treacherous role in the Afghan drama. He also recognized the problem centered in the territory straddling the eroding border between Pakistan and Afghanistan. In fact, he and his advisors began speaking of this territory as Af-Pak, treating it as a single entity that could be considered separately, in some sense, from the two states flanking it. On all these counts, the new president was correct: he saw the problem.

Good. Now—what was the solution?

Obama decided to send in more troops. This was not exactly a visionary break with the past. The troop count in Afghanistan had been rising steadily throughout the Bush years. The number of US combat troops in

Afghanistan stood as follows at the end of each year of the George W. Bush administration:[1]

- 2002:   5,200
- 2003:   10,400
- 2004:   15,200
- 2005:   19,100
- 2006:   20,400
- 2007:   23,700
- 2008:   30,100

Notice a trend? These numbers refer only to fighters actively enrolled in the US military. The war effort was also aided by private firms providing support services to the US military; their work force kept increasing too. By December 2008, they had 71,555 employees in Afghanistan.[2]

Other countries had troops there too, under NATO command, providing security throughout the country as the ISAF. In 2006, overall command of the war officially passed into NATO hands, by which time these countries, from Canada to Australia, had escalated their military presence as well. Great Britain, for example, was now contributing five thousand soldiers to the effort.

At the start of Obama's first term, NATO nations including the United States had a total of 56,000 soldiers stationed in Afghanistan. When you add private contractors, the number reaches 127,000. Even that number is deceptive, because it leaves out yet *another* military force operating in the country, the private security firms (not to be confused with the private military contractors who support the US military effort with such services as cooking, laundry, and maintenance). The private security firms were purely military operations, accountable only to their clients: they protected people and companies for money. Nearly a hundred of these firms sprouted in Afghanistan, and at their height they fielded about 40,000 operatives.

So when Obama decided to send more troops to Afghanistan he wasn't exactly making a radical break with existing policy. In the Bush years, the troops had been increased without fanfare to avoid undercutting the message that Afghanistan was almost fixed now, well in hand.

With Obama, the message changed. Obama said Iraq had been a mistake, the real enemy was in Af-Pak, and he would go after this real enemy. Shortly after his inauguration, he announced seventeen thousand more troops for Afghanistan. I couldn't help noticing that this number coincided with the size of the British community that had fled Kabul in 1842 and had come notoriously to grief in the Hindu Kush passes. But the president soon blunted the symbolic force of that number by adding another four thousand soldiers to his escalation.

Obama also sacked Bush's military commander and put a swashbuckler named Stanley McChrystal in charge. McChrystal was not some smooth operator who won his stars schmoozing in Washington. He was a man's man and a soldier's soldier, the kind of guy who slept four hours a night and ran several miles every morning before breakfast. The men he commanded reportedly revered him because he subjected himself to even greater rigors than he demanded of them. In Iraq, he had distinguished himself by hunting down and killing the notorious terrorist al-Zarqawi. It was hoped that in Afghanistan he could work a similar miracle with regards to Osama bin Laden.

At his confirmation hearing, McChrystal told Congress he was going to pursue a new strategy in Afghanistan, which he called a counterinsurgency approach. Counterinsurgency meant he would focus on bringing the Afghan people over to the American side by giving them good government and a sense of security, and he would achieve this by attacking the Taliban head-on, right in their strongholds, right in Helmand and Kandahar and adjacent provinces—clear the territories, hold them, and call in the civilians. He would measure success not by how many terrorists were killed but by how many Afghan civilians felt safer. He would also impose strict rules of engagement to make sure American forces did not keep killing civilians by mistake. He warned, however, that his approach might lead to more American casualties initially because it would involve American soldiers, unprotected by body armor, interacting face-to-face with more Afghans, any of whom might be intent on killing Americans. The public should brace itself to stay the course.

Vice President Biden opposed this strategy. He favored the more pinpoint strategy known as the counterterrorism approach. Biden wanted to remove most of the combat troops and reduce the American military footprint in Afghanistan to a handful of highly trained Special Forces who would focus strictly on identifying, hunting down, and killing key militants. His approach guaranteed that most Afghans would never have direct contact with American troops, which, ideally, would keep them from turning against America. His approach would also entail fewer American casualties, thereby keeping the American public from turning against the war—which in turn would give the administration breathing room to pursue its goals in Afghanistan as long as necessary.

Biden also favored expanding the use of drones—remotely guided pilotless vehicles operated from video game–like consoles in Arizona that could fire rockets at precise targets on the ground. Drones would *really* reduce American casualties.

Obama weighed these two approaches and liked them both. He authorized more troops for McChrystal—another thirty thousand, but he also sent in more specialists. Thereafter, arrests of suspected Taliban went up. NATO typically used the "night raid" method to arrest Taliban suspects. The team would hit a suspect's house in the dead of night when least expected, with minimum warning and maximum noise. Wearing bulletproof body armor and night-vision goggles, they would sweep in, grab the suspect, bag him, and get out at lightning speed. Sometimes they acted on erroneous information and arrested an innocent man, but such mistakes occurred only rarely, it seems. But, even when the night raid netted a bona fide insurgent, it traumatized the rest of his social cluster—wives, children, relatives, others living with him, people whose involvement in the insurgency might have been peripheral up to that point.

Bismillah Iqbal, who worked as an interpreter for the American military, described going on a night raid to me once.

> You *can't* go in the daytime. If they know you're coming, forget it. They start shooting. Even if you reach the front door, they're gone, they have ways. But when you come in the middle of the night, you burst in, people are asleep all over the floor, bodies in the dark—children, teenagers—no one knows who you are or why you're there—before they can move, you've dragged out some guy. One time, I remember seeing this kid cringing in a corner, wrapped in blankets. He must have been about ten. He'd been dreaming, and now he was awake and he was

in a nightmare. We had our goggles on, so he couldn't see our faces. I don't know *what* we looked like to him! We dragged away whoever it was—his father maybe? His older brother? I don't know. Women were hollering, children screaming, babies crying—you wouldn't believe the commotion! And this kid blinking into the lights, I saw his eyes, and I thought, "Whoa. We'll be back for *him* someday."

The Obama administration increased its use of drones dramatically. In 2008, the US military had carried out about 35 drone attacks. In the first year of the Obama administration, the United States conducted 140 drone attacks, killing nearly two hundred people. Inevitably, disputes arose about who they were killing. US and NATO officials insisted they were killing only terrorists; the villagers who had been attacked usually claimed they had nothing to do with insurgency and had suffered random civilian casualties for no reason. The truth, I'm guessing, lay somewhere in between.

Because the problem was said to be centered in Af-Pak, the drones not infrequently fired rockets at targets on the Pakistan side of the line. This infuriated Pakistanis of all walks of life, forcing the Pakistan government to protest the drone attacks. Ironically, the Pakistan government was busy purchasing drones from the United States and deploying them against the same insurgents in the same areas at the very time that it was issuing diatribes about US use of drones.[3]

In short, by the end of 2009, the United States and NATO were carrying out both a broad counterinsurgency campaign and a pinpoint counterterrorism campaign in Afghanistan (and Af-Pak). NATO had well over a hundred thousand combat troops stationed in the country, and there were also 107,000 private contractors there, of whom 26,000 were foreigners. (The other 81,000 were Afghans working for the United States or one of the other NATO nations.) The whole force far exceeded what the Soviets had deployed in Afghanistan at their peak. Even so, the insurgency kept spreading.

In 2010, McChrystal organized the biggest pitched battle of the war in Marjah, a small town twenty miles from Lashkargah, the capital of Helmand Province. McChrystal called Marjah the headquarters of the insurgency and said that taking this town would break the back of the Taliban.

The battle was fierce, the outcome inevitable: NATO won in a week. As soon as all "the Taliban" had been killed or driven underground, Mc-Chrystal's troops unloaded a so-called government in a box. In short order, Marjah's schools had reopened, clinics were operating, police were patrolling the streets, infrastructure was being maintained, and life looked good.

The only problem was that isolated episodes of violence kept troubling the town and its environs—no pitched battles, no militia attacks, nothing the police and military couldn't handle: it was more like crime than like war, but still, the bottom line was, violence kept happening and happening and happening. . . . Lady Sale's book *A Journal of the Disasters in Afghanistan* gave a similar picture of the situation the British experienced in Kabul in 1841. McChrystal triggered an uproar a few months later when he called Marjah a "bleeding ulcer," but he wasn't far wrong. The real problem for NATO was that its troops couldn't distinguish the people they were fighting against from the people they were fighting to protect. This wasn't their fault. One had to be on the inside to know the difference, and even there the boundaries were often blurred.[4]

Whatever momentum McChrystal built up, he broke it in July 2010 by consenting to a strange interview with *Rolling Stone* magazine in which he expressed blatant contempt for President Obama.[5] He told the reporter the president had looked "intimidated" when he met with his own military commanders. He derided Vice President Biden even more severely, pretending not to know his name and allowing his aide to suggest the name might be "Bite me." The general was called to Washington by his commander in chief for further instruction in military protocol, and the legendary General David Petraeus was installed in his place.

Conventional wisdom saw Petraeus as the man who had made "the surge" work in Iraq—*surge* meaning the sudden deployment of many additional troops. Petraeus endorsed McChrystal's fight-the-Taliban-in-their-strongholds strategy, but he let up on the tight rules of engagement. The rules had, in any case, been honored more in the breach than in the observance, and Petraeus said he could not in good conscience add to the dangers his own troops faced. The day he took charge, a NATO air strike killed thirty-nine civilians, mostly women and children, near the city of Kandahar. That fall, General Petraeus launched an even bigger battle than the one in Marjah. He decided to conquer Kandahar itself, the country's second-biggest city and the very birthplace of the Taliban.

During early skirmishes in the suburbs of Kandahar, American forces dropped twenty-five tons of bombs on a village called Tarok Kolache, erasing it from the face of the earth. (The residents had been warned to evacuate beforehand; official sources said there were no civilian casualties.)[6] Finally, after about two months of fighting, the United States claimed victory in the battle for Kandahar. Unfortunately, the gains made in Marjah had largely eroded by that time, and the insurgency was spreading virulently north.

Even in Kandahar, the extent of NATO control came into question on the night of April 25, 2011, when some eight hundred prisoners escaped from the main prison there. They left through a tunnel they had been digging for several months without anyone noticing. So many prisoners escaped that they were streaming out for four hours, also without anyone noticing. They came up in the compound across the street from the prison. From there, cars took them to more distant locations, where at least some of them completed their getaway in *taxicabs*. Only after all of them were gone did the alarm sound.[7]

The killing of Osama bin Laden on May 2, 2011, should have marked a turning point, given that when the United States went into Afghanistan in 2001, capturing Bin Laden and defeating al Qaeda were the avowed purpose of the war. The Taliban came into it only because they had abetted Bin Laden. As for the Afghans in general, they were defined as the intended beneficiaries of the intervention. Bin Laden's mysterious escape in 2001 and his subsequent silence left the War on Terror in Afghanistan without a marker that could define a victory. What would winning consist of? Other than Bin Laden and al Qaeda, there was no ruler to topple, no organization to bust up, no capital city to take. In Bush's war, the other side was never going to say "we surrender" because the "other side" in Afghanistan was not a "we," not a state, syndicate, or fixed entity of any kind, but a condition: a brew of poverty, impotence, resentment, humiliation, and aggression cooked into a movement by an angry ideology that had come to permeate the Islamic world. Anything the United States did to break the insurgency tended only to add to the humiliation and thus fuel the fires of resentment: fighting the war became the thing that was causing the war. Fighting it harder only made the fires burn hotter. Over the years, the "jihadism" of al Qaeda and its ilk melted into the enduring older dramas of Afghan history, including that long struggle between outward-looking Kabul and the inward-looking world of the Afghan countryside, a conflict the United States and NATO could not possibly solve. Instead, their attempts to "fix" Afghanistan devolved into a campaign that many Afghans now perceive as a war on Afghan culture.

Until May 2011, political considerations made it difficult for any US president to simply end the war and bring the troops home. His domestic political rivals would have accused him of accepting a defeat. But when a small team of Navy Seals dropped into a compound in the Pakistani city of Abbottabad, less than a mile from the Pakistan Military Academy, and shot Osama Bin Laden dead, they achieved the only definable objective of the war. Surely now it would be possible to declare victory and go home. But, as it turned out, it was too late for that. The United States was too thoroughly embroiled in Afghanistan to disengage so easily, even though the Obama plan to train an Afghan national army and police force and hand the country over to them remained on the books.

After Bin Laden's death, the Afghan insurgency demonstrated seemingly growing power with a series of strikes. In June 2011, gunmen and suicide bombers launched a five-hour attack on the Intercontinental Hotel in Kabul, where foreign dignitaries were meeting to discuss the future of Afghanistan. That September, insurgents fought an all-day battle in the capital, raining rockets on the US embassy and detonating four suicide bombs simultaneously in disparate parts of the city. One week later, assassins killed Burhanuddin Rabbani, head of the Northern Alliance and former president of the country, who was serving as leader of an ineffectual "peace council" commissioned by Karzai to negotiate with the Taliban. In April 2012, insurgents carried out another series of attacks in Kabul, another all-day battle. One month later, they assassinated another leading member of "the peace council." And so it went.

Ominously, more and more attacks were carried out by men in Afghan police or Afghan army uniforms. One suicide bomber blew himself up in the very heart of the Ministry of Defense. In 2012, killers dressed as policemen murdered two American officers in the most heavily secured area of the Ministry of Interior. This was no passion killing but a carefully plotted crime by someone made up to look like "one of ours." Were the insurgents stealing uniforms, or were they infiltrating the Afghan army and police forces that NATO was trying to build up? Which would be worse? Hard to say. The government, in any case, responded by forbidding tailors to make military uniforms.

As the ferocity of the insurgency mounted, US and NATO forces kept pouring fuel on the fire with a string of crimes and blunders that reinforced among Afghans a sense of the West as an invader at war with them. In the summer of 2011, the trial of the Stryker Brigade "kill team" began. These were a dozen soldiers who had formed a murder club in Kandahar to hunt and kill Afghan civilians for sport and who had kept (and traded) fingers and other body parts of their victims—details that emerged during the trials. In January 2012, a video of four US Marines urinating on the corpses of Afghans went viral on YouTube. In February, American troops at Bagram incinerated copies of the Qur'an in a trash fire, echoing another episode a year earlier, when a pastor in Florida burned Qur'ans as a deliberately provocative act that sparked deadly riots throughout Afghanistan. In March 2012, an American soldier went on a rampage in Kandahar and massacred sixteen random Afghan civilians.

American presidential candidate Newt Gingrich, reacting to the massacre and the subsequent unrest, said the United States should withdraw from Afghanistan posthaste because it was not going to "fundamentally change Afghan culture"[8]—reifying the assumption that the point of all these troops and firepower had all along been to "fundamentally change Afghan culture."

35

All That Glitters

THESE DEVELOPMENTS PROBABLY MAKE AFGHANISTAN LOOK HOPELESS. Whoever the Taliban might be, they're on the march, and nothing can now stop them from plunging Afghanistan back into the darkness of the late nineties . . . or so it seems.

That judgment, however, may be premature. The other side is pushing forward full throttle as well, fueled partly by the fact that big money is at stake now. In July 2010, right after McChrystal was fired, a major piece of good news began competing with all the awful war reports coming out of unhappy Afghanistan. It began with a *New York Times* piece revealing that this country has at least $1 trillion worth of undeveloped mineral wealth. The report was based on geological surveys commissioned by the Pentagon in 2009, but it wasn't really news: Alexander the Great knew of Afghanistan's copper. Marco Polo mentioned its mineral wealth. I first heard that mining would save Afghanistan in 1978, from an Afghan Ministry of Mines official visiting the Asia Foundation, where I worked at the time. Later, the Soviets mapped the minerals. According to the *Times*, however, few realized how rich these lodes were until the recent survey.

Afghanistan has the world's second-largest unexploited deposits of copper at a place called Mes Aynak. It has one of the largest deposits of unexploited high-grade iron ore in all of Asia. It has gold and precious gems, cobalt and phosphorus, barium, strontium, and uranium. It has plenty of natural gas and even a small quantity of oil.

Most interesting of all is the abundance of "rare earth minerals," including lithium, lanthanum, cerium, neodymium, and thirteen other metals that I confess I never heard of until they were discovered in Afghanistan. "Rare earth" minerals are actually no more rare than tin, but normally they are so thinly dispersed through layers of rock and soil that extracting commercial quantities of them is difficult. Extracting them is well worth the effort today, however, because technologies such as fiber optics, computer displays, hard drives, cell phone batteries, laptop batteries, low-energy lighting, solar conversion cells, hybrid car engines, and satellite communications would be impossible without them. Rare earth minerals also figure in a host of advanced military devices, such as guidance and control systems for smart bombs, drones, precision missiles, laser weaponry, signal-jamming devices, and military radar. The technologies essential to power and prosperity over the next century will depend on rare earth minerals, so you can bet those minerals will be as much the basis of wealth in the near future as oil was in the recent past. And poor Afghanistan is located right on the line of scrimmage again between the many powers that will be fighting for those riches.

China has the world's largest known reserves of rare earth minerals, about thirty-six million tons. Russia is next with nineteen million tons, and then comes the United States with thirteen million. No one knows how much Afghanistan has, but US military geologists have estimated that less than one square mile of the Helmand Valley contains about 1.5 million tons. If that is the sum total of rare earth minerals in Afghanistan, it's still a lot for one small country. There might be much more, though it's hard to tell right now, because the rare earth minerals are located exactly where the insurgency is raging most ferociously—in Kandahar and Helmand provinces.

Coincidence?

Yes, I'm pretty sure it is. Sorry, conspiracy theorists, but the factors that make these provinces so truculent predate the technologies that make rare earth minerals so precious. Most of the inhabitants of Helmand and Kandahar know nothing of the wealth they're standing on—yet. That will change.

I called the mineral wealth of Afghanistan good news, but really it's a good news/bad news situation. The minerals would be an unmitigated boon for a country with the technical know-how to develop its own resources, the strength to hold hungry outsiders at bay, and the social institutions needed to ensure that the wealth benefits the whole society and not just a favored few. As matters stand, foreign companies are the ones in line to develop these resources. Afghans will get something out of them through leases and partnerships, but they have yet to develop the political and social mechanisms to absorb even this portion of the wealth equitably and without conflict. Sadly, such mechanisms might not develop in the pressure cooker of great-power contention that has always put the squeeze on Afghanistan and will go on doing so.

In the race for Afghanistan's minerals, China has emerged as the big winner so far. The year before the *New York Times* broke the news about Afghanistan's enormous trove of copper ore, the Chinese company Metallurgical Corp signed a $3.5 billion deal for the country's copper. (This is the deal for which the Afghan minister of mines allegedly took the big kickback.) In late 2011, China's National Petroleum Corporation announced a joint venture with the Afghan-owned Watan Company to develop the country's oil and gas. Over the next ten years, the Afghan government expects to reap $5 billion from royalties and taxes on this operation. No word yet on what money changed hands privately to grease this deal. Maybe none did. Miracles do happen.

The Colorado-based Newmont Mining Corporation, America's biggest gold producer, bid on Afghanistan's major iron deposits but lost out to a consortium of seven Indian companies. The Indian investors plan to spend between $7 and $11 billion on developing the iron. Meanwhile, British, Iranian, and Turkish companies have been circling like hungry hawks over the other mineral resources of Afghanistan, competing to form joint ventures with Afghan companies to develop the gold, the uranium, the cobalt, and more.

The Chinese have committed no troops to Afghanistan nor spent a yuan on military operations there, so it's ironic that they are winning the rights to so much of the country's minerals. Then again, their lack of any military footprint may have given them an edge. At Mes Aynak, the Chinese company's contract binds it to building schools, roads, mosques, and a 400-megawatt coal-fired electric power plant in the area. The mining will displace some villagers, but Metallurgical Corp has reportedly offered to hire the displaced people to build new villages for themselves outside the affected area, replicating the ones that will be destroyed. The villagers get new homes and also get good jobs building them. At least that's the promise.

As it happens, French and Afghan archaeologists have found a Buddhist monastery at Mes Aynak, built in the seventh century BC. This amazing site is loaded with enough precious artifacts to fill the Kabul Museum to overflowing, but the Chinese mining operations will destroy it. The Chinese had planned to start mining in 2011, but they agreed to hold off for three years, supposedly to let the archeologists complete their excavations. Actually, it will take at least that long to set up the mining operation, so it's not clear that the Chinese made any financial sacrifices, and archeologists working on the site say they will need at least ten years to complete their work. Still, the Chinese reaped good PR out of their postponement announcement.

Afghanistan never had a single railroad in the past, but thanks to the mining it will soon have three and maybe more. The Chinese are building one railroad from Afghanistan's northern border to Logar Province, south of Kabul, in order to extract the copper from Mes Aynak. The Indians will need a railroad to mine the iron at Hajigak, so they're building one from Bamiyan Province, just west of Kabul, all the way to the Iranian port of Charbahar. Once built, these railroads will be available to transport other goods within and beyond Afghanistan. Meanwhile, a railroad running from Uzbekistan to the northern city of Mazar-i-Sharif was completed in 2012 and is carrying passengers and freight today.

In Mazar-i-Sharif, the capital of Balkh Province, economic development is flourishing despite the insurgency. Turkish investors have built factories here that produce edible oils and canned food products for domestic consumption and export. The province has textile mills, garment factories, and a motorcycle assembly plant.

In fact, business is flourishing throughout much of the country right alongside the violence. An Afghan-owned company (headquartered in Dubai) has signed a $60 million deal with Pepsi to distribute its products in Afghanistan. Another Afghan company with ties to business interests in the UAE is planning to invest $100 million to develop 3-G telecom services. It expects to add six million new subscribers to the millions of Afghans who already have cell phone service provided by three companies founded since 9/11. One of these companies offers sophisticated banking by phone, allowing people to conduct business from anywhere in the country that has cell phone towers.

Millions of Afghans are mired in grim poverty, yet Kabul and other cities are booming. The abundance of cash sloshing around becomes obvious when you look at the wedding celebrations of the nouveau super-rich. Afghans have always mounted extravagant weddings and funerals as badges of family honor. Even in the old days, young men sometimes couldn't get married simply because they couldn't host a wedding sufficiently grandiose to uphold their family's image in the community.

But the weddings of recent years have put the conspicuous consumption of the past to shame. Guests at these weddings routinely number in the hundreds. The sons and daughters of the richest power brokers have been known to host two thousand guests at a single party. (*Power broker* has replaced *warlord* as the standard title for a big shot in Afghanistan.) Even middle-class families straining to maintain appearances host celebrations that drag them to the edge of financial ruin.

The upside of this excess is the economic stimulus it provides. There is good money to be made operating a wedding hall, a palatial building fitted out specifically for these outlandish parties. Kabul has more than eighty such palaces now.[1] The expenses of a wedding may be one person's road to ruin, but they're another person's road to wealth, for this industry has opened up numerous jobs for Afghan women and afforded new opportunities for female entrepreneurs. Beauty shops have flourished, because men with money will open their wallets to enable their womenfolk to look stylish at these events. Women who make fancy gowns do a brisk business. A catering industry has spun off from the wedding trade. Pot and dish rental companies are flourishing. Musicians have no trouble getting work in modern Kabul.

In fact, the celebrations have been so extravagantly over the top that the government has tried to pass laws restraining big fat Afghan weddings—to no avail. People who want to flaunt their success by spending enough money to ruin themselves will find a way to do it, no matter what the law might say.

In 2001, shortly before the events of 9/11, development worker Idrees Ahmad Rahmani traveled extensively around rural Afghanistan; he reported that as soon as he left any road big or small, he found villages with no electricity, no municipal plumbing, no mail service, and no phones—inward-looking settlements so cut off from news of the outside world they didn't even know what was happening in Kabul, much less Pakistan, much less Paris or Peoria. In 2010, Rahmani made the same journey as a researcher and said he found no untouched villages of this type. The Afghan rural world had changed more in a decade than it had in a thousand years. How could this be?

Rahmani attributed the change partly to television. In every village he visited, he saw at least one set, always attached to a satellite dish, and often installed in a communal building that functioned as a town hall, where villagers could gather in the evening to watch programs from around the world.

Where do they get the electricity to run their TV sets? They have gas-powered generators, says Rahmani, which they own because the Chinese have been marketing generators cheap enough for almost every village to afford at least one. How do they get gas to run the generators? Well, says Rahmani, the elders send the young men of their village on regular runs to the nearest towns, on motorcycles, to bring back gas. And how can the young men afford motorcycles? You guessed it: the Chinese and Iranians have been producing rugged bikes at prices so cheap, every village can afford a few.[2] What's more, solar panels are popping up in rural Afghanistan. Where do villagers in remote places get the money to buy solar panels, motorcycles, or even the cheapest generators, much less the gas to run them? Rahmani didn't say, but the answer seems obvious. Many villagers throughout Afghanistan have a type of currency negotiable in world markets: opium.

When drug exporters tied in with the Taliban come to out-of-the-way villages to buy narcotics that they can smuggle abroad and resell in order to fund their insurgency, they don't necessarily pay with cash. Often they pay with commodities such as cell phones, television sets, motorcycles, SUVs, and even computers.[3] The Taliban are generally (and correctly) seen as a force that is trying to drag Afghanistan back to the seventh century socially, yet they are helping to diffuse technology throughout the country, thereby inadvertently facilitating the flow of information and cultural influences into the Afghan countryside, which may render their core project hopeless: for when villagers gather around their communal

TV sets, they can see shows from all over the world, thanks to their satellite dishes. Rahmani claims some even watch pirated HBO shows. I have no way to confirm that they do, but I guess they could.

Even if they watch only programs coming out of Kabul, rural Afghans have plenty of eye-openers to choose from. They can watch *Afghan Star*, a reality show modeled after *American Idol*. Singers perform for a panel of judges, some are eliminated, and some are approved to go on to the next round, a thinning process that eventually produces a single winner. Even in its first year, a couple of women made it into the final rounds. One of them, Herati singer Setara, shocked the Afghan audience by dancing without a head scarf when she sang her final number—and by dancing I don't mean Afghan wedding dancing, which involves side-to-side head movements, serpentine arm gestures, and eye flirting; I mean disco dancing complete with wiggling hips. Don't get me wrong: in America, her dancing would have been considered downright prim; in Afghanistan, it earned her death threats.

The death threats made the international news, reinforcing the theme of regressive barbarity so often associated with Afghanistan; but for me, the big news was that women were *competing* in this show and making it into the late rounds, not to mention the fact that the contestants included Pushtoons, Tajiks, and Hazaras; that the winner is selected by a television audience of millions voting by cell phone; and that when a Hazara guy won the first year, no one found his ethnicity worth remarking upon.

Afghan Star is not the only show of its kind. Another TOLO TV offering is a game show based on *Who Wants to Be a Millionaire?* In 2010, a dramatic series called *The Secrets of This House* premiered on TOLO. This was a soap opera produced entirely in Kabul and written by award-winning writer Atiq Rahimi, who came back from exile in France to work on the show.[4] *Eagle Four*, a cop show funded largely by the American Embassy, also began a run on TOLO in 2010. It featured an antiterrorism unit within the Afghan national police force that hunts down evildoers without bothering too much about the picayune niceties of the so-called regulations, much like the Kiefer Sutherland vehicle *24*. The team is coed, which is not completely fanciful, because the first women accepted into the police training program graduated in 2010 and joined the force. So did the first women to enter the officer ranks of the ANA. And, in 2012, I saw a reality show in Kabul about recent kidnappings in the country, which featured documentary footage interspersed with dramatic re-enactments.

The arts are back with astonishing vigor. In 2011, impresario Rameen Javed brought a collection of thirty avant-garde paintings by new Afghan artists on a gallery tour of America. Turquoise Mountain Foundation, founded by British author Rory Stewart but run entirely by Afghans now, has paired up aging Afghan artisans with aspiring younger ones to keep traditional arts alive. Shireen Pasha's documentary *Slowly, Slowly, Mud and Lotus* offers a stunning glimpse of these artisans and their work.[5] In 2011, Turquoise Mountain launched a project to restore the intricate labyrinth of buildings and narrow alleys comprising Kabul's oldest neighborhood, a neighborhood devastated in the urban civil wars of the nineties. Here, some of the last living masters of traditional Afghan arts and crafts—woodworkers, ceramicists, tile workers, metalsmiths, and such—are carrying out this restoration in conjunction with their young apprentices.

Film arts remain alive so far as well. German-Afghan director Burhan Qurbanni's feature *Shahada* made it into the prestigious Berlin International Film Festival. Two month later, Sonia Nassery Cole's movie *Black Swan* opened in Kabul's Ariana Cinema. Filmed entirely in Afghanistan, Cole's movie follows the travails of a Kabul family trying to run a cafe that stages poetry readings. Her film suffered a tragic blow when reactionaries kidnapped the actress playing the lead role and cut off her feet to punish her for her supposed infidelity to religion—whereupon Cole herself stepped into the role to finish the film.

And master musicians such as drummer Asif Mohammed and singer Farhad Darya have returned to their country from exile. The National Museum is being refurbished. Afghan entrepreneurs have built a National Sports Museum in Kabul, and Afghanistan sent athletes to the Olympics again in 2012, including female sprinter Tahmina Kohistani, who ran in the 100-meter event wearing a headscarf, and Rohullah Nikpai, who won a bronze medal in tae kwon do, as he did in 2008.

Afghanistan may be a tragedy but is not without its comedians. There's Amanullah Mujaddedi, for example, a prankster in the Andy Kaufman mode. Once, he set up a checkpoint at a public road and stopped cars, as so many thugs have done in Afghanistan, but instead of demanding a toll, he gave money away, real money—to the consternation and befuddlement of his "victims." His comedy sketches have featured a "jihadi gangsta" character he has developed, who wears gold robes and dark glasses and is attended by suggestively-clad, burqa-wearing female attendants. Making fun of jihadis in Afghanistan gives new meaning to the phrase "edgy comedy." You might suppose a fellow like this comes from a long line of cultural radicals; in fact, his uncle is Subghatullah Mujaddedi, the conservative religious leader who headed up one of those seven main Mujahideen parties based in Peshawar during the anti-Soviet war.

In short, the contest is not over. The rural conservatives keep pressing in upon the cities, sending their suicide bombers into crowded markets and trying as hard as they can to subvert the social cohesion developing around modernist ideas and values; but the other side is fighting fiercely to pull the country into an unknowable future and a full engagement with the great, wide world.

The money keeps pouring into the country, the thievery is beyond belief, the energy is uproarious, the days and nights are shattered by bombs and rockets and gunfire, and the singers keep singing and the comedians go on cracking jokes. Afghanistan, a project often interrupted but just as often resumed, is a country still coalescing—into what is anybody's guess.

Postscript

The Big Picture

THERE'S NO BRINGING THIS CHRONICLE TO THE PRESENT MOMENT, GIVEN that the present is a moving platform; and yet I do want to end this book by speaking of Afghanistan today, because "today," after all, is part of a larger pattern in Afghan history, a pattern generated by enduring factors.

For Afghanistan, the most important of these has always been location. This is the land-in-between, the land squeezed between mighty powers wrestling for stakes much bigger than Afghanistan. In ancient times, it was here that Turkish, Persian, and Indian civilizations went head-to-head. Afghans partook of all three civilizations and belonged to none. The people intermingled, but the territory never simply became the frontier of Persia or the northernmost edge of India. There was always a here here. Through the ages, the great powers kept changing, the contention never ended, and yet the land-in-between never disappeared. Far from being absorbed, Afghanistan keeps absorbing elements from all who encroach upon it, reconfiguring itself endlessly as an entity distinct from its neighbors and invaders.

In 2002, just after the original Taliban had been ousted, I visited Kabul for the first time in thirty-seven years and roamed the countryside north as far as Panjsher Valley, onetime headquarters of Ahmad Shah Massoud. Fully one-third of the capital had been reduced to rubble, perhaps more, and the plains north of the city were still charred from the fires of recent wars, and yet, in crucial ways, I found Afghanistan much the same as it had been when I left.

My friends and I could still stop at a random spot by the Panjsher River and within minutes find ourselves surrounded by local shepherds and farmers who strolled by to see who we were and to offer us fresh mulberries and hot tea. Everywhere, strangers casually engaged us in storytelling and conversation that lasted for hours, though I could not remember later what we talked about. The material world had sustained unbelievable damage, but the culture retained that calm indifference to deadlines and time, not to mention an aggressive sociability that had always characterized Afghan life at ground level, no matter what sultan was currently abiding his hour or two upon the country's throne.

But also, despite all the blood that had been shed over gender roles, Afghanistan remained a world divided into public and private realms, with the public world belonging almost entirely to men and with women still living mostly within compound walls, sequestered from the eyes of strangers. Yet, as an Afghan privy to the hidden world of at least my own clan and family, I can attest that these women remained as forceful, voluble, and vigorous as ever.

I visited Afghanistan again ten years later and found that much had changed—but much had not. In 2002, the city had been cluttered with the rubble of bombed-out buildings. In 2012, it was still cluttered, but with the rubble of new construction. In 2002, hardly anyone had a telephone. Now, although no one had a landline, almost everyone had at least one cell phone, and many had two. On my earlier visit, although I saw few people riding donkeys within the city limits anymore, I saw many riding them in the country. Now, I still saw donkeys in the countryside, but the people riding them were sometimes packing computers in their saddlebags.

In 2002 Kabul had been a city of about 350,000, crammed with cars but equipped (as far as I could tell) with only two traffic lights. It made for a clamorous chaos that no one seemed to notice. In 2012, Kabul had become a metropolis of many millions. How many? The Associated Press said three, many people in Kabul said five, and a few estimated ten, but no one really knew or knows. And yet, as I say, much remained unchanged. This metropolis of millions *still* seemed to have only two traffic lights. Traffic jams were endemic, and *still* no one seemed to care. They just conducted business on their cell phones while they waited. "If I weren't here, I'd be somewhere else," one guy shrugged, adding, "God is great."

The countryside retained something of that old, underlying calm. A hundred miles from Kabul, in a seemingly uninhabited valley, we stopped to change a tire, and we'd scarcely loosened the nuts before a grizzled local from a village we couldn't even see came moseying by to invite us home for tea. In the city, that deep sense of unhurried calm had given way to a frenzied hubbub ignited by the money and technology screaming down upon Afghanistan—yet this was just another aspect of the Afghan character rising to the surface, for paradoxically enough this has always also been a society of freewheeling deal makers, networking relentlessly as they scope out angles to play in a jungle gym of personal relationships. As it was in the days of Ahmad Shah Baba, so it still is today.

Ten years ago, people in Kabul seemed to regard traffic regulations as quaint foreign imports unsuited to this climate. They still do. People joke that driving in Kabul is like playing buzkashi. Cars are constantly bursting out of their lanes, even into supposedly one-way streets to drive against the prevailing flow because their drivers have spotted openings. You might suppose that here there are no rules.

You would be wrong. If there really were no rules, one would see thousands of car accidents. What I saw were thousands of near misses: not one collision. The rules may not be obvious to foreigners, but they exist and Afghans understand them. And the same is undoubtedly true of the country's social and political life.

The rules may be hard to discern in part because there isn't just one set. Afghanistan probably had a consistent culture when it first began coalescing as a nation-state in the eighteenth century, and, although it was evolving, it was doing so within a coherent framework.

Then the country experienced a series of incursions emanating out of Europe, which gave rise to a maelstrom of conflicting currents. Within the country, the multitudes whose cohesion derived only from traditional tribal and Islamic values expected their rulers to honor and defend those values with their lives and to otherwise leave them alone. Afghan rulers could not simply comply, however, for looking outward they always saw two or more well-equipped Western goliaths facing off against each other, with hapless Afghanistan situated between them on their line of scrimmage. Each goliath was intent on moving into this space to keep the other goliath from moving into it. Each expected to succeed with Afghans because it presumed it would bring cultural and material improvements to the country. Each was happy to deal with Afghan leaders so long as they operated on cultural ground familiar to Europeans.

Trying to negotiate between the local and global forces, between the inner and outer worlds, put Afghan rulers in a double bind. Anyone who wanted to rule this country had to secure the sponsorship of the strongest foreigners impinging on the country at that moment; yet no Afghan could rule this country for long without the allegiance of the country's deepest traditional forces. To the dominant outside power, therefore, every would-be ruler had to portray himself as a partner. At the same time, to his country's internal forces, he had to portray himself as a tough guy standing up to foreign bullies. The kings who best succeeded in this balancing act did so by covertly pursuing "modernization" while overtly proclaiming themselves champions of conservative social and religious values.

The same thing is happening again now. Afghans see the Karzai government signing one agreement after another with the Americans, and they shake their heads in disbelief. Americans see Karzai approving ever more reactionary social laws and issuing outlandish threats to join the Taliban, and they wonder if the president of Afghanistan has lost his mind. Actually, anyone in Karzai's role would exhibit similar schizophrenia. His seemingly erratic actions don't necessarily reflect personal instability but the surreal contradictions of his position in the bigger picture.

The concatenation of forces pervading and surrounding Afghanistan has given rise to competing visions for the nation's identity. Every foreign force that comes crashing in thinks it's intervening in "a country," but it's actually taking sides in an ongoing contest among Afghans about what this country is. Every foreign intervention founders therefore on the same rock. Routinely, the foreign power puts a proxy on the throne and tries to govern the country through him. But the very authority given to this proxy, because it comes from foreigners, weakens his authority among the traditional forces of old Afghanistan. The foreign power essentially tries to swing the pot by grasping its handle, but the pot shatters, and the foreign power is left holding only a handle. The British had their Shah Shuja and then their Yaqub Khan. The Soviets had their Taraki and then their Babrak Karmal. Shah Shuja, Yaqub Khan, Taraki, Karmal—they're all the same guy, just with different names. And now, America and NATO have Hamid Karzai.

Foreign interventions in Afghanistan don't just undermine the designated proxy but the authority of Kabul within Afghanistan. The erosion of central authority releases the country's propensity to fragment, and so in the end the foreign power finds itself facing a burgeoning chaos that saps its resources, leaving little time or strength for carrying out the original intentions of the intervention, whatever those were. The problem is not that Afghans unite and then cannot be conquered; the problem is that Afghans fragment and then cannot be governed. The great powers have a stake in making Afghanistan more governable, but the only people who can achieve this happy result are Afghans—because it depends on the resolution of contradictions within Afghan culture. Once the foreign power withdraws in disgust from a country it has helped render ungovernable, some new permutation of the Afghan urban (or rural) ruling classes comes back to power, its prestige renewed by the role it has (supposedly) played in driving out foreigners. The pendulum then swings back from fragmentation toward centralization, as a reinvigorated government sets to work trying to compress and shape this hodgepodge of peoples into a coherent state.

Every Afghan government must renew this project; no Afghan government can simply let go and watch the society come apart, because the foreigners are out there always. If it isn't the United States, it will be China. If not China, Iran. If not Iran, then India or Russia or some combination of Arab powers or of those central Asian republics—Uzbekistan, Turkmenistan, Tajikistan. . . .

As soon as new rulers secure credibility among Afghans, they do two things: one, they move toward a cautious accommodation with some chosen outside force while publicly asserting nonalignment in world politics; and two, they start trying to push Afghan customs and values into alignment with those of the world at large. If they do it artfully, they survive for a while; if they do it clumsily they go down.

This will happen again, whether elections bring another DC-approved modernist to the presidency or "the Taliban" overwhelm the cities and take power again. It will happen because, confoundingly enough, the constant threat of Great Power interventions make the centralizing power in Kabul outward-looking and oriented toward membership in the modern world. If "the Taliban" succeed in taking over, you can be sure they will develop this same outward-looking orientation and attraction to some version of modernity very shortly.

The world's great powers have a choice. They can take turns trying to conquer Afghanistan, or they can act together as neutral referees to promote Afghan reconciliation. Ironically, the interests of all outside powers are best served by a reconciliation that enables Afghans to form a sovereign country—sovereign culturally as well as politically. I say "ironically" because, as soon as Afghanistan achieves that sovereignty, it will adopt a foreign policy of dogged neutrality, which will serve no other country's interests fully. This might lead any given country to decide that conquering Afghanistan is the better option after all, but that option is never really on the table. The actual choices are (1) neutral-Afghanistan-serving-nobody's-interest-fully or (2) awful-quagmire-Afghanistan-sucking-down-yet-another-hapless-great-power.

The real question for the United States, then, is not how America can forge true democracy in Afghanistan or end corruption in Afghanistan or change the status of Afghan women: those questions are for Afghans to settle, and Afghans *will* settle them if left to their own devices. The real question for the United States is how to liberate Afghanistan from the United States—and all other outside powers. The conference that can best accomplish this is one that brings to the table not just NATO and Afghanistan but all countries with a potential interest in this territory—which is a lot of countries. And what this conference must hammer out is an agreement among all nations to accord Afghanistan the status of a central Asian Switzerland.

Once outside pressure abates, Afghans can begin to resolve their cultural contradictions. The path has been thorny, but that process may be under way already. For so long, this country has been wracked by the wrestling match between its rural and urban souls, but that distinction is growing fuzzier. Ten years ago, my family's ancestral village was a hamlet well outside Kabul. No formal road ran to it. To get there, you had to know where to depart from the highway and then which direction to go, over hill and dale, on foot, on a donkey, or in a rugged vehicle. Today, my relatives are busy filing formal claims to lands they've always farmed because New Kabul is coming, and when it does the government will appropriate undocumented properties, after which Deh Yahya will be just another neighborhood within the capital.

In 2012, I met a Pushtoon from rural Wardak working in Kabul as a driver. When he found out I was writing a book about Afghanistan, he begged me to tell the world about his people. "Everyone thinks we just want to fight and hurt and kill. It isn't true! Look at me! Am I not the sweetest, most well-behaved of men?" (He was in fact one of the sweetest fellows I had met in a long time.) He went on to say, "This government paved the road to my village. Before, it took four hours to get to Kabul. Now it takes forty-five minutes. If my mother gets sick and I need to get her to a hospital in Kabul, don't you think I'm glad the road is paved? We're not against roads! We're not against hospitals! We just want to live in peace, the way we've always lived."

On that same trip, I had a chance to visit Bamiyan, the valley where the giant Buddhas stood, before the Taliban blew them up. I had been there at the age of two but retained no images of the place in my head, of course, except from photographs. Yet, as we drove into the little town at the heart of the province, everything looked strangely familiar. For one thing, the bazaar of Bamiyan looked pretty much like all the small-town bazaars of my childhood and even like the one in Dehbouri, our neighborhood in Kabul. It was a narrow street flanked by room-sized stalls. Some were butcher shops, vending fresh meat hanging from hooks. Others were selling local fruits and vegetables piled high in baskets, still others miscellaneous dry goods such as matches, batteries, pencils, mascara, and toys. In the shops, storekeepers were drinking tea with their customers. On the sidewalks, street vendors were hawking motley goods and services. I saw one guy sitting on a stool with a little table in front of him and for a moment I thought he was a dalak, one of those itinerant barber/surgeons who used to cut hair on the streets in the old days.

He wasn't a dalak, of course. Those no longer exist. When I got close, I saw that this man had a personal solar panel the size of an attaché case standing next to his stool. It was hooked up to a 12-volt car battery. The battery was running a laptop computer. The laptop was wirelessly connected to the Internet, which this guy could access, even in central Afghanistan.

He was making money downloading songs from some website in Kabul or India and selling them to passersby to load into their cell phones as apps. The singers' voices were electronically modulated, but the songs, though modern in style, recognizably derived from the sort of music I used to hear on Kabul Radio in the fifties, which came out of the folk music of the hills, which went back to the twelfth century and before—just as surely as country music in modern America goes back through Appalachian bluegrass to English country music in Tudor times, or grunge rock goes back through Mississippi Delta blues to roots in Africa.

Here in Afghanistan, the twenty-first century lies directly atop the twelfth, but the contradictory currents of the country's culture and history may at last be melding into some new blend. Standing in that Bamiyan bazaar, under an enormous Buddha-shaped cavity in the cliffs, I felt suddenly that I was not surrounded by today nor by the past. It was the future rising around me, out of the swamp of Afghan history, something whose eventual shape I could not imagine. It struck me then that Afghanistan is like a laboratory. So many currents have flowed through this territory from so many places over so many centuries. The country is rife with contradictions—but then so is the planet. And if Afghanistan succeeds in blending its many strains into a cohesive cultural whole, well, then, maybe there's hope for the planet too.

ACKNOWLEDGMENTS

I AM GRATEFUL TO SO MANY PEOPLE FOR INFORMATION, CONVERSATIONS, and advice contributing to this book—Akbar Nowrouz, Ghafar Lakanwal, Bismillah Iqbal, Yalda Asmatey, Humaira Ghilzai, Idrees Rahmani, Anwar Rezayee, Abdul Hayy, Bashir Sakhawarz, Zahir and Shafiqa Ansary, Farid and Saman Ansary, Akhtar Jamal Ansary, Fazluddin, Najibullah Sedeqe, Wahid Omar, Zmarak Shalizi, Kasem Gardezi, and others too numerous to list. My thanks also goes to Joe Quirk for his invaluable feedback, and above all to my wife, Deborah Krant, for reading the manuscript again and again and patiently discussing it with me, acting as a second eye the likes of which no writer should be without. Thanks as well to Susan Hoffman for setting up the class at Berkeley's Osher Institute of Lifelong Learning that helped me formulate this book, to my agent Carol Mann, and to Lisa Kaufman for her always insightful editing.

NOTES

CHAPTER 1: FOUNDING FATHER

1. Pohand Abdul Hayy Habibi, *Tarikh-i-Mukhtasar-i Afghanistan* [Concise History of Afghanistan] (Arlington, VA: Association of Afghan Refugees, 1989), 256–257.

2. Mohammed Ali, *Cultural History of Afghanistan* (Kabul: Mohammed Ali, 1964), 217–220.

3. Saira Shah, "'Afghaniyat' Is Alive and Well in Afghanistan," *Guardian*, April 7, 2011, http://www.guardian.co.uk/commentisfree/2011/apr/07/afghanistan -nation-building-alive-well.

CHAPTER 2: AHMAD SHAH'S AFGHANISTAN

1. Hasan Kawun Kakar, *Afghanistan: The Soviet Invasion and the Afghan Response, 1979–1982* (Berkeley: University of California Press, 1995), 135–140.

2. Ali, *Cultural History of Afghanistan*, 198–199.

3. This picture of the *qala* comes partly from conversations with Akbar Nowruz, whose family had a qala in Logar.

4. See the discussion of Afghan society in Hasan Kawun Kakar, *Government and Society in Afghanistan: The Reign of Amir 'Abd al-Rahman Khan* (Austin: University of Texas Press, 1979), 50–66.

5. Description of *dalak* drawn heavily from Akbar Nowroz's accounts plus personal experience with dalaks of my day.

6. Ali, *Cultural History of Afghanistan*, 199.

7. Kakar, *Government and Society in Afghanistan*, 124–126.

8. *Zarb-ul Masal-ha*, Afghan proverbs collected by Dr. Ja'far Taheri, 129.

CHAPTER 3: FARANGIS ON THE HORIZON

1. This description of Dost Mohammed comes, in part, from Alexander Burnes, *Travels into Bokhara: Being the Account of a Journey from India to Cabool, Tartary, and Persia* (Philadelphia: E. L. Carey and A. Hart, 1835), 2:23.

2. Mir Ghulam Mohammed Ghobar describes Afghan trade goods, in *Afghanistan Dar Maseer-i-Tareekh, Juld-i Awal* [Afghanistan in the Course of History, Volume 1] (Kabul: Government Publications Department, 1967), 573, although he claims the economy suffered under Dost Mohammed. Fraser-Tytler has a more complimentary view of his reign. W. K. Fraser-Tytler, *Afghanistan: A Study of Political Developments in Central and South Asia* (London: Oxford University Press, 1950), 127.

CHAPTER 4: BETWEEN THE LION AND THE BEAR

1. The phrase appears in *The Wealth of Nations*, bk. 4, chap. 7, pt. 3. Smith actually qualifies the description by describing England as "a nation whose government is influenced by shopkeepers." The book can be found at http://www.gutenberg.org/files/3300/3300-h/3300-h.htm#2HCH0027.

2. Burnes, *Travels into Bokhara*, 1:127.

3. Ibid., 1:128.

4. Ibid., 1:178.

5. Ibid., 1:210–217.

6. Ibid., 1:234.

7. Ibid., 2:15–17.

8. Quoted in Ben Macintyre, *The Man Who Would Be King: The First American in Afghanistan* (New York: Farrar Straus Giroux, 2004), 201.

9. Quoted in Karl Ernest Meyer and Shareen Brysac, *Tournament of Shadows: The Great Game and the Race for Empire in Central Asia* (New York: Basic Books, 2006), 85.

10. Quoted by Fraser-Tytler, *Afghanistan*, 110. For the full text of the manifesto, see Abdul Hakim Tabibi, *Afghanistan: A Nation in Love with Freedom* (Cedar Rapids, IA: Igram Press, 1985), 144–148.

CHAPTER 5: AUCKLAND'S FOLLY

1. See Terence Blackburn, *The Extermination of a British Army: The Retreat from Kabul* (New Delhi: APH, 2008), ix–x, for a detailed breakdown.

2. Jules Stewart, *Crimson Snow: Britain's First Disaster in Afghanistan* (Gloucestershire: Sutton Press, 2008), 78, refers to eight hundred wives. Lady Florentia Sale, in her *A Journal of the Disasters in Afghanistan* (Franklin, TN: Tantallon Press, 2002; originally published in 1843), 48, refers to the king's womenfolk, including wives, daughters, and serving maids, as numbering in the eight hundreds.

3. Mohan Lal, Hindu interpreter for the British, reported this information but didn't mention the woman's name. His report was quoted by M. Saeed, *Women in Afghan History*, http://www.scribd.com/doc/30234527/Women-in-Afghan-History, 13.

4. Louis Dupree, *Afghanistan* (Princeton, NJ: Princeton University Press, 1980), 384. Fraser-Tytler, *Afghanistan*, 114.

5. Sale, *Journal*, 6–20.

6. Dupree, *Afghanistan*, 382–383, quoting John William Kaye, *History of the War in Afghanistan, Third Edition* (London, 1874), 2:130.

7. Stewart, *Crimson Snow*, 102–103

8. Fraser-Tytler, *Afghanistan*, 114

9. I found this diary on the Internet, but unfortunately it has vanished now. I am, however, amused to see that the phrase "frighteningly willing" made its way into the Afghan Chamber of Commerce's account of the First Anglo-Afghan war here: http://www.afghanchamber.com/history/englishinvation.htm. They must have seen the same diary as I.

10. David Loyn, *In Afghanistan* (New York: Palgrave MacMillan, 2009), 35–46.

11. Macintyre, *Man Who Would Be King*, 259–260.

12. Dupree, *Afghanistan*, 386.

13. Ibid., 389.

14. John William Kaye, *History of the War in Afghanistan* (New York: Palgrave MacMillan, 2009), 368–370.

15. Ibid., 376.

16. Ibid.

CHAPTER 6: THE SECOND COMING OF DOST MOHAMMED

1. Ghobar, *Afghanistan Dar Maseer-i-Tareekh*, vol. 1, 573.

2. Ibid., 587–588.

3. Ibid., 573.

4. Ibid.

5. Ibid.

6. Habibi, *Tarikh-i-Mukhtasar-i Afghanistan*, 290.

7. Ghobar, *Afghanistan dar Maseeri Tarikh*, vol. 1, 547.

8. Ibid., 583.

9. Ibid., 588.

CHAPTER 7: EIGHT OR TEN GOOD YEARS

1. Abdul Hakim Tabibi, *The Politicial Struggles of Syed Jamaluddin al-Afghani* (Kabul: Muassisa Intasharat Baihaqi, 1977). Also see Jamil Ahmad, "Jamaluddin Afghani," http://www.renaissance.com.pk/julletf94.html. For the Iranian-origins argument, see Nikki Keddie, *Sayyid Jamal al-Din "al-Afghani": A Political Biography* (Berkeley: University of California Press, 1972).

2. Saeed, *Women in Afghan History*, 15.

3. Ghobar, *Afghanistan Dar Maseer-i-Tareekh*, vol. 1, 594–595.

4. Habibi, *Tarikh-i-Mukhtasar-i Afghanistan*, 291–293.

5. Ghobar, *Afghanistan Dar Maseer-i-Tareekh,* vol. 1, 595–596.
6. Ibid., 594. Sherpoor is within the city limits of today's Kabul.

CHAPTER 8: INTERRUPTED AGAIN

1. Niall Fergusson, *Colossus, The Price of America's Empire* (New York: Penguin Books, 2004), 15.
2. Paul Kennedy, *The Rise and Fall of Great Powers* (New York: Random House, 1987), 151.
3. Maud Diver, *Kabul to Kandahar* (London: Peter Davies, 1935), 21.
4. Ibid., 29.
5. Ibid., 48.
6. Ibid., 54.
7. Ibid., 55.
8. Ibid., 58.
9. Ibid., 61.
10. Ibid., 94.
11. Ibid., 98.
12. Ibid., 100.

CHAPTER 9: A TIME OF BLOOD AND IRON

1. Kakar, *Government and Society in Afghanistan,* 3–6.
2. Habibi, *Tarikh-i-Mukhtasar-i Afghanistan.*
3. Kakar, *Government and Society in Afghanistan,* 48.
4. Ibid., 13.
5. Ibid., 16; also mentioned in Saeed, *Women in Afghan History,* 17. The story of female bodyguards comes from a conversation with Bob Darr/Abdul Hayy, author of *Spy of the Heart.*
6. Kakar, *Government and Society in Afghanistan,* 98–100.
7. Ibid., 105.
8. Ibid., 103–105.
9. Ibid., 40.
10. Ibid., 35.
11. Ibid., 38–39.
12. Ibid., xxiii.

CHAPTER 10: STARTING FRESH

1. Ghobar, *Afghanistan in the Course of History,* vol. 2, 19–23.
2. Rameen Moshref, "The Life and Times of Amir Habibullah," *Afghanistan Online,* http://www.afghan-web.com/bios/detail/dhabib.html. See also Dupree, *Afghanistan,* 408–409.

3. Khalili, *Yawd-dasht hai Ustad Kahlili* [Memoirs of Master Khalili] (As told to his daughter Marie) (Herndon, VA: Marie and Mohammed Afzal Nassiri, 2010), 25–27.

4. Ibid., 37–38.

5. Senzil Nawid, "Political Advocacy in Early Twentieth Century Afghan Persian Poetry," *Afghanistan Studies Journal* 3 (1992): 5–15.

6. Saeed, *Afghan Women in History*, 19.

7. Rhea Talley Stewart, *Fire in Afghanistan* (Garden City, NY: Doubleday, 1973), 11.

8. Ludwig W. Adamec, *Afghanistan, 1900–1923: A Diplomatic History* (Berkeley: University of California Press, 1967), 95.

9. Rhea Talley Stewart, *Fire in Afghanistan*, 20–21.

10. Ibid., 20.

11. Khalili, *Yawd-dasht hai Ustad Kahlili*, 28–31.

12. Ibid., 32.

13. Ibid., 36.

14. Ibid.

CHAPTER 11: KING OF THE RADICALS

1. Rhea Talley Stewart, *Fire in Afghanistan*, 23.

2. Ibid., 37.

3. Ibid., 43.

4. Ibid., 61.

5. Ibid., 73.

6. Ibid.

CHAPTER 12: KING'S LAW VERSUS GOD'S LAW

1. Rhea Talley Stewart, *Fire in Afghanistan*, 188.

2. Sana Haroon, *Frontier of Faith: Islam in the Indo-Afghan Borderland* (New York: Columbia University Press, 2007), 117–119.

3. Rhea Talley Stewart, *Fire in Afghanistan*, 346.

4. Khalili, *Yawd-dasht hai Ustad Kahlili*, 55–59.

5. Rhea Talley Stewart, *Fire in Afghanistan*, 378.

6. Ibid., 377–379, 403–405.

CHAPTER 13: THINGS FALL APART

1. Rhea Talley Stewart, *Fire in Afghanistan*, 416–417. Also see Saqao's "own" accounts of his exploits in his supposed autobiography: Habibullah Kalakani, *My Life from Brigand to King* (London: Octagon Press, 1990), 54–59, 66–68, 71–82.

2. For a discussion of Saqao's image, see Ludwig Adamec, "The Two Faces of Habibullah Kalakani," *Afghanistan Studies Journal* 2 (1990–1991): 85–90.

3. Rhea Talley Stewart, *Fire in Afghanistan*, 425–426, 435–437. Saqao's autobiography gives an amusingly different account of this episode. Kalakani, *Brigand to King*, 115–116, 118–120.

4. Rhea Talley Stewart, *Fire in Afghanistan*, 480. These stories were still being told when I was growing up in Kabul twenty-five years later. The poet Khalili's memoir gives a far more admiring picture of Bacha (59–60, 71–82), as does his biography of Amir Habibullah Kalakani.

5. Khalili, *Yawd-dasht hai Ustad Kahlili*, 71–73. Rhea Talley Stewart, *Fire in Afghanistan*, 438.

6. Kalakani, *Brigand to King*, 158–180.

7. M. H. Anwar, *Memories of Afghanistan* (Bloomington, IN: AuthorHouse, 2004), 127–129.

CHAPTER 14: AFTER THE STORM

1. Anwar, *Memories of Afghanistan*, 131–132.

2. Ghobar, *Afghanistan in the Course of History,* vol. 2, 96–97.

3. Khaled Siddiq Charkhi recounts the destruction of the Charkhi elders and the subsequent fate of surviving family members in *From My Memories: Memoirs of Political Imprisonment from Childhood in Afghanistan* (Bloomington, IN: AuthorHouse, 2010). See 1–37.

4. Ghobar, *Afghanistan in the Course of History,* vol. 2, 68.

5. Anwar, *Memories of Afghanistan*, 200–201, 212–215, 228, 225–226, 262–277.

6. Ghobar, *Afghanistan in the Course of History,* vol. 2, 151–161.

7. Amin Saikal, *Modern Afghanistan: A History of Struggle and Survival* (New York: I. B. Taurus, 2004), 114–115.

CHAPTER 15: NONALIGNED NATION

1. Dupree, *Afghanistan*, 510.

2. When Mao Tse-tung invented the term "Third World," he meant to label the Soviet Union and the United States together the "first world," the developed second-tier powers such as France and Germany the "second world," and all the undeveloped countries, including China, the third world. In common usage, First World came to mean the Capitalist West, Second World the Soviet-led Communist countries, and Third World everybody else. The exact meaning of the terms has remained ambiguous.

3. Dimensions from Dupree, *Afghanistan*, 483.

4. Ibid., 513–522.

CHAPTER 16: DEVELOPMENT, NO BRAKES

1. I remember hearing these speeches without understanding them when I was a little boy growing up in Kabul.
2. Dupree, *Afghanistan*, 546–548.

CHAPTER 17: THE DEMOCRACY ERA

1. Dupree, *Afghanistan* 549.
2. From private conversations with Nasser Hosseini, former ambassador to France, Mazar Ansary, and others.
3. Dupree, *Afghanistan*, 501.

CHAPTER 18: RISE OF THE LEFT

1. Raja Anwar, *The Tragedy of Afghanistan: A First-Hand Account* (London: Verso, 1988), 45.
2. Bashir Sakhawerz, author of the novel *The Snake Charmer*, described these events to me in July 2011; so did Ghulam Ebadi, author of an unpublished memoir, "In Quest of Khalil," which I was editing when he unexpectedly passed away.
3. Anwar, *Tragedy of Afghanistan*, 39–45.
4. Mentioned by Khaled Hosseini, who heard it from his father's associates in the government.

CHAPTER 19: CHANGE BY DECREE

1. Conversation with Ghaffar Lakanwall, former minister of agriculture in the Karmal government, August 16, 2005.
2. Ibid.
3. *Kabul Times*, page 1, August 9, 1979.
4. Conversation with Idrees Ahmad Rahmani, June 17, 2011.
5. Anwar, *Tragedy of Afghanistan*, 129, cites a 1978–1979 survey that claims 2.5 million Afghans—one out of every six—were nomadic or seminomadic at that time.
6. Fred Halliday, "The War and Revolution in Afghanistan," *New Left Review*, no. 119 (January–February, 1980): 31.
7. Anwar, *Tragedy of Afghanistan*, 179–180.
8. My cousin Farid, who was studying in New York at the same time as Amin, recollects Amin's fruitless but sincere attempt to recruit him into the Afghan Communist Party.

9. Kakar, among others, gives the twenty-five thousand figure in his book *Afghanistan: The Soviet Invasion and the Afghan Response, 1979-1982*. Anwar, *Tragedy of Afghanistan*, 156–157, gives the eight hundred number.

10. See Anwar, *Tragedy of Afghanistan*, 166–173, for a detailed account of this debacle.

11. The Russian General Staff, *The Soviet-Afghan War: How a Superpower Fought and Lost* (Lawrence: University Press of Kansas, 2002), 15.

CHAPTER 20: THE SOVIET OCCUPATION

1. Conversation in the summer of 2002 with Malia Zulfiqar, former minister of women's affairs in the Amin government, who resigned (and then defected) because she was required to take part in episodes like this.

2. Russian General Staff, *Soviet-Afghan War*, 21–22.

3. This detail comes from Mahtab Mujaddedi, who fought in Afghanistan as a Mujahid in the eighties.

CHAPTER 21: THE MUJAHIDEEN

1. Kakar, *Afghanistan*, 80.

2. Ibid., 138.

3. In a conversation with the author.

4. Chronicled in Ghulam Ebadi's unpublished personal essay "The Prince and the Lion."

5. From Abdullah Qazi, "Biography: Ahmad Shah Massoud," *Afghanistan Online*, http://www.afghan-web.com/bios/yest/asmasood.html, 2001, updated 2007.

CHAPTER 22: COLD WAR ENDGAME

1. In the nationwide speech delivered on July 15, 1979, Carter used the phrase "crisis of confidence," but his advisor Patrick Caddell had used the word "malaise" in his memo to Carter about the address, which became known ever after as Carter's "malaise" speech.

2. Reagan first evoked the phrase in a speech to the National Association of Evangelicals, March 8, 1983, in Orlando, Florida.

3. If you don't believe me, just Google "Gorbachev, birthmark, anti-Christ."

4. Nixon used variations of this phrase in his campaign speeches leading to the presidential election of 1972 and explicitly in a speech on January 23, 1973, describing the Paris Peace Accords his negotiators had just signed with the North Vietnamese.

5. Kamal Matinuddin, *The Taliban Phenomenon: Afghanistan 1994–1997* (Oxford: Oxford University Press, 1999), 53. Steve Coll, *Ghost Wars* (New York:

Penguin, 2004), puts the number distributed by the CIA at twenty-three hundred, 337.

CHAPTER 23: FROM HORROR TO CHAOS

1. In a conversation with the author, July 2, 2002.
2. Coll, *Ghost Wars*, 337, says six hundred remained in Afghan hands in 1996.
3. Mark Urban, *War in Afghanistan* (New York: St. Martin's Press, 1988), 241–243.
4. http://www.youtube.com/watch?v=p_Kp21GGccE.

CHAPTER 24: OUT OF THE CAMPS

1. Peter Tomsen, *The Wars of Afghanistan* (New York: Public Affairs, 2011), 17.
2. Matinuddin, *Taliban Phenomenon*, 18.
3. Ibid., 20.
4. Ahmad Rashid, *Taliban: Militant Islam, Oil, & Fundamentalism in Central Asia* (New Haven: Yale Note Bene, Yale University Press, 2000), 178.
5. http://www.infoplease.com/ipa/A0762181.html.
6. For a complete list of countries in the coalition and their troop contributions, see http://www.cryan.com/war/AlliedForces.html.
7. Various sources, such as BBC news reports, http://news.bbc.co.uk/2/shared/spl/hi/middle_east/02/iraq_events/html/desert_storm.stm.
8. Department of Defense (http://www.defense.gov/news/newsarticle.aspx?id=45404) official count of Americans killed in this war is 147. CNN (http://articles.cnn.com/2003-04-17/world/sprj.irq.casualties_1_combat-deaths-casualties-coalition-deaths?_s=PM:WORLD) set total coalition casualties at 358. For casualties on the Iraqi side, see http://www.cryan.com/war/AlliedForces.html. The accuracy of this count is open to discussion since official US Defense Department sources avoid estimating Iraqi casualties, as discussed by John Heidenrich, "The Gulf War: How Many Iraqis Died?" *Foreign Policy*, no. 90 (Spring 1993): 108–125.
9. Michael Klare, *Resource Wars: The New Landscape of Global Conflict* (New York: Henry Holt, 2001), 2–3; also see CIA estimates of oil reserves worldwide at https://www.cia.gov/library/publications/the-world-factbook/rankorder/2178rank.html.
10. Matinuddin, *Taliban Phenomenon*, 65–66.
11. Michael Griffin, *Reaping the Whirlwind: The Taliban Movement in Afghanistan* (London: Pluto Press, 2001), 36–37.
12. Ibid., 40.
13. Matinuddin, *Taliban Phenomenon*, 49–50. According to US State Department cables, however, US intelligence believed Pakistan directly funded and

armed the Taliban. See http://www.gwu.edu/~nsarchiv/NSAEBB/NSAEBB227/index.htm#15#15.

CHAPTER 25: TALIBAN VERSUS MUJAHIDEEN

1. Matinuddin, *Taliban Phenomenon*, 87.
2. For a full picture, see Abdul Salam Zaeef, *My Life with the Taliban*, ed. Alex Strick van Linschoten and Felix Kuehn (New York: Columbia University Press), 2010.
3. Tomsen, *Wars of Afghanistan*, 20.
4. Ibid., 17.

CHAPTER 27: AMERICA ENTERS THE PICTURE

1. Coll, *Ghost Wars*, 548.
2. Ibid., 538.
3. Ibid., 543.
4. Zaeef, *My Life with the Taliban*, 141–143.
5. http://www.nytimes.com/interactive/2011/06/22/world/asia/afghanistan-war-timeline.html.

CHAPTER 28: THE BONN PROJECT

1. Ahmad Rashid, *Descent into Chaos: The United States and the Failure of Nation Building in Pakistan, Afghanistan, and Central Asia* (New York: Viking, 2008), 90–93.

CHAPTER 29: KABUL SPRING

1. This data is collected from a variety of sources including Lydia's Poole's report to Global Humanitarian Assistance at http://www.globalhumanitarianas-sistance.org/wp-content/uploads/2011/02/gha-Afghanistan-2011-major-resourc e-flows.pdf. Also see GAO report found at http://www.gao.gov/new.items/d05742.pdf.
2. Interviewed in the movie *Defying Silence* by Stacia Teele and Ed Robbins.
3. http://www.pbs.org/independentlens/afghanistanunveiled/film.html.
4. http://old.bfi.org.uk/sightandsound/feature/242.
5. Joel Brinkley, "Pity Afghanistan's Children," *San Francisco Chronicle,* November 6, 2011.

CHAPTER 30: THE PERSISTENCE OF TROUBLE

1. Gayle Lemmon, "Raisins Give Hope to Afghan Farmers," *New York Times,* October 8, 2010.

2. This statistic was cited by a speaker at a September 2003 fund-raising event in Marin County for Roots for Peace, an NGO dedicated to removing land mines from war-torn areas and planting grapevines in the clear soil.

3. http://www.infoplease.com/ipa/A0933935.html.

4. General Accountability Office Report to Congressional Committees, July 2005, *Afghanistan Reconstruction: Despite Some Progress, Deteriorating Security and Other Obstacles Continue to Threaten Achievement of U.S. Goals* (Washington, DC: GAO, 2005), http://www.gao.gov/new.items/d05742.pdf.

5. Tomsen, *Wars of Afghanistan*, 640; and Sayid Sattar Langary, *Women from Afghanistan in Diaspora* (Bloomington, IN: AuthorHouse, 2010), xii.

6. Lydia Poole, *Afghanistan: Tracking Major Resource Flows, 2002–2010* (Wells, UK: Global Humanitarian Assistance), http://www.globalhumanitarian assistance.org/wp-content/uploads/2011/02/gha-Afghanistan-2011-major-resource-flows.pdf.

7. Fariba Nawa, "Deconstructing the Reconstruction: A Corpwatch Investigative Report," http://www.corpwatch.org/article.php?id=14076, 15.

8. Afghan Amabassador Tayeb Jawad (in a speech at the University of California–Berkeley, April 2007) claimed that two-thirds of the money allocated to aid in Afghanistan was banked in America. See also Matthew Nasuti, "America's 'Phantom Aid' to Afghanistan," *Atlantic Free Press*, November 4, 2009, http://atlanticfreepress.com/news/1/12194-americas-qphantom-aidq-to-afghanistan.html.

9. A June 2011 Majority Staff Report to the Senate Foreign Relations Committee estimated that posting one US civilian in Afghanistan costs half a million dollars, excluding security expenses and salary. *Evaluating U.S. Foreign Assistance to Afghanistan* (Washington, DC: US Government Printing Office, 2011), http://www.foreign.senate.gov/imo/media/doc/SPRT%20112-21.pdf, 7.

10. Conversation with James Ritchie, June 14, 2006.

11. Conversation with Wahid Mohmand, 2006.

CHAPTER 31: DRUGS AND CORRUPTION

1. Fariba Nawa, *Opium Nation: Child Brides, Drug Lords, and One Woman's Journey Through Afghanistan* (New York: Harper Perennial, 2011), 100–101. See also Gretchen Peters, "The Taliban and the Opium Trade," in Antonio Giustozzi, ed., *Decoding the New Taliban* (New York: Columbia University Press, 2009), 14.

2. Nawa, *Opium Nation*, 142–144.

3. Joshua Partlow, "Afghan Minister Accused of Taking Bribe," *Washington Post*, November 18, 2009, http://www.washingtonpost.com/wp-dyn/content/article/2009/11/17/AR2009111704198_2.html?sid=ST2009111800831.

4. Jonathan Landay, "Factory, Coal Mine Show Connections Matter Most in Afghan Business," *McClatchy Newspapers, Washington Bureau*, November 14,

2010, http://www.mcclatchydc.com/2010/11/14/v-print/103393/afghan-busi
ness-model-connections.html.

5. Dr. Nadir Atash, *Turbulence: The Tumultuous Journey of One Man's Quest for Change in Afghanistan* (New York: Planetpix Productions, 2009), 188–189.

6. Ben Farmer, "Karzai Under Pressure After Investigations Target 15 Officials on Corruption Charges," *Telegraph*, November 23, 2009, http://www.tele graph.co.uk/news/worldnews/asia/afghanistan/6636999/Karzai-under-pressure -after-investigations-target-15-officials-on-corruption-charges.html.

7. Arthur Kent, "West's Afghan Mission Undone by Farcical Spy vs. Spy Bribes," *Sky Reporter*, August 31, 2010, http://skyreporter.com/blog/page/2/20 100830_01/.

8. Conversation with Humaira Ghilzai, January 2, 2012.

9. Jonathan Steele, "US Convinced Karzai Half-Brother Is Corrupt, Wik-iLeaks Cables Say," *Guardian*, December 2, 2010, http://www.guardian .co.uk/world/2010/dec/02/us-karzai-half-brother-wikileaks; see also Dexter Filkins, Mark Mazzetti, and James Risen, "Brother of Afghan Leader Said to Be Paid by C.I.A.," *New York Times*, October 27, 2009, http://www.nytimes .com/2009/10/28/world/asia/28intel.html?_r=1.

10. Dexter Filkins, "Iran Is Said to Give Top Karzai Aide Cash by the Bagful," *New York Times*, October 23, 2010, http://www.nytimes.com/2010/10/24/ world/asia/24afghan.html?pagewanted=all.

CHAPTER 32: TALIBANISM

1. Christopher Reuter and Borhan Younus, "The Return of the Taliban in Andar District," in Giustozzi, *Decoding the New Taliban*, 101, 105.

2. Tim Golden, "In U.S. Report, Brutal Details of 2 Afghan Inmates' Deaths," *New York Times*, May 20, 2005, http://www.nytimes.com/2005/05/20/inter national/asia/20abuse.html?pagewanted=all. Also see Carlotta Gall, "U.S. Ex-amines Death of Afghan in Custody / Pathologist Described It as a Homicide," *San Francisco Chronicle*, March 3, 2003, A-5, http://www.sfgate.com/cgi-bin/arti cle.cgi?f=/c/a/2003/03/04/MN204728.DTL#ixzz1dtkZHw3U.

3. Reuter and Younus, "Return of the Taliban," 102–103.

4. Duncan Campbell and Kitty Logan, "The Man Who Thinks He's George Clooney. A Story of Today's Kabul," *Guardian*, July 9, 2004.

5. Reuter and Younus, "Return of the Taliban," 109–110.

6. Joanna Nathan, "Reading the Taliban," in Giustozzi, *Decoding the New Tal-iban*, 25–26.

7. Peters, "The Taliban and the Opium Trade," in Giustozzi, *Decoding the New Taliban*, 13–14.

8. Tom Coghlan, "The Taliban in Helmand: An Oral History," in Giustozzi, *Decoding the New Taliban*, 119–120.

CHAPTER 33: THE TIPPING POINT

1. "UNICEF Alarmed as Attacks on Afghan Schools Rise," *Unicef News*, http://www.unicef.org/infobycountry/media_35196.html. See also Carlotta Gall, "Taliban Behead High School Teacher in Southern Afghanistan," *New York Times*, January 4, 2006, http://www.nytimes.com/2006/01/04/international/asia/04cnd-afghanistan.html.

2. See, for example, Abdul Awaal Zabulwal, "Taliban in Zabul: A Witness Account," 184–186, and David Kilcullen, "Taliban and Counter-Insurgency in Kunar," 238–240, both in Giustozzi, *Decoding the New Taliban*.

3. Mohammed Osman Tariq Elias, "The Resurgence of the Taliban in Kabul, Loar, and Wardak," in Giustozzi, *Decoding the New Taliban*, 50–52.

4. Nawa, *Opium Nation*, 176.

CHAPTER 34: OBAMA'S SURGES

1. Amy Belasco, *Troop Level in the Afghan and Iraq Wars, FY2001–1012* (Washington, DC: CRS Report for Congress, July 2, 2009), http://www.fas.org/sgp/crs/natsec/R40682.pdf.

2. Moshe Schwartz and Joyprada Swain, *Department of Defense Contractors in Afghanistan and Iraq* (Washington, DC: CRS Report for Congress, May 13, 2011), http://www.fas.org/sgp/crs/natsec/R40764.pdf.

3. Quoting an English language radio station in Islamabad. "U.S. to Provide 85 Drones for Pakistan," *Xinhua News Agency*, April 22, 2011, http://www.afghanistannewscenter.com/news/2011/april/apr222011.html#16.

4. Sayyaf, a leading Mujahideen commander, and Amin, the Communist president, were related by marriage: their wives were sisters. In my village, some men were affiliated with Hezb-i-Islam while their cousins fought for Parcham.

5. David Hastings, "The Runaway General: The *Rolling Stone* Profile of Stanley McChrystal That Changed History," *Rolling Stone*, June 22, 2010, http://www.rollingstone.com/politics/news/the-runaway-general-20100622.

6. Spencer Ackerman, "25 Tons of Bombs Wipe Afghan Town Off Map," *Wired*, January 19, 2011, http://www.wired.com/dangerroom/2011/01/25-tons-of-bombs-wipes-afghan-town-off-the-map/.

7. Taimour Shah and Alyssa Rubin, "Taliban Proudly Describes Secrets of Great Escape," *Sydney Morning Herald*, April 27, 2011.

8. Geneva Sands, "Gingrich: 'I Don't See a Path Ahead' for Reform in Afghanistan," *Hill*, March 13, 2012, http://thehill.com/video/campaign/215749-gingrich-i-dont-see-a-path-ahead-for-reform-in-afghanistan-.

CHAPTER 35: ALL THAT GLITTERS

1. Kirk Semple, "Big Weddings Bring Afghans Joy, Debt," *New York Times*, January 14, 2008, http://www.nytimes.com/2008/01/14/world/asia/14weddings.html?pagewanted=all.

2. Conversation with Rahmani, now doing his doctoral studies at UCLA, June 17, 2011.

3. Peters, "The Taliban and the Opium Trade," 9.

4. Elizabeth Rubin, "Studio Kabul," *New York Times Sunday Magazine*, October 24, 2010, 40.

5. http://www.imdb.com/title/tt1506942/.

GLOSSARY

badmash Common thug.

Bala Hissar Fortress and palace complex overlooking Kabul.

buzkashi Equestrian sport in which riders struggle for possession of a goat carcass, which they compete to move to designated goal posts.

chad'ri Full-body covering worn by traditional Afghan women in public; also called a *burqa*.

dalak Itinerant rural barber and dental surgeon.

Deobandism Fundamentalist Islamic movement born at the Deoband religious seminary in India.

Eid Either of the year's two major Islamic holidays.

Farangi Foreigner, but specifically connoting European. A corruption of *Frank*.

fatwa A precedent-setting legal ruling by an authorized religious scholar.

ghulam bacha (slave son) A boy taken from his parents and raised at court to serve as a factotum for the king.

hazrat Term of respect for a religiously important man.

Hezb Political party.

imam One who leads prayer and takes care of a mosque; also, term of respect for a person with religious credentials.

Jeshyn Celebration. Specifically, a later summer festival celebrating Afghan independence; suspended in Communist times.

jihad Armed struggle in defense of Islam or the Islamic community.

Jihadism A fundamentalist Islamic movement that regards jihad as the primary duty of Muslims.

jirga A village council; also a meeting of the village council.

kafir Infidel.

kahrez Underground irrigation canal.

kalantar An agent of the state, elected by locals but charged with reporting on local affairs to the king.

khan Title for a feudal lord, usually a big landowner.

Kohistan A region just north of Kabul; literally "land of mountains."

kotwal An employee of the Ministry of the Interior, appointed by the state to keep an eye on local events.

kuchi Nomad. Literally, "one who moves."

loya jirga A grand council attended by delegates from all the tribes of Afghanistan, convened to consider matters of national importance.

madrassa Islamic school; seminary.

malik Village headman.

mawlawi Eminent religious scholar.

Mes Aymak An area south of Kabul containing immense deposits of copper ore.

mirab Respected village elder responsible for adjudicating irrigation water disputes.

mirza A privileged bureaucrat responsible directly to the king. Abbreviated from "Amir zada" or "Amir's child." Mirzas usually started out as ghulam bachas.

muezzin One who chants the call to prayer from the minaret of a mosque.

mufti A religious scholar who advises judges on legal interpretations.

muhtasib Officer of state morality police, charged with enforcing Islamic conduct.

mujahid One who participates in jihad, usually an Islamic guerilla.

mujahideen Plural of *mujahid*.

mullah A cleric who performs the religious ceremonies of daily life.

mustaufi Exchequer, equivalent to treasurer.

Nizamnama A secular legal code promulgated in the 1920s.

Paylucha A Kandahar street gang that later rebranded themselves as Mujahideen. Literally "the barefoot boys."

purdah The practice of secluding women from the sight of men who are not close relatives.

Pushtoonwali Unwritten code of conduct traditional among Pushtoons. Its tenets include the obligation to shelter travelers, practice hospitality, lavish generosity on guests, defend the sexual honor of female relatives, and avenge harm done to one's kin.

q'root A dried yogurt used in most Afghan gourmet dishes.

qala Rural fort belonging to a feudal lord; sometimes housed an entire clan.

qazi Judge.

Ramadhan The month when Muslims are enjoined to fast during the day.

Shari'a The code of conduct elaborated over the centuries by Islamic scholars. It includes a complete legal code covering civil and criminal matters as well as injunctions pertaining to religious and daily life.

shura Islamic term meaning "council."

Taliban A radical Islamist movement originating out of the Afghan refugee camps in Pakistan. Literally, plural of *talib*: "seeker" or "student."

wazir A king's chief office; equivalent to a (cabinet) minister.

Wikh-i-Zalmayan Student activist group of the 1940s that embraced modernism and Pushtoon nationalism.

BIBLIOGRAPHY

Ackerman, Spencer. "25 Tons of Bombs Wipe Afghan Town Off Map." *Wired*, January 19, 2011. www.wired.com/dangerroom/2011/01/25-tons-of-bombs-wipes-afghan-town-off-the-map/.

Adamec, Ludwig W. *Afghanistan, 1900–1923: A Diplomatic History.* Berkeley: University of California Press, 1967.

———. *Afghanistan's Foreign Affairs to the Mid-Twentieth Century: Relations with the USSR, Germany, and Britain.* Tucson: University of Arizona Press, 1974.

———. "The Two Faces of Habibullah Kalakani." *Afghanistan Studies Journal* 2 (1990–1991): 85–90.

Ahmad, Jamil. "Jamaluddin Afghani." www.renaissance.com.pk/julletf94.

Ali, Mohammed. *A Cultural History of Afghanistan.* Kabul: Mohammed Ali, 1964.

Anwar, M. H. *Memories of Afghanistan.* Bloomington, IN: AuthorHouse, 2004.

Anwar, Raja, *The Tragedy of Afghanistan: A First-Hand Account.* London: Verso, 1988.

Arnold, Anthony. *Afghanistan: The Soviet Invasion in Perspective.* Palo Alto, CA: Hoover Institution Press, 1981.

———. *Afghanistan's Two-Party Communism.* Stanford, CA: Hoover Institution Press, 1983.

Atash, Nadir. *Turbulence: The Tumultuous Journey of One Man's Quest for Change in Afghanistan.* New York: Planetpix, 2009.

Belasco, Amy. *Troop Level in the Afghan and Iraq Wars, FY2001–1012.* Washington, DC: CRS Report for Congress, 2009. www.fas.org/sgp/crs/natsec/R40682.pdf.

Blackburn, Terence. *The Extermination of a British Army: The Retreat from Kabul.* New Delhi: APH, 2008.

Burnes, Alexander. *Travels into Bokhara: Being the Account of a Journey from India to Cabool, Tartary, and Persia.* 2 vols. Philadelphia: E. L. Carey and A. Hart, 1835.

Campbell, Duncan, and Kitty Logan. "The Man Who Thinks He's George Clooney. A Story of Today's Kabul." *Guardian*, July 9, 2004.

Charkhi, Khaled Siddiq. *From My Memories: Memoirs of Political Imprisonment from Childhood in Afghanistan.* Bloomington, IN: AuthorHouse, 2010.

Chayes, Sarah. *The Punishment of Virtue: Inside Afghanistan after the Taliban.* New York: Penguin Books, 2006.

Coll, Steve. *Ghost Wars.* New York: Penguin Press, 2004.

Cooley, John K. *Unholy Wars: Afghanistan, America, and International Terrorism.* London, Pluto Press, 1999.

Coghlan, Tom. "The Taliban in Helmand: An Oral History." In Giustozzi, *Decoding the New Taliban*, 119–154.

Darr, Abdul Hayy Robert. *The Spy of the Heart.* Louisville, KY: Fons Vitae, 2006.

Diver, Maud. *Kabul to Kandahar.* London: Peter Davies, 1935.

Dupree, Louis. *Afghanistan.* Princeton, NJ: Princeton University Press, 1980.

Edwards, Lucy Morgan. *The Afghan Solution: The Inside Story of Abdul Haq, the CIA and How Western Hubris Lost Afghanistan.* London: Pluto Press, 2011.

Elias, Barbara, ed. *Pakistan: "The Taliban's Godfather"? National Security Archive Electronic Briefing Book No. 227.* Washington, DC: George Washington University National Security Archives, 2007.

Elias, Mohammed Osman Tariq. "The Resurgence of the Taliban in Kabul, Logar, and Wardak." In Giustozzi, *Decoding the New Taliban*, 43–56.

"The English in Afghanistan." *North American Review* 55, no. 116 (July 1842): 45–72.

Farmer, Ben. "Karzai Under Pressure After Investigations Target 15 Officials on Corruption Charges." *Telegraph*, November 23, 2009. www .telegraph.co.uk/news/worldnews/asia/afghanistan/6636999/Karzai

-under-pressure-after-investigations-target-15-officials-on-corrup tion-charges.

Fergusson, Niall. *Colossus: The Price of America's Empire.* New York: Penguin Books, 2004.

Ferris, John. "Invading Afghanistan, 1838–2006: Politics and Pacification." *Journal of Military and Strategic Studies,* 9, no. 1 (Fall 2006). www.jmss.org/jmss/index.php/jmss/article/view/119/131.

Filkins, Dexter. "Iran Is Said to Give Top Karzai Aide Cash by the Bagful." *New York Times,* October 23, 2010. www.nytimes.com/2010/10/24/world/asia/24afghan?pagewanted=all.

Filkins, Dexter, Mark Mazzetti, and James Risen. "Brother of Afghan Leader Said to Be Paid by C.I.A." *New York Times,* October 27, 2009. www.nytimes.com/2009/10/28/world/asia/28intel?_r=1.

Forbes, Archibald. *The Afghan Wars.* New York: Scribner, 1892. Reprint, Kessinger, 2004.

Fraser-Tytler, W. K. *Afghanistan: A Study of Political Developments in Central and South Asia.* London: Oxford University Press, 1950.

Gall, Carlotta. "Taliban Behead High School Teacher in Southern Afghanistan." *New York Times,* January 4, 2006. www.nytimes.com/2006/01/04/international/asia/04cnd-afghanistan.

———."U.S. examines death of Afghan in custody / Pathologist Described It as a Homicide." *San Francisco Chronicle,* March 3, 2003, A-5. www.sfgate.com/cgi-bin/article.cgi?f=/c/a/2003/03/04/MN 204728.DTL#ixzz1dtkZHw3U.

Gandhi, Sajit, ed. *The September 11th Sourcebooks.* Vol. 8, *The Taliban File.* Washington, DC: The GWU National Security Archives, 2003.

Ghaus, Abdul Samad. *The Fall of Afghanistan: An Insider's Account.* Washington, DC: Pergamon-Brassey, 1988.

Ghobar, Mir Ghulam Mohammed. *Afghanistan Dar Maseer-i-Tareekh, Juld-i Awal.* [Afghanistan in the Course of History, Volume 1]. Kabul: Government Publications Department, 1967.

———. *Afghanistan in the Course of History.* Vol. 2. Translated by Sherief Fayez. Alexandria, VA: Hashmat Gobar, 2001.

Girardet, Edward. *The Soviet War.* London: Palgrave Macmillan, 1986.

Giustozzi, Antonio, ed. *Decoding the New Taliban,* New York: Columbia University Press, 2009.

Gohari, M. J. *The Taliban: Ascent to Power.* Oxford: Oxford University Press, 1999.

Golden, Tim. "In U.S. Report, Brutal Details of 2 Afghan Inmates' Deaths." *New York Times,* May 20, 2005. www.nytimes.com/2005/05/20/international/asia/20abuse?pagewanted=all.

Government Accountability Office. *Afghanistan Reconstruction: Despite Some Progress, Deteriorating Security and Other Obstacles Continue to Threaten Achievement of U.S. Goals.* Washington, DC: GAO, 2005.

Griffin, Michael. *Reaping the Whirlwind: The Taliban Movement in Afghanistan.* London: Pluto Press, 2001.

Gross, Nassrine Abubakr, ed. *Qassarikh-i-Malalai ya Khaterat-e Awaleen Leesa-ye Dokhtaran-e Afghanistan* [Memories of Malalai, the First Girls' School in Afhganistan]. Falls Church, VA: KabulTec, 1998.

Habibi, Pohand Abdul Hayy. *Tarikh-i-Mukhtasar-i Afghanistan* [Concise History of Afghanistan]. Arlington, VA: Association of Afghan Refugees, 1989.

Hafvenstein, Joel. *Opium Season: A Year on the Afghan Frontier.* Guilford, CT: Lyons Press, 2007.

Halliday, Fred. "Revolution in Afghanistan." *New Left Review,* no. 112 (November–December 1978): 3–44.

———. *Soviet Policy in the Arc of Crisis.* Washington, DC: Institute for Policy Studies, 1981.

———. "The War and Revolution in Afghanistan." *New Left Review,* no. 119 (January–February 1980): 20–41.

Haroon, Sana. *Frontier of Faith: Islam in the Indo-Afghan Borderland.* New York: Columbia University Press, 2007.

Hastings, David. "The Runaway General: The *Rolling Stone* Profile of Stanley McChrystal That Changed History." *Rolling Stone,* June 22, 2010. www.rollingstone.com/politics/news/the-runaway-general-20100622.

Heidenrich, John. "The Gulf War: How Many Iraqis Died?" *Foreign Policy,* no. 90 (Spring 1993): 108–125.

Jones, Ann. *Kabul in Winter: Life Without Peace in Afghanistan.* New York: Metropolitan Books, 2006.

Joya, Malalai. *A Woman Among Warlords.* New York, Scribner, 2009.

Kakar, Hasan Kawun. *Afghanistan: The Soviet Invasion and the Afghan Response, 1979–1982.* Berkeley: University of California Press, 1995.

———. *Government and Society in Afghanistan: The Reign of Amir 'Abd al-Rahman Khan.* Austin: University of Texas Press, 1979.

Kalakani, Habibullah. *My Life from Brigand to King.* London: Octagon Press, 1990.

Kaplan, Robert D. *Soldiers of God: With the Mujahidin in Afghanistan.* New York: Houghton Mifflin, 1990.

Kaye, John William. *History of the War in Afghanistan.* 3 vols. London: Richard Bentley, 1858.

Keddie, Nikki. *Sayyid Jamal al-Din "al-Afghani": A Political Biography.* Berkeley: University of California Press, 1972.

Kennedy, Paul. *The Rise and Fall of Great Powers.* New York: Random House, 1987.

Kent, Arthur. "West's Afghan Mission Undone by Farcical Spy vs. Spy Bribes." *Sky Reporter*, August 31, 2010. http://skyreporter.com/blog/page/2/20100830_01/.

Khalili, Khalilullah. *Yawd-dasht hai Ustad Kahlili* [*Memoirs of Master Kahlili*] (As told to his daughter Marie). Herndon, VA: Marie and Mohammed Afzal Nassiri, 2010.

Kilcullen, David. "Taliban and Counter-Insurgency in Kunar." In Giustozzi, *Decoding the New Taliban*, 231–246.

Lal, Mohan. *Life of the Amir Dost Mohammed Khan of Kabul.* London: Longman, Brown, Green, and Longmans, 1846.

Landay, Jonathan. "Factory, Coal Mine Show Connections Matter Most in Afghan Business." *McClatchy Newspapers, Washington Bureau*, Nov. 14, 2010. www.mcclatchydc.com/2010/11/14/v-print/103393/afghan-business-model-connections.

Langary, Sayid Sattar. *Women from Afghanistan in Diaspora.* Bloomington, IN: AuthorHouse, 2012.

Loyn, David. *In Afghanistan.* New York: Palgrave MacMillan, 2009.

MacEachin, Douglas. *Predicting the Soviet Invasion of Afghanistan: The Intelligence Community's Record.* Langley, VA: CSI Publications, 2007.

Macintyre, Ben. *The Man Who Would Be King: The First American in Afghanistan.* New York: Farrar Straus Giroux, 2004.

Majority Staff Report to the Senate Foreign Relations Committee. *Evaluating U.S. Foreign Assistance to Afghanistan.* Washington, DC: US

Government Printing Office, 2011, 7. www.foreign.senate.gov/
imo/media/doc/SPRT%20112-21.pdf.

Matinuddin, Kamal. *The Taliban Phenomenon: Afghanistan 1994–1997.*
Oxford: Oxford University Press, 1999.

Meyer, Karl Ernest, and Shareen Blair Brysac. *Tournament of Shadows:
The Great Game and the Race for Empire in Central Asia.* New York:
Basic Books, 2006.

Moshref, Rameen. "The Life and Times of Amir Habibullah." *Afghanistan
Online.* www.afghan-web.com/bios/detail/dhabib.

Nathan, Joanna. "Reading the Taliban." In Giustozzi, *Decoding the New
Taliban*, 23–42.

Nasuti, Matthew. "America's 'Phantom Aid' to Afghanistan." *Atlantic
Free Press*, November 4, 2009. http://atlanticfreepress.com/news/
1/12194-americas-qphantom-aidq-to-afghanistan.

Nawa, Fariba. "Deconstructing the Reconstruction: A Corpwatch Investigative Report." www.corpwatch.org/article.php?id=14076.

———. *Opium Nation: Child Brides, Drug Lords, and One Woman's Journey Through Afghanistan.* New York: Harper Perennial, 2011.

Nawid, Senzil. "Political Advocacy in Early Twentieth Century Afghan
Persian Poetry." *Afghanistan Studies Journal* 3 (1992): 5–17.

Noelle, Christine. *State and Tribe in Nineteenth-Century Afghanistan: The
Reign of Amir Dost Mohammed Khan.* London: Curzon Press, 1997.

Overby, Paul. *Getting Out of Afghanistan.* New York: Foothills Press, 2012.

———. *Holy Blood: An Inside View of the Afghan War.* Westport, CT:
Praeger, 1993.

Partlow, Joshua. "Afghan Minister Accused of Taking Bribe." *Washington
Post.* November 18, 2009. www.washingtonpost.com/wp-dyn/
content/article/2009/11/17/AR2009111704198_2?sid=ST200911
1800831.

Peters, Gretchen. "The Taliban and the Opium Trade." In Giustozzi, *Decoding the New Taliban*, 7–22.

Poole, Lydia. *Afghanistan: Tracking Major Resource Flows, 2002–2010.*
Wells, UK: Global Humanitarian Assistance. www.globalhuman
itarianassistance.org

Qazi, Abdullah. "Biography: Ahmad Shah Massoud." *Afghanistan Online.*
www.afghan-web.com/bios/yest/asmasood, 2001, updated 2007.

Rashid, Ahmad. *Descent into Chaos: The United States and the Failure of Nation Building in Pakistan, Afghanistan, and Central Asia.* New York: Viking, 2008.

———. *Taliban: Militant Islam, Oil, & Fundamentalism in Central Asia.* New Haven: Yale Note Bene, Yale University Press, 2000.

Reuter, Christopher, and Borhan Younus. "The Return of the Taliban in Andar District." In Giustozzi, *Decoding the New Taliban,* 101–118.

Robson, Brian. *The Road to Kabul: The Second Afghan War 1878 to 1881.* Gloucestershire, UK: History Press, 2008.

Rotberg, Robert, ed. *Building a New Afghanistan.* Cambridge: World Peace Foundation; and Washington, DC: Brookings Institute Press, 2007.

Rubin, Elizabeth. "In the Land of the Taliban." *New York Times Magazine,* October 22, 2006, 86–94.

———. "Studio Kabul." *New York Times Magazine,* October 24, 2010, 40.

Russian General Staff. *The Soviet-Afghan War: How a Superpower Fought and Lost.* Lawrence: University Press of Kansas, 2002.

Sadeed, Suraya. *Forbidden Lessons in a Kabul Guesthouse.* New York: Hyperion, 2011.

Saikal, Amin. *Modern Afghanistan: A History of Struggle and Survival.* New York: I. B. Taurus, 2004.

Sale, Florentia. *A Journal of the Disasters in Afghanistan.* Franklin, TN: Tantallon Press, 2002. Originally published in 1843.

Sands, Geneva. "Gingrich: 'I Don't See a Path Ahead' for Reform in Afghanistan." *Hill,* March 13, 2012. www.thehill.com/video/campaign/215749-gingrich-i-dont-see-a-path-ahead-for-reform-in-afghanistan.

Savranskaya, Svetlana, ed. *Afghanistan, Lessons from the Last War: The Soviet Experience in Afghanistan: Russian Documents and Memoirs. National Security Archive, Document 21.* Washington, DC: George Washington University National Security Archives, 2001.

Savranskaya, Svetlana, and Thomas Blanton, eds. *National Security Archive Electronic Briefing Book No. 272, Afghanistan and the Soviet Withdrawal, 20 Years Later.* Washington, DC: George Washington University National Security Archives, 2009.

Schwartz, Moshe, and Joyprada Swain. *Department of Defense Contractors in Afghanistan and Iraq.* Washington, DC: CRS Report for Congress, May 13, 2011. www.fas.org.

Semple, Kirk. "Big Weddings Bring Afghans Joy, Debt." *New York Times*, January 14, 2008. www.nytimes.com/2008/01/14/world/asia/14weddings?pagewanted=ala.

Shah, Saira. "'Afghaniyat' Is Alive and Well in Afghanistan." *Guardian*, April 7, 2011. www.guardian.co.uk/commentisfree/2011/apr/07.

Shah, Taimour, and Alyssa Rubin. "Taliban Proudly Describes Secrets of Great Escape." *Sydney Morning Herald*, April 27, 2011.

Shalizi, Abdussattar. *Afghanistan: Ancient Land with Modern Ways*. Kabul: Ministry of Planning, 1964.

Steele, Jonathan. "US Convinced Karzai Half-Brother Is Corrupt, Wiki-Leaks Cables Say." *Guardian*, December 2, 2010. www.guardian.co.uk/world/2010/dec/02/us-karzai-half-brother-wikileaks.

Stewart, Jules. *Crimson Snow: Britain's First Disaster in Afghanistan*. Gloucestershire: Sutton Press, 2008.

Stewart, Rhea Talley. *Fire in Afghanistan*. Garden City, NY: Doubleday, 1973.

Tabibi, Abdul Hakim. *Afghanistan: A Nation in Love with Freedom*. Cedar Rapids, IA: Igram Press, 1985.

———. *Talashhayi Siyasi Sayyed Jamaluddin Afghani* [The Political Struggles of Sayid Jamal ad-Din Afghani]. Kabul: Muassisa Intasharat Baihaqi, 1355/1977.

Taheri, Mohammed Ja'far. *Zarb'ul Masal-ha* [Proverbs]. Arlington, VA: Asghar Taheri, 1389/1991.

Tomsen, Peter. *The Wars of Afghanistan*. New York: Public Affairs, 2011.

"UNICEF Alarmed as Attacks on Afghan Schools Rise." *Unicef News*. www.unicef.org/infobycountry/media_35196.

Urban, Mark. *War in Afghanistan*. New York: St. Martin's Press, 1988.

"U.S. to Provide 85 Drones for Pakistan." *Xinhua News Agency*, April 22, 2011. www.afghanistannewscenter.com/news/2011/april.

Zabulwal, Abdul Awaal. "Taliban in Zabul: A Witness Account." In Giustozzi, *Decoding the New Taliban*, 179–190.

Zaeef, Abdul Salam. *My Life with the Taliban*, edited by Alex Strick van Linschoten and Felix Kuehn. New York: Columbia University Press, 2010.

INDEX

VICTOR DALLONS

TAMIM ANSARY is the author of *Destiny Disrupted: A History of the World through Islamic Eyes* and *West of Kabul, East of New York,* among other books. For ten years he wrote a monthly column for Encarta.com, and has published essays and commentary in the *San Francisco Chronicle,* Salon, Alternet, TomPaine.com, *Edutopia, Parade,* the *Los Angeles Times,* and elsewhere. Born in Afghanistan in 1948, he moved to the United States in 1964. He lives in San Francisco, where he is director of the San Francisco Writers Workshop.

PublicAffairs is a publishing house founded in 1997. It is a tribute to the standards, values, and flair of three persons who have served as mentors to countless reporters, writers, editors, and book people of all kinds, including me.

I. F. STONE, proprietor of *I. F. Stone's Weekly*, combined a commitment to the First Amendment with entrepreneurial zeal and reporting skill and became one of the great independent journalists in American history. At the age of eighty, Izzy published *The Trial of Socrates*, which was a national bestseller. He wrote the book after he taught himself ancient Greek.

BENJAMIN C. BRADLEE was for nearly thirty years the charismatic editorial leader of *The Washington Post*. It was Ben who gave the *Post* the range and courage to pursue such historic issues as Watergate. He supported his reporters with a tenacity that made them fearless and it is no accident that so many became authors of influential, best-selling books.

ROBERT L. BERNSTEIN, the chief executive of Random House for more than a quarter century, guided one of the nation's premier publishing houses. Bob was personally responsible for many books of political dissent and argument that challenged tyranny around the globe. He is also the founder and longtime chair of Human Rights Watch, one of the most respected human rights organizations in the world.

·   ·   ·

For fifty years, the banner of Public Affairs Press was carried by its owner Morris B. Schnapper, who published Gandhi, Nasser, Toynbee, Truman, and about 1,500 other authors. In 1983, Schnapper was described by *The Washington Post* as "a redoubtable gadfly." His legacy will endure in the books to come.

Peter Osnos, *Founder and Editor-at-Large*